The Dictionary of
DEMOGRAPHY

ROLAND PRESSAT

The Dictionary of
DEMOGRAPHY

Edited by
CHRISTOPHER WILSON

Blackwell Reference

First published in French as *Dictionnaire de Démographie*
English translation first published 1985
© Roland Pressat's contributions
Presses Universitaires de
France, Paris
© Editorial organisation and contributions other than
those by Roland Pressat, Basil Blackwell Ltd 1985

Basil Blackwell Ltd
108 Cowley Road, Oxford OX4 1JF, England

Basil Blackwell Inc.
432 Park Avenue South, Suite 1505
New York, NY 10016, USA

British Library Cataloguing in Publication Data
Pressat, Roland
The dictionary of demography.
1. Demography – Dictionaries
I. Title   II. Dictionnaire de démographie.
English
304.6'03'21   HB849

ISBN 0-631-12746-1

Library of Congress Cataloging in Publication Data

Pressat, Roland.
The dictionary of demography.

Translation of: Dictionnaire de démographie.
Includes index.
1. Demography – Dictionaries.   I. Wilson, Christopher.
II. Title.
HB849.2.P7413 1985   304.6'03'21   84-28407
ISBN 0-631-12746-1

Typeset by Katerprint Co. Ltd, Oxford
Printed in Great Britain by
Bell and Bain Ltd, Glasgow

Contents

Acknowledgements

The Editor and Publishers are most grateful to Mrs Sarah Matthew who undertook the translation of the French edition of the Dictionary and to Dr Maxine Merrington who compiled the index. They also acknowledge permission from copyright holders to redraw and reproduce line illustrations on the following pages: Academic Press 63; Basic Books Inc. 67; HMSO 17, 186–7, 206; Institut National D'Études Démographiques 57, 127, 137; Plenum Press 122; the Population Information Program, the Johns Hopkins University 114; the Population Investigation Committee, the London School of Economics 157, 206, 214, 221; the Population Reference Bureau Inc. 25, 172, 179; and the Swedish Bureau of Statistics 6.

Preface

A great many people have made contributions to this dictionary; they all receive my thanks. Pride of place must be given to Roland Pressat whose entries, written originally for the French dictionary, form the core of this book and the inspiration for the entire work. I am also grateful to the other contributors for finding time in their hectic schedules to write such concise and erudite entries.

I would also like to note the contributions made by three people at Blackwell. John Davey was the initiator of this project and his enthusiasm for it saw it through several missed deadlines on my part. Janet Godden gave much care and thought to editing the text, and Ray Addicott organised the technical aspects of the work's production with great facility.

Stella Wilks not only typed most of the text, she acted as an extra editor, a sort of unofficial long-stop catching previously unnoticed slips in grammar or style. Doreen Castle of the Population Investigation Committee made available micro-computer facilities for the input of the text. The preparation of material was mainly undertaken at the London School of Economics, but was completed in the highly congenial environment of the Office of Population Research in Princeton. My debt to both institutions is great.

Finally I have one personal comment. Whatever help the dictionary may prove to be in informing or assisting others, there is already one person who has gained immensely from it – I myself. Editing it has required me to read widely on the entire range of subjects embraced by demography; an excellent general education in the discipline and one which I would otherwise have missed. For this, my sincerest thanks to all the others involved in its creation.

Christopher Wilson
May 1985

Note

The work under consideration derives from the project to translate the French edition of my *Demographic Dictionary*. The reader who compares the two versions will see the extent of the difference in editorial spirit between the two.

In the French version I tried above all to fix the language with the desired precision, given the woolliness of the subject. After all, a great part of it consists of technical terms. As a consequence of this point of view the encyclopaedic aspect was a little reduced. Ultimately, my objective was to select only the most assured entries, from the point of view of vocabulary and method.

Chris Wilson, who has made a fine job of the English adaptation, wisely holds a different view. And this is not simply a matter of different personalities, but of his feel for the requirements of the English-speaking reader. It is with a certain regret that I note, however, a certain looseness in the terminology which is likely to be a reflection of the nature of the Anglo-American demography, which is manifestly more liberal than its French counterpart. The French reader would notice, too, that a significant portion of the present work is devoted to techniques more fitting to British or trans-Atlantic, than to French-speaking methods. In short, the distinction which some people are prone to make between French and British demographic practices is evident in a reading of the two versions. This frank adaptation of the dictionary to the expectations of its intended readers is undoubtedly necessary from this point of view and I do not resent the liberties taken with my version, which along with broader encyclopaedic treatments and bibliographical references, may be seen as a token of the work's greater success with an interested public.

Roland Pressat
February 1985

Contributors

John G. Blacker **JGB**
Centre for Population Studies, London

John Bongaarts **JB**
Population Council, New York

Mead T. Cain **MTC**
Population Council, New York

John C. Caldwell **JCC**
Australian National University

J. G. Cleland **JGC**
World Fertility Survey, London

Joel E. Cohen **JEC**
Rockerfeller University, New York

Tim Dyson **TD**
London School of Economics

Douglas Ewbank **DE**
University of Pennsylvania

Griffith Feeney **GF**
East-West Population Institute Honolulu

Allan Hill **AH**
London School of Hygiene and Tropical Medicine

Kenneth Hill **KH**
National Academy of Sciences, Washington

R. J. Johnston **RJJ**
University of Sheffield

Chris Langford **CML**
London School of Economics

Ronald D. Lee **RDL**
University of California, Berkeley

P. N. Mari-Bhat **PNM-B**
University of Pennsylvania

Michael Murphy **MM**
London School of Economics

Hilary Page **HP**
Interuniversity Programme in Demography, Vrije Universiteit, Brussels

Roland Pressat **RP**
Institut National D'Études Démographiques, Paris

Pat Quiggin **PQ**
Australian National University

Philip Rees **PR**
University of Leeds

Eve Roman **ER**
London School of Hygiene and Tropical Medicine

Roger Schofield **RSS**
Cambridge Group for the History of Population and Social Structure

Christopher Scott **CS**
World Fertility Survey, London

Richard Smith **RMS**
All Souls' College, Oxford

David C. Souden **DCS**
Emmanuel College, Cambridge

James Trussell **JT**
Princeton University

Helen Ware **HW**
Human Rights Commission, Canberra

Christopher Wilson **CW**
London School of Economics

E. A. Wrigley **EAW**
London School of Economics

Guillaume Wunsch **GW**
Université Catholique de Louvain

Basia Zaba **BZ**
UNECLA, Trinidad

Editor's Introduction

The technical language of an academic discipline provides its various practitioners with a convenient lexicon of concepts and terms for use in the unambiguous exchange of ideas. Unfortunately it can also act as a barrier to non-specialists who are unfamiliar with the complexities of the vocabulary. To some extent this has been true of demography. Although similar to that of related subjects such as statistics, sociology or economics, the terminology used in demography is subtly different from them, often projecting an arcane and unnecessarily complex image. With the increasing importance of demography, and the much wider use of its methods, this sort of impediment to general communication is a serious problem. One of the purposes of this dictionary is to make demography accessible to other social scientists and to interested non-specialists.

In any subject as large and dynamic as demography the methods, concepts and philosophy of the discipline are constantly evolving. A further purpose of this book, therefore, is to analyse new developments in all areas of demography and to show their relation to more traditional ideas, thereby providing specialists with a means of keeping abreast of current thinking and broadening their knowledge of the field in general.

The dictionary covers the whole range of demographic study, and is particularly strong in certain areas. In his introduction to the French dictionary, the translation of which forms the core of this work, Roland Pressat noted that technical concepts and measures were usually the ones least well-understood and the most in need of clarifiction. This is equally true of the English-speaking demographic scene; accordingly, they are given prominence here. In addition to strictly demographic entries the dictionary contains terms drawn from neighbouring disciplines which have come to be widely used in population analysis. This is especially true of statistical terms which play an important role in any quantitative subject.

Whether an entry relates to a basic concept or to a complex new technique, the reader will find that is conforms to a standard pattern. A clear, brief definition is given, followed by a more detailed discussion, the length of which is determined by the entry's importance. In all but the most straightforward of entries there are also suggestions for further reading which will enhance an understanding of the subject in question.

The author of each entry is indicated by the initials at the end of its text.

The entries are arranged alphabetically, and reference from one to another can be made in two ways. The first is through the *cross-referencing*. Within an entry, certain other entries are referred to in capital letters. Reading these will help place the original entry in its proper context in the discipline as a whole. The second is the *index*, from which the reader will be able to find other entries in which a term is used and gain a wider appreciation of its use.

As a final point I should mention the relationship between this dictionary and the French version. The English- and French-speaking worlds of demography are not identical. The relatively small size of the francophone demographic community lends its work a coherence of interest and methodology not seen in the larger, more heterogeneous, anglophone world. This difference is reflected in the two dictionaries, the present work covering a wider range of material and methodology than the French volume. Nevertheless, the heart of this book are the entries translated and adapted from Roland Pressat's original. They provide the conceptual framework that forms the very basis of the subject.

Christopher Wilson

A

abortion The termination of pregnancy before the foetus has become capable of sustaining an independent extrauterine life, i.e. while the foetus is *non-viable*. An abortion may occur spontaneously in the course of a pregnancy, when it is known as a miscarriage, or more technically as a SPONTANEOUS ABORTION, or it may be due to deliberate outside intervention, when it is termed an INDUCED ABORTION. In everyday use abortion often takes on the meaning solely of induced abortion.

Medical tradition bases the definition of the non-viability of the foetus on the duration of pregnancy. A foetus is assumed to be viable after 28 weeks of gestation counting from the date of the last normal menstrual period (the conventional duration of pregnancy). On average this is about 180 days of actual duration. After 28 weeks' duration, the loss of the foetus is known as a STILLBIRTH. This definition of viability was based on the observation that infants born before 28 weeks of pregancy, or weighing less than 1000 grams, had little chance of survival. Modern advances in the care of premature infants, however, have led to a re-evaluation of the concept of viability. Some infants born at less than 24 weeks' duration, or weighing less than 600 grams, are reported to have survived.

More exclusive definitions of non-viability are sometimes employed in defining the permissible limit for carrying out an induced abortion under legal conditions (LEGAL ABORTION). Assessment of ILLEGAL ABORTION is always problematical since accurate statistics are virtually non-existent. (See also FOETAL MORTALITY.)   RP

Reading

Tietze, C. 1983: *Induced abortion, a world review 1983*. New York: Population Council.

abortion rate A measure of the frequency of abortion in a population in a given period, normally a particular year. Abortions may be related to the total population, or to the number of women of REPRODUCTIVE AGE and may be further specified by age, parity or other characteristics. The term is used with a variety of definitions. Calculation of a rate which is closely related to fertility rates is particularly useful when attempting to measure the significance of INDUCED ABORTION. This is usually only to be recommended in cases where the legal possibilities of employing it are extensive, since it is frequently misleading to try to quantify ILLEGAL ABORTIONS.

In measuring the significance of induced abortion it is usual to calculate the ratio of abortions in a year to the live births in that year or the ratio of abortions to all known pregnancies. (These measures are termed abortion ratios rather than rates.) It is possible, however, to use the term rate for the ratio of abortions in a year to the mean population, which provides a crude abortion rate analogous to the CRUDE BIRTH RATE.

A further measure of abortion often calculated is the TOTAL ABORTION RATE. This is usually taken to be the sum of the age-specific abortion rates found at a particular time and so is a period measure analogous to the TOTAL FERTILITY RATE. It can be interpreted as the number of abortions to be expected over a lifetime by a woman who experiences the average chance of having an abortion at each age. It is expressed as the number of abortions either per woman or per 1000 women and is sometimes known as the lifetime abortion rate.   RP

Reading

Tietze, C. 1983: *Induced abortion, a world review 1983*. New York: Population Council.

abridged life table A LIFE TABLE in which values of the life table functions are presented for certain age groups only, rather than for every single year of age.

When dealing with mortality, data are most commonly given for infant mortality (deaths under age 1), early childhood mortality (ages 1 to 4) and for five-year age groups thereafter. The final value is an open-ended age group (e.g. 80 and above). The convenience of expressing information in fewer than 20 age groups, rather than for up to 100 or more ages, means that the abridged life table is the form most commonly used for the presentation of detailed mortality analysis. Moreover, in some circumstances (dealing with small populations, for example) an abridged life table is preferable even if complete age-specific information is available.

Beyond mortality analysis the use of LIFE TABLE METHODS is possible for any NON-RENEWABLE PROCESS (e.g. first marriage). In such cases abridged life tables are used with age groups appropriate to the problem in hand (most often the conventional five-year age groups).   RP

Reading

Pressat, R. 1972: *Demographic analysis: methods, results, applications*. London: Edward Arnold; Chicago: Aldine Atherton. Chapter 6.

Shryock, H.S., Siegel, J.S. et al. 1976: *The methods and materials of demography*. Condensed edition by E.G. Stockwell. London and New York: Academic Press. Chapter 15.

Woods, R. 1979: *Population analysis in geography*. London: Longman. Chapter 3.

abstinence The avoidance of sexual intercourse. Prolonged abstinence is a completely effective method of contraception. PERIODIC ABSTINENCE where couples hope to avoid conception by refraining from sexual intercourse at certain times of the woman's menstrual cycles is less effective.

Prolonged abstinence, usually associated with prolonged BREASTFEEDING, seems to have been widespread, most notably in Sub-Saharan Africa (Schoenmaeckers et al. 1981) and parts of Asia and the Pacific (Singarimbun and Manning 1976). These practices were traditionally justified on the benefits to health of child or mother, though their effects in reducing fertility were sometimes explicitly mentioned. In most cases women only were expected to abstain, men being allowed sexual relations outside marriage, or, in polygynous societies, with other wives. Although sometimes enforced by intense social pressure, the duration of abstinence appears to be declining virtually universally and to be of short durations in many parts of East and Southern Africa. The abandoning of prolonged abstinence and breastfeeding has led to significant increases in fertility in some parts of Africa.

Although documentary evidence is scanty it seems likely that abstinence played an important role in the reduction of fertility in nineteenth- and twentieth-century Europe. With the widespread availability of methods of contraception which require less motivation, however, abstinence has become of limited importance.   CW

References

Schoenmaeckers, R. et al. 1981: The child spacing tradition and the postpartum taboo in tropical Africa: anthropological evidence. In H.J. Page and R. Lesthaeghe, eds. *Child-spacing in tropical Africa: traditions and change*. London and New York: Academic Press. Pp. 25–71.

Singarimbun, M. and Manning, C. 1976: Breastfeeding, amenorrhea and abstinence in a Javanese village: a case study of Mojolama. *Studies in family planning* 7, pp. 175–9.

Reading

Page, H.J. and Lesthaeghe, R. 1981: *Child-spacing in tropical Africa: traditions and change*. London and New York: Academic Press.

accounting, demographic The process of constructing tables that show how populations, classified into a variety of states, change over time. These tables are known as demographic accounts.

The states used in demographic accounting must include all those in which people can originate and all those to which people can move over a specified period. Origin states include birth as well as existence in a region. Destination states cover, at a minimum, survival in a region and death in a region. Both origins and destinations must include a 'rest of the world' state in order to complete the account. These minimum origin and destination states can be further broken down into a variety of different socio-economic categories such as sex, age, race, occupation, educational grade and many others depending on the purpose of the demographic analysis. Demographic accounts differ according to their treatment of time (open or closed accounts), and because of differences in the nature of the flows incorporated (transition or movement accounts).

PR

Reading

Rees, P.H. and Wilson A.G. 1977: *Spatial population analysis*. London: Edward Arnold.
Stone, R. 1971: *Demographic accounting and model-building*. Paris: OECD.

activity rate See PARTICIPATION RATE.

actuarial methods Since the days of GRAUNT the techniques of demographers and actuaries have overlapped in many ways, especially in the use of LIFE TABLES. The focus of actuarial work, however, is the precise interpolation and graduation of probabilities of survival, and the resultant financial and insurance calculations.

Advanced methods consist of highly complex and precise examples of life table analysis and employ elaborate methods of smoothing and graduating observed data. To this end actuaries have long employed mathematical models and standard life tables and have made use of life tables for highly specific groups of individuals (e.g. the clients of an insurance company), known as life tables for selected heads.

CW

Reading

Benjamin, B. and Haycocks, H.W. 1970: *The analysis of mortality and other statistics*. London and New York: Cambridge University Press.
Ross, J.A. 1982: Actuarial methods. In J.A. Ross, ed. *International encyclopaedia of population*. New York: Free Press.
Smith, D.P. and Keyfitz, N., eds. 1977: *Mathematical demography: selected papers*. Berlin and New York: Springer.

acute disease A disease with one or more of the following characteristics: a sharp or severe incidence, a rapid onset and short course with pronounced symptoms. The opposite of CHRONIC DISEASE.

RSS

adolescent subfecundity The diminished capacity to reproduce during adolescence. It occurs in both the male and the female. In the female it is primarily caused by irregular ovulation after MENARCHE, and in the male by insufficient production of normal sperm. As a result FECUNDABILITY is reduced to relatively low levels.

JB

Reading

Hafez, E.S.E. 1980: *Human reproduction: conception and contraception*. Hagerstown, Maryland: Harper and Row.
Journal of biosocial science. 1977: Fertility in adolescence. Supplement 5.

age Although of self-evident significance and meaning, in demography age is expressed in a number of different ways. A distinction is made between EXACT AGE and AGE IN COMPLETED YEARS. Additionally, it is sometimes necessary, given the sources of data available, to express age as a difference between two specified years. This is known as a period difference. One further definition of age sometimes encountered, especially in statistics using DOUBLE CLASSIFICATION by both age and birth cohort, is AGE REACHED.   RP

age composition   See AGE-SEX STRUCTURE.

age distribution   See AGE-SEX STRUCTURE.

age effect   The position of individuals in any demographic state at a given time depends on several factors. Considering purely demographic characteristics we can identify age, duration of exposure to a particular 'risk', time period effects, and cumulated COHORT experience. An age effect occurs when age has an impact on individual experience independently of any other determinants.

To take a concrete example, the fertility of married women in a certain year can be thought of as being composed of effects due to their age, to the duration of their marriages, to the time period in question, and to the previous experience of each cohort. An age effect may explain differences in childbearing among women who are similar in terms of characteristics other than age. As in this example age effects normally need to be considered in conjunction with other effects.

Although age is a powerful determinant of all demographic processes it is nonetheless a surrogate for more fundamental measures, i.e. physiological state (ageing does not occur uniformly to all individuals) and duration of exposure to social norms and influences. In principle it would be better, whenever possible, to relate the variation seen in vital rates to these underlying variables for which age is a proxy. Nevertheless the biological origin of age effects usually endows them with a generality and regularity absent in cohort or time period effects.   RP

Reading

Fienberg, S.E. and Mason, W.M. 1979: Identification and estimation of age-period-cohort models in the analysis of discrete archival data. In K.F. Schuessler, ed. *Sociological methodology*. San Francisco: Jossey-Bass. Pp. 1–65.

Hobcraft, J., Menken, J. and Preston, S. 1982: Age, period and cohort effects in demography: a review. *Population index* 48, pp.4–43.

Page, H.J. 1977: Patterns underlying fertility schedules: a decomposition by both age and marriage duration. *Population studies* 31, pp. 85–106.

Pullum, T.W. 1980: Separating age, period and cohort effects in white US fertility, 1920–1970. *Social science research* 3, pp. 225–44.

age errors   Errors which can arise from several sources in reported age. The person supplying the information (who may or may not be the individual whose age is in question) may not know the real age, or may wish to conceal the truth, or the interviewer may prefer to estimate the individual's age rather than accept the response, or the age recorded on the interview schedule may not be properly coded for analysis.

Age reporting errors are particularly frequent in many developing countries. For example, studies in Gambia, Ghana, Nigeria and Pakistan found that only 30 to 40 per cent of persons aged 25 to 49 were reported in the same five-year age group both in a survey and in its follow-up reinterview. In the US census of 1970 the comparable figure was 92 per cent. The difficulties caused by age misreporting are exacerbated by the fact that reported ages are often based on other demographic characteristics such as marital status and family size. Studies of such phenomena as age at first birth and at first marriage can therefore be biased by the preconceptions used in the estimation of age.

Although there is a great deal of speculation about the reasons for biased age reports and about the kinds of people who are most likely to misreport their ages there has been little research to determine the most common forms of misreporting.

A few studies have compared ages reported in a survey with more accurate sources of age, but most work has been based on the impact of misreporting on the reported age distribution or on the reported intercensal survival rates for cohorts. Because of the lack of hard information it is difficult to estimate the importance of misreporting for various kinds of demographic analysis. Among the most common forms of age error are AGE HEAPING, AGE OVERSTATEMENT, and AGE SHIFTING.   DE

Reading

Ewbank, D.C. 1981: *Age misreporting and age-selective underenumeration: sources, patterns, and consequences for demographic analysis.* Report 4, Committee on Population and Demography, United States National Academy of Sciences. Washington DC: National Academy Press.

Gibril, M.A. 1979: *Evaluating census response errors: a case study for the Gambia.* Paris: OECD.

Shryock, H.S., Siegel, J.S. et al. 1976: *The methods and materials of demography.* Condensed edition by E.G. Stockwell. London and New York: Academic Press. Chapter 8.

age group   Individual years of age are relatively rarely employed in demographic analysis. Most work revolves around age groups, variously defined but frequently embracing five years (0 to 4 completed years, 5–9, 10–14 and so on). In certain contexts very broad age groups may be acceptable, even desirable. For example when considering the AGEING of the population it is valuable to deal with three broad age groups: children and young dependents, adults of working age, and pensioners and elderly dependents.
                                                   RP

age heaping   A general tendency to misreport a preferred number as one's age (for example a number thought to be lucky, such as seven, or honourable, such as 100) or to round one's age to a number ending with the digits zero or five. This type of age misreporting results in a false concentration of persons at particular ages or in particular age groups. (See also AGE ERRORS.)   RP, DE

age in completed years   Age expressed as the number of complete years lived by an individual. This is frequently termed the 'age at last birthday' and is the method of expressing age most commonly employed in the population at large. In many parts of East Asia, however, age next birthday is traditionally used.

In contrast to age expressed in completed years EXACT AGE offers a more precise definition of age. For example someone born on 19 January 1956 will be exactly 29 years and 3 months on 19 April 1985. This could be expressed as 29 years, 89 days, or as 29.24 years.

At midnight at the turn of the year all persons of a given age in completed years are the members of one BIRTH COHORT: At the very end of 1985, all persons aged 29 were born in the year 1985 minus 29, or 1956.   RP

age overstatement   Exaggeration of age in a census or survey. Since it is difficult to measure the accuracy of individual age reports, overstatement frequently refers to net overstatement, the net effect of both overstatement and understatement on the reported age distribution. Overstatement is generally most common among the elderly and for children aged under five. (See also AGE ERRORS.)   DE

age pattern   A term used to express the way in which the timing or TEMPO of a demographic process varies with the age of individuals. Most processes have distinctive age patterns: mortality shows a bimodal pattern with peaks for infants and old people, fertility is concentrated into the REPRODUCTIVE AGES with a maximum in the 20s, and migration is usually dominated by young adults. The term age profile is also used, so, somewhat confusingly, are age distribution and age structure.   CW

age pattern of fertility A term used to express the way in which FERTILITY varies with age. It often occurs in the context of schedules of age-specific fertility rates or age-specific marital fertility rates. Fertility is restricted to the reproductive ages (for women roughly 15 to 50), and within this range shows a characteristic pattern. An initial rise from low levels (see ADOLESCENT SUBFECUNDITY) to a peak, usually in the 20s, is followed by a decline. This pattern varies depending on a number of factors: the level of FECUNDITY, the prevalence of marriage or other sexual unions, the degree of family limitation and so on.

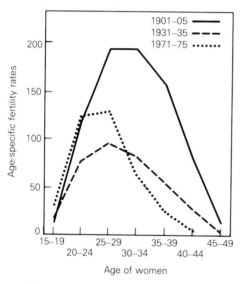

Sweden. Age-specific fertility rates 1901–05, 1931–35 and 1971–75.
Source: Swedish Central Bureau of Statistics 1976. Information i prognosfrågor. Stockholm.

Demographers have been able to model these age-specific patterns with some accuracy using descriptive models (see COALE-TRUSSELL FERTILITY MODEL), and with relation to the PROXIMATE DETERMINANTS OF FERTILITY. Since changes in the age pattern of fertility occur with the onset of the use of contraception in a population, studies of the demographic transition pay considerable attention to age patterns.   CW

Reading

Andorka, R. 1978: *The determinants of fertility in advanced societies*. London: Methuen.

Coale, A.J. 1977: The development of new models of nuptiality and fertility. *Population* 32, special number, pp. 131–54.

— and Trussell, T.J. 1974: Model fertility schedules: variations in the age structure of childbearing in human populations. *Population index* 40, pp. 185–258; also erratum *Population index* 41, p. 572.

Knodel, J. 1977: Family limitation and the fertility transition: evidence from age patterns of fertility in Europe and Asia. *Population studies* 31, pp. 219–49.

age pyramid See POPULATION PYRAMID.

age ratios Measures of the smoothness of a reported age distribution which are helpful in determining the age groups that are likely to be most affected by under-enumeration or by age misreporting.

The age ratio for an age group is normally taken as equal to the number reported in that age group divided by the number obtained from adding one-third of the numbers in the preceding and subsequent age groups and one-third of the reported number in the age group in question. (See also AGE ERRORS.)   DE

Reading

Shryock, H.S., Siegel, J.S. et al. 1976: *The methods and materials of demography*. Condensed edition by E.G. Stockwell. London and New York: Academic Press. Chapter 8.

age reached The age reached by the members of a particular COHORT in a specified period, normally a calendar year. It is employed most commonly in the context of DOUBLE CLASSIFICATION of vital events. When dealing with mortality, for example by specifying the age at death in completed years and in terms of age reached (i.e. the age which individuals reached in a year, or would have reached if they had survived), an exact estimate of mortality within each cohort can be reconstructed.   RP, CW

age shifting   Distortion of a reported age distribution caused by a general tendency to overstate or understate ages.

Examples of age shifting include age overstatement by the elderly and the common misallocation in older age groups of women aged 15–19 (especially those with children). With single-year age distributions upward shifting can result among children from the reporting of their age at nearest birthday rather than in completed years. Upward shifting can occur in five-year age distributions from rounding to ages which end in the digits zero or five since this rarely involves shifting to a lower age group. For example, if equal numbers of 28 and 32 year-olds report their age as 30, the single-year age distribution will not show a general shift, while the five-year distribution will show an upward shift. (See also AGE ERRORS.)   DE

age standardisation   See STANDARDISATION.

ageing (of the population)   Alteration in the age structure of a population in the direction of an increase in the relative importance of old persons, say those over 65, and usually reflected in an increase in the average age of the population. Such alteration generally takes the form of an increase in the numbers of the elderly, a fall in the number of children and young persons, and relative stability in the numbers in central age groups (see table).

Given such regularity, demographic ageing is normally studied with reference to three broad age groups representing the population of working age and young and old dependants. The exact ages chosen as the bounds of these groups vary, depending on the minimum age at leaving school and retirement age, but 0–14, 15–64 and 65 and over are commonly used, especially for international comparisons. Indeed, since the central age groups are generally little affected by ageing, it is common to address the issue by simply presenting the proportion aged 65 plus. A further often-quoted statistic is the DEPENDENCY RATIO which relates the size of the old and young age categories to the size of the central age group.

Although mortality and migration can have an impact on the process of population ageing, the principal determinant of ageing up to the present has been fertility behaviour. Since reduced fertility implies a diminution in the number of births its impact is marginal to the population at age zero, whereas mortality change is likely to affect many, possibly all, age groups. It is in countries where fertility (and hence population growth) has been reduced to low levels that ageing occurs – most notably Europe, North America and more recently Japan, where the rapid fall in fertility in the 1940s and 1950s is leading to accelerated ageing.

It should be noted, however, that mortality change in developed societies is becoming a factor in ageing. This is due to the fact that no significant further reduction is possible in mortality at young ages, the death rate being virtually zero in the first half of life. Any improvement must be among the elderly.

	England and Wales				
	Percentage of population in each age group				
Age group	1871	1901	1931	1961	1981
0–14	36.1	32.4	23.8	23.0	20.3
15–64	59.2	62.9	68.8	65.1	64.4
65 plus	4.7	4.7	7.4	11.9	15.3

Although rarely significant at the national level, emigration can have an appreciable effect on the ageing of local populations. Since migrants tend to be young adults, areas with high out-migration rates (often isolated rural areas and inner-cities) experience exaggerated ageing, not only because of the loss of migrants, but also because of the fall in births due to the depletion of persons in the reproductive ages.

These mechanisms of ageing can be generalised to any population. For example the lowering of recruitment into an institution or organisation will lead to ageing in just the same way as a fall in the birth rate. Similarly, raising the retirement age is equivalent to improving mortality at older ages and also leads to ageing. It has been pointed out that many large organisations have in the past had pyramidal age (and hence seniority) structures typical of rapidly growing populations. The changes required in such institutions to accommodate an older workforce may be considerable.

Ageing has its opposite in the rejuvenation of the population which arises from the opposite changes – increased fertility and immigration for whole populations and higher recruitment and lowering of the retirement age for an organisation. It is worth noting that ageing and rejuvenation are not always mutually exclusive. If, after a considerable period of low fertility, fertility rises, the numbers of young dependants will increase, while the process of ageing due to the preceding low fertility continues for some time. Such developments occurred in Western Europe, especially in France, following 1945.

The economic and social consequences of ageing are clearly considerable, particularly with regard to the increasing burden of dependency. There is a major distinction between young and old dependants. Although educational provision for children is a major government outlay, the cost of an aged dependant to the state is much larger than the cost of a child. (Clark and Spengler (1978) estimate three

times as much in the United States) owing to the much greater health care needs of the old. In contrast, the private cost of raising a child has been estimated to be higher than the outlay involved in supporting an average 60 year-old until death (Wander 1978).

A significant factor in the overall impact on the economy of an increased number of old persons is the question of retirement age. Livi-Bacci (1982) has pointed out that western societies have made it possible for elderly persons to retire at much earlier ages than was previously feasible, thus exacerbating an already increasing burden. Much depends on the economic participation rate of those aged 55 to 64 in determining the ability of society to provide for the elderly.

Finally, the ageing of the population may also affect the collective psychology of a population because of the increasing weight in the formation of attitudes of old people, who may be less open to change. This view is not without its critics, however, especially among the proponents of ZERO POPULATION GROWTH.

Whatever the drawbacks to ageing, contemporary populations will have to learn to adapt themselves to the new conditions which it implies since the process is unavoidable. In a finite world, where the population must progress towards a stationary state, a general movement towards a lower birth rate is unavoidable, to such an extent that the choice of growing or ageing, which still presents itself to some populations, will soon be limited everywhere to the second alternative.

RP, CW

References

Clark, R.J. and Spengler, J.J. 1978: Changing demography and dependency costs: the implications of new dependency ratios and their composition. In B. Herzog, ed. *Aging and income*. New York: Human Sciences Press.

Livi-Bacci, M. 1982: Social and biological ageing: contradictions of development. *Population and development review* 8, pp. 771–81.

Wander, H. 1978: Zero population growth now: the lessons from Europe. In T.J. Espenshade and W.J. Serow, eds. *The economic consequences of slowing population growth.* New York: Academic Press. Pp. 41–69.

Reading

Davis, K. and van den Oever, P. 1981: Age relations and public policy in advanced industrial societies. *Population and development review* 7, pp. 1–18.

Espenshade, T.J. and Serow, W.J., eds. 1978: *The economic consequences of slowing population growth.* New York: Academic Press.

Hauser, P.M. 1976: Aging and world-wide population change. In R.H. Binstock and E. Shanas, eds. *Handbook of aging and the social sciences.* New York: Van Nostrand Reinhold. Pp. 59–86.

Livi-Bacci 1982.

Wander 1978.

age-sex structure   The composition of a population according to the number or proportion of males and females in each age category. The age-sex structure of a population is well represented graphically by a POPULATION PYRAMID. When expressed as proportions, numbers are often given as a part per 1000, per 10,000 or per 100,000, etc. The age groups employed vary according to the aim of a particular study.

The age-sex structure of a population is the cumulative result of past mortality, fertility and migration, and demonstrates considerable variability caused by differences in these phenomena. Populations with rapid growth rates have young populations with a high proportion of children (up to half the population under age 15). More slowly growing or stationary populations have a smaller number of children with commensurately more adults and old persons.

The SEX RATIO at each age is also a feature of considerable importance, and one which varies considerably due to the impact of sex-selective mortality and migration.   RP, CW

Reading

Pressat, R. 1972: *Demographic analysis: methods, results, applications.* London: Edward Arnold; Chicago: Aldine Atherton. Chapter 9.

Shryock, H.S., Siegel, J.S. et al. 1976: *The methods and materials of demography.* Condensed edition by E.G. Stockwell. London and New York: Academic Press. Chapters 7 and 8.

age-specific fertility rate   The number of live births occurring to women of a particular age or age group per year, normally expressed per 1000 women (or sometimes per woman). Thus:

$$f_a = \frac{B_a}{FP_a} \times 1000$$

where f_a is the age-specific fertility rate at age a, B_a is the number of live births to women at that age and FP_a is the female mid-year population aged a.

Age-specific rates are INCIDENCE RATES and refer by implication to the female population. In theory, analogous male fertility rates could be calculated, given the appropriate statistics. In practice this is rarely done and the above definition is used without reference to sex. Five-year age groups from 15–19 to 40–44 or 45–49 are most commonly used.   RP

Reading

Pressat, R. 1972: *Demographic analysis: methods, results, applications.* London: Edward Arnold; Chicago: Aldine Atherton. Chapter 8.

Shryock, H.S., Siegel, J.S. et al. 1976: *The methods and materials of demography.* Condensed edition by E.G. Stockwell. London and New York: Academic Press. Chapter 16.

age-specific marital fertility rate   The number of live births occurring to married women of a particular age or age group, normally expressed per 1000 women (or sometimes per woman). Thus:

$$mf_a = \frac{B_{ma}}{FP_{ma}} \times 1000$$

where mf_a is the age-specific marital fertility rate at age a, B_{ma} is the number of live births to married women and FP_{ma} is the mid-year population of married women aged a. Five-year age groups from 15–19 to 45–49 are most commonly used. For countries with a very early start to childbearing the rate for ages 10–14 may also be given. The form of rate produced is an INCIDENCE RATE.

Since childbearing in many societies largely takes place within marriage these rates give a clearer indication of changes in actual childbearing than the more commonly quoted AGE-SPECIFIC FERTILITY RATES, which are also influenced by changes in marriage patterns. For this reason age-specific marital fertility rates are often used to test for the presence of FAMILY LIMITATION (see also COALE-TRUSSELL FERTILITY MODEL). In a population where control of fertility is widespread, however, age becomes a less significant determinant of marital fertility than the duration of marriage. In such cases DURATION-SPECIFIC MARITAL FERTILITY RATES may be more revealing.

RP, CW

Reading

Mineau, G.P. and Trussell, T.J. 1982: A specification of marital fertility by parents' age, age at marriage and marital duration. *Demography* 19, pp. 335–50.

Page, H.J. 1977: Patterns underlying fertility schedules: a decomposition by both age and marriage duration. *Population studies* 31, pp. 85–106.

Pressat, R. 1972: *Demographic analysis: methods, results, applications.* London: Edward Arnold; Chicago: Aldine Atherton. Chapter 8.

Shryock, H.S., Siegel, J.S. et al. 1976: *The methods and materials of demography.* Condensed edition by E.G. Stockwell. London and New York: Academic Press. Chapter 16.

age-specific rate A rate calculated to express the incidence of a demographic process at a given age or within a specified AGE GROUP. The size of age categories used varies according to the phenomenon studied, but five-year age groups are most common.

Age-specific rates are calculated for both period and cohort analyses and may be INCIDENCE RATES or ATTRITION RATES depending on the definition. When data are available classified by both cohort and age, i.e. DOUBLE CLASSIFICATION, it is possible to calculate two different age-specific rates using slightly different definitions. One is based on AGE IN COMPLETED YEARS and another, less common type, on AGE REACHED, which is a more precise indication of the birth cohort involved. However, calculations based on the age reached are rare owing to the paucity of data with DOUBLE CLASSIFICATION.

In the English language demographic tradition, age-specific rates are frequently presented and interpreted without comment on questions of selectivity and bias. In order to be strictly accurate reflections of underlying behaviour, however, these rates should be corrected for the influence of extraneous DISTURBING PROCESSES. If this is impossible because of lack of information on the disturbance it is necessary to assume that the disturbance is independent of the occurrence of the events under study. (See also NON-SELECTIVITY.)

RP, CW

Reading

Pressat, R. 1972: *Demographic analysis: methods, results, applications.* London: Edward Arnold; Chicago: Aldine Atherton. Chapters 2 and 3.

Wunsch, G. and Termote, M. 1978: *Introduction to demographic analysis.* New York and London: Plenum. Chapter 1.

age-structure effect The role played by the relative size of each age group in a population in determining the number of vital events in a particular period.

In various national populations, for instance, all of which exhibit a value of LIFE EXPECTANCY of around 70 years, a wide range of CRUDE DEATH RATES can be observed. These range from 5 per 1000 in populations with a relatively youthful age structure to nearly 15 per 1000 in countries with older populations.

Coping with age-structure effects is one of the main tasks of demographic analysis; it is achieved in various ways. One common approach is to employ STANDARDISATION, in either the direct or indirect forms; other approaches use TRANSLATION methods.

Age-structure effects are most prominent in the context of demographic phenomena characterised by large variance with age. Since the AGE PATTERN OF FERTILITY is concentrated into only those age groups comprising the REPRODUCTIVE AGES, the CRUDE BIRTH RATE is only moderately affected by age structure effects. In contrast, mortality exhibits its highest values at the extremes of the age range (i.e. both infants and old persons). In such circumstances the effect of age structure may be considerable.   RP, CW

Reading
Kitagawa, E.M. 1955: Components of a difference between two rates. *Journal of the American Statistical Association* 50, pp. 1168–94.
Pressat, R. 1972: *Demographic analysis: methods, results, applications.* London: Edward Arnold; Chicago: Aldine Atherton. Pp. 71–82 and 101–6.
Shryock, H.S., Siegel, J.S. et al. 1976: *The methods and materials of demography.* Condensed edition by E.G. Stockwell. London and New York: Academic Press. Pp. 221–8 and 241–6.

aggregate analysis   Analysis carried out on data referring to a unit of analysis other than the individual – commonly a nation – or an administrative unit within a nation. The term macro-level analysis is also encountered, as is aggregative analysis.

Strictly speaking it is the data rather than the analytical techniques which are inherently aggregated. Nevertheless the term is widely used. Aggregate analysis has been the conventional form of much demographic analysis, especially that based on official statistics. However, with the growth of sample surveys and the wealth of data they provide on individuals, micro-level or INDIVIDUAL ANALYSIS has gained popularity.   CW

algorithm   A step-by-step procedure which solves a particular problem. Algorithms are usually supported by a mathematical proof. The development of computers has led to a greater need for precise, formalised methodologies of problem solving, hence to a greater awareness of the importance of finding optimal algorithms. The word derives from the name Al-Ghorizmeh, a distinguished Arab mathematician of the sixth century.   CW

amenorrhoea   Absence of menstruation. Amenorrhoea results most commonly from sexual immaturity or advanced age, from pregnancy, or from the menstruation-inhibiting effect of frequent and intense breast-feeding. It can also occur under conditions of extreme malnutrition or as a result of endocrine disorders or medication.

The absence of menstruation is usually associated with the absence of ovulation and hence with a zero probability of conception. Since amenorrhoea is readily observable, whereas the presence or absence of ovulation is hard to detect, it is often used as a proxy variable for ANOVULATION in empirical demographic studies. The association between the two characteristics is far from perfect, however, since anovulatory menstrual cycles are not uncommon, particularly in the years near the beginning and end of the reproductive life span.   HP

Reading
Bongaarts, J. and Potter, R.G. 1983: *Fertility, biology and behavior: an analysis of the proximate determinants.* New York and London: Academic Press.
Gray, R.H. 1979: Biological factors other than nutrition and lactation which may influence natural fertility: a review. In H. Leridon and J. Menken, eds. *Natural fertility.* Liège: Ordina Editions. Pp. 217–51.
Tyson, J.E. and Perez, A. 1978: The maintenance of infecundity in post-partum women. In W.H. Mosley, ed. *Nutrition and human reproduction.* New York and London: Plenum.

annual measure   A measure calculated on the basis of observations made in one calendar year. Many demographic indices are presented on an annual basis and, where no explicit time reference is made, an annual dimension is often assumed.

When various rates are under consideration an annual rate is normally calculated using the formula – events divided by MID-YEAR POPULATION. Where a rate refers to data on a number of years, the term mean annual rate is employed. Rates or other measures calculated for periods of less than a year and adjusted to an annual dimension are termed ANNUALISED MEASURES.   RP

annualised measure   Any measure originally calculated on the basis of events that occur in a period other than a year, and then corrected to an annual dimension.

For example: if 48,000 deaths were recorded in February 1970 for a country of 52 million inhabitants the death rate that month would have been 48,000 divided by 52 million or 0.92 per thousand. This value is not comparable to annual crude death rates. It can, however, be adjusted to an equivalent annual value by estimating the number of deaths which would have occurred over 365 days given the death rate of February, i.e. by multiplying the value by 365/28. Thus an annualised crude death rate for February 1970 of 12.03 per thousand is obtained.

It should be noted that this correction effectively amounts to calculating the number of PERSON YEARS lived in February 1970 and uses this as the denominator of the rate.   RP

anovulation   Absence   of   ovulation (rupture of a mature ovarian follicle and release of an ovum), and hence zero probability of conception. A distinction can be made between:

(1) total anovulation (the relatively rare case of a woman who never ovulates throughout her life);
(2) the two long periods of anovulation that mark the beginning and end of a woman's reproductive life-span; and
(3) usually shorter anovulatory periods between the onset of ovulation and its final cessation:

(*a*) periods of spontaneous anovulation, most notably the anovulation that lasts through each pregnancy and continues for durations of up to 18 months or more after childbirth (the duration depending on how long the mother gives frequent and intensive breast-feeding (Howie and McNeilly 1982; Tyson and Perez 1979));
(*b*) anovulatory periods induced by ovulation-inhibiting medication, such as oral contraceptives.

Very few direct data on anovulation are available because ovulation itself is hard to detect. For all types of anovulation except that induced by medication a related variable that is readily observable – AMENORRHOEA – is often used instead. The correspondence between absence of ovulation and absence of menstruation is far from perfect, in particular anovulatory menstrual cycles are very common in the years immediately after menarche and before the menopause, and they may also occur in some cases during the first few months after the end of post-partum amenorrhoea.

Of the three types of anovulation the first appears to be rare and to have little impact on aggregate fertility levels. The second type sets the bounds of the potential reproductive life span, but we have too little reliable data to evaluate whether it is a major contributor to observed fertility differentials (Gray 1979). Variability in both the duration of post-partum anovulation and the use of ovulation-inhibiting medication is, however, known to be a major source of variations in fertility (Bongaarts 1982).   HP

References

Bongaarts, J. 1982: The fertility-inhibiting effects of the intermediate fertility variables. *Studies in family planning* 13, pp. 179–89.

Gray, R.H. 1979: Biological factors other than nutrition and lactation which may influence natural fertility: a review. In H. Leridon and J. Menken, eds. *Natural fertility*. Liège: Ordina Editions. Pp. 217–51.

Howie, P.W. and McNeilly, A.S. 1982: Breast-feeding and post-partum anovulation. *Inter-*

national Planned Parenthood Federation medical bulletin 16, pp. 1–3.

Tyson, J.E. and Perez, A. 1978: The maintenance of infecundity in post-partum women. In W.H. Mosley, ed. *Nutrition and human reproduction*. London and New York: Plenum.

Reading

Bongaarts, J. and Potter, R.G. 1983: *Fertility, biology and behavior: an analysis of the proximate determinants*. New York and London: Academic Press.

anthropological demography Strictly this term can be taken to refer to demographic studies of fertility, mortality and migration in the kinds of small human communities usually studied by anthropologists. However, the term, together with expressions such as 'demographic anthropology' and 'population anthropology', is commonly used to refer to the multitude of more general local-level population studies conducted by anthropologists, and increasingly by population scientists.

Examples of the first, more specifically demographic kind of study include the work of Borrie, Firth and Spillius (1957) on the demography of Tikopia, and Ardener and Carrier's study (1962) of divorce and fertility in West Africa. A recent example is Howell's investigation (1979) of the demography of the hunter-gatherer Dobe !Kung of Botswana. Notable among studies of the more general type are investigations into the work activities of children in peasant household economies, such as those conducted by White (1975) and Cain (1977), and more general investigations into the validity of the 'wealth flow' hypothesis on fertility trends in developing countries, such as those undertaken in south India by Caldwell, Reddy and Caldwell (1982).

More widely still the field can also be considered to cover a variety of studies that are not based on contemporary fieldwork investigation. Relevant here are studies of the prehistoric patterns of human population growth (see PALAEODEMOGRAPHY); SIMULATION experiments concerned with social rules (e.g. infanticide) and demographic processes in small

communities; and studies which address more general theoretical aspects of the relationship between social systems and their demographic processes. In this last context see for example Boserup (1965), Nag (1962) and, more recently, Kreager (1982).   TD

References

Ardener, E. 1962: *Divorce and fertility*, Nigerian social and economic studies 3. Lagos: Oxford University Press.

Borrie, W., Firth, R. and Spillius, J. 1957: The Population of Tikopia, 1929 and 1952. *Population studies* 10, pp. 229–52.

Boserup, E. 1965: *The consequences of agricultural growth*. Chicago: Aldine.

Cain, M. 1977: The economic activities of children in a village in Bangladesh. *Population and development review* 3.

Caldwell, J.C. Reddy, P.H. and Caldwell, P. 1982: The causes of demographic change in rural south India: a micro approach. *Population and development review* 8, pp. 689–727.

Howell, N. 1979: *The demography of the Dobe !Kung*. New York and London: Academic Press.

Kreager, P. 1982: Demography in situ. *Population and development review* 8.

Nag, M. 1962: *Factors affecting human fertility in non-industrial societies: a cross-cultural study*. New Haven, Connecticut: Yale University publications in anthropology 66.

White, B. 1975: The economic importance of children in a Javanese village. In M. Nag, ed. *Population and social organization*. The Hague: Mouton.

Reading

Kaplan, B.A. ed. 1976: *Anthropological studies of human fertility*. Detroit: Wayne State University Press.

Nag, M. ed. 1978: *Population anthropology: an international directory of contributors and their works*. Population Commission of the International Union of Anthropological and Ethnological Sciences.

Swedlund, A.C. and Armelagos, G.J. 1976: *Demographic anthropology*. Dubuque, Iowa: Wm. C. Brown.

Turnbull, C. 1972: Demography of small-scale societies. In G.A. Harrison and A.J. Boyce, eds. *The structure of human populations*. Oxford: Oxford University Press.

antinatalism The opposite of PRONAT-ALISM, and a term used for policies or theories which contain an explicit element of BIRTH CONTROL in order to limit births and hence population growth.

An alternative expression, population control, is also used. The term Malthusianism is also sometimes encountered, derived from Malthus's assertion of the need for control of population growth. He did not advocate FAMILY LIMITATION as the means to achieve this, but recommended control of marriage. However, those who took their inspiration from his writing, advocates of NEO-MALTHUSIANISM, regarded control of fertility within marriage as essential, and modern antinatalist policies stress the need to make means of CONTRACEPTION and INDUCED ABORTION freely available. (See also POPULATION THEORY.)   RP, CW

area sampling Characterising a type of sampling unit or sampling stage, rather than a complete SAMPLE DESIGN, the term refers to any sampling stage in which the sampling frame consists of areal units. Not all demographers would accept this definition; the term seems to be used in a variety of other senses, including (1) compact cluster sampling (see CLUSTER SAMPLING) and (2) any sample design in which some at least of the stages are based on areal units.   CS

assortative marriage See HOMOGAMY.

attrition rate A rate indicating the occurrence of a NON-RENEWABLE PROCESS in which the events under study are divided by the number of persons who have not yet experienced the event (or more exactly the person-years lived by them). They are sometimes also termed exposure rates.

Most frequently used are mortality rates where by definition only those still alive are taken in the denominator of the rate. However, any non-renewable process (marriage of single persons for example) may be analysed through these rates. Their distinguishing characteristic is that the experience of the event under study (the numerator of the rate) leads to removal of an individual from the population at risk and thus from the denominator. This distinguishes attrition rates from INCIDENCE RATES in which events are divided by the whole population irrespective of whether they have experienced the event in question. Attrition rates are closely related to the PROBABILITY of an occurrence at each age and thus facilitate analysis in terms of a LIFE TABLE.   RP

attrition table Synonym for LIFE TABLE. The term is sometimes used to indicate that LIFE TABLE METHODS can be applied to any NON-RENEWABLE PROCESS rather than just to mortality, as the use of the term life table might suggest. This applies equally to single- and multiple-decrement forms of the term life table analysis.

RP, CW

B

baby boom A significant increase in a time series of births, sustained for a number of years and typically longer. It is usually applied to the surge in births which occurred in much of Europe, North America and Australasia after World War Two, and peaked in the early 1960s. The terms 'miniboom' and 'boomlet' are also encountered. A sharp decline in births following a baby boom is sometimes referred to as a *baby bust*. RDL

Reading

Bouvier, L. 1980: America's baby boom generation: the fateful bulge. *Population bulletin* 35.

Easterlin, R. 1980: *Birth and fortune*. London: Grant McIntyre; New York: Basic Books.

Guilmot, P. 1978: The demographic background. In Council of Europe, *Population decline in Europe*. London: Edward Arnold; New York: St Martin's Press. Pp. 3–52.

back projection A technique, based on REVERSE SURVIVAL, for estimating the size of past populations where the available data are confined to simple totals of births and deaths stretching backwards from a reliable census which contains details of age structure. The technique does not require the population to be assumed to be closed to migration. It generates 'censuses' at regular intervals with details of age structure and estimates of net migration between successive 'censuses'. Having generated these 'censuses', estimates of expectation of life at birth, the gross reproduction rate and other measures are readily obtainable. EAW

Reading

Wrigley, E.A. and Schofield, R.S. 1981: *The population history of England 1541–1871: a reconstruction*. London: Edward Arnold; Cambridge, Mass.: Harvard University Press. Pp. 195–9 and appendix 15.

balancing equation An equation that expresses in simple form the way in which any population changes over time. It may be expressed as follows:

$$P_2 = P_1 + B - D + I - E$$

where P_1 and P_2 represent the population at two different dates and B, D, I and E stand for, respectively, births, deaths, immigrants (or inmigrants) and emigrants (or out-migrants) between the two dates. Expressed in this fashion the equation is simply a book-keeping identity and must hold in reality. However, the fact that errors of varying degrees may be present in the estimates of the population size and the vital events means that the identity of the equation is rarely found in practice. In this eventuality the logic of the equation can be used to estimate the size of errors.

The vital events contributing to the equation fall into two categories: $(B-D)$ gives the NATURAL INCREASE, while $(I-E)$ stands for NET MIGRATION. Given this, the equation may be re-expressed as:

$$P_2 = P_1 + NI + NM$$

with NI being natural increase and NM net migration. This re-expression is particularly useful when dealing with regional or local population where migration is frequently of more importance than at the national level. CW

Reading

Shryock, H.S., Siegel, J.S. et al. 1976: *The methods and materials of demography*. Condensed edition by E.G. Stockwell. London and New York: Academic Press. Pp. 4–5.

baseline event The event which marks the creation of a new COHORT. For a marriage cohort, the baseline event is marriage in a specified period; for a birth cohort, it is birth. The term event-origin, drawn from French terminology, is also sometimes encountered.   CW

bastardy See ILLEGITIMACY.

bills of mortality Information collected about the incidence of mortality week by week within the jurisdiction of city authorities in Europe from the sixteenth century onwards. The authorities were especially concerned to be well informed about plague deaths and these were usually separately tabulated from the start. In the course of time numbers of baptisms as well as burials came to be routinely counted, and the mortality data became more detailed. In London, for example, a fairly full classification of burials by cause of death was adopted in the seventeenth century and age breakdowns were added later. Collections of bills of varying degrees of completeness exist for London, Norwich, Northampton, Carlisle, Chester and other towns in England. Comparable tabulations were also made in many continental cities.   EAW

Reading

Graunt, J. 1973: *Natural and political observations made upon the bills of mortality* (first printed London 1662). Reprinted with an introduction by P. Laslett in *The earliest classics: pioneers of demography*. Farnborough, Hants: Gregg International.
Wilson, F.P. 1927: *The plague in Shakespeare's London*. Oxford: Oxford University Press. Appendix 1.

binomial distribution A theoretical frequency distribution which indicates the likelihood of a particular result occurring in a sample, given the characteristics of the overall population.

Also known as the Bernoulli distribution, after James Bernoulli who used it in his posthumously published *Ars conjectandi* (1713), the distribution is fundamental to the theory of hypothesis testing. When dealing with a large sample the binomial is distributed as the NORMAL DISTRIBUTION.   CW

Reading

Blalock, H.M. 1979: *Social statistics*. Revised second edition. Chapter 10.

biological family Strictly defined this term is used to cover what is variously described as the NUCLEAR FAMILY or elementary family. It consists of a married couple with offspring or a widowed person with offspring. The unit of reproduction exists irrespective of either common residence or formal marriage.

Goody recognised three kinds of enduring domestic situations arising out of the reproductive union. They are based on the fact that the mother-child bond is intrinsically longer-lasting than are bonds between sexual partners, or between genitor and offspring, which may be limited to the level of casual contact or could even be 'semen in a bottle' (Goody 1972). In the first and simplest form the mother-child unit exists largely on its own (e.g. the Caribbean 'matri-focal' family); another form, the mother-child relationship with the mother's brother playing the role of long-term provider, is found in matrilineal societies; the most widely prevalent form is based on the copulating couple.

More loosely defined, an ego's biological family or kin group could be taken to include all ascending kin through ego's parents. These are usually referred to as ego's matrilineal and patrilineal kin, i.e. 'blood relatives' of his mother's and father's side respectively. However, sociologists and anthropologists insist that in practice a kin relationship is socially and not biologically determined.   RMS

Reference

Goody, J. 1972: *Domestic groups*. Reading, Mass.: Addison-Wesley.

Reading

Goody 1972.
Harris, C.C. 1969: *The family*. London: Allen and Unwin.

biometric analysis of infant mortality A method of analysing infant mortality which provides a simple, if approximate, means of separating infant deaths due to causes preceding or associated with birth (e.g. birth trauma and congenital malformation) from those attributable to the postnatal environment (e.g. infection and accidents). The former type of death is termed *endogenous* and the latter *exogenous*.

Devised and developed by Bourgeois-Pichat (1946, 1951), the method is based on the observation that the age pattern of mortality after the first month of life is largely independent of the level of mortality. Moreover, cumulated deaths vary linearly with age (i.e. all the points fall on one straight line), if age is expressed on a particular logarithmic scale, $log(n + 1)^3$, where n is age in days since birth. By assuming that all deaths after the first month are exogenous and that exogenous deaths within the first month are related to age in the same linear fashion simple extrapolation of the straight line to age zero should indicate the level of endogenous deaths.

Although the technique has been widely used in studies of both historical and contemporary populations, it is sometimes open to a certain ambiguity owing to the cumulated deaths not falling on a straight line. Such deviations from linearity are closely related to BREASTFEEDING patterns in some populations (Knodel and Kintner 1977) and to changes in the age pattern of infant deaths at very low levels of mortality (Lantoine and Pressat 1984).   RP, CW

References

Bourgeois-Pichat, J. 1946: De la mésure de la mortalité infantile. *Population* 1, pp. 53–68.
— 1951: La mésure de la mortalité infantile. *Population* 6, pp. 223–48 and 459–80.
Knodel, J. and Kintner, H. 1977: The impact of breast feeding patterns on the biometric analysis of infant mortality. *Demography* 14, pp. 391–409.
Lantoine, C. and Pressat, R. 1984: Nouveaux aspects de la mortalité infantile. *Population* 39, pp. 253–64.

Reading

Knodel and Kintner 1977.
Pressat, R. 1972: *Demographic analysis: methods, results, applications.* London: Edward Arnold; Chicago: Aldine Atherton. Pp. 90–4.

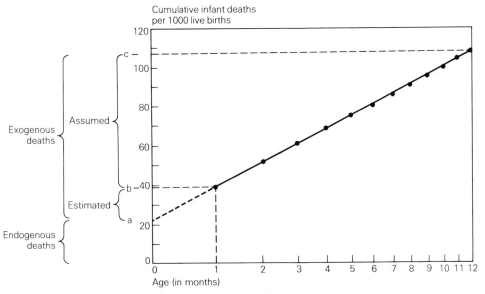

Rural counties of England and Wales 1905.
Source: *General Register Office 1907.* Sixty-eighth annual report of the Registrar General for England and Wales. London: HMSO. (Data also plotted in Knodel and Kintner 1977.)

biostatistics   The branch of statistics that deals with biological data and processes. The (bio)statistical analysis of demographic data most often involves hypothesis testing and estimation with standard techniques such as regression analysis and analysis of variance. In addition there are important more advanced applications, including the use of MARKOV CHAIN MODELS in the study of reproduction and migration, and the multivariate analysis of the LIFE TABLE with covariates.   JB

Reading

Bailey, N.T. 1959: *Statistical methods in biology*. London: English University Press.
Cox, D.R. 1972: Regression models and life tables. *Journal of the Royal Statistical Society* Series B, 34, pp. 187–220.
Sheps, M.C. and Menken, J.A. 1973: *Mathematical models of conception and birth*. Chicago: University of Chicago Press.

biostatistics of reproduction   A collection of statistical techniques and results relating to the biological determinants of human reproduction, for example, FECUNDABILITY, ANOVULATION, STERILITY and FOETAL MORTALITY, which, along with CONTRACEPTION and INDUCED ABORTION are directly involved in the reproductive process. Behavioural factors also play an important role; e.g. BREASTFEEDING leading to anovulation.

Much of the empirical basis of the biostatistical approach to fertility is based on the analysis of data from populations where FAMILY LIMITATION is not practised, and where, as a result, the effect of physiological factors is more clearly in evidence. While some of these data derive from the contemporary developing world most come from historical populations and form the basis for elaborate reproductive models (Bongaarts and Potter 1983; Leridon 1977). These models, in conjunction with observed data, give demographers detailed insights into the PROXIMATE DETERMINANTS OF FERTILITY, and the role played by each in human reproduction.   RP

References and Reading

Bongaarts, J. and Potter, R.G. 1983: *Fertility, biology and behavior: an analysis of the proximate determinants*. New York and London: Academic Press.
Leridon, H. 1977: *Human fertility: the basic components*. Chicago: University of Chicago Press.

birth   May be divided into STILLBIRTHS and live births, the combined total being termed total births. Although this distinction is retained in official statistics, when the resultant data are used in calculations of fertility rates and other measures 'births' often means solely 'live births'.

In addition to classification according to signs of life, births are classified in several ways. The duration of pregnancy (or sometimes the weight of the infant) is used to distinguish between *full term* or *at term* deliveries and premature births. A further physical criterion for distinguishing births is the number of children born in one confinement with an obvious distinction between single and multiple births. BIRTH ORDER is another significant characteristic.   RP, CW

birth cohort   A group of individuals born during a specified period of time, normally one calendar year or a number of years. The birth cohort is by far the most common form of COHORT used in demographic analysis; indeed the word 'cohort' is often used synonymously with 'birth cohort'. The term *generation* is also sometimes used with the same meaning as birth cohort.   RP

birth control   A term first popularised in the early decades of this century by Margaret Sanger, the American pioneer of modern FAMILY PLANNING in her magazine *The woman rebel*, and now taken to mean the behaviour of couples with the aim of preventing sexual intercourse from leading to a birth. The term is often used synonymously with CONTRACEPTION, FAMILY PLANNING and fertility regulation, although birth control is the most general of all these terms and refers to all forms of such behaviour without restriction with regard to methods.

While ABSTINENCE and prolonged BREASTFEEDING (which leads to ANOVULATION) may be used in some circumstances as explicit means of birth control, contraception and INDUCED ABORTION are the principal methods of controlling the occurrence of births, though in recent years, STERILISATION has also come to play a significant role. In addition to attempts to control final family size, birth control also embraces deliberate attempts at BIRTH SPACING, and thus the timing of births.

In contrast to this general term FAMILY LIMITATION has come to take on a more specific and limited use describing only attempts to limit family size after a certain *target* parity has been reached.   RP, CW

birth history   See MATERNITY HISTORY.

birth interval   The interval between two successive births or the interval between marriage (or more generally entry into sexual union) and a first birth. Intervals may be calculated on the basis of stillbirths as well as live births, but usually only involve the latter.

Starting from marriage, the time elapsed up to the first birth is conventionally termed the first birth interval, the duration from the first to the second birth the second birth interval and so on. The terms protogenesic and intergenesic intervals are also encountered for first and subsequent intervals respectively. In addition intervals may also be defined with reference to a particular time (e.g. a census or survey). From the point of view of the survey or census, intervals defined as above are termed CLOSED INTERVALS while the interval between the most recent birth and the survey or census is termed an OPEN INTERVAL. An interval which begins before and ends after the date in question is termed a straddling interval.

In recent years the analysis of birth intervals has gained wide acceptance as a

form of fertility analysis and many new analytic techniques have been applied. For example, examination of the COMPONENTS OF THE BIRTH INTERVAL has enabled links between the physiological and behavioural determinants of fertility to be more clearly identified (Leridon 1977). Similarly the fact that data on birth intervals refer to NON-RENEWABLE PROCESSES, (that is, a woman can have only one first birth (excluding multiple births), only one second birth and so on) makes birth intervals well suited to analysis by LIFE TABLE METHODS and HAZARDS MODELS (Smith 1980).   RP, CW

References

Leridon, H. 1977: *Human fertility: the basic components*. Chicago: University of Chicago Press.

Smith, D.P. 1980: *Life table analysis*. World Fertility Survey technical bulletin 6. Voorburg, The Netherlands: International Statistical Institute.

Reading

Chen, L.C., Ahmed, S., Gesche, M. and Mosley, W.H. 1974: A prospective study of birth interval dynamics in rural Bangladesh. *Population studies* 28, pp. 277–97.

Leridon 1977.

Page, H.J. and Lesthaeghe, R., eds. 1980: *Childspacing in tropical Africa: tradition and change*. London and New York: Academic Press.

birth order   The classification of births according to the number of previous births to the mother, or, less commonly, the number of previous births within the current marriage or sexual union. Birth order is normally based on live births only, although STILLBIRTHS are sometimes involved. An analogous classification is confinement order, which commonly takes into account all pregnancies lasting at least 28 weeks and counts MULTIPLE BIRTHS as one confinement. In the same way PREGNANCY ORDER may be used when information is known on the outcome of all pregnancies.

A distinction is frequently made

between *higher order* and *lower order* births (first, second and third births as lower order; fourth and above as higher). Such a distinction is useful in determining the origins of fertility change. For example, Ryder (1980) has shown that fertility fluctuations in the United States since the 1950s are mainly due to variation in lower order fertility. (See also PARITY.)   RP, CW

Reference

Ryder, N.B. 1980: Components of temporal variations in American fertility. In R.W. Hiorns, ed. *Demographic patterns in developed societies*. London: Taylor and Francis.

birth probability The probability, for women of a given family size, of giving birth within a specified time period, or at a specified duration of exposure to risk of doing so.

Although 'probabilities' are sometimes presented without reference to BIRTH ORDER or the PARITY of potential mothers (e.g. the probability of any woman giving birth in a particular year), such measures are not true probabilities since the women at risk may have more than one confinement in the year, giving a 'probability' greater than unity. The use of the term should be restricted to being the probability that a woman with a specified number of children, n, has a further birth (order $n + 1$) within a specified period, or more exactly, within a specified duration of the nth birth; or, in the case of first births within a specified duration of marriage (or since entry into a sexual union). It should, therefore, only be used within the context of BIRTH INTERVAL analysis or a PARITY-SPECIFIC analysis of fertility. Probabilities referring to a year of potentially fertile life are common, and in the case of the first interval monthly birth probabilities are sometimes calculated. (See also PARITY-SPECIFIC FERTILITY RATE.)   RP, CW

Reading

Pressat, R. 1972: *Demographic analysis: methods, results, applications*. London: Edward Arnold; Chicago: Aldine Atherton. Chapter 8. Shryock, H.S., Siegel, J.S. et al. 1976: *The methods and materials of demography*. Condensed edition by E.G. Stockwell. London and New York: Academic Press. Pp. 292–3. Wunsch, G. and Termote, M. 1978: *Introduction to demographic analysis*. New York and London: Plenum. Pp. 168–75.

birth rate See CRUDE BIRTH RATE.

birth spacing Deliberate action on the part of couples to space the births of their children at particular intervals. The synonyms child spacing and spacing behaviour are also used.

The term sometimes refers to traditional practices of prolonged breastfeeding or abstinence which have a spacing effect but may not be practised explicitly for contraceptive purposes.

Spacing is contrasted with STOPPING BEHAVIOUR where couples attempt to cease childbearing.   RP, CW

births averted A measure of the number of births which have not occurred because of the effects of a family planning programme. The estimation of the number of births averted involves making assumptions about several aspects of the reproductive process and inevitably involves a degree of uncertainty, though that can be minimised through the use of detailed reproductive models.   CW

Reading

Hermalin, A.I. 1982: Family planning programs: effects on fertility. In J. A. Ross ed. *International encyclopedia of population*. New York: Free Press.
Potter, R.G. 1970: Births averted by contraception: an approach through renewal theory. *Theoretical population biology* 1, pp. 251–72.

Bongaarts' decomposition A decomposition of fertility rates, designed to provide a simple and practical means of quantifying the impact of different PROXIMATE DETERMINANTS OF FERTILITY and hence of comparing the role of each determinant in different populations.

The decomposition focuses on four

determinants believed to be responsible for the bulk of the variation in fertility observed throughout the world, namely (1) the proportion of women married, (2) contraceptive use, (3) induced abortion and (4) the duration of the period of non-susceptibility to conception following a birth. This last determinant is closely related to the prevalence and intensity of breastfeeding. More detailed versions can be made by further breaking down these four factors.

The decomposition is multiplicative, the impact of each of the determinants being measured by a coefficient that indicates its impact in reducing fertility. More specifically, the decomposition is usually given as:

$$TFR = C_m \times C_a \times C_c \times C_i \times TF$$

where TFR is the TOTAL FERTILITY RATE, the coefficients reflect the effect in reducing fertility of marriage (C_m), abortion (C_a), contraception (C_c) and post-partum non-susceptibility (C_i), and TF represents the hypothetical maximum fertility or total fecundity.

The values of the coefficients can be estimated relatively easily from data on marital status, contraception, abortion and post-partum variables that are now widely available.   HP

Reading
Bongaarts, J. 1978: A framework for analyzing the proximate determinants of fertility. *Population and development review* 4, pp. 105–32.
— and Potter, R.G. 1983: *Fertility, biology and behavior: an analysis of the proximate determinants*. New York and London: Academic Press.

brain drain The emigration of highly-skilled, often professional, individuals to countries offering better economic and social opportunities. Recent examples are doctors, engineers and others leaving Third World countries to practise in the developed world. (See also INTERNATIONAL MIGRATION.)   CW

Brass techniques See INDIRECT ESTIMATION TECHNIQUES.

breastfeeding Lactation is studied by demographers because of its effects both in improving infant and child health and mortality, and in lengthening birth intervals and so reducing fertility.

Although long neglected, and even disparaged, as a major factor in demography, the importance of breastfeeding is now almost universally acknowledged. Evidence from historical Europe and North America and from contemporary developing countries attests its impact on mortality. This arises because breastmilk contains certain properties which make it superior to any alternative. It provides immunological protection against many common childhood diseases and contains the full nutritional requirements of the young infant in a form more easily digestible than other foods. Moreover, in conditions of poor hygiene and sanitation it is probably the only uninfected food available. The effects of these differences can be dramatic: during the 1890s in Berlin the death rate in the first year of life was 57 per 1000 among breastfed children but 376 per 1000 for those fed artificial foods. Even as late as 1946–7 the infant mortality rate in Great Britain for non-breastfed children was double the rate for those breastfed (Knodel 1977).

The effects of lactation on fertility are potentially very considerable. Indeed in societies where contraception and induced abortion are not widely available lactation is often the most important factor in keeping fertility below its physiological maximum. In Bangladesh, for example, where only an estimated 9 per cent of women currently use contraceptives, breastfeeding is prolonged leading to 18.5 months of AMENORRHOEA. If this duration fell to six months it has been estimated that the use of contraceptives would need to rise to 43 per cent to hold fertility at its present level. The physiological link between suckling and fertility is not entirely understood, but the main connections are apparent. The most plausible mechanism is for neural impulses from the nipple to reach the hypothalmus where they stimulate the release of beta endorphin. This in turn is thought to suppress hormone release leading to ANOVULATION. Analysis of the link between lactation and fertility is complicated, however, by the fact that both the duration and intensity of suckling are important. If alternative foods are used as partial substitutes for breastmilk the effect is reduced. Similarly, a few large feeds appear to have less impact than repeated short suckling. Many studies have failed to distinguish the various forms of breastfeeding and simply asked for the age at WEANING.

In many parts of the world the prevalence of breastfeeding is declining with potentially serious consequences for both mortality and fertility. In some Western countries, however, the incidence and average duration of lactation has increased in recent years from the very low levels of the 1960s as the benefits of breastfeeding receive more publicity.   CW

Reference

Knodel, J. 1977: Breast-feeding and population growth. *Science* 198, pp. 1111–15.

Reading

Knodel 1977.

— 1982: Breastfeeding. In J.A. Ross, ed. *International encyclopaedia of population.* New York: Free Press. Pp. 71–6.

McCann, M.F. et al. 1981: Breast-feeding, fertility and family planning. *Population reports,* series J, 24.

Short, R.V. 1984: Breastfeeding. *Scientific American* 250. 4, pp. 23–30.

built-in sample A sample survey built into a census. The two operations are carried out simultaneously and the more detailed questions of the survey replace the census in the selected units. The survey questionnaire includes the census questions so as to preserve the exhaustive census coverage.   CS

C

cancer   The second most common cause of death in developed countries after CARDIO-VASCULAR DISEASES, cancer is an uncontrolled proliferation of cells (hyperplasia). Normal cells, by a still unknown mechanism, stop dividing when their proper function is attained; malignant cells do not, and therefore produce an accumulation of tissue called tumour (see NEOPLASM). Another characteristic of cancer (metastasis) is the ability of malignant cells to detach themselves from the primary tumour and spread to other sites.

The origins of cancer are not well known: genetic and environmental factors are certainly involved. Among the numerous factors cited are the impact of various chemicals used in industry, radiation as in the form of X-rays, viruses (such as the EB virus), diet, tobacco smoking (in lung cancer), genetic susceptibility, and immune deficiency. The hope is that oncology (the study of tumours) will eventually control the mechanisms through which hyperplasia and metastasis occur. Among the promising approaches are stimulating the host defence mechanisms (the immuno-surveillance system) or inhibiting the vascularisation of the tumour. Another way of preventing cancer is to eliminate or reduce its various environmental and behavioural determinants, such as industrial carcinogens or smoking.

The monitoring of cancer trends is based on cancer deaths by site of cancer, as collected on the basis of the death certificate (see CAUSE OF DEATH) and then tabulated according to the INTERNATIONAL CLASSIFICATION OF DISEASES. Refined epidemiological studies require the existence of specific cancer registries, incorporating each new case of cancer as it occurs.

GW

Reading
Alderson, M. ed. 1982: *The prevention of cancer*. London: Edward Arnold.
Campbell, H. 1980: Cancer mortality in Europe. Patterns and trends – 1955 to 1974. *World health statistics quarterly* 33, pp. 241–80.
Fidler, I.J. 1979: Overview: cancer metastasis. In S.B. Day, ed. *A companion to the life sciences*. New York: Van Nostrand Reinhold.
Hiatt, H.H., Watson, J.D. and Winsten, J.A. 1977: *Origins of human cancer, book A*. Cold Spring Harbor, New York: Cold Spring Harbor Laboratory.
Kolata, G.B. 1980: Testing for cancer risk. *Science* 207, pp. 967–9.
Lilienfield, A.M., Levin, M.L. and Kessler, I.I. 1972: *Cancer in the United States*. Cambridge, Mass.: Harvard University Press.

cardiovascular disease   Disease of the heart and blood vessels. A list of the various forms of cardiovascular disease (CVD) can be found in the INTERNATIONAL CLASSIFICATION OF DISEASES, the major ones being coronary heart disease affecting the coronary arteries, and stroke affecting the brain (cerebral and carotid arteries).

CVD is currently the major cause of death in developed countries. The foremost etiological processes leading to CVD are atherosclerosis (a gradual blocking of the arteries due to the development of plaques composed predominantly of cholesterol), hypertension (a chronically elevated blood pressure), and congenital or rheumatic heart diseases (the latter resulting from the infection in childhood from specific streptococcal bacteria).

The causes of CVD are not all known: they probably include genetic, environmental and social factors. Individual life-style certainly has an impact on the major etiological processes, for example smoking, eating habits, and physical exercise. Prevention programmes have been set up in several countries with the aim of reducing the magnitude of CVD by changing life-styles and eliminating or reducing risk factors such as hypertension and obesity. (See also HEART DISEASE.)   GW

Reading

Dawber, T.R. 1980: *The Framingham study: the epidemiology of atherosclerotic disease.* Cambridge, Mass.: Harvard University Press.

Levy, R.I. and Moskowitz, J. 1982: Cardiovascular research: decades of rogress, a decade of promise. *Science* 217, pp. 121–9.

Marx, J.L. and Kolata, G.B. 1978: *Combating the #1 killer.* Washington DC: American Association for the Advancement of Science.

Shephard, R.J. 1981: *Ischaemic heart disease and exercise.* London: Croom Helm.

Rose, G.A. and Blackburn, H. 1968: *Cardiovascular survey methods.* Geneva: World Health Organisation.

World Health Organisation 1981: *Community control of cardiovascular diseases.* Copenhagen: Regional Office for Europe.

carrying capacity   The maximum number of persons sustainable by a given territory under specific conditions, e.g. at a given standard of living. The term was first employed in ecological studies and has been taken up widely by geographers. (See also MAXIMUM POPULATION.)   CW

case fatality rate   The proportion of fatal cases among persons contracting a specified disease. The rate, taken generally as the ratio of the number of deaths due to a particular disease to the number of cases of it, provides a measure of the virulence of the disease in question. It can also be viewed as the crude death rate for the population composed of those persons who contract the disease.   RP

cause of death   An illness or injury which leads to or contributes to death. Classification of deaths by cause is often complicated by the fact that there may be not one but several conditions contributing to the fatality. In such a case *multiple* or *joint* causes of death are said to apply. In order to distinguish among the various causes, the INTERNATIONAL CLASSIFICATION OF DISEASES (ICD) specifies that the death certificate must state the sequence of events leading to death and designate one cause as the *underlying* cause of death. This is the cause that the medical examiner judges to be the one which initiated the train of events ending in death, and which is sometimes different from the *immediate* cause of death. Another terminology contrasts *primary* or *principal* causes and *secondary, contributory,* or *associated* causes. In the case of injury or trauma, information is also required on the circumstances of the trauma: motor-vehicle accident, suicide, etc.

Although the ICD should in theory permit detailed comparability of cause of death statistics for all countries, in practice the quality of such data varies greatly. It depends to a large degree on the skill of the certifying medical attendant in diagnosing the cause of death and in describing it accurately on the death certificate, and to a lesser degree on the accurate coding of the information. One indication of the quality of cause of death information is the relative prominence of senility or other ill-defined conditions as causes of death. A high proportion of deaths in these indeterminate and vague catch-all categories is usually indicative of poor data.

A further, more general classification often made is between the two broad categories of EXOGENOUS MORTALITY and ENDOGENOUS MORTALITY. The former involves deaths which arise from environmental or external causes such as infectious diseases, the latter is principally due to the genetic make-up of the individual and includes such degenerative diseases as CANCER and CARDIO-VASCULAR DISEASE as well as conditions of early infancy, e.g. birth trauma.

In broad terms the history of developed countries can be seen as a move from

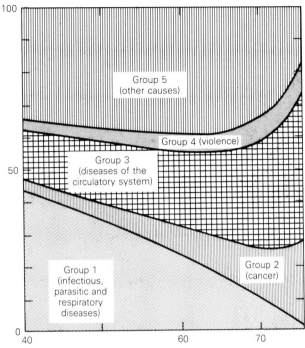

Percentage of Deaths

100

Group 5 (other causes)

Group 4 (violence)

Group 3 (diseases of the circulatory system)

50

Group 1 (infectious, parasitic and respiratory diseases)

Group 2 (cancer)

0

Life expectancy   40   60   70

Cause of death: Approximate percentage distribution of deaths at varying overall life expectancies.

exogenous to endogenous deaths. The virtual disappearance of infectious and parasitic diseases and their replacement with diseases associated with ageing has been given even greater significance by the growth of the aged population.

The impact of any one cause of death can be examined through the use of CAUSE-SPECIFIC DEATH RATES, and the result of eliminating any one cause can be assessed with a CAUSE-DELETED LIFE TABLE.   RP

Reading

Howe, G.M. 1976: *Man, environment and disease in Britain: a medical geography of Britain through the ages.* London: Penguin; New York: Barnes and Noble.

Preston, S.H. 1976: *Mortality patterns in national populations.* New York and London: Academic Press.

— and Nelson, V.E. 1974: Structure and change in causes of death: an international summary. *Population studies* 28, pp. 19–51.

cause-deleted life table A LIFE TABLE constructed using death rates lowered by the elimination of the risk of dying from a specified cause.

To construct a cause-deleted life table it is necessary to calculate probabilities of survival with one cause removed. Thus, if lx stands for the number of survivors at age x, $D_1(x,x+1)$ are the deaths between ages x and $x+1$ from the cause it is intended to remove and $D_2(x,x+1)$ are deaths due to all other causes, then the probability of death in the absence of one cause q_x^2 is given by:

$$q_x^2 = \frac{D_2(x, x+1)}{l_x - \dfrac{D_1(x, x+1)}{2}}$$

Unfortunately the data needed for this calculation are rarely available and the analyst has to resort to data on the proportion of deaths at age x due to the cause under consideration, K_x, which is more readily available. Thus, where q_x^2 is as above and q_x is the probability of dying from all causes, the following applies:

$$\log_e (1-q_x^2) = (1-K_x) \log_e (1-q_x)$$

These formulae assume that the various causes of mortality are independent of one another, which can never be strictly verified. Moreover, data on CAUSE OF DEATH are somewhat problematic even in the most developed countries and may be totally unreliable elsewhere. It is sensible, therefore, to regard cause-deleted life tables as a convenient, if somewhat conjectural, means of comparing the relative impact of different diseases.

The most common use of cause-deleted life tables is to calculate the gain in LIFE EXPECTANCY at birth which would result from the elimination of one cause. This was first attempted by Duvillard in 1806 who estimated that the removal of smallpox in France would improve life expectancy by 3.5 years. In modern populations the elimination of even the most widespread diseases would result in only modest gains in life expectancy. For example, if all cancer deaths were eliminated from the mortality of white males in the United States around 1970, a gain of only 2.3 years would accrue since the persons who did not die of cancer would still face substantial risks of dying from other causes. Other things being equal the age at which a particular cause is prevalent and its overall importance as a cause of death are the two factors which determine how much improvement could be expected from its elimination.   RP

Reading

Shryock, H.S., Siegel, J.S. et al. 1976: *The methods and materials of demography.* Condensed edition by E.G. Stockwell. London and New York: Academic Press. Chapter 15.

Wunsch, G. and Termote, M. 1978: *Introduction to demographic analysis.* New York and London: Plenum. Chapter 3.

cause-specific death rate The number of deaths attributable to a specified cause or group of causes during a year, convention-

ally expressed per 100,000 of the mid-year population. More generally it can be taken as the deaths due to a cause in any period divided by the PERSON-YEARS lived during that period.

These rates are most usefully expressed for specific age-groups, and according to sex rather than for the population as a whole. Another measure frequently calculated is the percentage of all deaths due to a particular cause, the cause-specific death ratio. This provides a convenient and simple measure of the relative importance of different diseases in a population.   RP, CW

Reading

Preston, S.H. and Nelson, V.E. 1974: Structure and change in causes of death: an international summary. *Population studies* 28, pp. 19–51.

Shryock, H.S., Siegel, J.S. et al. 1976: *The methods and materials of demography.* Condensed edition by E.G. Stockwell, London and New York: Academic Press. Chapter 14.

celibacy See MARRIAGE and MARITAL STATUS.

censoring See TRUNCATION.

census The total process of collecting, compiling and publishing data on the demographic, social and economic situation of all persons in a specified territory at a particular time.

With its governmental backing and large, sometimes vast, scale of operations, a census provides a primary source of information on the population of a country. Indeed, in some cases it is the only reasonably reliable data available. The operation of a census is usually governed by legal or constitutional arrangements which may fix its date and other aspects of its procedures, as well as making it obligatory for all respondents to answer truthfully. A modern census has four essential features: individual ENUMERATION, universality within a precisely defined territory, simultaneity, and defined periodicity. Where *individual enumeration* is not attempted and group enumeration is used the result is more accurately termed a head count rather than a census proper. This was the case in many early censuses. *Universality*, although always a goal, is never achieved in practice, virtually every census having some individuals not recorded. A distinction is made between *de facto* enumeration, which records where each individual was on census night, and *de jure* enumeration, which records usual residence. Each is widely used; the former in the United Kingdom and the latter in the United States, for example. *Simultaneity* is not always strictly observed either. In many cases there are practical advantages in spreading the process of enumeration over some time, for example where only a small number of trained interviewers is available. Nevertheless, the information recorded should always refer to the same date. In any event, it is necessary to take the census at a time of year when most people are least likely to be mobile, mobility being an obstacle to precise enumeration. Regular *periodicity* is a highly desirable feature of censuses: the United Nations recommends decennial or quinquennial censuses. Few countries feel able to mobilise the necessary resources for a census every five years (France for much of this century and post-war Japan are notable exceptions) and a census every decade has become the norm, with the UN recommending years ending in 0 for comparability.

Although census-taking of sorts has been attempted since ancient times (Egypt, Babylonia, China and Rome all conducted census-like operations) few results have survived and the counts were normally intended for taxation or military purposes. Extensive tax documents of a quasi-census kind have survived in many European countries dating from the fifteenth century or even earlier, the city-states of Italy being particularly well documented (see NOMINATIVE LISTING). The French colonies of Quebec (Nouvelle France) and Nova Scotia (Acadia) had 16 enumerations between 1665 and 1754, but it was in Scandinavia that the truly national census arose with counts in

Sweden in 1749, Norway in 1760, Denmark in 1769, and Iceland as early as 1703. France and Great Britain both took initial censuses in 1801 and the United States, following the tradition of colonial censuses dating back to 1624–25 in Virginia, held a national census in 1790. During the nineteenth century the use of censuses spread to all European states and to some of their overseas colonies, and the period since the second world war has seen the near-universality of census work.

Any national census entails a huge amount of preparatory work which may run over several years. Preliminary activities include elaborate mapping and preparation of lists of places, selecting questions and designing the questionnaire, planning data processing and analysis, running field trials or pre-tests, considerable publicity to ensure maximum public cooperation and the training of enumerators and supervisors, whose numbers may run into millions in the largest censuses.

The choice of questions varies greatly between countries though attempts by the United Nations to ensure at least a minimum of comparability have been partially successful. Whatever the questions, it is essential that the intended analyses are borne in mind from the outset since they may affect the design of the questionnaire and the training of enumerators. In addition to purely demographic characteristics such as age, sex and marital status, data are also gathered on housing, education, economic activity, religion, income and language as well as on household and family composition.

SAMPLING is also widely used within censuses in order to select a proportion of individuals for more detailed questioning. An elaborate LIFE HISTORY of an individual is sometimes drawn up in this manner to permit more elaborate analysis of, for example, migration or fertility. This is particularly true where alternative sources of data are unavailable.

Though the full processing and analysis of census material may take several years, provisional results (sometimes based on a

sample of individuals or areas) are frequently published very soon after the
completion of field operations, so that the
constantly changing make-up of the population may be grasped with the minimum
of delay, in spite of the problems caused
by over- or undercounts and other data
errors.

In many cases the census (as the most
accurate estimate of numbers) is used to
determine such matters as parliamentary
boundaries, the disbursement of government aid and other questions where population size is of consequence. In such circumstances the question of undercounting
often becomes highly emotive and may
lead to political and legal difficulties. In a
different context opposition to such a
large-scale governmental information-
gathering process may lead to controversy
over privacy. Moreover the expense of a
census also provokes unfavourable comment in many countries, especially those
where other sources of information are
comprehensive. Nevertheless, censuses re-
tain a number of distinct advantages over
alternative data collection methods such as
sample surveys: they provide a set of
detailed frames – lists of households, small
areas, etc. – which provide the basis,
perhaps the only one available, for subsequent surveys; they also provide up-to-
date information on very small areas,
something not feasible in the context of
sample enumeration.   RP, CW

Reading

Benjamin, B. 1970: *The population census*.
London: Heinemann.
Bulmer, M. and Warwick, D.P., eds. 1983:
Social research in developing countries.
Chichester and New York: Wiley.
Casley, D.J. and Lurey, D.A. 1981: *Data col-
lection in developing countries*. Oxford:
Clarendon Press.
Shryock, H.S., Siegel, J.S. et al. 1976: *The
methods and materials of demography*. Con-
densed edition by E.G. Stockwell. London and
New York: Academic Press. Chapter 3.
United Nations 1980: *Principles and recom-
mendations for population and housing cen-
suses*. Series M, statistical papers 67. New
York: Department of International Economic
and Social Affairs.
United States, National Academy of Sciences
1981: *Collecting data for the estimation of fer-
tility and mortality*. Panel on data collection,
Committee on Population and Demography.
Washington DC: National Academy Press.
Chapter 2.

central death rate The number of
deaths occurring in a specified period of
time (commonly one year) and in a specific age-sex category divided by the population at risk (i.e. in the appropriate age-
sex category), expressed in PERSON-YEARS.
The value is often multiplied by a convenient constant (e.g. 1000). In most calculations based on VITAL STATISTICS, the population at risk is taken to be the MID-YEAR
POPULATION. (See also LIFE TABLE and
LIFE TABLE FUNCTIONS).   MM

Reading

Elandt-Johnson, R.C. 1975: Definition of
rates: some remarks on their use and misuse.
American journal of epidemiology 102,
pp. 267–71.
Shryock, H.S., Siegel, J.S. et al. 1976: *The
methods and materials of demography*. Condensed edition by E.G. Stockwell. London and
New York: Academic Press. Chapter 14.

**Chandrasekar-Deming (C-D) tech-
nique** A method of correcting for the
underreporting of vital events when dual
reports on them are available for the same
population. (See DUAL RECORD SYSTEM.)
Suppose, after MATCHING of events
recorded in both reports, M is the number
of events reported by both sources, that
U_1 is the number of events reported by the
first source but missed by the latter, and
U_2 is the number of events reported by the
second source but missed by the former.
Then, by assuming that the two sources of
information were independent, an estimate of events missed by both sources, x,
is given by:

$$X = U_1 U_2 / M$$

and an estimate of total number of events,
E, is given by:

$$E = M + U_1 + U_2 + (U_1U_2/M)$$

Two sources of data are said to be independent when the events both included and excluded from one source have the same probability of inclusion in the other source. If any positive correlation between the two sources is present (i.e. if events not included in one source are also likely to be excluded from the other), the C-D technique would underestimate the number of events missed by both sources. Since a positive correlation may be expected even if there has been no collusion (because the chance of detecting a vital event is likely to vary in different demographic and socio-economic strata of the population), Chandrasekar and Deming (1949) suggested that their method be applied to homogeneous subgroups of the population and the total estimate be built upon from the estimates for subgroups. Because of the practical difficulties in MATCHING, the sensitivity of the C-D technique to erroneous matches or non-matches is of even greater consequence than the correlation bias. (Marks et al. 1974).   PNM-B

References

Chandrasekar, C. and Deming, W.E. 1949: On a method of estimating birth and death rates and the extent of registration. *Journal of the American Statistical Association* 44, pp. 101–15.
Marks, E.S., Seltzer, W. and Krotki, K.J. 1974: *Population growth estimation. A handbook of vital statistics measurement.* New York: Population Council.

Reading

Rumford, J. and Greene, S. 1979: A study of the correlation bias of unrecorded events by two independent enumeration systems. *Population studies* 33, pp. 181–8.
Greenfield, C.C. 1975: On the estimation of a missing cell in a 2 × 2 contingency table. *Journal of the Royal Statistical Society*, series A general, 138, pp. 51–61.
George, A. and Mathai, A.M. 1980: A method of estimating the total number of events from information supplied by several agencies. *Canadian studies in population* 7, pp. 1–7.

Chi square (χ^2) A statistic whose theoretical frequency distribution is often used as the basis of SIGNIFICANCE TESTS which present data in either the nominal or interval form.
It has two uses:

(1) to compare two observed distributions (the test indicates whether the two come from the same overall population)
(2) to compare an observed distribution with a theoretical one (the test shows whether actual data conform to the theoretical expectation).   CW

Reading

Blalock, H.M. 1979 *Social statistics.* Revised second edition. Chapter 15.

child spacing   See BIRTH SPACING.

child survivorship estimation   An INDIRECT ESTIMATION TECHNIQUE for estimating LIFE TABLE mortality measures from data on CHILDREN EVER BORN and children surviving.
The most widely used child survivorship estimation procedures utilise census or survey data for women classified in five year age groups. Brass discovered that proportions of deceased children among all children ever born to women aged 15–19, 20–24, and so on, closely approximate the life table PROBABILITY OF DYING by, respectively, ages 1, 2, 3, 5, 10, and so on. (See Brass 1975, chapter 8.) He developed a set of 'multipliers' to convert the proportions of deceased children into these probabilities.
Brass's technique, which formally assumes constant mortality, has been extended to allow for mortality change (see Feeney 1976, 1980). For each Brass estimate, a 'time ago' value is calculated which indicates the point, relative to the time of the census or survey, to which the estimate of mortality refers. Time ago values range from about one year for the youngest age group to nearly thirty years for the oldest age groups.
Child survivorship data may thus be used to estimate the trend of mortality for

several decades before a census or survey by using a MODEL LIFE TABLE family to translate the estimates from different age groups to a common base, such as the INFANT MORTALITY RATE. Where data are available from two or more sources at different points in time, the comparison of the overlapping portion of the estimated mortality trends provides a valuable check on data quality.

Hill and Trussell (1977) provide a useful overview of child survivorship and related indirect estimation techniques. On the estimation of mortality trends, see Feeney (1980) and Palloni (1981). Data collection errors are discussed in Blacker (1974), Blacker and Brass (1979) and Banister (1979).   GF

References

Banister, J. 1979: Census questions on fertility and child mortality: problems with questionnaire design. *Asian and Pacific census forum* 6.1, pp. 5–8.

Blacker, J. 1974: The estimation of vital rates from census data in Kenya and Uganda. In P. Cantrelle, ed. *Population in African development*. Dolhain, Belgium: Ordina editions.

— and Brass, W. 1979: Experience of retrospective demographic enquiries to determine vital rates. In L. Moss and H. Goldstein, eds. *The recall method in social surveys*. London: University of London, Institute of Education. Distributed by NFER Publishing Company.

Brass, W. 1975: *Methods for estimating fertility and mortality from limited and defective data*. Chapel Hill, North Carolina: Laboratories for Population Statistics. Chapter 8.

Feeney, G. 1976: Estimating infant mortality rates from child survivorship data by age of mother. *Asian and Pacific census newsletter* 3, pp. 12–6.

— 1980: Estimating infant mortality trends from child survivorship data. *Population studies* 34, pp. 109–28.

Hill, K. and Trussell, T.J. 1977: Further developments in indirect mortality estimation. *Population studies* 31, pp. 313–34.

Palloni, A. 1981: A review of infant mortality trends in selected underdeveloped countries: some new estimates. *Population studies* 35, pp. 100–19.

Reading

Brass 1975.

Brass, W., Coale, A.J. et al. 1968: *The demography of tropical Africa*. Princeton: Princeton University Press.

Hill, K. and Zlotnik, H. 1982. Indirect estimation of fertility and mortality. In J.A. Ross, ed. *International encyclopaedia of population*. New York: Free Press.

childbearing ages See REPRODUCTIVE AGES.

children ever born A woman who has reached reproductive age will have borne a certain number (perhaps zero) of children at any given time, of which a certain number will still be surviving. These numbers are referred to, respectively, as the children ever born and children surviving for this woman at this time. Data on children ever born and children surviving are collected in censuses, surveys, and vital registration systems, The term children ever born usually, but not invariably, refers to live births.

On the use of children ever born and children surviving data see INDIRECT ESTIMATION TECHNIQUES and CHILD SURVIVORSHIP ESTIMATION.   GF

child-woman ratio The number of children aged 0 to 4 (occasionally 0 to 9) divided by the number of women of childbearing age (usually 15 to 49), and commonly expressed per 1000.

This ratio is used as a rough indicator of fertility when more detailed measures are unavailable. Since it simply employs the most basic of census age data the ratio is calculable for any area for which an age-sex structure exists. For correct interpretation, however, considerable attention must be paid to the prevailing level of mortality, both of children and of adult women.   RP

Reading

Shryock, H.S., Siegel, J.S. et al. 1976: *The methods and materials of demography*. Condensed edition by E.G. Stockwell. London and New York: Academic Press. Pp. 297–301.

chronic disease A disease of long-continued duration or frequent recurrence. The opposite of ACUTE DISEASE.

RSS

circular migration Patterns of MIGRATION in which individuals or groups move away and then return to the place of origin over the course of a well-defined time.

Circular migration usually takes place along the established paths which characterise a MIGRATION FIELD. Apprentices and servants in towns in historic Europe (and *gastarbeiter* in contemporary Europe) who acquire skills or higher earnings before returning home, are prime examples. SEASONAL MIGRATION is a subset of circular migration, the moves usually being accomplished within a year or single agricultural cycle.

DCS

Reading

Tilly, C. 1978: Migration in modern European history. In W.H. McNeill and R.S. Adams, eds. *Human migration: patterns and policies*. Bloomington, Indiana and London: Indiana University Press.

circulation A term used to refer to geographical mobility of a short-term, repetitive or cyclical nature not usually leading to any permanent change of residence.

CIRCULAR MIGRATION is one form of circulation, though the concept is general and includes commuting, seasonal migration and transhumance. A considerable body of research on circulation in third world countries has developed, much of it stressing the role of circulation as a response to socio-economic disequilibrium.

CW

Reading

Chapman, M. 1982: Circulation. In J.A. Ross, ed. *International encyclopaedia of population*. New York: Free Press. Pp. 93–8.

citizenship See NATIONALITY.

civil registration See VITAL REGISTRATION.

closed interval A term most frequently employed in the analysis of BIRTH INTERVALS and referring to intervals which begin and end (i.e. open and close) before the date of a survey or census. Intervals which have begun before an interview of this kind but have not yet ended are termed open intervals, and those which begin before such a reference point and end after it are termed straddling intervals.

CW

closed population A population into and out of which there is no migration, and where, as a consequence, population growth depends entirely upon the difference between births and deaths. The concept is often invoked in models of population behaviour, though it is sometimes relaxed to requiring no net migration, i.e. immigration and emigration are equal. A contrast is made with an OPEN POPULATION where there may be migration.

CW

cluster sampling A type of SAMPLING. The term is used by some authors to mean a SAMPLE DESIGN of one or more stages in which each unit of the final sampling stage consists of a cluster of smaller units, all of which are covered by the inquiry. More commonly the term is used with the same meaning as MULTI-STAGE SAMPLING, and in this case the above design is termed compact cluster sampling.

CS

Coale-Demeny model life tables A series of MODEL LIFE TABLES providing compendious information on model mortality patterns and the associated STABLE POPULATIONS for 25 'levels' of mortality ranging from a LIFE EXPECTANCY of 20 years to one of 80 years (77.5 in the first edition), and for four families or 'regions' of mortality pattern. The exact age pattern of mortality varies from region to region at the same level. These tables are probably the most frequently employed of all model life tables in demographic research.

The original research took place in the 1940s, though the life tables were subsequently revised and improved before initial publication by Coale and Demeny in

1966. A second, even more detailed edition appeared in 1983. These tables are based principally on the vital statistics and censuses of Europe, North America and Australasia, with very little data from developing countries. Nevertheless, the consistency and generality of the patterns of mortality they reveal has led to their widespread use in research on all parts of the world. A further factor in their favour has been the sheer comprehensiveness of the tabulations presented, which means that they can be used with the minimum of effort on the part of researchers.   CW

References

Coale, A.J. and Demeny, P. 1966: *Regional model life tables and stable populations*. Princeton: Princeton University Press.
— with Vaughan, B. 1983: *Regional model life tables and stable populations*. Second edition. New York and London: Academic Press.

Reading

Coale and Demeny 1983.

Coale's fertility indices

Four indices expressing the level of fertility (general, marital and non-marital) and the prevalance of marriage, devised by A.J. Coale (1967) and widely used, especially in historical studies.

The measures were suggested by Coale as a way of exploiting the wealth of information contained in the censuses and vital statistics of later-nineteenth and early-twentieth-century Europe. They have been used as the principal form of expressing the fertility of these populations in a detailed, continent-wide study led by Coale and based at Princeton University. The project has provided, for the first time, consistent and readily comparable indicators of fertility during the DEMOGRAPHIC TRANSITION in Europe.

The four indices are based on the technique of INDIRECT STANDARDISATION which involves applying a standard set of age-specific marital fertility rates to the observed age distribution of women in each country. A comparison is then made between the observed number of births and the number expected if the standard rates applied. As a standard, Coale selected the fertility of the HUTTERITES, a religious group living on the High Plains of the United States and Canada, whose women had the highest fertility ever recorded in detail. Coale's fertility indices therefore show how close the fertility being measured comes to the theoretical maximum of the Hutterites: I_f indicates this for general fertility, I_g for marital fertility and I_h for non-marital fertility. The index I_m provides a measure of the proportions married in each age, weighted by the Hutterite fertility rate. As a result of these definitions the measures can be related by the simple expression:

$$I_f = I_m \times I_g + (1 - I_m) I_h$$

RP

Reference

Coale, A.J. 1967: Factors associated with the development of low fertility: an historic summary. In United Nations *Proceedings of the World Population Conference, 1965*. New York: Department of Economic and Social Affairs. Volume 2, pp. 205–9.

Coale-Trussell fertility model

A FERTILITY MODEL devised by Coale and Trussell (1974) with the intention of capturing the range of AGE PATTERNS OF FERTILITY typically observed in human populations.

The schedule of AGE-SPECIFIC FERTILITY RATES depends on four parameters: a_0, the age at which a consequential number of people form sexual unions; k, the speed with which cohabitation (or marriage) becomes a general phenomenon in the population; M, a measure of the maximum fertility experienced in the population under study (normally that of women aged 20–24); and m, the degree of fertility control.

The model is itself based on two sub-models, one describing the age of entry into marriage (or more generally cohabitation) (Coale and McNeil 1972), the other dictating the age schedule of fertility rates for married or cohabiting women (Coale 1971). Since fertility in many societies is largely confined to those who are married, the two sub-models can be viewed as models of marriage and marital fertility.

Unlike many other fertility models this one is empirically based, observed schedules of first marriage and marital fertility being used to construct standard distributions. The shape of the rising part of the fertility schedule is dominated by the schedule of entry into marriage while that of the falling part is determined by the degree of fertility control.

The nuptiality model has been shown to fit age patterns of marriage, as well as patterns of age at the birth of a first child (Rodriguez and Trussell 1980). The marital fertility model (Coale and Trussell 1974, 1978) has been used extensively in studies of the DEMOGRAPHIC TRANSITION (Knodel and van de Walle 1979). (See also MARRIAGE MODELS.)   TJT

References

Coale, A.J. 1971: Age patterns of marriage. *Population studies* 25, pp. 193–214.

— and McNeil, D. 1972: The distribution by age at first marriage in a female cohort. *Journal of the American Statistical Association* 67, pp. 743–9.

Coale, A.J. and Trussell, T.J. 1974: Model fertility schedules: variations in the age structure of childbearing in human populations. *Population index* 40, pp. 185–258 and Erratum, *Population index* 41 p. 572.

— 1978: Finding the two parameters that specify a model schedule of marital fertility rates. *Population index* 44, pp. 203–13.

Knodel, J. and van de Walle, E. 1979: Lessons from the past: policy implications of historical fertility studies. *Population and development review* 5, pp. 217–45.

Rodriguez, G. and Trussell, T.J. 1980: *Maximum likelihood estimates of the parameters of Coale's model nuptiality schedule from survey data*. World Fertility Survey technical bulletins 7. Voorburg, The Netherlands: International Statistical Institute.

Reading

Coale, A.J. 1977: The development of new models of nuptiality and fertility. *Population* 32, pp. 131–54.

Knodel and van de Walle 1979.

coding The translation of material (usually responses to a QUESTIONNAIRE) into categories which can be represented concisely and systematically within a DATA PROCESSING system (manual or electronic). A coding frame is developed with categories that allocate all possible responses among mutually exclusive codes, usually numerical but sometimes alphabetical. For some purposes, particularly with occupational, industrial and medical categorisation, an internationally agreed coding scheme may exist. Where an item is intrinsically numeric (e.g. age) or has categories that can be predicted with confidence (e.g. sex) precodes can be incorporated in the data collection instrument and transcribed directly into the data processing system (closed questions). Where such a prediction cannot be made (e.g. opinion questions) space must be provided for the respondent or interviewer to write in the answers and for these to be categorised ('coded') in a subsequent office operation (open-ended questions). Some questions can have multiple answers (e.g. types of contraceptive methods known) and special arrangements must be made to process all the answers given. Coding may be combined with office or manual editing. (See also EDITING).   JGC

Reading

International Labour Organization. 1968: *International standard classification of occupations*. Geneva: ILO.

Montgomery, A.C. and Crittenden, K.S. 1977: Improving coding reliability for open-ended questions. *Public opinion quarterly* 41, pp. 235–43.

Muehl, D. 1961: *A manual for coders*. Ann Arbor, Michigan: Survey Research Center, University of Michigan.

United Nations 1980: *National migration survey. Manual VII*. Bangkok: Economic and Social Commission for Asia and the Pacific.

Woodward, J.L. and De Lott, J. 1952: Field coding versus office coding. *Public opinion quarterly* 16, pp. 432–6.

World Fertility Survey 1976: *Editing and coding manual*. Basic documentation 7. Voorburg, The Netherlands: International Statistical Institute.

World Health Organization 1977: *Manual of the international statistical classification of diseases, injuries and causes of death, 1975 revision*. Geneva: WHO.

cohabitation   The living together of two persons of opposite sex in a conjugal union. The term is normally restricted to those in non-marital unions.

CONSENSUAL UNIONS are common in many countries, most notably in Latin America and the Caribbean. In recent years most countries in Western Europe, North America and Australasia have also seen marked increases in cohabitation. A variety of forms are apparent. In Scandinavia many couples form life-long *de facto* unions without acquiring legal sanction, while in many other societies cohabitation seems to be part of a sequence of events usually leading to legal marriage and may be most sensibly viewed as a stage in the process of courtship.   CW

cohort   A group of persons who experience the same significant event in a particular time period, and who can thus be identified as a group in subsequent analysis.

For example, all babies born in 1980 are the BIRTH COHORT of that year, while those marrying in 1980 form a similar MARRIAGE COHORT. Although birth and marriage are the most common reference points for the definition of a cohort, the concept is completely general and any significant occurrence can be taken as the original or BASELINE EVENT; entry into the labour force may be a suitable choice for analysis of employment, and divorce for the study of remarriage, to take just two examples.

COHORT ANALYSIS which follows the experience of individuals over time has many advantages over PERIOD ANALYSIS especially for phenomena such as marriage or childbearing where individual choice may play a significant role in the timing of events. (See also HYPOTHETICAL COHORT and COHORT EFFECT).   RP, CW

Reading
Ryder, N.B. 1968: Cohort analysis. In D.E. Sills, ed. *International encyclopaedia of the social sciences*. Pp. 546–50.

cohort analysis   Demographic analysis using COHORTS as the unit of study. The behaviour of the group of individuals experiencing a specified event in a given time period is noted over successive years, building up a picture of their collective history. The term longitudinal analysis is also employed.

Cohort analysis implies studying the experience of each cohort spread over many years (up to a whole life span), whereas PERIOD ANALYSIS deals with the demographic events observed in a specified period, normally one calendar year, and in this way deals with many cohorts simultaneously. Ryder (1964) has suggested that analysis in demography moves in a logical sequence from individual occurrences (e.g. birth, marriage, death) to cohort processes (fertility, nuptiality, mortality), and thence to cohorts classified by duration since the BASELINE EVENT that defines the cohort. The demographic events of a particular period are thus composed of the experiences of different cohorts, at various durations. For this reason period analysis may be less revealing than cohort analysis, especially when the timing of events is largely under individual control, e.g. nuptiality and fertility, and where past experience plays a role in determining present behaviour. However, the fact that cohort measures of fertility are less volatile than analogous period rates may not imply any theoretical superiority of cohort analysis since almost any moving average of period rates seems to produce similar stability of experience to that of true cohorts.   RP, CW

References
Hobcraft, J., Menken, J. and Preston, S. 1982: Age, period and cohort effects in demography: a review. *Population index* 48, pp. 4–43.

Ryder, N.B. 1964: Notes on the concept of a population. *American journal of sociology* 61, pp. 447–63.

Reading

Hobcraft, Menken and Preston 1982.

Ryder, N.B. 1968: Cohort analysis. In D. E. Sills, ed. *International encyclopaedia of the social sciences*. Pp. 546–50.

Shryock, H.S., Siegel, J.S. et al. 1976: *The methods and materials of demography*. Condensed edition by E.G. Stockwell. London and New York: Academic Press. Pp. 550–3.

cohort component methods   See COM-PONENT METHODS.

cohort effect   The demographic behaviour of an individual at any time is always conditioned by a number of factors: the effects of age, the impact of current circumstances and the accumulated experience of the individual. Since this latter will be largely shared with other members of the same COHORT, it is often termed a cohort effect.

Age, period and cohort effects have been central to much demographic analysis. Most demographic processes demonstrate marked age-specific patterns, variation from period to period may also be considerable, and the role of the past in determining present actions may be similarly noticeable. To take one example, suppose that the proportion of ever-married persons at age 45 is higher than at age 50 in a population at a certain time. The normal increase in the population of ever-married persons with age cannot explain such an anomaly. Clearly something in the past experience of the two cohorts has caused their marriage histories to vary; a cohort effect is said to apply.

Attempts to quantify rigorously the scale of cohort effects have not been common, and a recent review by Hobcraft et al. (1982) suggested that, while the conventional age-period-cohort approach may be suitable for mortality analysis, for fertility, more elaborate models related to theories of reproductive behaviour were needed.   RP, CW

Reference and Reading

Hobcraft, J., Menken, J. and Preston, S. 1982: Age, period and cohort effects in demography: a review. *Population index* 48, pp. 4–43.

cohort fertility   The reproductive performance of particular birth or marriage COHORTS. A contrast is made between this and the fertility of a particular period (commonly one calendar year), referred to as current or PERIOD FERTILITY.

Although in many cases information is only directly available on period fertility, cohort measures have significant advantages: they are often less variable over time, they come closer to describing the sequential nature of fertility behaviour and they are often more convenient for the projection of future population. A commonly calculated measure of cohort fertility is CUMULATIVE FERTILITY which is the summation of a cohort's childbearing experience from the beginning of EXPOSURE TO RISK until some later date. The terms COMPLETED FERTILITY or lifetime fertility are used to refer to cumulated fertility at the end of the reproductive age span.   CW

Reading

Pressat, R. 1972: *Demographic analysis: methods, results, applications*. London: Edward Arnold; Chicago: Aldine Atherton. Chapter 8.

Shryock, H.S., Siegel, J.S. et al. 1976: *The methods and materials of demography*. Condensed edition by E.G. Stockwell. London and New York: Academic Press. Pp. 550–3.

cohort life table   A LIFE TABLE constructed to describe the mortality of a particular COHORT rather than to represent the conditions of a specified period.

Much conventional use of life tables is for periods, assuming that the importance of past experience on current death rates is limited, and that the construction of HYPOTHETICAL COHORTS based on period data is thus justified. In fact, clear cohort effects can be demonstrated for many aspects of mortality. Early work by actuaries (Derrick 1927, Kermack et al. 1934) on data for England and Wales demonstrated cohort effects, and recent studies of parts of the developing world (Mata 1978) and of nineteenth-century

France (Preston and van de Walle 1978) both found enduring effects of early childhood illness.

One drawback with cohort life tables derives from the longevity of human beings. A complete life table for a cohort must give data on deaths occurring over a period of around a century, perhaps longer. This may be partially overcome by considering truncated cohort experience, examining deaths up to certain ages only. An alternative approach is to study cohorts between two specific ages, i.e. to examine only a segment of the whole life span. Studies of particular diseases, rather than overall death rates, also often employ a cohort perspective.   CW

References

Derrick, V.P.A. 1927: Observations on (1) errors of age in the population statistics of England and Wales, and (2) the changes in mortality indicated by the national records. *Journal of the Institute of Actuaries* 58, pp. 117–46.

Kermack, W.O., McKendrick, A.G. and McKinlay, P.L. 1934: Death rates in Great Britain and Sweden: some general regularities and their significance. *The Lancet* 1, pp. 698–703.

Mata, L. 1978: *The children of Santa María Cauqué: a prospective field study of health and growth*. Cambridge, Mass.: MIT Press.

Preston, S.H. and van de Walle, E. 1978: Urban French mortality in the nineteenth century. *Population studies* 32, pp. 275–97.

Reading

Cox, P.R. and Scott, W.F. 1977: International studies in generation mortality (with discussion). *Journal of the Institute of Actuaries* 104, pp. 297–333.

Hobcraft, J., Menken, J. and Preston, S. 1982: Age, period and cohort effects in demography: a review. *Population index* 48, pp. 4–43.

cohort rate   A rate which shows the experience of a demographic event within one or several cohorts. It is contrasted to rates referring to experience within a specific time period, known as period rates.
                                                    RP

coital rate   A measure of the frequency of intercourse, defined as the number of times intercourse occurs per person (or per couple) and per unit of time, e.g. the number of times per woman per month.

Since coitus can lead to a conception only if it occurs during a relatively short period within the woman's ovulatory cycle (the 'fertile period'), coital frequency and timing are direct determinants of conception rates. For example, if the timing of intercourse is random and intercourse takes place at most once per day, then the probability, p, of coitus occuring during the fertile period is given by

$$p = 1 - \binom{M-F}{n} \Big/ \binom{M}{n}$$

where F is the duration of the fertile period in days and n is the number of times intercourse occurs in an interval of M days between two menstrual periods that includes the fertile period. In general, FECUNDABILITY tends to increase with increasing coital frequency, the effect being less at high frequencies than at low ones.
                                                    HP

Reading

Barrett, J.C. 1971: Fecundability and coital frequency. *Population studies* 25, pp. 309–13.

Barrett, J.C. and Marshall, J. 1969: The risk of conception on different days of the menstrual cycle. *Population studies* 23, pp. 455–61.

Bongaarts, J. 1976: Intermediate fertility variables and marital fertility rates. *Population studies* 35, pp. 227–41.

Leridon, H. 1977: *Human fertility: the basic components*. Chicago: Chicago University Press.

Schwartz, D., MacDonald, P.D.M. and Henchel, V. 1980: Fecundability, coital frequency and the viability of ova. *Population studies* 34, pp. 397–400.

common-law marriage   See CONSENSUAL UNION.

complete life table   Also known as 'unabridged life table', the term refers to a

LIFE TABLE which contains data for every year of age from birth to the last applicable age. ABRIDGED LIFE TABLES, which present data on summary age groups rather than individual years of age are less cumbersome and more commonly employed.   RP

completed duration The time since a specified date expressed in the number of complete time-units that have elapsed. A marriage which took place on 3 June 1980 can be classified on 5 July 1981 as being of one completed year's duration if years are used as the unit of time, or of 13 completed months if months are used. The concept is analogous to the expression of AGE IN COMPLETED YEARS.   RP

completed fertility The CUMULATIVE FERTILITY at the end of the REPRODUCTIVE AGES. The term is used to refer variously to individual women, to marriages, and to birth or marriage COHORTS, the latter two being the most common usages. The term lifetime fertility is also encountered.

A careful distinction must be made between the use of the term to describe the average childbearing experience, over a lifetime, of all women and its use for married women only. For the former, values in the range 1.5 to 8 children per woman have been observed while the latter has exceeded 10 in some populations, for example French Canada in the eighteenth century and the HUTTERITES of North America in this century. Both measures, when correctly used give good indications of the level of fertility prevailing in a population and variations in each measure are clearly linked to many social and biological factors, above all the extent of BIRTH CONTROL.

The impact of mortality on the level of reproduction may also be taken into account. If the fertility rate at each age is multiplied by the PROBABILITY OF SURVIVAL up to that age, the sum of the products may be termed the completed *net*

fertility, a measure closely related to the NET REPRODUCTION RATE.   RP

Reading
Pressat, R. 1972: *Demographic analysis: methods, results, applications.* London: Edward Arnold; Chicago: Aldine Atherton. Chapter 8.
Shryock, H.S., Siegel, J.S. et al. 1976: *The methods and materials of demography.* Condensed edition by E.G. Stockwell. London and New York: Academic Press. Pp. 281–94.

completeness See COVERAGE.

component methods Methods of estimating the size and AGE-SEX STRUCTURE of a population, and of making demographic PROJECTIONS, which rely on breaking down overall population change into its component parts: births, deaths and migration. If each age group is estimated, the term cohort-component methods is employed.

Whether individual cohorts or simply estimates of overall population are involved the methods rely on the fundamental BALANCING EQUATION:

$$P_2 = P_1 + B - D + I - E$$

where P_1 and P_2 represent the population at two different dates and B, D, I and E are the births, deaths, immigrants and emigrants between the two dates. Cohort-component methods simply extend this identity to apply to each cohort. Numerous variations of the basic component methodology for estimating population size have been suggested, utilising mathematical models, correcting for observed deficiencies in data or exploiting additional data sources. (Shryock and Siegel 1976).

Elaboration of the basic method for making projections has been even more extensive particularly with regard to the handling of fertility measures: for example, PROXIMATE DETERMINANTS OF FERTILITY, such as marriage, may be built into the projection model. Whatever the exact methodology employed, a variety of projections, based on varying assumptions about fertility trends, are generally made.

Component methods are by far the most widely used techniques of projection and have the advantage of providing estimates of many demographic processes, mortality, fertility, etc. giving the overall projections a more detailed form. In recent years, however, a number of alternative approaches to projection and forecasting have been proposed (United Nations 1979).   RP, CW

References

Shryock, H.S., Siegel, J.S. et al. 1976: *The methods and materials of demography*. Condensed edition by E.G. Stockwell, London and New York: Academic Press. Chapter 22.

United Nations 1979: *Prospects of population: methodology and assumptions*. New York: Department of International Economic and Social Affairs.

components of the birth interval   Birth intervals are defined in general as the intervals between two successive births, i.e. as interbirth intervals. A distinction should be drawn between intervals defined in terms of live births, and intervals defined in terms of all births whether live or still. The interval between marriage and first birth (the 'first birth interval') is often considered as a special case.

Whatever the definition used, birth intervals are conveniently and revealingly analysed in terms of their main components. The simplest decomposition is based on just three components (see fig. below).

I_p The period following childbirth during which the woman is not at risk of a new conception, i.e. the post-partum non-susceptible period. By definition this component is absent from the first birth interval.

I_e The waiting time to the conception that will lead to the next (live) birth. This interval is sometimes referred to as the 'exposure interval', although strictly speaking this would be the correct term only if the woman is exposed to the risk of conception throughout. And I_g The period of gestation leading to the next (live) birth.

The second component I_e can be subdivided to allow explicitly for time taken by any pregnancies that end in an abortion (or stillbirth).   HP

Reading

Bongaarts, J. 1976: Intermediate fertility variables and marital fertility rates. *Population studies* 35, pp.227–41.

— and Potter, R.G. 1983: *Fertility, biology and behavior: an analysis of the proximate determinants*. New York and London: Academic Press.

Leridon, H. 1977: *Human fertility: the basic components*. Chicago: Chicago University Press.

composition   A term used to describe the distribution of the members of a population according to characteristics such as age, sex, marital status, socioeconomic status and so on. The terms composition and structure are often used interchangeably, although the latter is sometimes restricted to breakdown according to age and sex only (see AGE-SEX STRUCTURE). The term population distribution usually refers to the spatial distribution only, though it sometimes appears as a synonym of composition and structure.   CW

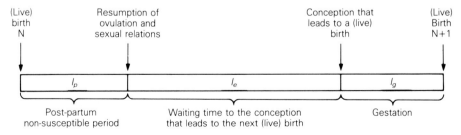

conception   Two distinct events which occur about a week apart: the fertilisation of the ovum by a sperm cell or spermatozoon, which marks the beginning of a PREGNANCY, and the implantation of the fertilised ovum in the wall of the uterus, termed nidation, which occurs a few days after fertilisation.   RP

conception rate   The ratio of conceptions occurring during a specified period to the number of women who might conceive. Alternative definitions of the women included in the denominator imply that a variety of rates may be calculated within this general term.

For example the calculation may be restricted to women in sexual unions and outside the post-partum NON-SUSCEPTIBLE PERIOD. These women are most directly at risk of conceiving, and calculations based on experience of this kind are generally employed in studies of CONTRACEPTIVE EFFECTIVENESS such as the well-known PEARL RATE. Analysing only the first conceptions occurring after the onset of a study provides ideal data for analysis using LIFE TABLE METHODS, which have been employed extensively in this context, producing both rates and probabilities in any given month of observation.

The term conception rate is sometimes used when all women, or all married women, form the denominator. In this case the rate often represents simply data on births back-dated by 9 months to indicate the approximate date of conception. Although occasionally useful, particularly when studying seasonal fluctuations in fertility, such measures are at best approximate since they take no account of ABORTIONS either induced or spontaneous. (See also FECUNDABILITY.)   RP

Reading

Leridon, H. 1977: *Human fertility: the basic components*. Chicago: University of Chicago Press.

confidence interval   An indication of the degree of uncertainty in estimating the value of a particular measure. The confidence interval shows the limits within which the estimated quantity may be expected to lie with a specified probability. The concept is widely used, especially when sampling is involved in the data collection.   CW

confinement   The outcome of a PREGNANCY which has lasted long enough for the foetus to become capable of independent life outside its mother, i.e. it is assumed to be 'viable'.

Viability is commonly taken to occur after 28 weeks of pregnancy (sometimes 20 weeks). Additional factors such as birth weight or size of foetus are also occasionally employed in classification. A confinement therefore involves one or more BIRTHS, either still- or live births. Termination of pregnancy before the foetus reaches viability is termed an ABORTION. The term *delivery* is used as a synonym of confinement and, in British statistics, the term *maternity* is similarly employed. Because of the possibility of MULTIPLE BIRTHS the number of confinements experienced by a woman may differ from the number of children born, leading to use of the term confinement order, as distinct from BIRTH ORDER.

Confinements are often specified as either *at term* or *premature*, according to the duration of pregnancy at the confinement. Various definitions of prematurity are employed, though a common one is any delivery before 37 weeks duration since the last normal menstrual period.
                           RP

consensual union   A term used to describe a *de facto* sexual union of a stable nature without recorded legal sanction.

In many countries (most notably in Latin America and the Caribbean, though increasingly in Europe and North America), unions which come into being without any solemnisation by legal or religious authorities are well known. A variety of terms are employed to describe these unions. Customary marriages, common-law marriage or companionate marriage imply a certain social recognition, though the extent of this, and of legal recognition, varies widely in different countries. These terms normally also connote cohabitation, whereas free unions, temporary unions or visiting unions may not. The term conjugal union is sometimes used to include all stable unions, including marriages.

In demographic data collection and analysis for countries where such unions are significant, it is essential that their true nature is recognised. For example, in Caribbean countries early censuses counted only legal marriages, with no reference to consensual unions, making the analysis of the resultant data on nuptiality and fertility problematic.   RP, CW

continuity, condition of   In some demographic literature, particularly that inspired by the French tradition, continuity is a term employed, along with the further condition of independence, to formulate certain mathematical bases of demographic measures. Both conditions were defined by Henry (1966) as necessary if observed rates and probabilities were to be interpreted as unaffected by the various DISTURBING PROCESSES which interfere with the observation of demographic phenomena. Although still quoted (Wunsch and Termote 1978), the two conditions have been shown to be replaceable by the single condition of NON-SELECTIVITY (Hoem 1972, 1978).   RP, CW

References

Henry, L. 1966: Analyse et mésure des phénomènes démographiques par cohortes. *Population* 21, pp. 465–82.
Hoem, J. 1972: Inhomogeneous semi-Markov processes, select actuarial tables, and duration dependence in demography. In T.N.E. Greville, ed. *Population dynamics*. New York and London: Academic Press. Pp. 251–96.
— 1978: Demographic incidence rates. *Theoretical population biology* 14, pp. 329–37.
Wunsch, G. and Termote, M. 1978: *Introduction to demographic analysis*. New York and London: Plenum.

contraception   Conscious action taken by individuals or couples to prevent conception.

Although there is evidence for the existence of contraceptive knowledge throughout recorded history it is probably only in recent times (about the last 200 years) that the practice has become at all widespread. The variety of CONTRACEPTIVE METHODS is considerable and their relative efficacy in preventing contraception is assessed in various measures of CONTRACEPTIVE EFFECTIVENESS. The termination of pregnancy in INDUCED ABORTION is distinguished from contraception, though both are means of birth control, family planning or family limitation.   RP

contraceptive effectiveness   The extent to which a contraceptive method reduces the chance of conception.

Three definitions of effectiveness are used.

(1) Theoretical effectiveness, sometimes called physiological effectiveness, refers to the efficacy of a contraceptive in ideal laboratory conditions. It is determined solely by the characteristics of the method.
(2) USE-EFFECTIVENESS, also termed clinical effectiveness, is a measure of practical protection, i.e. allowing for failure to use the method correctly.
(3) Extended use-effectiveness takes into account conceptions following the cessation of use (e.g. if the method is not well tolerated) as well as failures during use.

Theoretical effectiveness is often hard to assess and analysis usually focuses on the last two definitions. Quantitative assessment of effectiveness involves the comparison of the chances which contraceptive users and non-users have of conceiving in a given period. The standard measure of this was introduced by R.G. Potter (1960), and defines effectiveness e as:

$$e = 1 - \frac{f_r}{f_n}$$

where f_n is natural FECUNDABILITY, i.e. the probability that a fecund woman will conceive in one month, and f_r is the residual fecundability among contraceptors. With a perfect contraceptive f_r is zero and so e is 1. Because of difficulties in assessing fecundability, however, few studies provide estimates of effectiveness.

Alternative strategies involve assessing the number of women who become pregnant unintentionally, using cumulative failure rates or PEARL RATES. The latter relates the number of contraceptive failures to the number of months of EXPOSURE TO RISK and is usually expressed per 100 woman-years (Pearl 1939). Since individuals differ significantly with respect both to coital frequency and to contraceptive use, however, exposure at different durations of use of a specific method are not truly comparable. Henry (1968) has suggested an 'improved Pearl rate' restricting observation to a fixed interval, commonly a year. This rate is very similar to the cumulative failure rate which is calculated using LIFE TABLE METHODS. In the life table the confounding effects of women who become no longer exposed to risk for reasons other than pregnancy (e.g. discontinuing the contraceptive) can be eliminated (Tietze and Lewit 1973; Trussell and Menken 1982).

Because of the difficulty in obtaining genuinely comparable estimates of effectiveness the most useful comparative approach is an examination of cumulated use-failure rates. Results from a survey taken in 1973 in the United States for example, show one-year values ranging from 0.020 for oral contraceptives and 0.042 for IUDs, to 0.191 for periodic abstinence (rhythm method). These correspond to use-effectiveness of 99 per cent, 97 per cent and 87 per cent respectively (Vaughan et al. 1977; Bongaarts and Potter 1983).   RP, CW

References

Bongaarts, J. and Potter, R.G. 1983: *Fertility, biology and behavior: an analysis of the proximate determinants*. New York and London: Academic Press. Chapter 3.
Henry, L. 1968: Essai de calcul de l'efficacité de la contraception. *Population* 23, pp. 265–78.

Pearl, R. 1939: *The natural history of population*. London: Oxford University Press.
Potter, R.G. 1960: Length of observation period as affecting the contraceptive failure rate. *Milbank Memorial Fund quarterly* 38, pp. 140–52.
Tietze, C. and Lewit, S. 1973: Recommended procedures for the statistical evaluation of intrauterine contraception. *Studies in family planning* 4, pp. 35–42.
Trussell, J. and Menken, J. 1982: Life table analysis of contraceptive failure. In A. Hermalin and B. Entwisle, eds. *The role of surveys in the analysis of family planning programs*. Liège: Ordina.
Vaughan, B.J., Trussell, J., Menken, J. and Jones, E.F. 1977: Contraceptive failure among married women in the United States 1970–1973. *Family planning perspectives* 9, pp. 251–8.

Reading

Bongaarts and Potter 1983.
Tietze, C. and Lewit, S. 1968: Statistical evaluation of contraceptive methods: use effectiveness and extended use-effectiveness. *Demography* 5, pp. 931–40.

contraceptive failure See CONTRACEPTIVE EFFECTIVENESS.

contraceptive methods Techniques of CONTRACEPTION. A distinction is made between 'traditional' and 'modern' methods though this terminology may be misleading since some societies have no tradition of contraception and some modern methods are of relatively long standing.

ABSTINENCE and coitus interruptus are both clearly classifiable as traditional methods and both probably played a major role in the reduction of fertility during the nineteenth and twentieth centuries in Western countries. Both, however, require high motivation for effective use. A more restricted application of abstinence is the so-called rhythm method or PERIODIC ABSTINENCE in which couples refrain from sexual relations during a part of each of the woman's menstrual cycles. The use of condoms and various spermicides has been known for several generations, though their refinement and widespread use is a more recent phenomenon.

Similarly diaphragms, cervical caps and other ways of blocking the passage of sperm have been improved in recent decades. Among the most significant departures in contraceptive use have been the development of INTRA-UTERINE DEVICES and ORAL CONTRACEPTIVES. One area of considerable controversy is that of INJECTABLE CONTRACEPTIVES which release contraceptive steroids slowly over the intervals between quarterly injections. Although widely accepted on medical grounds, the use of injected contraceptives is still not allowed in many countries. The use of POST-COITAL CONTRACEPTION is regarded by some as more akin to induced abortion than contraception since it aims to prevent the implantation of a fertilised ovum. STERILISATION is a permanent form of contraception.

The effectiveness of each method is often hard to determine; abstinence (when complete) and sterilisation potentially offer complete effectiveness, but with other methods a range of estimates is common. A distinction is made between theoretical CONTRACEPTIVE EFFECTIVENESS and USE-EFFECTIVENESS, the latter being lower than the former. A further reduction is usual in assessing the continued efficacy of methods in terms of extended use-effectiveness.

Most research on techniques of contraception has focused on ways of disrupting the female reproductive process. This arises in part from the inherently more fragile and controllable nature of the female contribution to conception, but it may also derive from the assumption that reproduction, and hence its control is primarily a female responsibility. As a consequence, with the exception of vasectomy, little progress has been made in the development of forms of male contraception. No effective pharmacological male contraceptive with acceptably slight side effects has yet been developed. Future contraceptive methods are likely to exploit more fully the complex bio-chemical nature of reproduction, taking advantage of progress in molecular biology.   RP, CW

Reading

Segal, S.J. et al. 1982: Contraceptive methods: overview. In J.A. Ross, ed. *International encyclopaedia of population*. New York: Free Press. Pp. 103–9.

conurbation   A continuous built-up area which has arisen from the coalescing of formerly separate settlements which, while retaining some administrative or economic independence, form one agglomeration. The term is often used synonymously with METROPOLITAN AREA.
                                                                CW

co-resident group   Those who share the same physical space for the purposes of eating, sleeping and taking rest and leisure, growing up, child rearing and procreating.

Hammel and Laslett (1974), who have provided perhaps the most ambitious attempt to categorise co-resident group structures, argued that the co-resident group is the group of persons brought together by the 'intersection of different activities within a particular space'. As their concern with group size and structure rests on considerations of both residence and activity, Hammel and Laslett prefer to use the term co-resident domestic group to define the units of analysis.

It should be noted that in certain respects the above definition is wider than that of the HOUSEHOLD which has often, especially in the majority of modern censuses, been taken to be the group of persons who regularly take meals together derived from a common stock of food (Hajnal 1982). This implicitly assumes that in order to eat together all working members (whose locus of employment need not be within the space occupied by the co-resident domestic group) pool their income (Wall 1983).   RMS

References

Hajnal, J. 1982: Two kinds of pre-industrial household formation systems. *Population and development review* 8, pp. 449–94.

Hammel, E.A. and Laslett, P. 1974: Comparing household structure over time and between cultures. *Comparative studies in society and history* 16, pp. 73–109.

Wall, R. 1983: 'Introduction to R. Wall, ed. *Family forms in historic Europe*. Cambridge: Cambridge University Press.

Reading

Goody, J. 1972: *Domestic groups*. Reading, Mass.: Addison Wesley.

Hammel and Laslett 1974.

corrected measure Any measure in which an explicit correction is made for deficiencies. It may take account of deficiencies in the original data (e.g. under-enumeration) or correct for inappropriate methods yielding results that could be misleading for the purpose in hand. Some corrections explicitly take account of the impact of a DISTURBING PROCESS, for example NET RATES which take into account the way in which mortality disturbs other processes.   RP, CW

cost of children See VALUE OF CHILDREN.

cost-benefit analysis A method for the evaluation of investment in projects of various kinds and a set of techniques used to assess individual decision-making.

   Cost-benefit analysis was first employed in economics for the assessment of major construction schemes; it has been used in demography mainly to examine the impact of family planning programmes. A common approach is to compare the costs of a particular programme with the hypothesised benefits (e.g. savings on health and education caused by fewer births). Such analyses, like all cost-benefit analyses, involve many assumptions and are hard to verify. Direct assessment of programmes is often made using the number of BIRTHS AVERTED or the number of COUPLE-YEARS of protection.

   A rather different use of cost-benefit models appears in studies of migration, where models are applied to individuals, assuming that a person migrates if the economic benefit of moving outweighs the cost of doing so. Although non-economic costs are hard to evaluate in any detail, such models have been useful in studying rural-urban migration in developing countries (Todaro 1976).   CW

Reference

Todaro, N.P. 1976: *Internal migration in developing countries: a review of theory, evidence, methodology and research priorities*. Geneva: International Labour Organisation.

Reading

Gorosh, M.E. 1982: Family planning programmes: management and evaluation. In J.A. Ross, ed. *International encyclopaedia of population*. New York: Free Press. Pp. 225-8

Lapham, R.J. and Mauldin, W.P. 1972: National family planning programs: review and evaluation. *Studies in family planning* 3, pp. 29-52.

couple Two persons of opposite sex living in a stable union. In many circumstances this implies a married couple, but it can refer to any CONSENSUAL UNION. RP

couple-years A measure of the duration of EXPOSURE TO RISK of conception widely used in the assessment of family planning programmes. It is a form of the general concept of PERSON-YEARS.

   The use of couple-years of contraceptive use (often termed protection from risk of conception) enables different durations of use by different couples to be aggregated into an appropriate index of overall usage. A more elaborate measure, standard couple-years of protection has also been suggested. This attempts to take into account the varying fertility expectations of couples, the overlap between contraceptive use and the post-partum non-susceptible period, and the effectiveness of each type of contraceptive method. RP, CW

Reading

Hermalin, A.I. 1982: Family planning programs: effects on fertility. In J.A. Ross ed. *International encyclopedia of population*. New York: Free Press. Pp. 228-35.

coverage The definition of the population groups and the time period to be included in a CENSUS or registration system or in the sampling universe for a

SURVEY. The word is often used to refer to the achieved rather than the intended coverage.

For a census coverage is generally defined as the resident population (de jure or de facto) of a geographic area on a particular date. This definition is usually expanded to explicitly include or exclude such groups as citizens temporarily overseas, persons in transit, and foreign nationals within the enumeration areas.

Accurate estimates of census coverage errors are rare. However, POST-ENUMERATION SURVEYS suggest undercounts of about 10 per cent for Liberia in 1974 and about 5 per cent for Korea and Malaysia in 1970. For United States whites, estimated census undercounts are 6 per cent for 1880 and 2 per cent for 1960. Net coverage varies greatly according to such variables as age, sex, marital status and household composition.   DE

Reading

Ewbank, D.C. 1981: *Age misreporting and age-selective underenumeration: sources, patterns, and consequences for demographic analysis.* Report 4, Committee on Population and Demography, National Academy of Sciences. Washington: National Academy Press. Pp.18–69.

Shryock, H.S., Siegel, J.S. et al. 1976: *The methods and materials of demography.* Condensed edition by E.G. Stockwell. London and New York: Academic Press. Chapter 3.

criminal abortion See ILLEGAL ABORTION.

crisis, mortality A sudden and pronounced rise in the death rate, for whatever cause. The degree of upward fluctuation considered sufficient to constitute a 'crisis' varies according to the subjective preferences of individual authors.

Much attention has been paid to crises in pre-industrial Europe; indeed, since Graunt's work using the BILLS OF MORTALITY for London, discussion of crisis mortality has been a recurrent theme. Much of the discussion in the 1950s and 1960s stressed FAMINE as a cause of crises (Meuvret 1965); more recent analysis has tended to give precedence to epidemic mortality. The scale of crises in the pre-industrial era was sometimes huge, most strikingly in the Black Death of 1348 to 1350 (bubonic plague) which is thought to have been responsible for the deaths of 25 million people (a quarter of the total population of Europe).

The overall importance of crises compared with endemic mortality has, however, been questioned. Wrigley and Schofield (1981) have demonstrated that in England between the sixteenth and nineteenth centuries, even in the worst years, only a minority of individual parishes experienced a crisis in any given year. Nevertheless the gradual disappearance of crises may have played some role in the improving mortality conditions in Europe from the late eighteenth century onwards.

Contemporary developing countries have seen a rapid improvement in mortality in this century, especially since 1945, and the incidence of crises has been greatly reduced. Most of the mortality crises of the 1970s, for example, arose when famine coincided with or was caused by political problems (such as the food shortages in Bangladesh and Ethiopia, as well as the better-known example of Kampuchea).

RSS, CW

References

Meuvret, J. 1965: Demographic crisis in France from the sixteenth to the eighteenth century. In D.V. Glass and D.E.C. Eversley, eds. *Population in history.* London: Edward Arnold.

Wrigley, E.A. and Schofield, R.S. 1981: *The population history of England, 1541–1871: a reconstruction.* London: Edward Arnold; Cambridge, Mass.: Harvard University Press. Appendix 10.

Reading

Charbonneau, H. and Larose, A. eds. 1979: *The great mortalities: methodological studies of demographic crises in the past.* Liège: Ordina editions.

Wrigley and Schofield 1981.

cross-sectional data A term used to describe material collected from a population at a time, that purports to represent the state of affairs prevailing in the population at that moment. The term cross-sectional analysis is also sometimes used as a synonym of PERIOD ANALYSIS.

The main sources of demographic cross-sectional data are the population CENSUS and SURVEYS. Indeed, according to the United Nations (1980) one of the key criteria of a modern census is that it should approximate to simultaneity. Censuses and surveys thus provide information on the 'stock' characteristics of the population at a given time, and the corresponding function for such data is the 'proportion' or 'percentage' (Cox 1976). Though common, causal inferences from cross-sectional data are hazardous and may be better attempted from information collected longitudinally.   TD

References

Cox, P.R. 1976: *Demography*. Fifth edition. Cambridge: Cambridge University Press.

United Nations 1980: *Principles and recommendations for population and housing censuses*. Series M, statistical papers 67. New York: Department of International Economic and Social Affars.

Reading

Blalock, H.M. 1964: *Causal inferences in nonexperimental research*. Chapel Hill, North Carolina: University of North Carolina Press.

Cox 1976.

Moser, C.A. and Kalton, G. eds. 1971: *Survey methods in social investigation*. Second edition. London: Heinemann; New York: Basic books (1972).

crude birth rate   The ratio of live births in a specified period (usually one calendar year) to the average population in that period (normally taken to be the MID-YEAR POPULATION, which is equivalent to the number of PERSON-YEARS lived). The value is conventionally expressed per 1000.

Sometimes referred to simply as the birth rate, the crude birth rate is the simplest and commonest measure of fertility. As with any CRUDE RATE, it is influenced both by the level of the process it attempts

to measure, fertility, and by the AGE-SEX STRUCTURE of the population. Nevertheless, the relative number of women of childbearing age in the population as a whole does not vary greatly in most populations, so the crude birth rate is less affected by variations in the age structure than is the CRUDE DEATH RATE. In other ways the adjective 'crude' is more appropriate for the crude birth rate, since it takes no account of the proportions of women married, or in other reproductive unions, which makes it impossible to distinguish the respective impact of marriage and marital fertility.

The range of values observed for the crude birth rate is considerable, from around 10 per 1000 in some developed countries today, to 55 or more in some parts of the developing world. The most important factor in determining such variation is the prevalence of CONTRACEPTION and INDUCED ABORTION. However, even where modern methods of family planning are not widely employed, and where age-sex structures and marriage patterns are similar, crude birth rates may still show marked variation from population to population. Such divergencies are attributable to certain socio-cultural characteristics: the duration of breastfeeding and the prevalence of post-partum abstinence, for example. Additionally, poor hygiene and the widespread incidence of diseases affecting the reproductive organs (particularly common in parts of tropical Africa) may lead to reductions in the crude birth rate.   RP

Reading

Pressat, R. 1972: *Demographic analysis: methods, results, applications*. London: Edward Arnold; Chicago: Aldine Atherton. Pp. 172–9.

Shryock, H.S., Siegel, J.S. et al. 1976: *The methods and materials of demography*. Condensed edition by E.G. Stockwell. London and New York: Academic Press. Pp. 273–8.

crude death rate   The ratio of deaths in a year to the MID-YEAR POPULATION or, more generally, the ratio of deaths in any specified period to the number of PERSON-

YEARS lived in that period. The value is conventionally expressed per 1000.

The most elementary and one of the most frequently quoted of all measures of mortality, the crude death rate (also called simply the death rate) is strongly influenced by the AGE-SEX STRUCTURE of the population. Other things being equal, the higher the proportion of old people, the higher the death rate. It is, therefore, a very poor indicator of the comparative mortality conditions of different countries. The estimated crude death rates for both the United Kingdom and Guatemala was 12 per 1000 in 1980, for example, whereas life expectancy at birth (a much clearer indication of mortality levels) was 72 years in the United Kingdom and 58 years in Guatemala. However, for short periods and for one country, comparisons made on the basis of crude death rates are more valid since the age-sex structure of the population changes only slowly.

The lowest crude death rates should theoretically occur in rapidly growing, and hence youthful, populations with a high life expectancy; and the highest rates should occur in slow-growing old populations with low life expectancy. Today, although the former set of circumstances holds (in 1980 Kuwait, Hong Kong, Singapore and Taiwan all had crude death rates of 5 per 1000, and Costa Rica 4 per 1000), the latter does not occur in national populations. All countries with high proportions of old people have achieved long life expectancies, and the remaining parts of the world with poor mortality conditions (life expectancy of around 40) have young populations owing to high fertility. As a consequence crude death rates above 20 per 1000 are becoming increasingly rare, and rates of 30 are now unknown for national populations in normal circumstances. In the past, crude death rates of over 50 per 1000 could not have been sustained for any length of time as the population would have died out. More common values in historical populations were 30 to 40 per 1000, with crisis years reaching rates perhaps twice as high.   RP

Reading

Shryock, H.S., Siegel, J.S. et al. 1976: *The methods and materials of demography*. Condensed edition by E.G. Stockwell. London and New York: Academic Press. Chapter 14.

Woods, R. 1979: *Population analysis in geography*. London: Longman. Chapter 3.

Wunsch, G. and Termote, M. 1978: *Introduction to demographic analysis*. New York and London: Plenum. Chapters 2 and 3.

crude divorce rate   The ratio of divorces in a given period (normally a year) to the average population in that period or to the number of PERSON-YEARS lived in the period.

The distortions and qualifications of other crude rates are apparent in this measure, the values it gives being influenced by the AGE-SEX STRUCTURE, marriage patterns and underlying mortality conditions of a population, as well as its patterns of divorce. Moreover, the variation in the legal provision for divorces in different countries makes any use of this rate as a comparative indicator of marital instability highly dubious.   RP

crude marriage rate   The ratio of marriages in a given period (usually a year) to the average population in that period (normally the MID-YEAR POPULATION), or to the number of PERSON-YEARS lived in the period.

The rate, sometimes termed simply the marriage rate, is influenced by many factors. The AGE-SEX STRUCTURE is one, as it is in any crude rate, but underlying behavioural factors play an even more important part, particularly the social norms with regard to age at marriage, divorce and remarriage. Frequent remarriage, following divorce or widowhood, may lead to high crude marriage rates. Although the values of the rate are subject to large short-run variations, especially in times of economic crisis or war and the periods of recovery which follow them, long-term variation is limited. This is attributable to the fact that in most cases the number of marriages per person and the timing of marriage in terms of age vary within a relatively narrow band. Occasionally crude first marriage rates are presented. These overcome difficulties caused by remarriage, but are still the outcome of many contributory factors.   RP

crude rate   A rate which consists of the ratio of the demographic events occurring in a specified period (usually a year) to the average total population in that period (normally the MID-YEAR POPULATION), or to the number of PERSON-YEARS lived during the period.

Although widely quoted these rates are generally poor indicators of the processes they attempt to measure since the total population is taken as the denominator and large numbers of people irrelevant to the demographic experience in question are therefore included in the calculation: for example, men, children and older women are incapable of giving birth but are taken into account in the calculation of the CRUDE BIRTH RATE. A further problem is that these rates take no account of the AGE-SEX STRUCTURE of the population. Given the highly age-specific nature of many demographic phenomena and the considerable variation in the relative size of different age groups in different populations these rates are liable to give doubtful or spurious results when comparisons of different populations are made. Yet another difficulty is that crude rates do not permit the analysis of the separate contributions to their values. For example the effects on the crude birth rate of changes in marriage and marital fertility may be quite distinct, but this is not detectable using crude rates. However, though these problems make the use of crude rates as comparative indicators doubtful, over short periods and within one population they can act as useful indices.

Rates based on more carefully specified numerators and denominators are more interpretable than are crude rates; an example is the AGE-SPECIFIC RATE, which allows the AGE PATTERN of a process to be studied. Another approach is that of STAN-DARDISATION, in which an attempt is made to control the possible influence of confounding factors.

In spite of all their drawbacks the simplicity and apparent comprehendibility of crude rates makes them, particularly in non-specialist work, the most frequently quoted of all measures.   RP

Reading
Pressat, R. 1972: *Demographic analysis: methods, results, applications*. London: Edward Arnold; Chicago: Aldine Atherton. Chapter 3.

crude rate of natural increase   The ratio of the increase in population during a specified period (usually a year) that is attributable to the difference between births and deaths (the NATURAL INCREASE) to the average population in the period (usually the MID-YEAR POPULATION). This is equivalent to the difference between the CRUDE BIRTH RATE and the CRUDE DEATH RATE.

In contemporary populations this rate is rarely negative for national units, although low fertility has produced such values in parts of Europe, notably in both East and West Germany. Values of around 1 per cent are common in developed countries, while developing countries frequently demonstrate much higher values, with some in Africa and the Middle East approaching 4 per cent. High values such as these arise from the combination of improved mortality conditions (a crude death rate of 10 per 1000 or less), a young population, and high fertility (a crude birth rate of 40 to 50 per 1000 or even higher).   RP

cumulative fertility   The number of live births experienced by a woman, or a cohort of women, according to age (in a BIRTH COHORT) or to duration of marriage (in a MARRIAGE COHORT). The cumulative value is equivalent to the sum of the various age-specific or duration-specific fertility rates up to a given age or duration, and is a commonly-quoted measure of COHORT FERTILITY. The term is also sometimes used to refer to the cumulation of age-specific fertility rates observed in a particular period, which are treated as a HYPOTHETICAL COHORT. It can be defined as

$$F_x = \sum_{a=0}^{x} f_a$$

where F_x is the value of cumulative fertility at age x, and f_a is the AGE-SPECIFIC FERTILITY RATE at age a, or the DURATION-SPECIFIC MARITAL FERTILITY RATE at duration a. Cumulative fertility at the end of the REPRODUCTIVE AGES is termed COMPLETED FERTILITY for a true cohort and the TOTAL FERTILITY RATE for a hypothetical cohort.

Various further elaborations of these measures may be made. One valuable exercise is to calculate net cumulative fertility, which involves multiplying the duration- or age-specific fertility rates by the appropriate probability of survival before summation, yielding a measure which indicates the joint effect of mortality and fertility. The resulting values, which are referred to as cumulative net fertility, are closely related to the NET REPRODUCTION RATE.   RP, CW

Reading

Henry, L. 1976: *Population: analysis and models*. London: Edward Arnold. Chapter 6.

Pressat, R. 1972: *Demographic analysis: methods, results, applications*. London: Edward Arnold; Chicago: Aldine Atherton. Chapter 8.

current analysis   A synonym for PERIOD ANALYSIS referring to the present moment. It is contrasted with COHORT ANALYSIS. CW

current fertility   The fertility observed during a particular period. The term is a synonym for PERIOD FERTILITY, used when referring to the fertility levels of the present, in contrast to COHORT FERTILITY.
CW

curve fitting   The fitting of mathematical equations to demographic data. Although data may not conform exactly to any mathematical abstraction demographers have long used equations in numerous ways.

One purpose of such an exercise is to graduate or smooth observed data which may contain irregularities and errors. Another use of curve fitting is to provide MODELS of demographic behaviour; this was first attempted for mortality. For more than a century, since the time of Gompertz, demographers and actuaries have tried to deduce mathematical laws to describe the age-specific pattern of mortality; this led ultimately to the development of MODEL LIFE TABLES. Similar attempts to model fertility, nuptiality and migration have been made in recent years, often fitting RELATIONAL MODELS to observed data. (See also GRADUATION, INTERPOLATION, FERTILITY MODELS, MARRIAGE MODELS, MIGRATION MODELS).   CW

Reading

Shryock, H.S., Siegel, J.S. et al. 1976: *The methods and materials of demography*. Condensed edition by E.G. Stockwell. London and New York: Academic Press. Appendix C.

customary marriage   See CONSENSUAL UNION.

D

data cleaning The transformation of a file of data (normally held on a computer) to a state in which analysis can be conducted smoothly with minimum distortion of results from errors.

Data from a survey or other form of inquiry as first entered into a computer file will contain many errors and discrepancies which may have arisen at the data capture, CODING or data entry stage. In this initial state the data are called 'raw data'. Cleaning is often done in two stages. First, where the structure of the file is at all complex, e.g. where there are many records ('cards') per case or variable length records, any inconsistencies in the file structure, in particular missing or duplicated records, are detected and resolved. Second, once the file is well structured or sorted into some rational sequence within-record data checking can be done. This may include the following types of check: missing or redundant information; the absolute range of item (e.g. number of individuals aged less than 15 or more than 64); contradiction between two or more variables (e.g. the recorded age at death of an individual is greater than the number of years since the date of birth); and implausibility (e.g. an individual with 10 or more years of schooling who cannot read).

The resolution of errors of any type can be of three sorts. (1) If the original data (e.g. QUESTIONNAIRES) are available a check against them will often solve the problem. (2) If they are not, a generally plausible solution may be derived by examining the record as a whole. (3) It is possible to devise automatic corrections and additions to be made by program ('imputation'). This may include the assigning of missing or not stated codes in specified instances.

Several passes through the error checking programs may be necessary before the data can finally be pronounced 'clean'. Both because many undetectable errors may exist and because resolution of detected errors often contains an element of informed guesswork, a clean data set cannot be regarded as error-free. Researchers vary widely in the perceived importance and thoroughness of data cleaning.

JGC

Reading
Banister, J. 1980: Use and abuse of census editing and imputation. *Asian and Pacific census forum* 6.3. Honolulu: East-West Population Institute.

Fellegi, I.P. and Holt, D. 1976: A systematic approach to automatic edit and imputation. *Journal of the American Statistical Association* 71.353, pp. 17–35.

Sande, I.G. 1982: Imputation in surveys: coping with reality. *American statistician* 36.3, pp. 145–52

data collection The mechanisms whereby information on the age structure, births, deaths, migration and other related topics are compiled. The most important of these techniques are CENSUSES, sample SURVEYS, and civil registration which embraces both VITAL REGISTRATION and POPULATION REGISTERS. Detailed recommendations on all these forms of data collection are provided by the United Nations (1969, 1971, 1973, 1980). Data on migration are normally collected through records compiled for persons entering or leaving the country at land frontiers, seaports or airports.

The actual methods by which the information is collected in censuses and surveys vary considerably according to the level of development of the country and the sophistication of the respondents. In most developed countries census forms are completed by the householders, and the role of the enumerator is simply to deliver the forms, collect them and check that they have been correctly completed. In developing countries on the other hand, where large proportions of the population are illiterate, the forms are completed by the enumerators on the basis of oral answers given by the householders. Sample surveys also take a variety of forms: they may be single-round RETROSPECTIVE SURVEYS or they may be multi-round longitudinal PROSPECTIVE SURVEYS. In developed countries some survey questionnaires are delivered through the post, and the respondents are asked to complete them themselves (e.g. the 1946 'Family Census' of Great Britain); but most surveys are conducted by face-to-face interviews between the enumerators and the respondents.

The instruments of data collection sometimes take the form of verbatim questionnaires, the enumerators being required to read the questions out as they have been printed or they take the form of a simple 'schedule' in which the nature of the question is indicated by an abbreviated column heading. In the latter case the enumerators are left to word the questions as they think fit and in some developing countries this may involve translating the questions into the local language when the form itself has been printed in another. Registration procedures also vary. In most countries the responsibility for registering a birth or death lies with the immediate relatives; the registrar plays an essentially 'passive' role, and simply waits for people to come and register. Sometimes, however, especially in developing countries, it is the responsibility of registrars to ascertain what births and deaths have occurred within their areas, to visit the relevant households, and to record the necessary particulars of the birth or death. These

active procedures may mean that the registrars make regular visits to all the households in their areas. In these circumstances the distinction between an active registration system and a prospective survey can become hazy. JGB

References

United Nations 1969: *Methodology and evaluation of population registers and similar systems*. Series F, studies in methods 15. New York: Department of Economic and Social Affairs.

— 1971: *Methodology of demographic sample surveys*. Series M, statistical papers 51. New York: Department of Economic and Social Affairs.

— 1973: *Principles and recommendations for a vital statistics system*. Series M, statistical papers 19, revision 1. New York: Department of Economic and Social Affairs.

— 1980: *Principles and recommendations for population and housing censuses*. Series M, statistical papers 67. New York: Department of International Economic and Social Affairs.

Reading

Benjamin, B. 1968: *Health and vital statistics*. London: Allen and Unwin.

— 1970: *The population census*. London: Heinemann.

Bulmer, M. and Warwick, D.P., eds. 1983: *Social research in developing countries*. Chichester and New York: Wiley.

Casley, D.J. and Lury, D.A. 1981: *Data collection in developing countries*. Oxford: Clarendon Press.

Moser, C.A. and Kalton, G., eds. 1971: *Survey methods in social investigation*. Second edition. London: Heinemann; New York: Basic Books (1972).

Seltzer, W. 1973: *Demographic data collection: a summary of experience*. New York: Population Council.

Shryock, H.S., Siegel, J.S. et al. 1976: *The methods and materials of demography*. Condensed edition by E.G. Stockwell. London and New York: Academic Press. Chapter 3.

United States, National Academy of Sciences, Committee on Population and Demography 1981a: *Collecting data for the estimation of fertility and mortality*. Report 6. Washington DC: National Academy Press.

— 1981b: *Data collection: a statement for administrators*. Report 7. Washington DC: National Academy Press.

data processing The stage of a project, following collection and receipt of the original material and preceding report-writing, during which the information is entered onto a machine-readable medium (or directly into a computer system) and eventually used to produce tabulations and statistical analyses.

The following stages may be involved: editing, coding, DATA CLEANING, and re-arrangement of information to form a summary set of variables amenable to analysis. In modern practice the latter stages are based exclusively on computer-related devices and the punch card methods of the past are rapidly disappearing. A wide range of general purpose software is available but complex surveys or special analyses may still require specific programs.   JGC

Reading

Francis, I. 1981: *A comparative review of statistical software*. New York: North Holland.

Rattenbury, J. 1980: Survey data processing – expectations and reality. *World fertility survey conference 1980*. Record of proceedings. Voorburg, The Netherlands: International Statistical Institution. Volume 3, pp. 95–142.

Rowe, B. and Scheer, M. 1977: *Computer software for social science data*. London: Social Science Research Council.

World Fertility Survey 1980: *Data processing guidelines*. Basic documentation number 11. Voorburg, The Netherlands: International Statistical Institute.

de facto population The population enumerated in a census according to where people are staying on census night, rather than according to their place of usual residence (a *de jure* count, see below).

The *de facto* census lists individuals present in each HOUSEHOLD at the time of the census and is more common, on a world-wide basis, than the *de jure* census. The latter, however, is employed in many developed countries, notably North America and continental Europe.   RP

Reading

Benjamin, B. 1970: *The population census*. London: Heinemann.

Shryock, H.S., Siegel, J.S. et al. 1976: *The methods and materials of demography*. Condensed edition by E.G. Stockwell. London and New York: Academic Press. Chapter 3.

de jure population The population normally resident in a specified area. Also known as the resident population, it includes temporary absentees but excludes visitors or transients.

In a *de jure* census, all persons who usually live in a HOUSEHOLD are listed, whether or not they are present at the time of enumeration. This presents certain conceptual difficulties since a normal residence may not be strictly defined; legal residence or some other criterion may be used, and there can often be some ambiguity about where an individual 'belongs'. Moreover, practical arrangements for ensuring the correct enumeration of persons away from their normal home, often involving special forms and procedures, give an additional complication to census operations. Partly as a consequence of such problems, *de jure* censuses are largely restricted to developed countries in continental Europe and North America, *de facto* definitions (see above) being employed elsewhere.   RP, CW

Reading

Benjamin, B. 1970: *The population census*. London: Heinemann.

Shryock, H.S., Siegel, J.S. et al. 1976: *The methods and materials of demography*. Condensed edition by E.G. Stockwell. London and New York: Academic Press. Chapter 3.

death The permanent disappearance of all evidence of life at any time after birth. As defined by the World Health Organization a death can only occur after a live birth, so the definition does not encompass STILLBIRTH or ABORTION both of which are classified as foetal mortality.
                                CW

death rate   See CRUDE DEATH RATE.

decrement table   See LIFE TABLE.

delivery   See CONFINEMENT.

demographic ageing   See AGEING.

demographic analysis   A form of statistical analysis which employs, for the most part, a modest array of mathematical and statistical techniques to deal with the data produced by censuses, surveys and vital registration systems.

There is a fundamental distinction between COHORT ANALYSIS, in which the behaviour of a specific group of individuals is followed through time, and PERIOD ANALYSIS, dealing with the events of a particular period. In both forms age has long been recognised as a critical determinant of the variation in vital rates, and as a result the description of demographic processes in ways which enable age-specific patterns to be examined has been central to demographic analysis; first among these is the LIFE TABLE. Attempts to 'control' for the effects of age also led both to the development of various summary indices such as LIFE EXPECTANCY, TOTAL FERTILITY RATE, and NET REPRODUCTION RATE, all of which attempt to provide measures independent of age structure, and to ideas of STANDARDISATION, involving the imposing of the age structure of one population arbitrarily on another for the purpose of comparison. Such elementary algebraic techniques are both appealing and widely used and their simplifying assumptions have provided a common set of tools for analysis. However, with the wider availability and use of computers, demographic analysis is moving closer to other forms of statistical analysis.

Demographic analysis plays a central role in any population research; properly carried out it provides illuminating insights into changes in population structure and behaviour, pinpointing causal relationships and refining interpretation. Moreover, it is able to call into question

the basis of assumptions grounded on apparent common-sense alone.   RP, CW

Reading
Hobcraft, J., Menken, J. and Preston, S. 1982: Age, period and cohort effects in demography: a review. *Population index* 48, pp. 4–43.
Pressat, R. 1972: *Demographic analysis: methods, results, applications.* London: Edward Arnold; Chicago: Aldine Atherton.
Shryock, H.S., Siegel, J.S. et al. 1976: *The methods and materials of demography.* Condensed edition by E.G. Stockwell. London and New York: Academic Press.

demographic transition   A description of the observed long-term trends in fertility and mortality, and a model attempting to explain them. As Demeny (1972) has succinctly put it: 'In traditional societies, fertility and mortality are high. In modern societies, fertility and mortality are low. In between there is the demographic transition.'

The precise timing of the demographic transition has varied with respect to both date of onset and duration in the different countries experiencing it. For European societies general mortality improvements may have begun in the later eighteenth century, though the control of fertility within marriage is not apparent until the later nineteenth century, except for France where family limitation seems to have been practised in some regions as early as the 1780s and for certain small groups in other countries at even earlier dates. By the eve of the Second World War most of Northern and Western Europe and North America had reached low levels of fertility, with the rest of the continent following in the post-war decades. In the developing world virtually all populations have experienced dramatic improvements in mortality, and at a rate far exceeding the changes experienced in nineteenth-century Europe. Many countries are also moving towards a lower birth rate, though in few is it as yet declining fast enough to avoid population growth on a scale unprecedented in human history.

Demographic transition theory can be

broadly classified into three parts:

(1) a description of changes over time in fertility and mortality
(2) the construction of theoretical causal models explaining these changes
(3) predictions for future changes, especially in the developing world.

All three aspects are found in the work of the first proponents of the theory, Thompson (1929), Davis (1945) and, perhaps most clearly, Notestein (1945). From their writings came what is now termed 'classical' transition theory. Baldly stated, they argued that the initial trigger of change was a fall in mortality, to which fertility responded by declining after some lag, and that prime responsibility for these changes lay in the development of industrial and urban societies in which traditional values supporting high fertility were undermined.

These notions have been very widely employed and, until recently, largely accepted without significant modification. To quote Demeny (1972) once more, transition theory has become 'the central preoccupation of modern demography', principally because of the light it claims to shed on current rapid population growth in developing countries. In recent years, however, improved availability of data on both historical and contemporary populations have revealed considerable weaknesses in the classical formulation.

Much of the revision has been necessitated by new data on European populations, especially those produced under the auspices of the European Fertility Project supervised by A.J. Coale at Princeton University. This project has provided detailed statistics on fertility, both marital and non-marital, and on marriage patterns for regional units on a continent-wide basis. Summarising the results, Knodel and van de Walle (1979) have pointed out that no simple association exists between socio-economic development and demographic change. Some countries, such as France, demonstrated widespread control of fertility while still at low levels of in-

dustrial, urban and social development and lowered both fertility and mortality more or less simultaneously. Other countries, most notably Britain, were at high levels of development in all respects before any noticeable fertility control took place. Moreover, within individual countries regional cultural factors, such as language and religion, seem to have been more important sources of variation in fertility in many cases than economic variables.

In step with these revisions of the historical record, experience in the Third World has led demographers to question the validity of transition theory. It is clear, for example, that substantial declines in fertility have occurred in a number of countries with only a limited amount of development, and often with quite low average incomes. Sri Lanka, Thailand, China and possibly Indonesia are cases in point: all are overwhelmingly rural and poor yet they all exhibit certain developmental characteristics: education (for both sexes) is well established, health care has improved, extra-familial welfare institutions (of at least a minimum level) exist, and all have good communications and transport.

A further critique of classical ideas has been put forward by Caldwell (1976) who has stressed the importance of the transmission of idea, especially the ideas of the NUCLEAR FAMILY, rather than economic change *per se*. In short what Caldwell terms 'westernisation' is thought to be more relevant than industrialisation. This suggestion has not gone unchallenged. R. M. Smith for example (1982) pointed out that the nuclear family was established in Western Europe for centuries before the demographic transition, and Sun et al. (1978) have shown that the Taiwanese EXTENDED FAMILY has remained largely intact despite spectacular falls in fertility and increases in economic development.

In general, therefore, it appears that the simplistic and deterministic models of classical transition theory must be revised to take account of the cultural diversity of human experience. In this light Coale

C

54   demography

(1973) claims that three conditions are necessary for any sustained fall in fertility, and that unless all three are satisfied little or no change can be expected. His conditions are: (1) that fertility control is perceived by couples as economically and socially advantageous, (2) that control is ethically and morally acceptable and (3) that adequate means of control are available.   RP, CW

References

Caldwell, J.C. 1976: Toward a restatement of demographic transition theory. *Population and development review* 2, pp. 579–616.

Coale, A.J. 1973: The demographic transition. In *International population conference, 1973*. Liège: International Union for the Scientific Study of Population.

Davis, K. 1945: The world demographic transition. *Annals of the American Academy of Political and Social Science* 273, pp. 1–11.

Demeny, P. 1972: Early fertility decline in Austria-Hungary: a lesson in demographic transition. In D.V. Glass and R.Revelle, eds. *Population and social change*. London: Edward Arnold.

Knodel, J. and van de Walle, E. 1979: Lessons from the past: policy implications of historical fertility studies. *Population and development review* 5, pp. 217–45.

Notestein, F.W. 1945: Population: the long view. In T.W. Schultz, ed. *Food for the world*. Chicago: University of Chicago Press.

Smith, R.M. 1982: Fertility, economy and household formation in England over three centuries. *Population and development review* 7, pp. 595–622.

Sun, T.-H., Lin, H.-S. and Freedman, R. 1978: Trends in fertility, family size preferences and family planning practice: Taiwan, 1961–1976. *Studies in family planning* 9, pp. 54–70.

Thompson, W. 1929: Population. *American journal of sociology* 34, pp. 959–75.

Reading

Coale 1973.

Freedman, R. 1982: Fertility decline. In J.A. Ross, ed. *International encyclopaedia of population*. New York: Free Press. Pp. 258–66.

Knodel and van de Walle 1979.

Teitelbaum, M.S. 1975: Relevance of demographic transition theory for developing countries. *Science* 188, pp. 420–5.

demography The study of human populations in relation to the changes brought about by the interplay of births, deaths and migration. The term is also used to refer to the actual phenomena observed, as in phrases such as the demography of tropical Africa.

The word was coined by the Belgian statistician Achille Guillard in 1855 though the subject has much older roots in the intellectual tradition of Europe, and its present diversity is such that it cannot be defined in a single phrase. The attempt above deals only with its most specific aspect: the study of populations as dynamic bodies, constantly subject to the processes of renewal and change. Though there is no strict division a contrast is frequently made between *pure* or *formal* demography and POPULATION STUDIES or social demography. The former is concerned mainly with the collection and analysis of data, while the latter implies a wider frame of reference drawing in work from related fields.

The scope of demographic work can be seen as falling into three main areas:

(1) The size and make-up of populations according to diverse criteria (age, sex, marital status, educational attainment, spatial distribution, etc.). In short, pictures of a population at a fixed moment.
(2) The different processes which directly influence this composition (fertility, mortality, nuptiality, migration, etc.).
(3) The relationships between these static and dynamic elements and the social, economic and cultural environment within which they exist.

A similar three-part division can be drawn for the methodology of demographic studies:

(1) DATA COLLECTION in the form of the CENSUS, VITAL REGISTRATION, or specialised SURVEYS, which may go beyond the collection of facts to examine attitudes and beliefs.
(2) DEMOGRAPHIC ANALYSIS, which provides a way of turning raw data into

more precisely directed measures.

(3) Interpretation of the data and its location within the wider context of social statistics, drawing upon such neighbouring disciplines as economics, history, sociology, psychology, law or biology.

In addition to a more detailed understanding of the causes of demographic phenomena, the aim of many studies is to provide a basis for some degree of FORE-CASTING future trends.

The diversity of subject matter and techniques is such that the discipline can in fact be regarded as a series of sub-disciplines, loosely united by a central core of techniques. Among these sub-disciplines are ECONOMIC DEMOGRAPHY, HISTORICAL DEMOGRAPHY and MATHEMATICAL DEMOGRAPHY. Works dealing with POPULATION THEORY and POPULATION POLICY are also sometimes distinguished as separate subject areas, while GENETICS and EPIDEMIOLOGY are outside disciplines with close links to certain forms of demographic research.   RP

demometrics   The science of measuring the relationships between demographic indicators and socio-economic variables.

The relationships studied are the influences of socio-economic factors on demographic characteristics and the influences of demographic factors on socio-economic characteristics either separately or simultaneously. The term was first used by Rogers (1978), although a substantial body of work preceded that coining. Of particular interest in demometrics has been the relationship between migration and employment change (see Lowry 1966; and Ledent 1978).   PR

References

Ledent, J. 1978: Regional multiplier analysis: a demometric approach. *Environment and planning A* 10, pp. 537–60.
Lowry, I.S. 1966: *Migration and metropolitan growth*. San Francisco: Chandler.
Rogers, A. 1978: Demometrics of migration and settlement. In A. Rogers and F. Willekens, eds. *Migration and settlement: measurement*

and analysis. Research report RR-78-13 Laxenburg, Austria: International Institute for Applied Systems Analysis.

density of population   A comparative measure of the number of people resident within a standard unit of area. The most elementary measure is the number of persons per square kilometre, per hectare, per square mile, etc. Such definitions are useful for small units but more refined measures are better for large regions and nations. Typical measures calculated relate population to cultivatable land or some other economic factor. In urban areas density may be expressed as persons per household, or even persons per room, and used as an index of crowding.   DCS

Reading

Clarke, J.I. 1972: *Population geography*. Second edition. Oxford and New York: Pergamon. Chapter 4.

Deparcieux, Antoine (1703–1768)   A French astronomer responsible for several studies of mortality. His work both consolidated certain techniques and foreshadowed later developments.

Deparcieux was one of the first scholars to appreciate and use the wealth of information contained in statistics on life annuities. These he used to construct LIFE TABLES which he first published in 1746 in his *Essay on the probabilities of the length of human life*. He also employed data on mortality within religious communities which enabled him to follow statistics on individuals over a number of years. Along with KERSSEBOOM, Deparcieux can be credited with the development of rigorous mortality analysis, including the correct use of the concept of EXPOSURE TO RISK. Perhaps even more interestingly, in his attempts to establish values for LIFE EXPECTANCY AT BIRTH, for which data on infant and child mortality were required, he undertook an elementary RETRO-SPECTIVE SURVEY, asking women at the end of their reproductive lives about the survival of their children. From this survey, which prefigures a great deal of current demographic work with surveys, Deparcieux was able to calculate life expectancies for various subgroups, thereby setting in motion, probably for the first time, a data collection exercise with purely demographic objectives, and one well constructed to avoid potential errors and biases.   RP

dependency ratio The ratio of the economically dependent parts of the population to the productive part. Dependency ratios do not usually use detailed breakdowns of the population according to economic activity, but are normally calculated purely on the basis of the AGE-SEX STRUCTURE, leading to the use of the term *age dependency ratio*. The ages chosen to represent the number of individuals in the LABOUR FORCE are largely arbitrary, 15 to 64 being a common range useful for international comparisons. The ratio would be defined as the number of persons below 15 or above 64 years of age divided by the number between those ages.

The overall ratio is sometimes decomposed into its two constituent parts – the burden of children and of the elderly. These are termed the child dependency and the old-age dependency ratios. Countries with rapidly-growing and hence young populations show the highest dependency ratios, though the interpretation of the measure is made difficult by the fact that the size and nature of the burden of aged dependents is often quite different from that of children. In particular, the costs may be shared differently between families and the state in the two cases. (See also AGEING.)   RP, CW

Reading

Clark, R.J. and Spengler, J.J. 1978: Changing demography and dependency cost: the implications of new dependency ratios and their composition. In B. Herzog, ed. *Aging and income*. New York: Human Sciences Press.

Hauser, P.M. 1976: Aging and world-wide population change. In R.H. Binstock and E. Shanas, eds. *Handbook of aging and the social sciences*. New York: Van Nostrand Reinhold. Pp. 59–86.

depopulation A reduction in the population of a given area. This may arise as a consequence of migration or it may be caused by an excess of deaths over births.

In historical times famines, war and other forms of CRISIS may have led to depopulation. In the contemporary world migration is largely responsible, and the process is almost exclusively a feature of rural areas. Since migration is most common among young adults rural areas are depleted of couples of childbearing age which may lead to an excess of mortality over fertility, further increasing the rate of population decline. Although negative rates of population growth have been observed in some developed countries since the later 1970s, significant depopulation at a national level is unknown in the developed world.   RP, CW

derived projection A demographic PROJECTION in which estimates of specified socio-economic characteristics of the population are made after an initial projection of the AGE-SEX STRUCTURE and from which more detailed projections are derived. In order to obtain the specific projections required the projected age distribution is combined with estimates of the age-specific pattern of characteristics (e.g. labour force PARTICIPATION RATES, SCHOOL ENROLMENT RATE, household HEADSHIP RATES, etc.).   RP

Reading

Shryock, H.S., Siegel, J.S. et al. 1976: *The methods and materials of demography*. Condensed edition by E.G. Stockwell. London and New York: Academic Press. Chapter 23.

desired family size In attempts at a fuller understanding of the motivation of couples with regard to childbearing, demographers often examine statements of the desired family size. A distinction is sometimes made between the family size desired by a particular couple or woman, and the ideal family size for the population in general, though the two terms are often used synonymously. A contrast is commonly made between a theoretical desired family size and actual intended family size.

Questions relating to these concepts are frequently asked in fertility surveys, although the reliable interpretation of the responses may be problematic. As Lesthaeghe et al. (1981) have noted, they may be 'rather slippery pieces of information'. In some societies the very idea of individual control over fertility may be foreign, leading many respondents to answer that family size is 'up to God' or to make some similar objection. In such circumstances a numerical estimate of desired size, even if obtained, may have little meaning. In spite of potential difficulties the expressed desired family size in Third World countries is often compared with current fertility levels. A desired size significantly below current levels is commonly taken as indicative of a latent desire for greater availability of facilities for family planning.

Difficulties also arise in interpreting declarations of desired fertility in western countries. Statements on the matter are not independent of current family size – initially 'unwanted' births may be subsequently incorporated into the stated desired number. In addition the variation of desired sizes is usually much less than that of actual fertility; few responses cite zero or high values (5 plus) as desired sizes, two children being overwhelmingly preferred in most cases. In general, trends in desired fertility seem to move in step with trends in actual births, although most studies suggest that desired family size is generally greater than the observed average. This has led some demographers to argue that socio-economic conditions in western societies prevent couples from fully realising their desires for children (Girard and Roussel 1982). Others interpret such discrepancies as being due to social norms on the acceptability of stating certain desires (e.g. a couple may not desire any children at all, but may not wish to say so). As Ryder (1978) has noted, 'responses to behavioral and attitudinal questions tend to be biased in the direction of normative adherence.'

In addition to their use in the understanding of fertility trends reproductive intentions have also been used as inputs to PROJECTIONS of future population. The sophistication of such methods is often considerable, though their additional value beyond conventional methods is as yet unproven.   RP, CW

References

Girard, A. and Roussel, L. 1982: Ideal family size, fertility and population policy in Western Europe. *Population and development review* 8, pp. 323–45.

Lesthaeghe, R. et al. 1981: Child-spacing and fertility in Lagos. In H.J. Page and R. Lesthaeghe, eds. *Child-spacing in tropical Africa: traditions and change*. London and New York: Academic Press. Pp. 147–79.

Ryder, N.B. 1978: Some problems of fertility

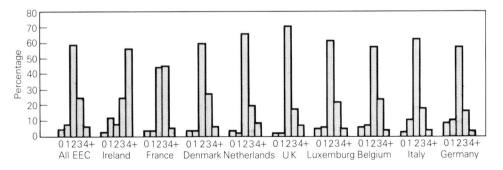

Reported ideal family size in EEC countries 1979.
Source: Girard and Roussel 1982.

research. In K.E. Taeuber, L.L. Bumpass and J.A. Sweet, eds. *Social demography*. New York and London: Academic Press. Pp. 3–13.

Reading

Lee, R.D. 1980: Aiming at a moving target: period fertility and changing reproductive goals. *Population studies* 34, pp. 205–26.

Ryder 1978.

Westoff, C. and Ryder, N.B. 1977: The predictive value of reproductive intentions. *Demography* 14, pp. 431–53.

differential fertility Differences in the fertility of subgroups within a population observed either in a given period or within specific cohorts.

The assessment of fertility differentials is usually made on the basis of the final family size (the TOTAL FERTILITY RATE in period terms), and less commonly on the basis of measures of the timing or tempo of fertility. Conventional divisions are residence (urban-rural), religion, economic or educational characteristics, and ethnic or regional groupings. Physiological factors may sometimes be involved, but the most widely cited causes for differentials are economic constraints and variation in desired family size. Demographers increasingly also attempt to explain differentials in terms of the PROXIMATE DETERMINANTS, notably contraceptive use, the incidence of abortion, marriage patterns and breastfeeding.

Broad generalisations, often qualified in particular studies, are that increased education, especially female education, participation by women in jobs outside the home and increased urbanisation all act to lower fertility and create differentials. Social class or status is also often cited as a factor, though in some developed countries, for example the UK, class differences in fertility are now small.

Differential fertility often plays a major role in determining the relative socio-economic and political status of different groups, especially those divided by ethnic, linguistic or religious status. Examples are relations between Walloons and Flemings in Belgium, between the Jewish and Arab population in Israel or between French and English speakers in Canada.   RP

Reading

Rindfuss, R.R. and Sweet, J.A. 1977: *Postwar fertility trends and differentials in the United States*. London and New York: Academic Press.

Taeuber, K.E., Bumpass, L.L. and Sweet, J.A. 1978: *Social demography*. New York and London: Academic Press.

Thompson, J.H. 1982: Differential fertility among ethnic minorities. In D.A. Coleman, ed. *Demography of immigrants and minority groups in the United Kingdom*. London and New York: Academic Press.

Thompson, J.H. and Britton, M. 1980: Some socio-economic differentials in fertility in England and Wales. In R. W. Hiorns, ed. *Demographic patterns in developed societies*. London: Taylor and Francis.

differential mortality Differences in MORTALITY found among various subpopulations either at a particular time or between different COHORTS.

These differences may be analysed in a variety of ways according to the availability of data and the precise objectives of the analysis. The application of LIFE TABLES and the STANDARDISATION of death rates to control for differences in age structure are among the most common. The subpopulations chosen for analysis are highly varied, groups being classified by residence (urban or rural), social class, level of education, occupation and so on.

The various factors affecting differential mortality are far from being clearly understood; climate, diet and life style more generally are all subjects of current research. Moreover, there may be strong underlying interaction factors since the choice of residence, occupation and so on may be related to health in the first place, leading to selectivity among the subpopulations studied. For example, the higher mortality of single persons, above that of the married population may be due in part to celibacy being almost inevitable for individuals in very poor health.

Among the most intriguing differentials in mortality are those apparent between different social classes. Definitions of SOCIO-ECONOMIC STATUS vary considerably from country to country, and even within a single country are often subject to modification and revision. The most common approach has been to use the occupation of males to determine socio-economic status for all persons, i.e. to attribute to children and wives the status of the husband or father. Two major problems in this context are that the socio-economic status of an individual may well change during a lifetime, introducing potential life-cycle effects as well as purely class differentials, and that the status of women (especially the unmarried) may be handled incorrectly. The life-cycle problem may in theory be partially resolved by techniques of RECORD LINKAGE enabling a more detailed LIFE HISTORY to be developed, but it is in practice often unresolvable. In some studies, particularly in North America, income has been used to represent socio-economic status, but this is not always the best guide since non-financial elements of status, notably educational level, seem to be particularly important.

Whatever the difficulties with definition, social class differentials are often highly significant at all ages, including infancy. For example in England and Wales in 1970–72, the standardised mortality ratio, set at 100 for the sum of all classes, was 77 for the highest social class, and 137 for the lowest.

Early proponents of welfare services in developed countries envisaged the eventual disappearance of differentials of this kind, but this has not generally occurred. A recent summary by Vallin (1981) concluded that 'inequality in respect of death is only one dimension of social inequality. It was an illusion to imagine that the one could be eliminated without the other.'

RP, CW

Reference

Vallin, J. 1981: Socio-economic determinants of mortality in industrialized countries. In

United Nations *Population bulletin* 13, pp. 26–41.

Reading

Adelstein, A.M. and Ashley, J.S.A. 1980: Recent trends in mortality and morbidity in England and Wales. In R.W. Hiorns, ed. *Demographic patterns in developed societies.* London: Taylor and Francis.

Kitagawa, E. and Hauser, P. 1973: *Differential mortality in the United States: a study in socio-economic epidemiology.* Cambridge, Mass.: Harvard University Press.

Vallin 1981.

digit preference A tendency for census or survey respondents to misreport age, showing a preference either for numbers ending in certain digits (usually 0 or 5 or, to a lesser degree, even numbers) or for numbers which are regarded as lucky or honourable.

Various indices of digit preference have been used. Two of the most common are Whipple's index which examines heaping on ages ending in 0 or 5 in the age range 23 to 62, and MYER'S INDEX which gives a similar indication taking into account the effects of mortality and varying cohort size. (See also AGE ERRORS)   RP

Reading

Ewbank, D.C. 1981: *Age misreporting and age-selective underenumeration: sources, patterns, and consequences for demographic analysis.* Report 4, Committee on Population and Demography, United States National Academy of Sciences. Washington DC: National Academy Press.

direct standardisation A technique used to adjust CRUDE RATES in order to eliminate the effect of differences in AGE-SEX STRUCTURE, or any other extraneous factors, so as to facilitate the comparison of rates for different populations.

Age is by far the most common variable for which STANDARDISATION is undertaken, and the general principle of the methodology can be well understood by considering how direct standardisation is made for age. A 'standard' population is selected and its age structure is applied to the age-specific rates for each population. The number of events (births, deaths etc.) which would result from this hypothetical combination of population and vital rates is then calculated and a standardised rate arrived at by dividing this hypothetical number of events (births, deaths, etc.) by the total size of the standard population. The resultant rate represents what the crude rate would be if the population from which the age-specific rates are taken had the same age structure as the standard. In essence the method is analogous to taking a weighted average of each set of age-specific rates, with the same weights (the standard age structure) applied to each case.

This methodology permits any number of comparisons to be made between different populations but the choice of a standard population is purely arbitrary, and the standardised rates are of values only within the context of a particular comparison and have no intrinsic value. One of the real populations for which standardisation is to be undertaken may be used as the standard, or some population unrelated to the comparison in question; the choice of standard may play a noticeable role in the ultimate values of the standardised rates. Direct standardisation is applicable in principle to any demographic process; in practice it is most commonly used in mortality analysis.   RP, CW

Reading

Fleiss, J.L. 1981: *Statistical methods for rates and proportions*. New York and Chichester: Wiley. Chapter 14.

Shryock, H.S., Siegel, J.S. et al. 1976: *The methods and materials of demography*. Condensed edition by E.G. Stockwell. London and New York: Academic Press. Pp. 241–5.

Wunsch, G. and Termote, M. 1978: *Introduction to demographic analysis*. New York and London: Plenum. Chapter 2.

disease and malnutrition   In very poor human populations infections and parasite diseases frequently interact synergistically with various kinds of nutritional deficiency to bring about a period of sustained

sickness that ends in death. This so-called 'synergism of infectious disease and malnutrition' is particularly important in accounting for high levels of infant and child mortality in contemporary developing countries, where studies indicate that it may be implicated in some way in almost 60 per cent of all early-age deaths (Puffer and Serrano 1973).

An initial disease episode often promotes (or in the case of low birth weight babies sustains) a condition of nutritional deficiency which in turn reduces the body's ability to cope with a further disease attack. A downward vicious circle of interaction ensues in which it is difficult to determine which component – the disease or malnutrition – is more important because of their mutually reinforcing influences. The synergism is highly complex and variable in its mechanisms and components. With young children, diarrhoeal disease and measles usually play important roles, and among those mechanisms promoting malnutrition consequent upon infection are loss of appetite and withdrawal of food from those who are sick. Diarrhoeal diseases in particular tend to reduce the body's capacities to absorb food nutrients, leading to both fluid and salt loss.   TD

Reference

Puffer, R.P. and Serrano, C.B. 1973: *Patterns of mortality in childhood*. Scientific publication 262. Washington DC: Pan American Health Organization.

Reading

Chen, L.C. 1978: Control and diarrhoeal disease, morbidity and mortality, some strategic issues. *American journal of clinical nutrition* 31, pp. 2284–90.

—, Chowdhury, A.K.M. and Huffman, S.L. 1980: Anthropometric assessment of energy-protein malnutrition and subsequent risk of mortality among pre-school aged children. *American journal of clinical nutrition* 31, pp. 1836–44.

Morley, D.C., Bicknell, J. and Woodland, M. 1968: Factors influencing the growth and nutritional status of infants and young children in a Nigerian village. *Transactions of the Royal*

Society of Tropical Medicine and Hygiene 62,
pp. 164–99.
Puffer and Serrano 1973.

dissolution of marriage   See DIVORCE.

distribution of population   In demographic work the term distribution is used
mainly to refer to the spatial or geographical distribution of a population. It
indicates the way in which the members of
a population are physically dispersed,
while the term structure is used to refer to
an age-specific breakdown, as in the AGE-
SEX STRUCTURE.   CW

disturbing process   A demographic process which disturbs the observation of
some other process when the latter is the
principal focus of interest.

In practice as opposed to theory demographic processes are never fully independent of one another (the study of fertility,
for example, is disturbed by the interference of mortality and migration) and
the elimination of the extraneous influences of such disturbances has traditionally, if implicitly, been one of the main purposes of demographic analysis. Mortality,
as an ever-present possibility, is potentially a disturbance of all other processes
and has received most attention as such.
The concept is completely general:
mortality may disturb the study of nuptiality by preventing some persons from
marrying but equally, if the focus of interest is the mortality of single persons, marriage acts as a disturbance by removing
them from the single state. (See also NON-
SELECTIVITY.)   RP

Reading
Wunsch, G. and Termote, M. 1978: *Introduc-
tion to demographic analysis.* New York and
London: Plenum. Chapter 1.

divorce   The final legal dissolution of a
marriage, involving the separation of husband and wife by a judicial decree which
confers on each the right of remarriage
according to the laws of individual countries.

Within this broad definition the legal
situation with regard to divorce varies
from being altogether illegal (in some predominantly Catholic countries) to requiring only a statement of intent by the husband (in much of the Islamic world). The
incidence of divorce is, not surprisingly,
greatly influenced by such conditions and
it tends to vary inversely with the difficulty of obtaining a decree. Moreover,
divorce is a rather unsatisfactory measure
of marital breakdown since separation and
informal living apart may be common,
especially where divorce is illegal or difficult to obtain. Because of this, the most
accurate data on the prevalence of marital
instability often come from census or
survey questions.

The most useful measures of divorce are
those provided by a DIVORCE SCHEDULE
which gives rates of divorce according to
age or, preferably, by duration of marriage. These enable the calculation of the
proportion of marriages that will end in
divorce, probably the most informative
single indicator of trends and levels. Even
this, however, needs careful interpretation
at a time of rapid change (Preston 1975).

In no population yet observed has
divorce been the outcome of a majority of
marriages, although this may ultimately be
observed for marriages contracted in the
United States in recent years. Analysis of
period data for the 1970s suggests levels of
about 15 to 17 per cent of marriages in
France ending in divorce and of about 25
to 35 per cent in Britain, the United States,
Scandinavia and parts of Eastern Europe.
International comparisons are particularly
hazardous owing to variation in legal conditions, but it is clear that significant increases in divorce have occurred in most
of the developed nations since the second
world war, especially since the 1960s, as
liberalised divorce laws came into effect in
many countries.

The factors which make couples more
likely to divorce have received a good deal
of attention. In the United States increased
likelihood of divorce has been noted
among persons marrying at a young age

(especially during the teens), among those with low educational attainment and among couples in which the bride was pregnant at marriage. There is also some evidence that remarried persons are more likely to divorce than others, and that individuals whose parents divorced during their childhood are similarly more likely to do so (Bumpass and Sweet 1972). Analogous differentials have been identified in many countries.

The social and economic consequences of increased divorce are clearly substantial and few countries have developed adequate and equitable legal and financial arrangements to cope with them (Chester 1983).   RP, CW

References

Bumpass, L.L. and Sweet, J.A. 1972: Differentials in marital instability, 1970. *American sociological review* 37, pp. 754–66.

Chester, R. 1983: A social agenda: policy issues relating to the family. In *Papers of the British Society for Population Studies, Bath Conference*. Office of Population Censuses and Surveys, occasional papers 31. London: OPCS. Pp. 96–105.

Preston, S.H. 1975: Estimating the proportion of American marriages that end in divorce. *Sociological methods and research* 3, pp. 435–60.

Reading

Carter, H. and Glick, P.C. 1976: *Marriage and divorce: a social and economic study*. Revised edition. Cambridge, Mass.: Harvard University Press.

Preston 1975.

Sweet, J.A. 1982: Marriage and divorce. In J.A. Ross, ed. *International encyclopaedia of population*. New York: Free Press. Pp. 429–36.

divorce rate   A term used in a variety of ways to indicate the incidence of divorce in a population, and often put forward with various qualifiers to specify more exactly its meaning.

One measure sometimes referred to in this way is the CRUDE DIVORCE RATE, which is simply the ratio of divorces in a particular year to the average population and as such largely uninformative. Relat-

ing divorces to the total number of marriages, as in the divorce rate for married persons, is similarly highly approximate and open to compositional distortions. More refined measures are rates which are age-specific or, more usefully, duration of marriage specific. These are presented in a divorce schedule and allow the proportion of marriages ending in divorce to be calculated.   RP

Reading

Haskey, J. 1982: The proportion of marriage ending in divorce. *Population trends*, 27.

Preston, S.H. and McDonald, J. 1979: The incidence of divorce within cohorts of American marriages contracted since the Civil War. *Demography* 16, pp. 1–25.

Shryock, H.S., Siegel, J.S. et al. 1976: *The methods and materials of demography*. Condensed edition by E.G. Stockwell. London and New York: Academic Press. Pp. 344–7.

divorce schedule   A series of divorce rates indicating the likelihood of divorce within a specific MARRIAGE COHORT, according to the duration of marriage. An analogous schedule is sometimes produced for divorces within a specified period, though cohort analysis is generally preferable.

Since divorce is a NON-RENEWABLE PROCESS, at least as far as any given marriage is concerned, the duration-specific divorce rates may be transformed into probabilities of divorce at each duration, and LIFE TABLE METHODS employed to analyse them. The proportion of marriages ending in divorce is easily calculable on this basis and provides the most informative single indicator of the level and trend of divorce (Preston 1975). Similarly, expressing data on divorce in the form of a life table makes it suitable for modelling by HAZARDS MODELS (Menken et al. 1981).   RP, CW

References

Menken, J., Trussell, T.J., Stempel, D. and Babakol, O. 1981: Proportional hazards life table models: an illustrative analysis of sociodemographic influences on marriage duration in the United States. *Demography* 18, pp. 181–200

Number of years

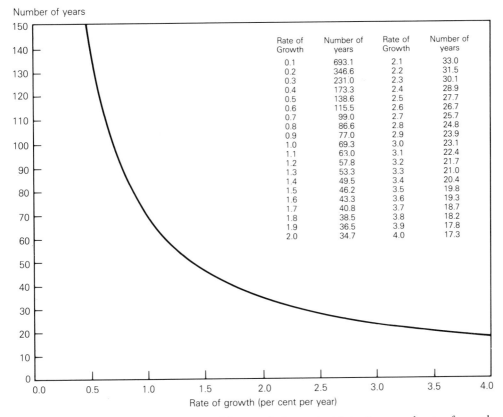

Rate of Growth	Number of years	Rate of Growth	Number of years
0.1	693.1	2.1	33.0
0.2	346.6	2.2	31.5
0.3	231.0	2.3	30.1
0.4	173.3	2.4	28.9
0.5	138.6	2.5	27.7
0.6	115.5	2.6	26.7
0.7	99.0	2.7	25.7
0.8	86.6	2.8	24.8
0.9	77.0	2.9	23.9
1.0	69.3	3.0	23.1
1.1	63.0	3.1	22.4
1.2	57.8	3.2	21.7
1.3	53.3	3.3	21.0
1.4	49.5	3.4	20.4
1.5	46.2	3.5	19.8
1.6	43.3	3.6	19.3
1.7	40.8	3.7	18.7
1.8	38.5	3.8	18.2
1.9	36.5	3.9	17.8
2.0	34.7	4.0	17.3

Rate of growth (per cent per year)

Doubling time: Number of years required for population to double in size at each rate of growth.
Source: Shryock, Siegel et al. 1976.

Preston, S.H. 1975: Estimating the proportion of American marriages that end in divorce. *Sociological methods and research* 3, pp. 435–60.

Reading

Carter, H. and Glick, P.C. 1976: *Marriage and divorce: a social and economic study.* Revised edition. Cambridge, Mass.: Harvard University Press.
Preston 1975.

double classification The classification of the demographic events recorded in vital statistics according to both the age, or duration of EXPOSURE TO RISK, (in completed years) and the BIRTH COHORT of the individuals involved. In any one year the deaths of persons of any given age will be those of people born in two different calendar years: some of the persons dying in 1990 at age 20 will have been born in 1970 and others in 1969. Classification by birth cohort and age will reveal the exact numbers involved, allowing the calculation of exact cohort measures. Although this has theoretical advantages the practical use of double classification is limited. Statistics of this type are most widely prepared and used in France.   RP, CW

doubling time The number of years required for a specified population to double its size, given the current rate of population growth. See figure above.

The growth rate of a population is not always immediately interpretable to non-specialists. The doubling time is often used, therefore, as a fairly dramatic indication of the consequences of rapid growth. Doubling time is calculated by dividing the number 69.3 (the natural log of 2, multiplied by 100) by the growth rate in per cent per year. A population growing at 2 per cent per year would take (69.3/2) or just under 35 years to double. At 3 per cent, the time needed would be only 23 years. Some populations today, with annual growth rates well above 3 per cent, are set to double in size within 2 decades. Although no more than a very crude way of estimating future population size, the doubling time is a convenient and vivid way of demonstrating the implications of current growth rates.   CW

Reading

Shryock, H.S., Siegel, J.S. et al. 1976: *The methods and materials of demography*. Condensed edition by E.G. Stockwell. London and New York: Academic Press. Chapter 13.

dual record system   A system of collecting information on VITAL EVENTS in a geographical area, or for a sample population, by two independent data-gathering operations. Terms also in use are dual collection system and dual report system.

Although two similar methods of data collection could be used in combination, in practice most dual record systems have two features:

(1) A continuous recording of vital events in which a locally resident registrar takes active steps to find out through his informants what vital events are occurring instead of waiting for people to come to him for registration.
(2) A multi-round survey in which repeated visits are made to households in the area to ascertain what vital events have occurred during the intervals between the visits.

These periodic surveys provide both a regular update on the population base required for rate computation and an independent check on registered vital events. As the MATCHING of events recorded in both procedures form an integral part of the dual record system, requisite data for

matching are also collected in both operations. Most dual record systems also aim at estimating events missed by both procedures using the CHANDRASEKAR-DEMING TECHNIQUE.   PNM-B

Reading

Blacker, J.G.C. 1977: Dual record demographic surveys: a re-assessment. *Population studies* 31, pp. 585–97.

Coale, A.J. 1961: The design of an experimental procedure for obtaining accurate vital statistics. *International population conference, New York*. Volume 2. London: International Union for the Scientific Study of Population.

Krotki, K.J., ed. 1978: *Developments in dual system estimation of population size and growth*. Edmonton: University of Alberta Press.

Marks, E.S., Seltzer, W. and Krotki, K.J. 1974: *Population growth estimation. A handbook of vital statistics measurement*. New York: Population Council.

duration effect   See AGE EFFECT.

duration of pregnancy   This is open to two definitions: (1) the true duration, measured from the exact day of conception; and (2) the duration since the last normal menstrual period sometimes termed the *conventional* duration.

The latter (on average two weeks more than the former), is more frequently employed since specification of the precise day of conception is rarely feasible. In any case conception comprises two separate things, fertilisation and implantation, which occur about a week apart.   RP

duration-specific marital fertility rate   The number of live births occurring to married women of a particular duration of marriage, normally expressed per 1000 women (sometimes per woman).

In populations with low fertility, duration-specific rates are often preferable as indicators of fertility to the more frequently quoted age-specific rates, since it is marriage rather than age to which marital fertility is related. Rates classified by both age and duration are even more informative sources of information.   RP

Reading

Mineau, G.P. and Trussell, T.J. 1982: A specification of marital fertility by parents' age, age at marriage and marital duration. *Demography* 19, pp. 335–50.

Page, H.J. 1977: Patterns underlying fertility schedules: a decomposition by both age and marriage duration. *Population studies* 31, pp. 85–106.

Pressat, R. 1972: *Demographic analysis: methods, results, applications.* London: Edward Arnold; Chicago: Aldine Atherton. Chapter 8.

Shryock, H.S., Siegel, J.S. et al. 1976: *The methods and materials of demography.* Condensed edition by E.G. Stockwell. London and New York: Academic Press. Chapter 16.

Duvillard, Emmanuel (1755–1832) A French statistician whose LIFE TABLE, produced in 1806, is frequently taken as representative of mortality conditions in France in the later eighteenth century.

Duvillard's life table appears to be a compilation of data from various sources, including information used by earlier authors (e.g. Deparcieux, Moheau and Buffon), and statistics from Geneva. The total amounted to 101,542 deaths. A further drawback with Duvillard's life table is that it was arrived at by arranging the deaths in order of age, with no reference to the population at risk. This is a form of life table construction valid only when dealing with a STATIONARY POPULATION – not an entirely plausible assumption in this case. In spite of these problems, Duvillard's life table is widely quoted as a precursor of later work. Particularly interesting is his attempt to estimate, on the basis of the life table, the likely gain in LIFE EXPECTANCY which would accrue from the elimination of smallpox. He estimated an improvement of 3.5 years, from 28.76 to 32.26. His methods of analysis (which drew on work by Bernoulli in 1760) inaugurated the technique of CAUSE-DELETED LIFE TABLES.

RP

E

early childhood mortality This is usually defined as pertaining to children aged between one and five years. The term refers to deaths occurring before the fifth birthday, but specifically excludes deaths in infancy.

The early child mortality rate is the number of deaths of children aged 1–4 per 1000 population of the same ages. This rate is well under one in most developed countries, where the few early child deaths that occur are mostly due to accidents and congenital defects. But in some developing country populations where DISEASE AND MALNUTRITION are rife, early child death rates well in excess of 160 per 1000 have been found (Cantrelle and Leridon 1971). In such circumstances early age deaths are not sharply restricted to the first year of life, and the probability of dying during early childhood may well exceed that of dying in infancy. (See also CHILD SURVIVORSHIP TECHNIQUES.)   TD

Reference

Cantrelle, P. and Leridon, H. 1971: Breast-feeding, mortality in childhood and fertility in a rural zone of Senegal. *Population studies* 25, pp. 505–33.

Reading

Ashworth, A. 1982: International differences in child mortality. *Human nutrition: clinical nutrition* 36.

Dyson, T. 1977: Levels, trends, differentials and causes of child mortality – a survey. *World health statistics report* 30, pp. 282–311.

Puffer, R.P. and Serrano, C.B. 1973: *Patterns of mortality in childhood.* Scientific publication 262. Washington, DC: Pan American Health Organization.

Easterlin hypothesis Two related but distinct theories:

(1) The fertility of a generation or couple is influenced positively by its 'relative income', that is, by the ratio of its actual income to its aspirations. This is known as the *relative income hypothesis.* Easterlin has added a special twist: that aspirations are formed in the adolescent years by exposure to the standard of living in the parental home. Thus intergenerational income trends influence fertility.

(2) The size of a cohort has a strong negative influence on its economic welfare and relative income, therefore fertility of a cohort will be negatively associated with its size (or the ratio of its size to that of the parental cohort). This may lead to cycles two generations long in fertility, births, and the age distribution, known as Easterlin cycles. See figure opposite.   RDL

Reading

Easterlin, R. 1980: *Birth and fortune.* London: Grant McIntyre; New York: Basic Books.

Population and development review 1976: Fertility, aspirations and resources: a symposium on the Easterlin Hypothesis. Volume 2, pp. 411–77. Articles by D. Freedman, R.A. Easterlin, R.D. Lee, H. Leibenstein, V.K. Oppenheimer, and W.C. Sanderson.

Smith, D.P. 1981: A reconsideration of Easterlin cycles. *Population studies* 35, pp. 247–64.

economic activity Any occupation or activity that contributes to the production of income. Details of activity according to occupation of work status provide a means of classifying the LABOUR FORCE, sometimes also referred to as the working or economically active population. Homemakers or housewives, students and retired workers are not normally regarded as

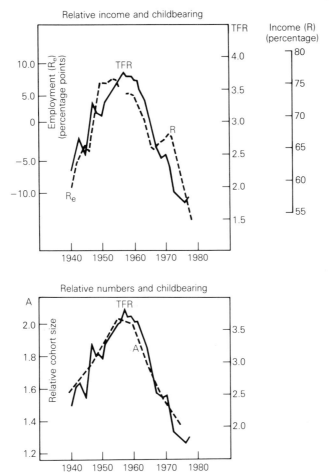

Relative income and childbearing

Relative numbers and childbearing

Easterlin hypothesis: Swings in US fertility measured by the Total Fertility Rate (TFR) match swings in relative employment and income of young men and relative cohort size.
Source: Easterlin 1980.

forming part of the labour force; it is, however, usually defined to include both unemployed and employed workers. The broad classifications of economic activity generally made often embrace a very wide range of individual jobs.   RP

Reading
Shryock, H.S., Siegel, J.S. et al. 1976: *The methods and materials of demography*. Condensed edition by E.G. Stockwell. London and New York: Academic Press. Chapter 12.
Standing, G. 1982: Labor force. In J.A. Ross, ed. *International encyclopaedia of population*. New York: Free Press. Pp. 391–8.

economic demography A branch of demographic research dealing with the relationship between population and economics. Both the range of topics covered and the variety of techniques of analysis employed are vast and highly diverse, embracing all aspects of demographic change.

Since little unity of approach or subject matter exists it is easiest to examine economic demography in terms of its use in the various phenomena to which economic analysis has been applied. Very general relationships between the economic organisation of a society and its overall demographic characteristics have been recognised since at least the time of MALTHUS, and a recurrent theme in much POPULATION THEORY has been the notion of an optimum size or optimum rate of population growth for any economic environment. In this vein recent research on pre-industrial Europe has explicitly linked economic and demographic change within the concept of a HOMEOSTATIC REGIME (Wrigley and Schofield 1981).

Discussions on the links between population growth and economic development in the Third World have often been marked by controversy and are now dominated by microeconomic approaches, often predominantly concerned with fertility decline (Cassen 1970, Ridker 1976). In developed countries attention has recently focused on questions of AGEING and its economic consequences (Clark et al. 1982). A considerable increase in the proportion of national income spent on pensions and health care seems inevitable in most countries, with the range of further likely outcomes including changes in the savings ratio and patterns of consumption among others. There is, however, a considerable shortage of accurate information on many of the macroeconomic consequences of ageing, and in particular on productivity and life-cycle effects. In addition the full implications of changing DEPENDENCY RATIOS are unclear.

Economic models have also been widely used in analysing the components of demographic change. The declining importance of economics in determining mortality at a national level (Preston 1975) has, in general, led demographers to look elsewhere for applications of economics, in particular to fertility and migration. Two major schools of thought have developed in fertility research: the 'socio-economic' approach of Leibenstein (1975) and Easterlin (1975), and the 'new home economics' approach of Becker (1965) and Schultz (1976). The former attempts to link economic models to more widely-defined social factors, while the latter insists on the primacy of economic decision making within a household framework. A further strand of thought, also based on household economics, is the study of the VALUE OF CHILDREN, a concept with social and psychological, as well as economic, implications (Fawcett 1982). Economic factors have long been cited as factors in migration; in the nineteenth century, Ravenstein in his 'laws' of migration stated that economic causes were of primary importance. Historical and contemporary evidence, as well as commonsense, demonstrate that major migration flows exist from low-income to higher-income areas. However, Todaro (1976) has shown that it is perceived income and employment opportunities, rather than real differences, which are of most importance.   RP, CW

References

Becker, G.S. 1965: A theory of the allocation of time. *Economic journal* 75, pp. 493–517.
Cassen, R.H. 1970: Population and development: a survey. *World development* 4, pp. 785–830.
Clark, R.L., Kreps, J. and Spengler, J.J. 1982: Aging population: United States. In J.A. Ross, ed. *International encyclopaedia of population*. New York: Free Press. Pp. 31–40.
Easterlin, R.A. 1975: An economic framework for fertility analysis. *Studies in family planning* 6, pp. 54–63.
Fawcett, J.T. 1982: Value of children. In J.A. Ross, ed. *International encyclopaedia of population*. New York: Free Press. Pp. 665–71.
Leibenstein, H. 1975: The economic theory of fertility decline. *Quarterly journal of economics* 89, pp. 1–31.
Preston, S.H. 1975: The changing relation between mortality and level of economic development. *Population studies* 29, pp. 231–48.
Ridker, R.G., ed. 1976: *Population and development: the search for selective interventions*. Baltimore: Johns Hopkins University Press.
Schultz, T.P. 1976: Determinants of fertility: a micro-economic model of choice. In A.J. Coale, ed. *Economic factors in population growth*. New York: Wiley.
Todaro, M.P. 1976: *Internal migration in de-

veloping countries: a review of theory, evidence, methodology and research priorities. Geneva: International Labour Organisation.
Wrigley, E.A. and Schofield, R.S. 1981: *The population history of England, 1541–1871. A reconstruction*. London: Edward Arnold: Cambridge, Mass.: Harvard University Press.

Reading
Cassen 1976.
Findley, S.E. 1982: Internal migration: determinants. In J.A. Ross, ed. *International encyclopaedia of population*. New York: Free Press. Pp. 344–51.
Jones, G.W. 1982: Fertility determinants: sociological and economic theories. In J.A. Ross, ed. *International encyclopaedia of population*. New York: Free Press. Pp. 279–86.

economically active population See LABOUR FORCE.

EDA See EXPLANATORY DATA ANALYSIS.

editing The identification and removal of errors from a data set. Editing may be performed before either the data have been entered onto a computer file (field, or office/manual editing) and/or afterwards (machine editing). Field or office editing may include the following checks: verification of the sample and identification of the number of individual cases; the adequacy and legibility of material; the existence of missing or redundant information; the internal consistency and plausibility of items; and the uniformity of interpretation by interviewers. Resolution of these errors may be based on reference to related material for the same case, by discussion and clarification with the person who collected the data or by returning to the original source (e.g. re-interview). Field or manual editing may be combined with CODING. Machine editing is synonymous with DATA CLEANING.   JGC

Reading
United Nations 1980: *National migration surveys, manual VII. Manual for office editors and coders*. Bangkok: Economic and Social Commission for Asia and the Pacific.

World Fertility Survey 1976: *Editing and coding manual*. Basic documentation 7. Voorburg, The Netherlands: International Statistical Institute.

embryo See PREGNANCY.

emigration The process of international MIGRATION viewed from the standpoint of the nation from which the movement occurs. Emigrants, therefore, are persons leaving one country to establish residence in another. The word out-migrant is used to refer to people leaving a given area and moving to another part of the same country.   RP

emigration rate The ratio of the number of emigrants leaving a specified country or region within a given period to the average population in that period, or to the number of person-years lived. The rate may refer to the total population, producing a crude emigration rate (analagous to other CRUDE RATES), or it may be made specific to each age group.
Because of theoretical and practical difficulties only limited use has been made of rates in the study of INTERNATIONAL MIGRATION, and no particular set of rates has yet become standard. (See also MIGRATION.)   RP, CW

Reading
Shryock, H.S., Siegel, J.S. et al. 1976: *The methods and materials of demography*. Condensed edition by E.G. Stockwell. London and New York: Academic Press. Chapter 20.

endemic disease A disease that is constantly present in a particular locality. The opposite of EPIDEMIC.   RSS

endogamous circle See MARRIAGE MODELS.

endogamy Marriage predominantly, or exclusively, between members of the same social, geographical or ethnic group. A population of limited size where marriage is entirely endogamous is known as an ISOLATE. Various qualifiers such as occupational or religious endogamy are sometimes found. The opposite term is exogamy. Homogamy and its synonyms assortative marriage or assortative mating indicate marriage between persons with certain common characteristics, either social, physical or mental. The opposite is heterogamy.   RP

endogenous mortality   Mortality due to genetic makeup or to circumstances arising before or during birth. It is contrasted with EXOGENOUS MORTALITY which is attributable to environmental or external causes.

This general distinction can be enlarged by consideration of mortality in various age groups. A newborn infant often has a substantial risk of dying partly attributable to endogenous factors, such as congenital malformations which arise from its constitution and may be regarded as reflecting its intrinsic viability (or lack of viability). After the immediate postpartum period, however, exogenous risks such as infections or accidents become increasingly more important. Between the ages of about 1 and 10 or 15 virtually all deaths are due to exogenous factors. After this point mortality due to ageing (above all heart disease and cancers) appears and gradually increases. Deaths attributable to ageing are also termed endogenous.

Although medicine has made considerable progress in eliminating exogenous deaths, endogenous mortality has proved more resistant. In spite of the large increase in LIFE EXPECTANCY the permanence of endogenous mortality renders the maximum length of life unchanged at about 110 to 115 years. Even the total removal of all exogenous mortality would seem to lead to a life expectancy only a few years longer than that observed in the most favourable cases (see LONGEVITY).

The distinction between endogenous and exogenous mortality is most commonly attempted for infant deaths using the BIOMETRIC ANALYSIS OF INFANT MORTALITY but even there the exact determination of the two quantities is uncertain, owing to variation in the age-pattern of deaths within the first year of life.   RP, CW

Reading
Benjamin, B. and Pollard, J.H. 1980: *Analysis of mortality and other actuarial statistics.* London: Heinemann.
Bourgeois-Pichat, J. 1952: Essai sur la mortalité biologique de l'homme. *Population* 7, pp. 381–94.
Knodel, J. and Kintner, H. 1977: The impact of breast feeding patterns on the biometric analysis of infant mortality. *Demography* 14, pp. 391–409.
McKeown, T. 1977:*The modern rise of population.* London: Edward Arnold.
Pollard, J. 1979: Factors affecting mortality and the length of life. In International Union for the Scientific Study of Population, *Population science in the service of mankind: conference on science in the service of life, Vienna 1979.* Liège: IUSSP. Pp. 53–79.
Pressat, R. 1972: *Demographic analysis: methods, results, applications.* London: Edward Arnold; Chicago: Aldine Atherton. Pp. 82–101.

enumeration   An operation designed to provide information about the members of a population. It represents the data collection phase of a census. A distinction is made between information gathered by direct interview, the enumerator being responsible for filling in the census form, and self-enumeration, which is the responsibility of the members of each household.

The direct interview has the advantage that the form is filled in by a trained enumerator familiar with the questions asked. This may be the only possible type of enumeration in populations with low levels of literacy, although the expense of recruiting, training and employing the vast numbers of enumerators needed in any census is a powerful countervailing factor. The result is that direct enumeration by interviewer tends to be limited to developing countries, although the United States used direct interviews for every census up to 1960.

In self-enumeration the census forms

are distributed, usually one to each household, and the required information is entered by one or more household members. If the forms are collected by census officials checking for correctness and completeness is often carried out on collection, and in a mail census special visits or correspondence may be used to verify the data. Self-enumeration is generally preferred on cost grounds in developed countries but even where it is the norm, particular sectors of the population such as transients and other highly mobile groups, may need a different form of enumeration.

RP, CW

Reading

Benjamin, B. 1970: *The population census.* London: Heinemann.

Bulmer, M. and Warwick, D.P. eds. 1983: *Social research in developing countries.* Chichester and New York: Wiley.

Casley, D.J. and Lurey, D.A. 1981: *Data collection in developing countries.* Oxford: Clarendon Press.

United Nations 1980: *Principles and recommendations for population and housing censuses.* Series M, statistical papers 67. New York: Department of International Economic and Social Affairs.

United States, National Academy of Sciences 1981: *Collecting data for the estimation of fertility and mortality.* Panel on Data Collection, Committee on Population and Demography. Washington DC: National Academy Press. Chapter 2.

epidemic A mass outbreak in a particular locality of a disease which spreads and then disappears within a relatively brief period. When it appears over a wide area it is known as a pandemic.

In contrast to endemic disease, which is permanently present in a population and is, by its very nature, regular and (in the aggregate at least) predictable in occurrence, the irregularity and sudden increase of illness and death associated with epidemics has endowed them with a special significance throughout history. The populations of pre-industrial Europe viewed epidemics (especially the bubonic plague)

with fear, occasionally with terror, although endemic mortality was the greater killer.

The term is sometimes used loosely to indicate any high level of MORBIDITY or mortality, or even applied to the widespread occurrence of any phenomenon perceived as undesirable, e.g. an 'epidemic' of teenage pregnancy.   RSS, CW

Reading

Charbonneau, H. and Larose, A., eds. 1979: *The great mortalities: methodological studies of demographic crises in the past.* Liège: Ordina Editions.

epidemiology Commonly defined as 'the study of the distribution of a disease or a physiological condition in human populations and of the factors that influence this distribution' (Lilienfeld 1978).

It is primarily concerned with population groups and not with individuals. Most epidemiological studies are concerned either with investigating the etiology of a specified condition or with evaluating a preventative procedure. Many of the methods and techniques employed are derived from other disciplines such as statistics, demography, social science and biological science. One area in which epidemiological work has had a significant impact on demography is the mathematical modelling of disease (see Bailey 1975).

ER

References

Bailey, N.J.T. 1975: *The mathematical theory of infectious diseases.* Second edition. London: Charles Griffin.

Lilienfeld, D.E. 1978: Definitions of epidemiology. *American journal of epidemiology* 107, pp. 87–90.

Reading

Lilienfeld, A.M. and Lilienfeld, D.E. 1980: *Foundations of epidemiology.* Second edition. Oxford: Oxford University Press.

MacMahon, B. and Pugh, T.F. 1970: *Epidemiology principles and methods.* Boston: Little, Brown and Company.

Sinnecker, H. 1976: *General epidemiology* Chichester and New York: Wiley.

ergodicity The property of having the present state of a population independent of its make-up in the remote past, and determined only by the birth and death rates recently experienced. It is a crucial element in the construction of mathematical models of demographic change.

Not all populations display ergodicity. Those that do are ergodic because births occur simultaneously to parents from different earlier cohorts, gradually smoothing the time series of births.

When the current state of a population is specified by a census solely according to age, it is determined by the age-specific rates of birth, death and possibly migration. When the present state of the population is specified by age, sex and characteristics such as geographical location or educational status, it is determined by birth, death and migration rates specific to age, sex and the other characteristics.

Ergodicity can be proved to be a property only of mathematical models of populations, and is imputed to a real population on the hypothesis that the real population is well described by some mathematical model that has been shown to be ergodic. Strong ergodic theorems assume that the vital rates of a population model are fixed over all time. The theory and applications of STABLE POPULATIONS are based on strong ergodic theorems. Weak ergodic theorems assume that populations experience a given deterministic sequence of possibly time-varying vital rates.

Stochastic ergodic theorems assume that the sequence of vital rates experienced by a population is not deterministic but is modelled by a stochastic process. A stochastic ergodic theorem asserts that in the long run the probability distribution of the population model will depend on the stochastic process that has been governing the vital rates and not on the initial state of the population model.   JEC

Reading

Arthur, W.B. 1981: Why a population converges to stability. *American mathematical monthly* 88, pp. 557–63.

Cohen, J.E. 1979: Ergodic theorems in demography. *Bulletin of the American Mathematical Society* NS 1, pp. 275–95.

ethnic group A group of persons bound together by a common culture, language, customs, religion or race. The term is often used in the context of minority groups differentiated from a larger population by these characteristics.

The term is of broader meaning than the more controversial usage racial group, although the two may in some circumstances be coterminous. The precise definitions of ethnic groups in official statistics vary widely. In the US census a variety of categories is used, some reflecting race and others national origin. The question is, in essence, a matter of self-identification. In many countries place of birth has been used in an attempt to identify ethnicity, and one or more of the specific attributes of the group (language, religion, etc.) may also be employed. In some countries, for example the United Kingdom, ethnic status is regarded as too 'sensitive' an issue to be included in the census at all.   RP, CW

Reading

Bean, F.D. and Frisbie, W.P., eds. 1978: *The demography of racial and ethnic groups*. New York and London: Academic Press.
Shryock, H.S., Siegel, J.S. et al. 1976: *The methods and materials of demography*. Condensed edition by E.G. Stockwell. London and New York: Academic Press. Chapter 9.

eugenics The study of factors capable of improving the physiological and intellectual status of populations by their effect on the conditions of human reproduction and on the physical environment.

Eugenics was a prominent intellectual force of the late nineteenth and early twentieth centuries. Now associated in the minds of many with racism and sexism, it plays a much less explicit role in the study of present day populations. Nevertheless development of techniques and methodology in several disciplines, such as human biology, demography and statistics, owe much to work carried out with a eugenic motivation, and the subject now embraces a much wider range of social and environmental factors than its initial, purely genetic, considerations. The term negative eugenics is sometimes used to refer to the elimination of genetic defects. This is a subject of growing significance as medical sophistication increases and childbearing at older ages declines, since it is at these ages that mothers are most likely to bear handicapped offspring.   RP, CW

Reading

Cavalli-Sforza, L.L. and Bodmer, W.F. 1971: *The genetics of human populations*. San Francisco: W.H. Freeman. Chapter 12.

Smith, A. 1975: *The human pedigree*. Philadelphia and New York: J.B. Lippincott. Chapters 14 and 15.

Euler, Leonhard (1707–1783)   A Swiss mathematician whose development of the concept of the STABLE POPULATION foreshadowed and inspired the work of twentieth-century demographers on the same subject. His work, published in 1760, contained the key notions of the LIFE TABLE and an arbitrary rate of increase of population.   RP

Reading

Euler, L. 1970: A general investigation into the mortality and multiplication of the human species. (1760) Translated by N. Keyfitz and B. Keyfitz. *Theoretical population biology* 1, pp. 307–14.

event   See VITAL EVENT.

event history   See LIFE HISTORY.

ever-married   See MARRIAGE.

exact age   A person's age given as the exact difference between the date on which the calculation is made and the person's birthday. A person born on 19 January 1956 will be exactly 29.24 years (or 29 years, 89 days) old on 19 April 1985. In contrast with the more often encountered age in completed years, which does not change between birthdays, exact age increases continuously.   RP

excess male mortality   See SEX DIFFERENTIAL MORTALITY

exogamy   See ENDOGAMY.

exogenous mortality   Mortality due to external causes, such as accidents and parasitic or INFECTIOUS DISEASES. It is contrasted with ENDOGENOUS MORTALITY which is attributable to ageing or to congenital defects. The term is most widely used in analysis of infant deaths where the two forms of mortality may be distinguished (with some element of uncertainty) by use of the BIOMETRIC ANALYSIS OF INFANT MORTALITY.

Most of the improvement in LIFE EXPECTANCY has been due to the control of exogenous mortality, both through medical intervention and through improved environmental conditions. (Endogenous deaths are much less easy to prevent.)   RP

Reading

Benjamin, B. and Pollard, J.H. 1980: *Analysis of mortality and other actuarial statistics*. London: Heinemann.

Bourgeois-Pichat, J. 1952: Essai sur la mortalité biologique de l'homme. *Population* 7, pp. 381–94.

Knodel, J. and Kintner, H. 1977: The impact of breast feeding patterns on the biometric analysis of infant mortality. *Demography* 14, pp. 391–409.

McKeown, T. 1977: *The modern rise of population*. London: Edward Arnold.

Pollard, J. 1979: Factors affecting mortality and the length of life. In International Union for the Scientific Study of Population, *Population science in the service of mankind: Conference on science in the service of life, Vienna 1979*. Liège: IUSSP. Pp. 53–79.

Pressat, R. 1972: *Demographic analysis: methods, results, applications*. London: Edward Arnold; Chicago: Aldine Atherton. Pp. 82–101.

expectation of life   See LIFE EXPECTANCY.

exploratory data analysis (EDA)   Techniques of statistical analysis devised by Tukey (1977) which use relatively elementary arithmetic and graphical methods in order to calculate robust and informative descriptive statistics.

In contrast with more conventional, and more widely used, forms of statistical analysis based on the testing of various hypotheses and formal probability theory, EDA is aimed at providing a description of a body of data and its internal structure. Although its use in demographic research has increased only slowly EDA provides a series of straightforward and readily interpretable statistics which are particularly useful in the first stages of analysis and for the presentation of summary descriptions.

CW

Reading

Tukey, J.W. 1977: *Exploratory data analysis.* Reading, Mass.: Addison-Wesley.

exponential population growth   Population increase resulting from a constant rate of growth. In this situation the size of a population will increase without limit if the growth rate is positive and decreases steadily if it is negative. This can be defined as:

$$P_t = P_o e^{rt}$$

where P_o is the initial population size, P_t is the population after time t and r is the growth rate. An alternative expression is:

$$P_t = P_o(1 + r_1)^t$$

with r_1 defined as $\log_e(1 + r_1) = r$. The geometric increase postulated by Malthus is a special case of exponential growth. Although no real population has experienced exponential growth over a sustained period, the simplifying assumption to this form of increase was essential to the development of STABLE POPULATION theory.

RP

Reading

Keyfitz, N. 1977: *Applied mathematical demography.* New York and London: Wiley. Chapter 1.

exposure rate   See ATTRITION RATE.

exposure to risk   The circumstances in which a person is liable to experience a particular demographic event.

The word 'risk' rather than the more neutral 'chance' reflects the influence on demography of actuarial work, in which the event in question is death; it does not necessarily imply that the event is unwelcome, and phrases such as 'risk of marriage' are used. The concept is fundamental to demographic analysis and the most revealing measures are those which relate events to the number of persons who could have experienced them rather than to the whole population. The term 'population at risk' is widely used to indicate the subgroup of the population whose experience is the focus of a particular measure. Special attention is paid to the question of HETEROGENEITY, and it is normal to divide the population into subgroups which are more homogeneous with regard to the risk in question. The most important distinction of this type is age, which has a large impact on virtually all demographic phenomena. At times it is impossible to specify the true population at risk. When studying fertility, for example, it is common to distinguish between married and unmarried women, since they usually have differing likelihoods of giving birth, but it is rarely possible to exclude women who are physiologically unable to bear children since they are not an identifiable group.

RP

extended family   A term used initially by anthropologists to denote a domestic group or composite of domestic groups consisting of two or more NUCLEAR FAMILIES linked together through parent and child (patrilineal extended family, matrilineal extended family) or through siblings (fraternal or sororal extended family) (Kessing 1975).

In quantitative studies of the CO-RESIDENT GROUP an extended family HOUSEHOLD has been defined as one consisting of a conjugal family unit with the addition of one or more relatives other than offspring, the whole group living together on its own with servants. If the resident relative is of a generation earlier than that of the head of the household the extension is upwards; if the relative is a brother, sister or cousin of the head or his spouse it is sideways or lateral (Laslett 1972). A multiple family household comprises all forms of domestic group which include two or more conjugal family units connected by KINSHIP or marriage; these units can be simple or extended and can be disposed vertically and laterally.

In certain functionalist treatments of family extension of complexity, co-residence in the same dwelling may not be an absolutely necessary precondition, for instance in the cooperative exploitation of a common economic resource, even where that resource is land (Yanagisako 1979). Furthermore, certain census-takers do not define domestic groups with reference to their living under the same roof. In certain agricultural societies the eldest generation living after retirement in separate quarters without their own kitchens are treated as part of the household of their children (Berkner 1975).   RMS

References

Berkner, L. 1975: The use and misuse of census data for the historical analysis of family structure. *Journal of interdisciplinary history* 5, pp. 721–38.

Kessing, R.M. 1975: *Kin groups and social structure*. New York: Holt, Rinehart and Winston.

Laslett, P. 1972: Introduction. In P. Laslett and R. Wall, eds. *Household and family in past time*. London and New York: Cambridge University Press.

Yanagisako, S.L. 1979: Family and household. The analysis of domestic groups. *Annual review of anthropology* 8, pp. 161–205.

Reading

Laslett 1972.

F

factor analysis A form of statistical analysis consisting of finding latent un-measured variables, or factors which are hypothesised as being source variables accounting for the interrelations in the data. It is therefore assumed that the observed variables are influenced by several determinants, some shared by some or all variables (common factors), others affecting only each single observed variable (unique factors). It is further assumed that the common factors are smaller in number than the original variables.

Methods of deriving common factors are very similar to PRINCIPAL COMPONENTS ANALYSIS. However, as factor analysis assumes the existence of a residual variance due to the presence of unique factors, the part of the variance of the observed variables accounted for by the sole common factors (communality) is not known and has to be estimated from the data.

The solution obtained is not unique. A terminal solution is usually established by rotating the common factors to obtain a simple structure, assuming that these factors are either orthogonal (uncorrelated) or oblique (correlated). Factors are then named, taking into account the correlations (or factor loadings) between each observed variable and each factor (the factor structure matrix). A distinction is often made between exploratory factor analysis, which attempts to reduce the original number of variables to a smaller number of factors, and confirmatory factor analysis which assumes that there are a specific number of underlying factors and then tests this hypothesis.   GW

Reading
Harman, H.H. 1976: *Modern factor analysis*. Chicago: University of Chicago Press.

Kim, J.O. and Mueller, C.W. 1978: *Introduction to factor analysis*. Sage university papers series on quantitative applications in the social sciences. Beverly Hills and London: Sage Publications.

Rummel, R.J. 1970: *Applied factor analysis*. Evanston, Illinois: Northwestern University Press.

family It is conventionally argued in both anthropological and sociological literature that families are KINSHIP units and as such must be defined strictly in terms of kinship relationships and not in terms of co-residence. The empirical distinction is founded on the observation that in numerous societies families do not form HOUSEHOLDS, and that in even more instances CO-RESIDENT GROUPS are not composed of families (Yanagisako 1979; Bender 1967).

Demographers have used the word 'family' in ways that reflect its use in everyday speech and, perhaps more significantly, by the methodology or data-gathering principles of modern national census offices which treat the co-resident group or the dwelling unit as the unit of enumeration. 'Family demographers' tend therefore to be preoccupied with those kin co-residing in the same dwelling unit. Kin who do not share the same dwelling unit are not therefore part of the 'family' in the demographic sense, even though they may live close by and even though there may be considerable interaction between them and the 'family' (Burch 1979). This latter approach has met with considerable criticism from those who argue that co-resident group structure and kinship are so enmeshed that they must not be differentiated for analytic purposes (Berkner 1975; Wheaton 1975).   RMS

References

Bender, D. 1967: A redefinement of the concept of household: families, co-resident and domestic functions. *American anthropologist* 69, pp. 493–504.

Berkner, L. 1975: The use and misuse of census data for the historical analysis of family structure. *Journal of interdisciplinary history* 5, pp. 721–38.

Burch, T.K. 1979: Household and family demography: a bibliographic essay. *Population index* 45, pp. 173–94.

Wheaton, R. 1975: Family and kinship in Western Europe: the problem of the joint family household. *Journal of interdisciplinary history* 4, pp. 601–28.

Yanagisako, S.J. 1979: Family and household: the analysis of domestic groups. *Annual review of anthropology* 8, pp. 161–205.

Reading

Burch 1979.

family cycle   Attempts to characterise a society in terms of its CO-RESIDENT GROUP structure are complicated by substantial changes during the life time of an individual co-resident group. Aggregate data at any given moment catch co-resident groups at different stages of this life cycle and may thus obscure important temporal variations.

Beginning with Fortes's work (1949) on Ashanti domestic groups there has been an important series of efforts to reconstruct the longitudinal aspects of co-resident group structure from synchronic, cross-sectional data by tabulating information on co-resident group size and composition as a function of the age of its head (Berkner 1972). Freeman et al. (1978) found that in Taiwan most married couples of reproductive age had lived at one time in extended HOUSEHOLDS, even

though in a cross-sectional view of the sample data 60 per cent of households were nuclear. Idealised family development cycles have been suggested. For example the following sequence in present day western societies: (a) the courtship phase; (b) the initial phase of marriage; (c) the child-bearing and child-rearing phase; (d) the phase of disintegration (Turner 1969).

Such longitudinal studies are hampered by their inability to distinguish the current situation of successive cohorts from the consequence of secular changes either in household formation rules or in the exogenous conditions of household management (Watkins 1980).   RMS

References

Berkner, L. 1972: The stem-family and the developmental cycle of the peasant household: an eighteenth-century Austrian example. *American historical review* 77, pp. 398–418.

Fortes, M. 1949: Time and social structure: an Ashanti case study. In M. Fortes, ed. *Social structure*. Oxford: Clarendon Press.

Freeman, R. et al. 1978: Household composition and extended kinship in Taiwan. *Population studies* 32, pp. 65–80.

Turner, C. 1969: *Family and kinship in modern Britain*. London: Routledge and Kegan Paul.

Watkins, S.C. 1980: On measuring transitions and turning points. *Historical methods* 13, pp. 181–6.

Reading

Berkner 1972.
Turner 1969.
Watkins 1980.

family demography   The analysis of the patterns and determinants of the family and household.

Traditionally work by demographers on these subjects has reflected the official definition of households, rather than the more amorphous concept of family. The main concern of family demographers, therefore, has been with the analysis of kin living in the CO-RESIDENT GROUP. In addition to developing measurements of household size and structure, demographers have given considerable attention to the questions of life-cycle patterns.   CW

Reading

Burch, T.K. 1982: Household and family demography. In J.A. Ross, ed. *International encyclopaedia of population*. New York: Free Press. Pp. 299–307.

Ryder, N.B. 1975: Reproductive behaviour and the family life cycle. In United Nations *The population debate: dimensions and perspectives*. New York: Department of Economic and Social Affairs. Vol. 2, pp. 278–88.

family formation   The process of family building, usually taking into account both NUPTIALITY and FERTILITY. Studies of family formation generally pay particular attention to the timing of marriage, birth intervals and notions of the family cycle.
                                                                                CW

family limitation   Deliberate restriction of the number of children born to couples who have reached a certain family size or PARITY. Sometimes termed 'stopping behaviour', it is contrasted with more general terms such as BIRTH CONTROL or FAMILY PLANNING which may involve attempts to space births as well as to prevent them.

Although a number of factors leading to reduced fertility, most importantly prolonged BREASTFEEDING, can be observed for many pre-industrial societies both in the contemporary developing world and in historical populations, they do not seem to have been widely used as methods of family limitation. They were employed irrespective of family size and acted only as a form of BIRTH SPACING. So while the means to limit family size (abstinence, withdrawal, etc.) seem to have been potentially available at all times, the motivation to use them appears to have been generally absent. This has led some demographers, most lucidly Knodel (1977), to suggest that family limitation, which is essential to the reduction of fertility in the DEMOGRAPHIC TRANSITION, is a fundamental innovation in human society.

The recognition that it is necessary to distinguish between the means to control fertility and the motivation to do so is relatively recent but it has played a valuable role in the understanding of fertility decline, both in historical European populations and in the Third World today. For example, it can throw light on the fact that once family limitation becomes widely established, fertility falls (often rapidly and usually monotonically) to low levels. Equally, changes in mental outlook seem to offer more plausible reasons than changes in economic circumstances for the fertility declines seen in predominantly rural and agricultural countries (e.g. France and Bulgaria and, more recently, Thailand).

Direct evidence of the increased use of contraception to achieve family limitation is not generally available for historical populations. Demographers base their judgements, therefore, on the recorded evidence of births, in particular the examination of various fertility rates and indices. AGE-SPECIFIC MARITAL FERTILITY RATES are commonly analysed, as are convenient summary measures, such as those generated by the COALE-TRUSSELL MODEL. (See also NATURAL FERTILITY.)   RP, CW

Reference

Knodel, J. 1977: Family limitation and the fertility transition: evidence from the age patterns of fertility in Europe and Asia. *Population studies* 31, pp. 219–49.

Reading

Knodel 1977.

Knodel, J. and van de Walle, E. 1983: Fertility decline: European transition. In J.A. Ross, ed. *International encyclopaedia of population*. New York: Free Press. Pp. 268–75.

family planning   Conscious effort of couples or individuals to control the number and spacing of births.

Family planning is used synonymously with many terms – birth planning, birth control, fertility regulation, planned parenthood and many others. The term implies a general reproductive strategy, however, and should not be used to mean just contraception, since it comprises practices aimed both at preventing births at certain times and at inducing them at others.

Although in historical Europe and North America family planning was initially practised in the face of hostility or disapproval from administrative and religious authorities, in many countries today it is advocated and extensively promoted by governments. This has accelerated the growth of family planning programmes – involving either official or private organisations – to distribute contraceptives, and advise on their use. The scale and complexity of many of these programmes makes the assessment of their effectiveness a major research concern in demography.   RP, CW

Reading

Ross, J.A., ed. 1982: *International encyclopaedia of population*. New York: Free Press. Articles on family planning programmes by W. B. Watson, M. E. Gorosh, J. R. Foreit, J. G. Dryfoos, and A. I. Hermalin, pp. 205–35; and on family planning research pp. 235–40.

family reconstitution   A technique of RECORD LINKAGE which consists of linking together the vital events recorded by a registration system in order to reconstitute the history of individual families. Although sometimes used on data from civil registration systems, the majority of family reconstitution studies are based on the PARISH REGISTERS of historical populations in Europe and North America.

The technique of family reconstitution was developed in France in the 1950s as a means of exploiting the particularly rich data in French parish registers (Fleury and Henry 1956), and it has subsequently been extended to many populations in Western Europe and Colonial North America. The process is generally based around the family reconstitution form (FRF) on which the researcher assembles the facts relating to one marriage: the date of the marriage, the dates of birth of the spouses, the dates of birth and death of any children and, finally, the deaths of the spouses. Socio-economic information (e.g. occupation) is also included. The FRF provides a complete history of the marriage from which many demographic indices can in theory be calculated. Complications may be caused however by deficient registration, or, even where registration is complete, migration may remove individuals from observation. These considerations, together with the time-consuming nature of reconstitution, often mean that only a relatively small number of families is in fact available for detailed analysis, a problem which has led to doubts over the validity of reconstitution on grounds of representativeness and stochastic variation. Whatever its theoretical and practical difficulties, family reconstitution provides insights into past populations which would otherwise be unavailable. For example, studies of pre-industrial Europe have demonstrated the predominance of NATURAL FERTILITY as a form of childbearing, with FAMILY LIMITATION restricted to certain groups until the era of the DEMOGRAPHIC TRANSITION.

The lengthy nature of any reconstitution has prompted the development of computer-based techniques of linkage, though these are complicated by the difficulties of historical records (such as the highly variable spelling of names). The most extensive work in this direction has taken place in England, at the Cambridge Group for the History of Population and Social Structure, and at the University of Montréal, where an attempt is being made to reconstitute the history of the entire population of Colonial Quebec.   RP, CW

Reference

Fleury, M. and Henry, L. 1956: *Nouveau manuel de dépouillement et d'exploitation de l'état civil ancien*. Paris: Institut National d'Etudes Démographiques.

Reading

Hollingsworth, T.H. 1969: *Historical demography*. London: Hodder and Stoughton; Ithaca, NY: Cornell University Press.
Willigan, J.D. and Lynch, K.A. 1983: *Sources*

and methods of historical demography. New York and London: Academic Press.

Wrigley, E.A., ed. 1966: *An introduction to English historical demography*. London: Weidenfeld and Nicholson; New York: Basic Books.

Wrigley, E.A., ed. 1973: *Identifying people in the past*. London: Edward Arnold.

family size   In much demographic literature the everyday term family size is replaced with the technical term PARITY. 'Family size' is often used, however, in ways synonymous with parity, especially in the consideration of intentions, such as DESIRED FAMILY SIZE or intended family size.   RP, CW

famine   An extreme and general lack of availability of food. Famine may be acute or chronic in character. The extent to which it raises mortality depends on the social and economic circumstances of the relevant population.

In early research on pre-industrial Europe famine was regarded as a principal cause of crisis mortality. More recent work, has suggested that it played a lesser role in this respect than epidemics, although malnutrition interacts 'synergistically' with many diseases to exacerbate their effects (see DISEASE AND MALNUTRITION).

The impact of famine on fertility has also been a topic of interest to demographers. Recent research suggests that it is only in the most extreme cases that a significant impact on fertility is evident (Menken et al. 1981). Interestingly, data from the Dutch 'hunger-winter' famine of 1944–45 indicate that famine only slowly leads to reduction in births (as bodily resources are depleted) but that a return to adequate nutrition produces an almost instant recovery (Stein et al. 1975)   RSS, CW

References

Menken, J., Trussell, T.J. and Watkins, S.C. 1981: The nutrition-fertility link: an evaluation of the evidence. *Journal of interdisciplinary history* 11, pp. 425–41.

Stein, Z., Susser, M., Saenger, G. and Marolla, F. 1975: *The Dutch hunger winter of 1944–1945*. New York: Oxford University Press.

Reading

Dando W. 1980: *The geography of famine*. London: Edward Arnold.

Menken et al. 1981.

Sen, A. 1981: *Poverty and famines: an essay in entitlement deprivation*. Oxford: Oxford University Press.

Wrigley, E.A. and Schofield, R.S. 1981: *The population history of England, 1541–1871: a reconstruction*. London: Edward Arnold. Cambridge, Mass.: Harvard University Press. Chapters 8 and 9. (Chapter 9 by R.D. Lee.)

fecundability   The probability of conception in one menstrual cycle (or one month) among women who menstruate regularly but do not practise contraception.

Fecundability is normally calculated only for married women (or those in other stable unions) and is often referred to with a variety of qualifiers, some of which are incompatible with the above definition. *Total* fecundability refers to all conceptions in a given month, many of which will produce pregnancies of very short duration (i.e. not long enough to delay the next menstrual period) and are therefore undetectable, except in very elaborate medical studies. *Recognisable* fecundability refers to pregnancies which last long enough to delay a period and so are potentially detectable. Among these, however, some will end in miscarriage or stillbirth. *Effective* fecundability refers only to those conceptions which lead to live births. In addition to these definitions a contrast is sometimes made between *natural* and *residual* fecundability. The former qualifier is tautologous and simply implies the basic definition of fecundability, while the latter is the fecundability which pertains even in the presence of contraception. Comparisons of natural and residual fecundability have been used to assess CONTRACEPTIVE EFFECTIVENESS.

The concept of fecundability was introduced by Gini in 1924 (see Gini 1977) as a way of improving the understanding of birth intervals. Despite this early suggestion it was not until the 1950s, with the work of Henry (see Henry 1972), that the idea received wider use in models of reproduction. Estimates of fecundability have often been varied, partly on account of inappropriate forms of analysis. The results of the most reliable studies (based on the interval between marriage and first birth in non-contracepting populations) suggest that the mean fecundability varies between 0.15 and 0.30 for newly married couples, although there is considerable variation among women according to age and duration of marriage. The probability is substantially below 1 because fertilisation can only occur within a relatively short fertile period (of about 2 days), because of the occurrence of infertile (anovulatory) cycles, and because of the failure of ova to implant after fertilisation. The corollary of these probabilities is that women must wait several months on average before conception occurs. Typical mean waiting times are between 5 and 10 months, although for some women several years may elapse.   RP, CW

References

Gini, C. 1977: First investigations on the fecundability of a woman (1924). Translated by D. Smith, in D. Smith and N. Keyfitz, eds. *Mathematical demography: selected papers.* Berlin and New York: Springer-Verlag. Pp. 367–71.
Henry, L. 1972: *On the measurement of human fertility: selected writings.* Translated and edited by M.C. Sheps and E. Lapierre-Adamcyk. New York and London: Elsevier.

Reading

Bongaarts, J. 1975: A method for the estimation of fecundability. *Demography* 12, pp. 645–60.
Leridon, H. 1977: *Human fertility: the basic components.* Chicago: University of Chicago Press.

fecundity   The physiological capability of a man, woman or couple to produce a live birth. It is contrasted with FERTILITY which is the actual reproductive performance of an individual, a group or a society.

Although widely invoked as a factor in determining fertility differentials, fecundity is still imperfectly understood in quantitative terms. Analysis of the fertility

of populations not employing FAMILY LIMITATION (and thus where NATURAL FERTILITY prevails) show large variations in the level of fertility, though they do exhibit common age-specific patterns of childbearing. In terms of populations rather than of individuals it is probably possible only to assess fecundity with reference to various behavioural factors, the PROXIMATE DETERMINANTS, which are closely linked to reproductive physiology. The various components of fecundity are also open to study. The probability of conception in one month of exposure to the chance of doing so, FECUNDABILITY, has received attention, as has FOETAL MORTALITY. The impact of BREASTFEEDING has been analysed extensively because of its effect in inducing ANOVULATION.

RP, CW

Reading

Bongaarts, J. and Potter, R.G. 1983: *Fertility, biology and behavior: an analysis of the proximate determinants.* New York and London: Academic Press.
Leridon, H. 1977: *Human fertility: the basic components.* Chicago: University of Chicago Press.

female fertility   See FERTILITY.

fertile ages   See REPRODUCTIVE AGES.

fertility   The childbearing performance of individuals, couples, groups or populations. It is contrasted with FECUNDITY, the theoretical capacity to reproduce, which may or may not lead to fertility. Sometimes the term NATALITY is used to refer to the most general analyses of childbearing, though this usage is becoming less common, and the term fertility is commonly used to cover all aspects of reproduction. Measures of fertility normally refer only to live births.

Several different qualifiers are applied to fertility to specify more exactly the focus of analysis. By convention, most measures of fertility are related to mothers. In some cases they are limited to examining the way in which mothers give birth to daughters (female fertility), a definition which is most common in studies of the REPLACE-MENT of generations. In theory there is no reason why fertility rates expressed with reference to the father should not be calculated. In practice, difficulty in determining paternity and the less restrictive biological limits on the age range of male fertility, make measures problematic, so they are rarely calculated.

Most studies employ a relatively modest array of measures of fertility, generally based on conventional age and marriage duration specific rates, with the exact choice being determined by the nature of the available data and the particular problem being studied. A major distinction is that between current or PERIOD ANALYSIS and COHORT methods. The former, involving the study of fertility in a specified period (often one year), is frequently easier in terms of the statistics provided by official agencies. The latter, in following the experience of individuals through a period of time, comes closer to replicating the sequential process of family formation as it occurs in reality. A further distinction is often made according to the marital status of the mother, MARITAL FERTILITY and non-marital fertility (commonly termed legitimate and illegitimate) both being subsets of overall or GENERAL FERTILITY. In addition to very imprecise measures such as the CRUDE BIRTH RATE, demographers employ measures of fertility according to both the mother's age and the duration of marriage in an attempt to assess the underlying level and AGE-PATTERN OF FERTILITY.

Fertility rates have frequently been taken as the dependent variable in elaborate socio-economic models of reproduction, relatively little attention being paid to continued refinement of the measures of fertility. As Ryder and Westoff (1971) have dramatically noted, 'the subtleties of complex explanatory systems, employing sophisticated social, economic and psychological concepts, will provide meagre returns unless and until we learn to measure more accurately and dependent variables at the core of the analysis of fertility'.

A major improvement in the understanding of fertility has come from the many FERTILITY MODELS developed by mathematical demographers, especially from models of the PROXIMATE DETERMINANTS OF FERTILITY. Whatever the strictures of Ryder and Westoff, attempts to place fertility in its social, economic and cultural setting abound (see Jones 1982).

RP, CW

References

Jones, G.W. 1982: Fertility determinants: sociological and economic theories. In J.A. Ross, ed. *International encyclopaedia of population*. New York: Free Press, pp. 279–86.
Ryder, N.B. and Westoff, C.F. 1971: *Reproduction in the United States, 1965*. Princeton NJ: Princeton University Press.

Reading

Jones 1982.
Ryder, N.B. 1978: Some problems of fertility research. In K. E. Taeuber, L. L. Bumpass and J. A. Sweet, eds. *Social demography*. New York and London: Academic Press.

fertility distribution   See AGE PATTTERN OF FERTILITY.

fertility models Mathematical constructs aimed at describing or explaining fertility patterns. A major distinction can be made between models linking fertility to social or economic variables (see ECONOMIC DEMOGRAPHY) and others in which certain details of reproduction (e.g. the AGE PATTERN OF FERTILITY) are modelled in isolation.

Among the most mathematically sophisticated models are those related to the PROXIMATE DETERMINANTS OF FERTILITY, a series of physiological and behavioural factors through which social and economic variables must operate if they are to influence fertility. A particularly influential model is the BONGAARTS' DECOMPOSITION, which is relatively simple in structure. Other models of proximate determinants are generally more complex (Bongaarts 1976, Sheps and Menken 1973). A contrast can be made between deterministic and stochastic models in which the random nature of the processes of conception and birth are modelled (MODE 1975). SIMULATION by means of computer programs is often an important factor in the latter. (Dyke and MacCluer 1973). Descriptive models of age-specific patterns of fertility have also been developed, most successfully in the COALE-TRUSSELL FERTILITY MODEL, which is based on empirical studies.

Through the use of these various models, demographers have been able to investigate the impact on fertility of numerous factors: family planning programmes, the effectiveness of contraception, changes in marriage age and alteration in breastfeeding practices, to name only some. Moreover the formal rigour imposed by a mathematical definition of a process has often, of itself, helped to clarify the issues, interrelationships and implications of particular theories.   CW

References

Bongaarts, J. 1976: Intermediate fertility variables and marital fertility rates. *Population studies* 30, pp. 227–41.

Dyke, B. and MacCluer, J.W., eds. 1973: *Computer simulation in human population studies*. New York: Academic Press.

Mode, C.J. 1975: Perspectives in stochastic models of human reproduction: a review and analysis. *Theoretical population biology* 8, pp. 247–91.

Sheps, M.C. and Menken, J. 1973: *Mathematical models of conception and birth*. Chicago: University of Chicago Press.

Reading

Bongaarts, J. and Potter, R.G. 1983: *Fertility, biology and behavior: an analysis of the proximate determinants*. New York and London: Academic Press.

Coale, A.J. 1977: The development of new models of nuptiality and fertility. *Population* 32, special number, pp. 131–54.

Menken, J. 1975: Biometric models of fertility. *Social forces* 43, pp. 52–65.

fertility schedule   A series of FERTILITY rates calculated for various ages of women, or various durations of marriage. The most common schedule is that of AGE-SPECIFIC FERTILITY RATES, although the term is used to refer to any series of rates. The generality of usage is such that the term can be used to describe both COHORT and period data, and may also be refined to take into account certain births only (e.g. first births only).   RP, CW

fictitious cohort   See HYPOTHETICAL COHORT.

fictive cohort   See HYPOTHETICAL COHORT.

final family size   See COMPLETED FERTILITY.

first marriage   See MARRIAGE.

foetal mortality   A term used to cover all stillbirths, miscarriages and abortions.

Strictly speaking, foetal mortality does not include the termination of life at very early stages of pregnancy, which might more accurately be termed embryonic mortality. This distinction is rarely necessary since demographic studies usually start only after four weeks of pregnancy taking the first missed menstrual period as proof of conception. A distinction is made between spontaneous abortions or miscarriages, which are deaths before 28 weeks of pregnancy, and stillbirths, which are deaths after that duration, when the foetus is assumed to be capable of independent life outside the uterus. An alternative terminology, recommended by the World Health Organisation, is to group all these as foetal deaths, distinguishing early, intermediate, and late mortality according to the duration of pregnancy.

Many studies have attempted to measure the risk of foetal mortality. Unfortunately, most suffer from significant shortcomings with regard to methodology, biases or reporting, and only a few can be regarded as reliable (Leridon 1977). Only four studies, all made in the United States, provide apparently reliable estimates of foetal mortality by duration of gestation. Averaging the results from

84   foetus

these studies gives the values shown in the table below.

Time since last menses (weeks)	Foetal mortality (per cent)
4–7	8.1
8–11	5.9
12–15	2.9
16–19	1.0
20–23	0.6
24–27	0.3
28–31	0.2
32–35	0.2
36–39	0.3
40+	0.5
Total	20.0

Source: Bongaarts and Potter 1983.

Bongaarts and Potter suggest that this figure of 20 per cent of pregnancies ending in foetal death is a slight overestimate. It arises because there is a chance that some of the apparent foetal deaths in the first few weeks (especially weeks four and five) are simply unusually delayed, but normal, menstrual periods. Taking this into account they suggest an overall value of 17 per cent. With data of this quality it is possible to employ LIFE TABLE METHODS to obtain more refined measures.

Foetal mortality rates vary substantially with the age of the mother, being lowest in the early twenties, rising slowly to the mid-thirties and sharply thereafter. Women aged over 40 have a rate double that of younger women. Teenagers may also have a higher risk but this is not found consistently. Although the evidence is very limited it appears that there are relatively few differences in foetal mortality between developed and developing nations, presumably indicating that biological rather than social or medical factors are of primary importance. This is consistent with most of the foetal deaths occurring early in pregnancy. In contrast stillbirth rates, which do reflect health conditions, are generally higher in poor, developing countries.   RP, CW

References

Bongaarts, J. and Potter, R.G. 1983: *Fertility, biology and behavior: an analysis of the proximate determinants.* New York and London: Academic Press.

Leridon, H. 1977: *Human fertility: the basic components.* Chicago: University of Chicago Press.

Reading

Bongaarts and Potter 1983.

foetus See PREGNANCY.

follow-up survey A SURVEY design in which the same individuals are interviewed more than once. Although difficult to manage, because tracing individuals is not easy, especially in countries with poor address systems and mobile populations, the results are often of considerable scientific value.

Several definitive studies in demography and epidemiology, examining child growth and causes of child deaths, for example, have employed the follow-up design. Two features account for the follow-up survey's special strength. First, re-interview of the same subjects leads to close control of the quality of the data and opens up the possibility of the correction of errors from previous rounds. Secondly, the standard errors of measurements made repeatedly on the same number of people are much smaller than for the single-round design. As a result total sample size can usually be held down in follow-up surveys. All other things being equal, a follow-up design with a small number of cases allows the investigator to concentrate on data quality, allowing the measurement of events otherwise difficult to capture such as spontaneous abortions (miscarriages) and deaths of very young infants. One unfortunate feature of the follow-up design, apart from the difficulties of management, is that rare events cannot be studied in the general small samples characteristic of these surveys.

AH

Reading

Douglas, J.W.B. 1976: The use and abuse of national cohorts. In M. Shipman, ed. *The*

organization and impact of social research.
London: Routledge and Kegan Paul.

Moser, K. and Kalton, G., eds. 1971: *Survey methods in social investigation*. Second edition. London: Heinemann; New York: Basic Books (1972).

United States, National Academy of Sciences 1981: *Collecting data for the estimation of fertility and mortality*. Committee on Population and Demography, report 6. Washington DC: National Academy Press.

force of mortality   A synonym for the INSTANTANEOUS DEATH RATE, drawn from actuarial usage and employed mainly within the field of mathematical demography.   RP

forecast   The term demographic PROJECTION refers to the production of a set of internally consistent estimates of population variables under assumptions about fertility and mortality (and sometimes migration). If the projection is based on the view that the rates are likely to occur, the projection is a forecast. This is implicitly the case with most projections produced by official agencies.

Although conventional techniques of projection are normally used, a variety of alternative methodologies have come into being, many based on econometric or statistical forecasting methods (see Lee, in United Nations 1979). The reliability of various forecasting methods is often a sub-

ject of some controversy, and Keyfitz (1981) has suggested, on the basis of an empirical evaluation of official forecasts of total population, that typical errors for such estimates are 0.4 per cent per year.
                                        MM

References

Keyfitz, N. 1981: The limits of population forecasting. *Population and development review* 7, pp. 589–603.

United Nations 1979: *Prospects of population: methodology and assumptions*. New York: Department of International Economic and Social Affairs.

frequency distribution   A tabulation of the number of occurences in each category of the values of a variable.

Theoretical distributions generated by a particular algebraic formulation, such as the NORMAL DISTRIBUTION or the BINOMINAL DISTRIBUTION, are smooth because they are based on infinitely large populations. Empirically values are less regular, though methods of analysing them usually assume that they share certain properties with theoretical distributions. For example, errors are often assumed to be normally distributed.   CW

Reading

Blalock, H.M. 1979: *Social statistics*. Revised second edition. Chapter 4.

full life table   See COMPLETE LIFE TABLE.

G

genealogy The branch of knowledge devoted to establishing and authenticating descent lines and related matters. The techniques and problems involved are similar to those used in demography where nominal RECORD LINKAGE is used, as in the case of FAMILY RECONSTITUTION.

An interest in tracing lines of descent has been widespread in many societies time out of mind. Apart from its intrinsic interest it may be of the highest practical importance in connection with property, status, title and kinship obligations. It may also be of great significance for reasons connected with religious belief and observance.

The term is also used for the family histories created by genealogists and is sometimes used when referring to the results of family reconstitution. (See also HISTORICAL DEMOGRAPHY.)   EAW

Reading

Dyke, B. and Morrill, W.T. 1980: *Genealogical demography*. London and New York: Academic Press.

Gardner, D.E. and Smith, F. 1956 and 1959: *Genealogical research in England and Wales*. Two volumes. Salt Lake City: Bookcraft.

general fertility When measures calculated in the study of FERTILITY make no distinction according to the marital status of women they are said to refer to general fertility. The synonymous term overall fertility is also encountered. A further use of the qualifier 'general' is found in measures which relate births to the entire female population of childbearing age, e.g. the general fertility rate.   RP, CW

general fertility rate The ratio of the number of live births in a specified period

(often a year) to the average number of women of childbearing age (usually taken as 15 to 49) in the population during the period. It is commonly given as a value per 1000, and can be expressed as

$$GFR = \frac{B}{FP_{15-49}}$$

where B is the total number of births and FP_{15-49} is the female population in the reproductive age range. In some cases different age limits are employed, e.g. 15 to 44 in countries where fertility at ages beyond 45 is minimal. The rate is more refined than the CRUDE BIRTH RATE since it relates births more exactly to the age groups of women likely to experience them, eliminating some potential distortions caused by variation in the AGE-SEX STRUCTURE. It is still a relatively unsophisticated guide to fertility, taking no account of the AGE-PATTERN OF FERTILITY or of marriage patterns.   RP

general marital fertility rate The ratio of live births among married women in a given period (often a year) to the average number of married women of childbearing age in the population during that period. Commonly expressed per 1000, it can be defined as:

$$GMFR = \frac{B_m}{MFP_{15-49}}$$

where B_m are the births to married women and MFP_{15-49} stands for the married female population in the reproductive age range. Slight variations in the definition of these ages are sometimes found. This rate is less commonly quoted than the less specific GENERAL FERTILITY RATE which takes no account of the marital status of mothers.   CW

generation, mean length of   The average age of mothers at the birth of their daughters. This is regarded as the mean interval separating the births of one generation from those of the next. The term is an essential part of STABLE POPULATION theory where it is conventionally represented by the letter T.

In spite of the wide variety of fertility and mortality patterns observed in human populations the mean length of generation varies little, mostly within a small range around 29 years. In theory, and occasionally in practice, analogous measures for the male population are calculable, The difficulties in estimating male fertility discourage this, however, and the mean length of male generations is normally only computed when a researcher wishes to compare explicitly the population dynamics of the two sexes.   RP, CW

genetics   See POPULATION GENETICS.

gerontology   The study of all aspects of individual ageing and its consequences, especially its social and economic correlates.

The study of ageing has increased considerably in recent years. There are two main resons for this. In the first place the AGEING OF THE POPULATION has produced a much greater number of elderly people, and secondly the growth of public institutions and assistance (pensions, medical care, social security) has greatly increased the economic significance of ageing. In addition the psychological and social consequences of ageing, the physiological aspects of LONGEVITY, and the impact on family and household composition have all received attention from gerontologists.   RP

Reading

Burgess, E.W. 1960: *Aging in western societies.* Chicago: University of Chicago Press.

Clark, R.L. and Spengler, J.J. 1980: *The econ-*

omics of individual and population aging. Cambridge and New York: Cambridge University Press.

Gini, Corrado (1884–1965)   Italian statistician and demographer whose work in several areas was influential in the development of demographic concepts and techniques.

In 1924 Gini introduced the concept of FECUNDABILITY, the probability of a woman conceiving in one month (or one menstrual cycle). This concept, has been central in the development of mathematical models of the BIOSTATISTICS OF REPRODUCTION (Gini 1977). In other studies of fertility Gini used vital statistics to analyse patterns of marital fertility. In particular, he developed techniques of INDIRECT STANDARDISATION to estimate the total marital fertility rate. Another of his concepts which has been widely used is his index of concentration. It presents a quantitative estimate of the extent to which certain characteristics (e.g. income) are unequally distributed between subgroups of the population. It has also been used as a measure of urbanisation, expressing the relative concentration in communities of increasing size (Shryock and Siegel 1976).   RP

References

Gini, C. 1977: First investigations on the fecundability of a woman (1924). In D. Smith and N. Keyfitz, eds. *Mathematical demography: selected papers.* Berlin and New York: Springer-Verlag.

Shryock, H.S., Siegel, J.S. et al. 1976: *The methods and materials of demography.* Condensed edition by E.G. Stockwell. London and New York: Academic Press. Pp. 98–100.

Gompertz fertility model   A RELATIONAL MODEL of the AGE PATTERN OF FERTILITY. The basic premise underlying this model system, is that there is a linear relationship between the Gompertz (double exponential) transform, $Y(x)$, of CUMULATIVE FERTILITY $F(x)$, for all ages x, in any two populations. This can be defined as:

$$Y(x) = -\log_e \left\{ -\log_e \frac{F(x)}{T} \right\}$$

where T is the TOTAL FERTILITY RATE, i.e. $F(50)$. Denoting the two populations by subscripts A and B, the model postulates that:

$$Y_A(x) = \alpha + \beta Y_B(x)$$

By using a standard FERTILITY SCHEDULE, denoted by the subscript S it is possible to derive a whole range of model fertility schedules from it by varying the values of the parameters α and β in the relation:

$$Y(x) = \alpha + \beta Y_s(x)$$

and then employing the reverse transformation:

$$F(x) = T_e^{-e^{-Y(x)}}$$

In effect, this yields a three parameter model system for describing the variation of fertility with age: T being a level parameter; α a location parameter (positive values of α making the derived schedule younger than the standard); and a dispersion parameter β (values of β greater than unity making the derived schedule more concentrated about the modal age than the standard).   BZ

Reading
Booth, H. 1984: Transforming Gompertz's function for fertility analysis: the development of a standard for the relational Gompertz function. *Population studies* 38, pp. 495–506.

Gompertz formula A mathematical expression devised by the English actuary Benjamin Gompertz in 1825 in an attempt to provide a model for the observed age-specific pattern of mortality. Gompertz suggested the following relations:

$$q_x = B.c^x$$

$$l_x = l_o.g^{(c^{x-1})}$$

where q_x and l_x are the probability of dying at age x and the number of survivors at age x and B, c and g are constant. In effect this implies an exponential increase in the probability of dying with age which, Gompertz reasoned, corresponded with 'the increased inability to withstand destruction' (Gompertz 1825) that accompanied ageing. Gompertz's model has been extensively used in the smoothing of the q_x function of recorded LIFE TABLES, although it is only suitable for the age range with increasing mortality, roughly after about age 15. An improvement of Gompertz's 'law' was suggested by MAKEHAM, and has been used even more widely.   RP

Reference
Gompertz, B. 1825: On the nature of the function expressive of the law of human mortality. *Philosophical transactions of the Royal Society*, part 2.

Reading
Smith, D. and Keyfitz, N. 1977: *Mathematical demography: selected papers*. Berlin and New York: Springer-Verlag. Pp. 273–82.

graduation In demographic work it is sometimes valuable to replace an observed set of figures with another derived from it but showing greater regularity. The process of moving from the former to the latter is called graduation. The alternative term smoothing is also frequently used.

In its simplest form, graduation consists of running a smooth line by eye through a number of points in the observed data. This is termed graphic graduation, and is satisfactory in many cases. In situations where greater precision is required more complex methods of graduation are employed, making use of CURVE FITTING and mathematical formulae. While undoubtedly valuable in correction for deficiencies in observed data, these elaborate fitting procedures may on occasion disguise genuine fluctuations and variations by imposing mathematical abstractions on demographic behaviour.   CW

Reading
Shryock, H.S., Siegel, J.S. et al. 1976: *The methods and materials of demography*. Condensed edition by E.G. Stockwell. London and New York: Academic Press. Pp. 531–59.

Graunt, John (1629–1674) Author of *Natural and political observations made upon the bills of mortality*, first published in 1662 (reprinted 1973), in which he employed results from BILLS OF MORTALITY and from records of christenings in London to make a quantitative study of mortality and population growth in the city. Graunt's development of the LIFE TABLE has led to his being called the 'father of modern demography' (Smith and Keyfitz 1977).

For a self-educated London merchant Graunt's use of the information at his disposal was remarkable both in imagination and in understanding. Although many of his numerical calculations are based on highly unrealistic assumptions and suspect source material his methodology of the life table, though not taken up again until the work of HALLEY thirty years later, was nevertheless of fundamental importance. In addition he made estimates of the size and growth of the population of London, of the sex ratio at birth and the number of women of childbearing age. Causes of death and the relative healthiness of urban and rural localities were among the many subjects taken into consideration – testimony to Graunt's clear view of the interdependence of population processes.   RP

References

Graunt, J. 1973: *Natural and political observations made upon the bills of mortality*. First published 1662. Reprinted with an introduction by P. Laslett in *The earliest classics: pioneers of demography*. Farnborough, Hants.: Gregg International.
Smith, D. and Keyfitz, N., eds. 1977: *Mathematical demography: selected papers*. Berlin and New York: Springer-Verlag. (Contains extracts from Graunt's work, pp. 11–20.)

Reading

Glass, D.V. 1963: John Graunt and his *Natural and political observations*. *Proceedings of the Royal Society* series B, 159, pp. 2–37.

gravity model A description of the tendency for MIGRATION to decline with distance, a mathematical expression of one of RAVENSTEIN'S LAWS OF MIGRATION.

Though the term is usually used to describe the distribution of migration distances travelled by individuals within a given area, empirical studies also use gravity models to describe the geographical extent of a MIGRATION FIELD around a given place. Gravity models have been used in geographical literature to account for a wide variety of patterns of flow and interaction.   DCS

Reading

Shaw, R.P. 1976: *Migration theory and fact. A review and bibliography of current literature*. Philadelphia: Regional Science Research Institute.

gross A qualifier used in demographic terminology in two distinct ways.

First, it is used with reference to various measures dealing with observed values and making no explicit correction for the effects of DISTURBING PROCESSES on the observations. In contrast, measures which do take disturbances into account are termed NET values. The GROSS REPRODUCTION RATE for example is purely a measure of fertility, whereas the NET REPRODUCTION RATE also takes account of the impact of mortality in disturbing reproduction. The term gross in this sense is normally applied only in explicit comparison with net measures. In most circumstances it is implicit since the majority of measures do not involve explicit correction for disturbances.

The second use of the word gross occurs in the study of MIGRATION, where it stands for the total number of migratory moves (see below). Net migration, on the other hand, refers to the balance of moves into or out of a given territory.   RP, CW

gross migration The total movement into or out of a specified territory within a certain period. It is contrasted with NET MIGRATION, which is the difference between in- and out-flows.

A given level of net migration can result from a great variety of combinations of moves into or out of a territory; hence no simple relation exists between the two.

Since gross migration is a measure of the total number of moves made in a territory it is sometimes referred to as *migration turnover*. In many cases net migration, being the ultimate result of the many migratory moves, is the quantity upon which most attention is focused. However, the growth of MULTIREGIONAL DEMOGRAPHY, and its need for input data on gross flows, has led to greater concern with estimates of gross migration. (See also MIGRATION.)

RP, CW

Reading
Haenszel, W. 1967: Concept, measurement and data in migration analysis. *Demography* 4, pp. 253–61.

gross reproduction rate (GRR) The average number of daughters that would be born to a woman during her lifetime if she passed through the childbearing ages experiencing the average age-specific fertility pattern of a given period (often a year).

The most frequent use of the measure is in period analysis using the notion of a hypothetical cohort, but it is sometimes also quoted for true cohorts. The rate is related to the TOTAL FERTILITY RATE (TFR) in the following manner:

$$GRR = TFR \times \frac{\text{Proportion of}}{\text{female births}}$$

Since the SEX RATIO at birth varies little between populations (105 males per 100 females is general), the proportion of female births can be taken as 100/205, or 0.488, in the absence of more detailed information. The GRR was widely used in the 1930s and 1940s as an indicator of fertility trends, whereas the TFR is more often quoted in current work. The interpretation of either rate requires some caution since the value in a particular year may be greatly affected by short-term fluctuations. Values of the GRR for cohorts are sometimes encountered and are less prone to such ambiguities.

The GRR is contrasted with the NET REPRODUCTION RATE which takes account of mortality as well as fertility. Both are normally calculated solely for the female population, although analagous male reproduction rates are sometimes quoted.

RP, CW

Reading
Hajnal, J. 1959: The study of fertility and reproduction – a survey of thirty years. In *Thirty years of research in human fertility: retrospect and prospect.* New York: Milbank Memorial Fund. Pp. 11–37.
Shryock, H.S., Siegel, J.S. et al. 1976: *The methods and materials of demography.* Condensed edition by E.G. Stockwell. London and New York: Academic Press. Chapter 18.

growth balance methods Methods, based on refinements of the simple BALANCING EQUATION, used to assess the extent of under-registration in a vital registration system and to use the information contained to estimate the level of mortality.

Though conventionally regarded as forms of INDIRECT ESTIMATION TECHNIQUES, growth balance methods use conventional registration data and census age structures. Nevertheless the fact that they are mainly used in developing countries, and that the best known method was proposed by William Brass, author of many indirect techniques, leads to their inclusion in the repertoire of these techniques.

In any population the growth rate, r, birth rate, B, and death rate, D, are related simply (assuming no migration) as:

$$B = r + D$$

In a stable population this relationship holds for every age group, so that where $B(x+)$, $r(x+)$ and $D(x+)$ are the birth, growth and death rates for the population aged x and over, we have:

$$B(x+) = r(x+) + D(x+)$$

When ages other than zero are taken for x the 'birth rate' is simply the number aged x divided by the number x and older. If it is further assumed that the level of under-reporting is the same for all age groups (usually approximately true after childhood), the logic of the balancing equation indicates the deficiency of the numbers of reported deaths. In particular, if a graph is drawn with $B(x+)$ on the horizontal axis and $D(x+)$ on the vertical, the points for each group should fall on a straight line. The slope of the line indicates the degree of under-enumeration and the intercept is the value of $r(x+)$.

A number of refinements and extensions of this basic idea have been made (United Nations 1983). In all cases the quality of results depends on the validity of the underlying assumptions, in particular, on the quality of the age reporting in the data used. In spite of potential problems the methods have been successful in providing estimates of underreporting and mortality levels in many countries.   CW

References

Brass, W. 1975: *Methods for estimating fertility and mortality from limited and defective data.* Chapel Hill, NC: University of North Carolina, Laboratories for Population Statistics.

United Nations 1983: *Manual X: indirect techniques for demographic estimation.* New York: Department of International Economic and Social Affairs. Chapter 5.

Reading

Brass 1975.

Hill, K. and Zlotnick, H. 1982: Indirect esti-

mation of fertility and mortality. In J.A. Ross, ed. *International encyclopaedia of population.* New York: Free Press. Pp. 324–34.

United Nations 1983.

growth rate   The ratio of the total increase (or decrease) in a population during a given period to the average population in that period, taking into account all sources of population change (births, deaths and migration).

The value is commonly calculated from the population totals given in two successive censuses. Where r is the annual rate of growth, t is the time elapsed between censuses (in years), e is the exponential function and P_1 and P_2 stand for the population size in the first and second censuses, we have the following:

$$\frac{P_2}{P_1} = e^{rt}$$

and the growth rate is given by:

$$r = \frac{\log_e\left(\frac{P_2}{P_1}\right)}{t}$$

RP, CW

Reading

Woods, R. 1979: *Population analysis in geography.* London: Longman. Chapter 8.

H

Hajnal's method See SINGULATE MEAN AGE AT MARRIAGE.

Halley, Edmund (1656–1742) The well known astronomer and the author of one of the earliest examples of the LIFE TABLE.

In 1693 Halley published his findings based on the distribution of deaths according to age for the city of Breslau (now Wroclaw in Poland) for the years 1687 to 1691. Since Halley's calculations were based only on recorded deaths, with no data on the population at risk, his life table would, as he was aware, be correct only if it dealt with a STATIONARY POPULATION; it is doubtful whether Breslau met this strict requirement since, like most cities, it was greatly influenced by migration. Halley's life table was the first to be based entirely on actual data, and was a noticeable improvement on the semi-hypothetical calculations put forward by GRAUNT, but it was not until the work of MILNE in the nineteenth century that truly exact life table analysis was started. Interestingly, going beyond the life table, Halley ventured a number of comments on other aspects of demography, especially the powerful role of late marriage or celibacy in limiting population growth. RP

Reading

Halley, E. 1693: An estimate of the degrees of mortality of mankind. *Philosophical transactions of the Royal Society of London* 17, pp. 596–610. (Extracts reprinted in D. Smith and N. Keyfitz, eds. 1977: *Mathematical demography: selected papers*. Berlin and New York: Springer Verlag. Pp. 21–6.)

hazard function A mathematical representation of the chance of a non-renewable demographic event occurring at each age or duration.

The concept derives from SURVIVAL ANALYSIS in which the term instantaneous failure rate is used. The equivalent in mortality is the instantaneous death rate. Many demographic processes studied through LIFE TABLE METHODS are more naturally formulated and analysed in terms of hazard functions. Both parametric and non-parametric forms have been used in demographic work, and hazard functions have also been employed to justify RELATIONAL MODELS such as the LOGIT LIFE TABLE SYSTEM. (See also HAZARDS MODELS.)   MM

Reading

Elandt-Johnson, R.C. and Johnson, N.M. 1980: *Survival models and data analysis*. New York and Chichester: Wiley.

Trussell, J. and Hammerslough, C. 1983: A hazards-model analysis of the covariates of infant and child mortality in Sri Lanka. *Demography* 20, pp. 1–26.

hazards models Models of demographic processes which employ the HAZARD FUNCTION of a process as the dependent variable and use covariates to estimate the impact of various independent factors.

The estimation of LIFE TABLES with covariates can be easily accomplished with hazards models as proposed by Cox (1972). Though such models can be estimated with continuous covariates they can best be understood by imagining that all variables, including age, are categorical. The analyst begins by constructing separate matrices of events (e.g. deaths) and PERSON YEARS of exposure. Each cell represents a particular combination of covariate categories in a specific life table age interval. Next, the log of the the hazard or risk (the death rate) is modelled as the sum of an overall effect, an age interval effect, and covariate effects, plus any interaction effects. If there are no interactions between age intervals and covariates a particular combination of covariates simply raises the underlying risks of death at all ages by a constant multiplicative factor; these models are known as *proportional hazards* models.

Hazards models are clearly appropriate for multivariate analysis of any process for which a life table is the preferred methodology. Examples include analysis of contraceptive failure (Schirm et al. 1982), infant and child mortality (Trussell and Hammerslough 1983) and marital dissolution (Menken et al. 1981).   TJT

References

Cox, D.R. 1972: Regression models and life tables. *Journal of the Royal Statistical Society* Series B, 34, pp. 187–200.

Menken, J., Trussell, T.J., Stempel, D. and Babakol, O. 1981: Proportional hazards life table models: an illustrative analysis of socio-demographic influences on marriage dissolution in the United States. *Demography* 18, pp. 181–200.

Schirm, A., Trussell, T.J., Menken, J. and Grady, W. 1982: Contraceptive failure in the United States: the impact of social, economic and demographic factors. *Family planning perspectives* 14, pp.68–75.

Trussell, T.J. and Hammerslough, C. 1983: A hazards model analysis of the covariates of infant and child mortality in Sri Lanka. *Demography* 20, pp. 1–26.

head of household

There is no universally accepted rule as to who is considered the head of a household, and the concept may be of significance only as a part of the process of enumeration in a CENSUS.

Most systems assume that the members of the household (in practice the member responding to the questionnaire) will decide themselves who is to be considered the head for the purpose of the evaluation in question. In complex households the classification given may depend on who is cited as head and in these cases leaving the decision to household members may introduce a subjective element into the classification. This, however, is generally preferred as the best means of describing the social reality of the household as seen by its members. In recent years opposition to the term 'household head' (especially from feminists) has led to several censuses (e.g. the United States and the United Kingdom) replacing it with the term 'reference person'. It may not be easy to reconstruct the more conventional definition from this; a major drawback in assessing change over time in household composition.   CW

Reading

Burch, T.K. 1982: Household and family demography. In J.A. Ross, ed. *International encyclopaedia of population*. New York: Free Press. Pp. 299–307.

headship rate

The ratio of the number of heads of household to the total population in a specified age and sex category. Since there is, by definition, one head per household, the measure also indicates the ratio of households to population.

The headship rate is inversely related to the complexity of households – the simpler the structure the greater the number of households. It also gives an indication of LIFE CYCLE patterns in the formation and composition of households. It is widely used in HOUSEHOLD PROJECTIONS in which rates specified according to marital status, age, and sex are used, in conjunction with projections of total numbers of persons, to estimate the number of households expected to be in existence at some future date.   RP, CW

Reading

Burch, J.K. 1982: Household and family demography. In J.A. Ross, ed. *International encyclopaedia of population*. New York: Free Press. Pp. 299–307.

heart disease

Some forms of heart disease are congenital in origin, others are due to rheumatic fever caught in infancy and childhood. The main form of heart disease (ischaemic, or coronary, heart disease) is due, however, to the blocking of one or more of the coronary arteries supplying blood to the heart muscle. This cuts off the supply of oxygen to a part of the heart muscle (the myocardium) which becomes ischaemic, i.e. deprived of blood. If the blood flow is not resumed the ischaemic tissue of the heart muscle eventually dies, and the area is called an infarct. The terms heart attack, myocaridal infarction, coronary occlusion or thrombosis are all synonymous.

Ischaemic heart disease is mainly due to atherosclerosis, the gradual blockage of the arteries by the development of plaques. When the coronary arteries are partially blocked the heart muscle may not receive enough oxygen under exertion: chest pain results, a condition called angina pectoris.

The importance of monitoring trends in heart diseases as the most significant cause of death in developed countries has led several countries to set up heart attack registers as a complement to the death registration system. (See also CARDIOVASCULAR DISEASE, MORBIDITY.)   GW

Reading

Benditt, E.P. 1977: The origin of atherosclerosis. *Scientific American* 236, pp. 74–85.

Havlik, R. and Feinleit, M., eds. 1979: *Proceedings of the conference on the decline in coronary heart disease mortality.* Bethesda, Maryland: United States, National Heart, Lung, and Blood Institute.

Keys, A. 1980: *Seven countries. A multivariate analysis of death and coronary heart disease.* Cambridge, Mass.: Harvard University Press.

Moriyama, I.M., Krueger, D.E. and Stamler, J. 1971: *Cardiovascular disease in the United States.* Cambridge, Mass.: Harvard University Press.

World Health Organization 1976: *Myocardial infarction community registers.* Copenhagen: Regional Office for Europe.

heterogeneity Variation among the members of a population with respect to a particular demographic phenomenon.

Heterogeneity poses many theoretical problems for the interpretation of demographic measures. Analysis has conventionally attempted to overcome the question of heterogeneity by studying separate subpopulations, each assumed to be homogeneous. Where this is not feasible the assumption of homogeneity is extended to the whole population. It is common to divide populations by age, sex, race and socio-economic characteristics. Regardless of how many attributes are taken into account, however, the individuals in each category will differ in various other ways. Some of these ignored factors will affect their chances of experiencing particular events, and will affect analysis accordingly.

The nature of heterogeneity may be to produce apparent features at the level of a whole population which are not found in any individual. For example, if a population consists of two homogeneous subpopulations, each with constant risk of dying with age, but one much higher than the other, the combined death rate will fall as age increases because the members of the high-mortality population will die sooner than those with low mortality. The overall effect, therefore, is for mortality to be related to age, when this is not so for any individual. The scope for this type of effect is large – almost any age pattern of mortality (or any other phenomenon) could, in theory, be generated by heterogeneity unrelated to age. In practice such extreme cases are rare, but the potential for incorrect interpretation remains, especially when relating individual and aggregate data.   CW

Reading

Heckmann, J.J. and Singer, G. 1982: Population heterogeneity in demographic models. In K.C. Land and A. Rogers, eds. *Multidimensional mathematical demography.* New York and London: Academic Press.

Keyfitz, N. and Littman, G. 1980: Mortality in a heterogeneous population. *Population studies* 33, pp. 333–43.

Vaupel, J.W. and Yashin, A.I. 1983: The deviant dynamics of death in heterogeneous populations. In N.B. Tuma, ed. *Sociological methodology 1984.* San Francisco: Jossey Bass.

historic calendar An interviewing tool designed to improve the accuracy of reporting in censuses and surveys. It consists of a list of dates associated with certain significant events in the history of a country or region. Interviewers can refer to it when attempting to specify the date of the demographic events about which information is being collected.

The use of historic calendars is principally limited to countries where VITAL REGISTRATION is deficient and where the concepts of age and duration may be of little relevance and thus poorly known. A special form of historic calendar is the annual calendar, in which reference is made to aspects of the annual rhythm of a particular community in order to specify the season, or possibly the month, during which the demographic events occurred. Climatic changes, the sequence of annual festivals and the agricultural seasons are all possible calendars. Although in widespread use the value of all historic calendars has been called into question. A recent report by the US National Academy of Sciences noted that 'Studies of the use of historic calendars . . . indicate that this technique does not improve reporting significantly, even where interviewers bothered to use it properly' (NAS 1981).   RP, CW

Reference

United States, National Academy of Sciences 1981: *Collecting data for the estimation of fertility and mortality*. Committee on Population and Demography report 6. Washington DC: National Academy Press.

historical demography The application of the techniques of demographic analysis to historical source material, usually made in an attempt both to improve the understanding of the history of a particular population and to throw light on contemporary demographic patterns. An interest in past populations is probably as old as history itself while the techniques and fields of concern of historical demography today are of recent origin. Most have been developed during the last thirty years.

Every substantive branch of demography has its counterpart in historical demography; fertility, mortality, nuptiality, migration and their joint influence on age structure and household composition have all been analysed in historical populations. One feature of historical demography is the distinctiveness of its source materials. Although much work dealing with the later nineteenth century onwards in Europe and North America is able to make use of modern vital statistics and census material, earlier studies rely on the use of sources not collected with the demographer in mind. PARISH REGISTERS, a particularly valuable source, are a case in point: they record religious ceremonies (baptism and burial) rather than the associated demographic events (birth and death). Similarly the census-like NOMINATIVE LISTINGS of earlier eras were drawn up for reasons largely unrelated to the enumeration of population: tax gathering or the assessment of potential military manpower, for example. In addition to their distinctiveness these sources are also of limited availability. Even within Europe and the colonial settlements of European nations, where registers and listings were commonly kept, their survival has been patchy (Willigan and Lynch 1983). Beyond these regions the existence of usable records is very rare; only Japan seems to have data of analogous quality and quantity – particularly the nominative listings of the Shumon-aratame-cho (see Hanley 1974). In areas and periods devoid of any documentary sources the techniques of PALEODEMOGRAPHY, closely linked to physical anthropology and archaeology, come into play.

Given the particular nature of much of their source material historical demographers have developed a number of characteristic techniques of research. Pride of place goes to FAMILY RECONSTITUTION, a form of RECORD LINKAGE which reorganises the information in parish registers into family histories, enabling many conventional demographic measures to be calcu-

96   historical demography

lated. The technique was first developed
in France (Fleury and Henry 1965) and
has been widely used, especially in the
study of fertility.

One particular attraction of historical
data for analysis is the detailed information obtainable on populations with high
fertility, and on the period of the DEMO-
GRAPHIC TRANSITION. They are an excellent source for the examination of NATU-
RAL FERTILITY and FAMILY LIMITATION.
The analysis of fertility patterns has been
facilitated by the similarity between the
form of data created in family reconstitu-
tions and that based on contemporary
survey material – both provide a MATER-
NITY HISTORY for each woman. The area of
household composition and formation has
also been fortunate, with historical and
contemporary analysis running in similar
directions. The analysis of mortality and
migration has not benefited from any
similar convergence. In addition to family
reconstitution considerable progress has
been made in AGGREGATE ANALYSIS, particularly in the analysis of time-series of
vital events (Wrigley and Schofield 1981).

The results of historical demography
have often overturned earlier preconceptions of the nature of historical societies.
In a pioneering study of nineteenth-
century census material Hajnal (1965) was
able to demonstrate that pre-industrial
Western Europe was characterised by uni-
quely low nuptiality, high proportions of
women never marrying and those who did
doing so at a relatively late age. Laslett
(1972) found from household analysis that
the NUCLEAR FAMILY had been typical of
England and many other parts of Europe
since the sixteenth century. Smith (1979)
has suggested that the observations of
both Hajnal and Laslett are probably valid
for the Middle Ages as well. The notion of
uniformly high fertility in earlier centuries
has also been refuted. Different studies
demonstrate large variations in fertility
even in the absence of any family limitation, the variation being linked closely to
the duration of BREASTFEEDING undertaken by mothers. The picture of a largely

immobile peasantry fixed to the land has
also been shown to be false, at least for
England and the more economically
developed areas of Continental Europe. In
addition to these revelations of pre-
industrial times, research on the demographic transition in Europe has caused
major revisions of previous orthodoxy
since the supposedly axiomatic relationships between social and economic development and fertility decline cannot be
proved (Knodel and van de Walle 1979).

The consideration of such varied results
has led to new concepts of population
change and its place in a wider social,
economic and cultural setting. This has
given rise to many problems. First, many
results from historical studies are based on
small populations, and are difficult to gen-
eralise. Second, few historical studies are
able to present detailed non- demographic
data on the populations they study, especially at the level of INDIVIDUAL ANALYSIS.
In spite of these problems, a number of
conceptual frameworks linking population to other variables have been adduced,
most notably the idea of the HOMEO-
STATIC REGIME.   RP, CW

References

Fleury, M. and Henry, L. 1965: *Nouveau manuel de dépouillement et d'exploitation de l'état civil ancien.* Paris: Institut National d'Études Démographiques.

Hajnal, J. 1965: European marriage patterns in perspective. In D.V.Glass and D.E.C. Evers-ley, eds. *Population in history.* London: Ed-ward Arnold; Chicago: Aldine Atherton. Pp. 101–43.

Hanley, S.B. 1974: Fertility, mortality and life expectancy in pre-modern Japan. *Population studies* 28, pp. 127–42.

Knodel, J. and van de Walle, E. 1979: Lessons from the past: policy implications of historical fertility studies. *Population and development review* 5, pp. 217–45.

Laslett, P. 1972: Introduction. In P. Laslett and R. Wall, eds. *Household and family in past time.* London and New York: Cambridge Uni-versity Press.

Smith, R.M. 1979: Some reflections on the evi-dence from the origins of European marriage patterns in England. In C.C. Harris, ed. *The sociology of the family: new directions for Britain.* Sociological review monograph. University of Keele.

Willigan, J.D. and Lynch, K.A. 1983: *Sources and methods of historical demography.* New York and London: Academic Press.

Wrigley, E.A. and Schofield, R.S. 1981: *The population history of England 1541–1871: a reconstruction.* London: Edward Arnold; Cambridge, Mass.: Harvard University Press.

homeostatic regime   A term used to denote the existence of a system of relationships between the fertility, mortality and nuptiality characteristics of a community and its socio-economic circumstances such that any movement away from an initial position of equilibrium tends to provoke changes elsewhere in the system which restore the original state.

For example, an adventitious increase in population occurring for whatever reason in an agricultural community practising strictly impartible inheritance would result in an increase in the proportion of young men and women who did not marry or who married very late in life. The growth rate would thereby be reduced, or become negative. Equally, a fall in population would lead to higher fertility by earlier or more universal marriage. Similar links between population growth, real income trends and marriage opportunities may produce a similar effect.   EAW

Reading

Ohlin, P.G. 1961: Mortality, marriage and population growth in pre-industrial populations. *Population studies* 16, pp. 190–7.

Scott Smith, D. 1977: A homeostatic demographic regime: patterns in west European family reconstitution studies. In R.D. Lee, ed. *Population patterns in the past.* London and New York: Academic Press. Pp. 19–51.

Wrigley, E.A. and Schofield, R.S. 1981: *The population history of England 1541–1871: a reconstruction.* London: Edward Arnold; Cambridge, Mass.: Harvard University Press. Chapter 11.

Wynne-Edwards, V. 1965: Self-regulating systems in populations of animals. *Science* 147, pp. 1543–8.

homogamy   Marriage between individuals with similar characteristics. The synonym assortive marriage is also used, as is the term endogamy when qualified by reference to the characteristic under consideration, e.g. occupational endogamy. Socio-economic status, religion, educational attainment and ethnic status are the attributes of homogamous marriage most commonly studied.   RP

Reading

Johnson, R.A. 1980: *Religious assortative marriage in the United States.* New York and London: Academic Press. Chapter 2.

household   One or more persons who make common provision for food and other essentials for living. This is an abbreviated version of the definition of the household recommended by the United Nations (1980) for enumeration and aggregation of individuals in population and housing CENSUSES.

'Common provision for food' – often defined as sharing a hearth or cooking facilities – is the most frequent criterion used for identifying households in national censuses. The second most common criterion is the sharing of a dwelling or housing unit. This is often combined with common provision for food in defining households for census purposes, although in some cases – notably the United States and Canada – it is the only criterion. The organisation of domestic groups varies greatly cross-nationally, however, and, it is likely that no single definition of household can be universally applicable.   MTC

Reference

United Nations 1980: *Principles and recommendations for population and housing censuses.* Series M, statistical papers 67. New York: Department of International Social and Economic Affairs.

Reading

Burch, T.K. 1979: Household and family demography: a bibliographic essay. *Population index* 45, pp. 173–95.

Laslett, P. and Wall, R., eds. 1972: *Household*

and family in past time. London and New York: Cambridge University Press.

White, B.N.F. 1980: Rural households in anthropological perspective. In Binswanger, H.P. et al., eds. *Rural household studies in Asia*. Singapore: University of Singapore Press.

household composition A description of the HOUSEHOLD according to some aspect of its membership. Descriptive criteria for household composition include size (total number of persons in the household), number of children or adults, number of marital pairs or NUCLEAR FAMILIES, various characteristics of the head of household, such as age, sex, and marital status, and the characteristics of other members of the household, such as relationship to head. Important dimensions of household composition are summarised in typologies of household structure.   MTC

Reading

Kuznets, S. 1978: Size and age structure of family households: exploratory comparisons. *Population and development review* 4, pp. 187–223.

Laslett, P. and Wall, R., eds. 1972: *Household and family in past time*. London and New York: Cambridge University Press.

household projection A projection of future population expressed in terms of the number and composition of households. The most commonly used method for making household projections involves applying projected HEADSHIP RATES in each age and sex category to the projected population in that category at a certain future date.

The headship rate method is simple and based on, for example, the extrapolation of census data. Alternative methodologies have been suggested, but a review of these and the conventional approach by the United Nations (1973) concluded that: 'The headship rate method seems to be perhaps the most plausible and widely applicable method for many countries and for some years to come. Although this method does not directly take into account the dynamic aspects of the family

life cycle, namely formation, growth, contraction and dissolution of households and families, it certainly has methodological advantages over many other methods of projection.'   MM

Reference

United Nations 1973: *Methods for projecting households and families. Population studies* 54. New York: Department of Economic and Social Affairs.

Reading

Akkerman, A. 1980: On the relationship between household composition and population age distribution. *Population studies* 34, pp. 525–34.

household questionnaire A census-like form designed to obtain information on households, together with information about all or certain members of the HOUSEHOLD. It usually involves a listing of all persons in the household. In the absence of the HEAD OF HOUSEHOLD, the informant may be any adult member of the household. The information may also be used to identify respondents eligible for interview with an INDIVIDUAL QUESTIONNAIRE; questionnaires with this as their main purpose are often called *household rosters*. (See also QUESTIONNAIRE.)   JGC

household structure See HOUSEHOLD COMPOSITION.

Hutterites An anabaptist religious sect whose members live mostly on the High Plains of North America and who demonstrate very high levels of fertility. The fertility rates recorded for the group living in North Dakota in the 1920s are among the highest of any population, women marrying at age 20 bearing on average 10 or more children. This has led to data on their reproduction being used in a number of mathematical models of fertility. In addition, Coale used their AGE-SPECIFIC MARITAL FERTILITY RATES as a standard schedule of fertility in contrasting a number of widely quoted measures of fertility. (See COALE'S INDICES OF FERTILITY).   CW

Reading

Eaton, J. W. and Mayer, A.J. 1953: The social biology of very high fertility among the Hutterites: the demography of a unique population. *Human biology* 25, pp. 206–64.

hypothetical cohort A theoretical concept by which measures can be calculated for a particular period analogous to those calculable for a true COHORT.

In PERIOD ANALYSIS the age-specific or duration-specific occurrences of a given phenomenon are often cumulated as though they were observations relating to a cohort. The resulting construct is said to refer to a hypothetical cohort. The terms fictitious, fictive or synthetic cohort are also used with the same meaning.

Many common demographic measures are based on the hypothetical cohort. For example, if the age-specific mortality rates observed in a particular year are applied to a hypothetical birth cohort it is possible to estimate the LIFE EXPECTANCY of that cohort, and hence of the period. Similarly the TOTAL FERTILITY RATE for a period represents the average family size which a cohort of women would achieve if they experienced at each age the relevant age-specific fertility rate of the period. By implication most of the summary demographic indicators for a period are calculated on the basis of hypothetical cohorts. However the relationship between the hypothetical and actual cohorts is variable and interpretation based on the hypothetical version is sometimes questionable. First, the experience of a particular year may be a poor guide to longer-run trends (low fertility during a war, for example). Second, even if a given year is not peculiar, changes in the overall level of the process under consideration (the QUANTUM), and the timing or TEMPO of the process, may be taking place, leading to distortions in period rates. One potential means of overcoming these problems is the use of more elaborate TRANSLATION models. In practice most analysts employ the conventional hypothetical cohort approach, with the appropriate caution in interpretation.

RP, CW

I

ideal family size See DESIRED FAMILY SIZE.

illegal abortion INDUCED ABORTION, carried out in contravention of the law of a particular country. It is sometimes termed criminal abortion or clandestine abortion.

The prevalence of illegal abortion is extremely difficult to determine and reliable statistics do not exist. A direct inquiry into the subject runs up against a marked tendency to dissimulation on the part of those investigated, who have difficulty in admitting to a practice which carries legal sanctions of some severity and which may be the object of a degree of social disapproval. In order to overcome this difficulty, a method of inquiry, known as the RANDOMISED RESPONSE TECHNIQUE, has been devised which carries some possibility of the subject of the investigation being convinced of the total confidentiality of her information. Where this technique has been used it has been possible to revise upwards quite considerably the estimates provided by direct questioning though estimates of the exact value remain doubtful. For example, when questions using RRT were asked of a group of Taiwanese women known to have had abortions, only 40 per cent were estimated as having done so (Rider et al. 1976).

Most methods of indirect estimation of illegal abortion are highly dubious. Some rely on estimating deaths said to have been caused by the effects of an illegal abortion, others deal with reported medical complications. Neither is reliable, and they are useful only for giving an approximate order of magnitude to the phenomenon. They do nonetheless suggest a fact now more or less completely accepted, that the frequency of abortions varies greatly according to the group of women under consideration, a sizeable proportion never having recourse to it while a minority undergo several abortions. This seems to indicate, as common sense would suggest, that the incidence of illegal abortion stands in inverse proportion to the amount of information available to the population about CONTRACEPTION and the ease of access to contraceptive methods. Finally and above all, the significance of illegal abortions depends on the ease with which LEGAL ABORTION can be obtained, although this does not mean that a very liberal abortion law would make illegal abortions disappear altogether. Various reasons, among them a desire for the greatest possible secrecy, will always cause some women to seek illegal abortions. Carried out most frequently by people with no formal qualifications and under poor sanitary conditions, illegal abortion is the source of a variety of infections and complications, sometimes resulting in death.   RP

Reference
Rider, R.V. et al. 1976: A comparison of four methods for determining prevalence of induced abortion, Taiwan 1970–1971. *American journal of epidemiology* 103, pp. 37–50.

Reading
Henshaw, S.K. et al. 1982: Abortion and the public opinion polls: women who have had abortions. *Family planning perspectives* 14, pp. 60–2.

Rider et al. 1976.

Tietze, C. 1983: *Induced abortion, a world review 1983*. New York: Population Council.

illegal migration MIGRATION which contravenes the laws governing entry into or exit from a particular country. The term is commonly used to describe IMMIGRATION of individuals from poorer countries into countries with relatively high standards of living. The term undocumented migration is also encountered.

Particular attention has been given to illegal immigration into the United States, especially from neighbouring countries of Latin America. As it is a controversial and highly politicised subject popular estimates of its incidence are often greatly overstated. While some US government officials have suggested that over a million illegal immigrants enter the United States annually from Mexico, Heer (1979) has used data from the Current Population Survey to estimate a net figure of between 100,000 and 200,000 a year. CW

Reference

Heer, D. 1979: What is the annual net flow of undocumented Mexican immigration to the United States? *Demography* 16, pp. 417–23.

illegitimacy Broadly defined as the state of being of illegitimate birth (Latin: *illegitimus* meaning 'not in accord with the law'), that is, born outside a legal marital union. There can be no universally applicable definition because laws develop from the culture of particular societies or are imposed by particular groups, and because words and their meanings are socially constructed.

Malinowski (1930) put forward 'the principle of legitimacy' that 'no child should be brought into this world without a man – and one man at that – assuming the role of sociological father. . .'. Malinowski described this as 'a universal sociological law' and presumably in functionalist terms implied that it was to be found in every society as a principle supportive of marriage as a stable relationship. There are reasons for doubting Malinowski's claim, for it is known that in pre-industrial Japan, for instance, there

was neither a social concept of, nor a word for, illegitimacy (Hayami 1980). Where the concept is encountered demographers are obliged to work with statistics of illegitimate births that register a socially defined category specific to each individual society. RMS

References

Hayami, A. 1980: Illegitimacy in Japan. In P. Laslett, K. Oosterveen, and R.M. Smith, eds. *Bastardy and its comparative history.* London: Edward Arnold. Pp. 397–402.

Malinowski, B. 1930: Parenthood: the basis of social structure. In V.F. Calverton and S.D. Schmalhausen, eds. *The new generation.* London: George Allen and Unwin.

Reading

Davis, K. 1939: Illegitimacy and the social structure. *American journal of sociology* 45.

Hartley, S.F. 1975: *Illegitimacy.* Berkeley: University of California Press.

Laslett, P. et al., eds. 1980: *Bastardy and its comparative history.* London: Edward Arnold.

Teichman, J. 1982: *Illegitimacy: a philosophical examination.* Oxford: Basil Blackwell.

illegitimacy rate This indicates the extent to which women 'at risk', i.e. unmarried women (those single, widowed, divorced and separated), produce children out of wedlock.

$$IR = \frac{I}{UW_{15-49}}$$

where IR is the rate, I stands for the number of illegitimate births and UW is the number of unmarried women of childbearing age. The illegitimacy rate is a far less ambiguous measure than the ILLEGITIMACY RATIO. It is clearly possible for the two measures to diverge in the trends they display. Raising (or lowering) legitimate fertility rates would lower (or raise) the illegitimacy ratio if illegitimacy rates remained constant. If the rate remained constant in a period of declining nuptiality the ratio might rise as the number of legitimate births fell. The ratio and the rate are more likely to mirror each other when illegitimacy increases as the age and incidence of marriage fall and rise respectively, and falls when marriage age and incidence rise and fall respectively, as occurred in early modern England (Wrigley 1981).   RMS

Reference

Wrigley, E.A. 1981: Marriage, fertility and population growth. In R.B. Outhwaite, ed. *Marriage and society: studies in the social history of marriage*. London: Europa.

Reading

Drake, M. 1979: Norway. In R.W. Lee, ed. *European demography and economic growth*. London: Croom Helm. Pp. 299–306.

Knodel, J. and Hochstadt, S. 1980: Urban and rural illegitimacy in Imperial Germany. In P. Laslett, K. Oosterveen and R.M. Smith, eds. *Bastardy and its comparative history*. London: Edward Arnold. Pp. 285–9.

illegitimacy ratio   Usually expressed as the percentage of all births that are illegitimate, or the number of births out of wedlock per hundred births.

$$\text{Ratio} = \frac{I}{I + L}$$

where I and L stand, respectively, for illegitimate and legitimate births. The measure indicates the degree to which illegitimacy maintains its *relative* importance as fertility in general increases or decreases, and is more ambiguous in its significance than the ILLEGITIMACY RATE.
                                                    RMS

immigration   Movement into a given territory from another country. Immigration is conventionally taken to be a part of INTERNATIONAL MIGRATION, whereas movement into an area from a different part of the same country is termed IN-MIGRATION.   RP

immigration rate   A measure of the extent of immigration into a particular country or area. A variety of rates, analogous to those employed in the study of other phenomena, is used; for example, the crude immigration rate (the number of immigrants divided by the average population) and various age- or sex-specific rates. All are subject to the same fundamental objection: they relate migratory moves to the receiving population rather than to the sending population. Since the members of the receiving area cannot, by definition, contribute to the events in question this produces a rate of dubious value. The only justification for the calculation is that it enables comparisons to be made with the more justifiable EMIGRATION RATE and combines with it to estimate NET MIGRATION.   RP

incidence rate   A common calculation in epidemiological studies. The terminology can be extended more generally since many common demographic rates share the same broad definition, which helps to specify their nature.

In epidemiology, incidence rates are defined as the number of new cases of a disease occurring in a population during a specified period of observation, divided by the average population during the period. A significant feature of these rates is that persons who already have the condition under observation are not excluded from the denominator. This feature is shared by many demographic rates. Any rate which is calculated on the basis that the events occurring in the numerator do not affect the appearance of individuals in the denominator may be termed an incidence rate (Hoem 1978). In the calculation of age-specific fertility rates, for example, births are divided by the number of women in each age group and the occurrence of a birth does not remove a woman from the denominator. In this way age-specific fertility rates and many similarly defined rates are formally identical to incidence rates. Some researchers while recognising the similarity of the various demographic rates of this kind, have not drawn the parallel with epidemiology but have used alternative general terms for these rates, mostly drawing on French terminology. 'Reduced events' is one phrase of this kind.

Demographic incidence rates may refer either to renewable or to non-renewable processes. Just as some diseases can be contracted several times so that some people contribute more than once to illness incidence rates, so some demographic events can be experienced several times and affect the incidence rates accordingly. Whether dealing with renewable or non-renewable processes, the key feature of incidence rates remains. The denominator consists both of those who have experienced the event under consideration and also of those who have not.

When interpreting demographic incidence rates it is important to realise that they will be an exact reflection of actual population behaviour if and only if the various phenomena disturbing our observation (principally mortality, but also migration) do not act differently on individuals according to whether or not they have experienced the event studied. (For example, when studying marriage we assume that mortality is the same for single and married persons.) In many cases this condition of NON-SELECTIVITY is not entirely met although any errors introduced by this are normally small.

In contrast to incidence rates another major rates category is ATTRITION RATES, in which only those individuals who have not experienced the event studied are counted in the denominator. These rates deal exclusively with non-renewable processes: mortality is a prominent example, but marriage of single persons, and several other processes meet this criterion. Since the experience of the event studied leads automatically to the removal of a person from the population at risk, and hence from the denominator of the rate, they are best termed attrition rates.   RP, CW

Reference

Hoem, J. 1978: Demographic incidence rates. *Theoretical population biology* 14, pp. 329–37.

incidence rate (in epidemiology) In epidemiology an incidence rate is a measure of MORBIDITY and is defined as follows:

$$IR = \frac{N}{P} \times K$$

where IR is the incidence rate, N stands for the number of new cases of a disease beginning within a specified period, P is the number of persons exposed to the risk of contracting the disease during the period and K is a constant (normally 1000 but sometimes 100,000 for rare conditions).

An incidence rate estimates the probability, or risk, of developing a disease during a specified time period. The numerator can either be the number of persons presenting for the first time with the disease or the number of new spells of disease. The number of persons exposed to risk (denominator) is often estimated by the total or mid-period population, but a better estimate can be obtained from longitudinal or follow-up studies where PERSON-YEARS (or, if appropriate, person-weeks, etc.) of exposure to risk can be calculated.

Incidence and point prevalence are related as follows:

$$IR = PPR/Dur$$

where PPR stands for the point PREVALENCE RATE and Dur is the mean duration of disease per sick person.   RP, ER

Reading

Bradford Hill, A. 1977: *A short textbook of medical statistics*. London: Hodder and Stoughton Educational.
Lilienfeld, A.M. and Lilienfeld, D.E. 1980: *Foundations of epidemiology* . Second edition. Oxford: Oxford University Press.

increment-decrement life table A generalisation of the conventional LIFE TABLE which allows entries (increments) as well as exits (decrements) from given states.

These tables are widely used in analyses of such factors as working life, nuptiality and, especially, migration (where they form a central part of MULTIREGIONAL DEMOGRAPHY). The increment-decrement life table is usually based on a Markov chain assumption with a finite state space. Under this assumption it is possible to extend all the conventional life table functions, so that, for example, the expected number of years spent in a particular state by status at a fixed earlier time may be computed.

Although reflecting the dynamics of demographic systems more realistically than simpler models, these tables often require substantial and detailed data on transition probabilities. Moreover, the validity of the Markovian assumption is often open to question, in that, for example, migration rates will often depend on duration in the state as well as on age.   MM

Reading

Land, K.C. and Rogers, A., eds. 1982: *Multidimensional mathematical demography*. New York and London: Academic Press.

Rogers, A., ed. 1980: Essays in multistate mathematical demography. Special issue of *Environment and planning A* 12.

Willekens, F.J. et al. 1982: Multistate analysis of marital status life tables: theory and applications. *Population studies* 36, pp. 129–44.

independence, condition of   Some demographic literature, in particular that based on the French tradition, considers independence and another mathematical condition, continuity, to be fundamental theoretical bases of all demographic calculations. Taken together in the formulation by Henry (1966), the two conditions are held to be necessary if problems of bias and selectivity are to be overcome. Although still quoted (Wunsch and Termote 1978), these two conditions have been shown to be replaceable by the single condition of NON-SELECTIVITY (Hoem 1972, 1978).   RP, CW

References

Henry, L. 1966: Analyse et mésure des phéno-mènes démographiques par cohortes. *Population* 21, pp. 465–82.

Hoem, J. 1972: Inhomogeneous semi-Markov processes, select actuarial tables, and duration dependence in demography. In T.N.E. Greville, ed. *Population dynamics*. New York and London: Academic Press. Pp. 251–96.

— 1978: Demographic incidence rates. *Theoretical population biology* 14, pp. 329–37.

Wunsch, G. and Termote, M. 1978: *Introduction to demographic analysis*. New York and London: Plenum. Chapter 1.

indirect estimation techniques   A body of analytical techniques which have been developed for the estimation of the levels and trends in fertility, mortality and migration for all populations lacking the conventional sources of data, in particular a reliable and comprehensive system of vital registration. The word 'indirect' is used to denote the fact that many of these techniques utilise data which, although not such as would enable the main indices of fertility and mortality to be calculated directly, are nevertheless so closely correlated with these indices that estimates of them can readily be calculated from the data available.

Among the techniques which are clearly in this category are the estimation of infant and child mortality from proportions of children surviving among CHILDREN EVER BORN tabulated by age group of mother, and the estimation of adult mortality from data on orphanhood or widowhood. The term is also used to denote other techniques which involve the critical assessment of data of the conventional type (such as registered deaths by sex and age) by relating these data to another set of information in such a way that, on the basis of certain assumptions, a certain pattern of relationship may be expected. If this pattern is in fact reproduced, corrections of the data may be made. This type of technique includes the GROWTH BALANCE METHOD and the comparison of cumulated current fertility and average parity or P/F RATIO METHODS. A third body of techniques generally included under the heading of indirect methods is that which consists of the fitting of fertility and mortality models to fragmentary and incomplete data. These models include the relational GOMPERTZ FERTILITY MODEL and the COALE-TRUSSELL FERTILITY MODEL and Brass's LOGIT LIFE TABLE SYSTEM. Indirect methods of estimating emigration have also been devised, using reports by mothers on the numbers of their children and by siblings on the numbers of their brothers and sisters who are outside the country. JGB

Reading

Brass, W. 1975: *Methods for estimating fertility and mortality from limited and defective data.* Chapel Hill, North Carolina: University of North Carolina. Laboratories for Population Statistics.

— 1976: Indirect methods of estimating mortality illustrated by application to Middle East and North African data, *Population bulletin of the United Nations Economic Commission for Western Asia* 10 and 11.

Hill, K. and Zlotnik, H. 1982. Indirect estimation of fertility and mortality. In J.A. Ross, ed. *International Encyclopaedia of population.* New York: Free Press. Pp. 324–34.

United Nations 1967: *Manual IV: Methods of estimating basic demographic measures from incomplete data.* Series A, 42. New York: Department of Economic and Social Affairs.

— 1983: *Manual X: Indirect techniques for demographic estimation.* New York: Department of International Economic and Social Affairs.

indirect standardisation A technique used to calculate comparative measures of demographic phenomena by relating the observed number of events to the number which would be expected if the population under study experienced a 'standard' set of rates specific to each age, duration or other category.

Since age is the variable for which STANDARDISATION is most often undertaken the principle of the methodology can best be seen by consideration of an example of indirect standardisation for age in mortal-ity analysis. For each age group in the population studied an appropriate mortality rate is taken from a standard schedule. Multiplying the number of persons in the age group by the standard rate yields the number of deaths to be expected if this age group experienced the standard rate. Summing these products for all ages provides an expected total number of deaths. Division of the observed number of deaths by this hypothetical expected number gives a ratio expressing the difference between the mortality of the population studied and the standard. This ratio may be interpreted directly, or multiplied by the crude death rate of the standard population to generate a measure analogous to the crude rate but with the effects of population composition greatly reduced.

The principal advantage of indirect standardisation over the direct variety is that it requires only information on the total number of events occurring in a population rather than needing age-specific rates. This makes it possible to use it in many cases where direct standardisation is impossible (no age-specific data) or inadvisable (e.g. small populations with highly volatile age-specific rates). It may be used to analyse any phenomenon, and there is a particularly interesting use of it in Coale's fertility indices.

A certain caution is necessary in interpretation. The measures calculated by indirect standardisation are comparative. They enable a comparison of any given population with a 'standard', but any arbitrary set of rates can form that standard, and the particular set chosen may have a significant effect on the resulting indices. Although very widely used, both direct and indirect standardisation remain simple and essentially arbitrary procedures. Their currency in demographic analysis is an inheritance from the era before the development of high-speed computers and sophisticated multivariate techniques. In this light their value, in comparison with more theoretically sound methodologies, such as REGRESSION, is debatable. RP, CW

Reading

Fleiss, J.L. 1981: *Statistical methods for rates and proportions*. Second edition. New York and Chichester: Wiley. Chapter 14.

Kitagawa, E.M. 1964: Standardized comparisons in population research. *Demography* 1, pp. 296–315.

Shryock, H.S., Siegel, J.S. et al. 1976: *The methods and materials of demography*. Condensed edition by E.G. Stockwell. London and New York: Academic Press. Pp. 241–5.

Wunsch, G. and Termote, M. 1978: *Introduction to demographic analysis*. New York and London: Plenum. Chapter 2.

individual analysis Demographic analysis carried out at the level of individual persons rather than using aggregated information for groups, areas or countries.

Strictly speaking, since it is usually the data analysed rather than techniques of analysis which are inherently individual, it would be better to speak of individual data. The data are collected in many ways: retrospective surveys, prospective studies and record linkage all furnish such information.

Many demographic measures were first developed for AGGREGATE ANALYSIS using data from censuses or systems of vital registration. With the growth in recent years of sample surveys and other individual-level sources such as FAMILY RECONSTITUTION many of these methods have been transferred (not always successfully) to the analysis of individual behaviour. The inherently stochastic nature of demographic processes endows individual data with much greater variation (a problem compounded by small sample sizes). In addition many conventional measures do not exploit the full range of information commonly gathered in individual-level surveys. In fertility analysis, for example, the traditional approach concentrates on various age-specific rates while individual data may be more fruitfully analysed in terms of BIRTH INTERVALS. It has taken demographers many years to come to terms with such differences and to recognise the forms of analysis best suited to

individual data. The relationship between individual and group attributes is still a topic of considerable attention, especially in fertility analysis.   RP, CW

Reading

Ryder, N.B. 1978: Some problems of fertility analysis. In C.E. Taeuber, L.L. Bumpass and J.A. Sweet, eds. *Social demography*. New York and London: Academic Press. Pp. 3–13.

individual questionnaire A QUESTIONNAIRE intended to elicit information from, and in relation to, an individual. The term is used in contrast to HOUSEHOLD QUESTIONNAIRE.   JGC

induced abortion An ABORTION following deliberate intervention to terminate the pregnancy. Used colloquially the word abortion generally means induced abortion.

The term ILLEGAL ABORTION describes induced abortion occurring in contravention of the laws of the country in which the abortion takes place, whereas LEGAL ABORTION takes place within the framework countenanced by such laws. Illegal abortions, which are often performed by unqualified persons in unhygienic conditions, incur a much greater chance of injury, infection and death. Reliable statistics are non-existent and most assessments of their prevalence are highly conjectural. In contrast, statistical data on legal abortion are relatively plentiful and provide an accurate impression of its significance. The legal status of induced abortion varies widely from total prohibition (in some cases in the national constitution) to elective abortion at the request of the pregnant women. Tietze (1983) estimates that in mid-1982 10 per cent of the world's population lived in countries where abortion was illegal, and 18 per cent where it was allowed only to save the life of a pregnant woman. In contrast 39 per cent lived in countries permitting abortion on request. Between the two extremes various medical, social and judicial grounds are required to justify abortion. The vast majority of laws permitting abortions have been in operation only since the late 1960s.

The prevalence of induced abortion as a means of birth control also varies greatly. It is unlikely that any country has achieved a low level of fertility without widespread use of induced abortion, either as a primary method of control or as a back-up for contraception. In low-fertility countries the level of abortion seems to be a reflection of the availability and acceptability of contraception: countries with relatively poor provision of contraception (e.g. the Soviet Union, Eastern Europe and Japan) have high abortion rates. Recent liberalisation of abortion laws elsewhere seems in general to have led to a shift from illegal to legal abortions rather than a replacement of unwanted births by abortions. Few developing countries have liberalised their abortion laws, and of these fewer still collect comprehensive statistics on them. Nevertheless the incidence of illegal abortions is believed to be high in many urban areas in the Third World, especially in Latin America.

Although knowledge of folk methods of inducing an abortion is sometimes said to be widespread these methods are generally both ineffectual and highly dangerous. The range of modern medical techniques can be summarised in three groups: (1) the instrumental evacuation of the uterus by the vaginal route; (2) the induction of uterine contractions; (3) major surgery (Plaskon 1982). The first of these, which includes suction curettage, dilatation and curettage and menstrual regulation (or endometrial aspiration), is by far the most widely used (for over 90 per cent of abortions in most developed countries). The induction of contractions, either through the injection into the amniotic sac of various compounds, or by extra-amniotic injections or mechanical stimulation, is used in western countries principally for late abortions, although it is more widely used in Japan. Uterine surgery, that is, hysterotomy (or even hysterectomy, which also produces sterility) is usually performed only when other

methods fail or when unusual medical conditions of the pregnant woman intervene. It is also most common for late abortions.

The duration of pregnancy at the time of the abortion is of considerable importance, particularly in the evaluation of the morbidity and mortality associated with an induced abortion. The proportion of abortions at short durations of pregnancy (up to 12 weeks) has increased in recent years. In 1980 it was 82 per cent in England and Wales, 90 per cent in the United States and over 95 per cent in some countries. The increasing risk with longer duration can be seen in data from the United States 1972–80. At 8 weeks' duration or less, 0.4 deaths occurred per 100,000 abortions; at 13–15 weeks the rate was 4.2 per 100,000 and 14.0 at 21 weeks or later (Tietze 1983). Only this last value exceeds the risk associated with continuing the pregnancy to a live birth. Illegal or self-induced abortions carry much higher, but not easily quantifiable, risks. Assessment of other complications of abortions, especially effects on subsequent fertility, is beset by methodological problems. In general it appears that complications from early abortions are modest.   RP, CW

References and Reading

Plaskon, V. 1982: Abortion: medical techniques. In J.A. Ross, ed. *International encyclopaedia of population.* New York: Free Press. Pp. 8–11.

Tietze, C. 1983: *Induced abortion, a world review 1983.* New York: Population Council.

infant mortality Mortality of live-born infants who have not reached their first birthday. Infant mortality is a major contributor to deaths in populations with high mortality but is reduced almost to insignificance in many developed countries, marking one of the most striking aspects of mortality improvement.

A number of distinctions are made according to the age at death of the infant and the cause of death. Deaths in the first month (28 days) of life are termed neonatal, and deaths thereafter post neonatal. Mortality in the first week is sometimes called early neonatal. Although stillbirths are not normally taken into account in these terms, they are included in perinatal mortality, which normally deals with deaths in the first week of life and still-births occurring after 20 or 28 weeks' gestation. Precise definitions of perinatal mortality may vary with respect to the categories of deaths included. A further distinction is made between exogenous and endogenous infant mortality. The former involves deaths attributable to accidents and infections while the latter is a reflection of congenital malformation and birth trauma. The two may be separated in an approximate fashion by the BIOMETRIC ANALYSIS OF INFANT MORTALITY. As mortality improves the importance of exogenous infant mortality declines, to such an extent that in developed countries its virtual disappearance is a realistic hope. As with all endogenous mortality, that experienced by infants is less easily dealt with since it represents fundamental weaknesses in human make-up.

The most common measure of deaths during infancy is the infant mortality rate, defined conventionally as the number of deaths among infants below one year of age per 1000 live births in the same period. Rates for the various sub-classifications of age or cause are components of this overall rate. Refinements of the infant mortality rate sometimes lead to the use of a life table for deaths under one year of age in order to specify exactly the chance of survival at various ages.   RP

Reading

McNamara, R. 1982: *Infant and child mortality.* In J.A. Ross, ed. *International encyclopaedia of population.* New York: Free Press. Pp. 339–43.

Vallin, J. 1976: World trends in infant mortality since 1950. *World health statistics report* 29, pp. 646–58.

infant mortality rate The number of deaths during a specified period (often a year) of live-born infants who have not reached their first birthday, divided by the number of live births in the period, and usually expressed per 1000.

The precise meaning of the rate defined in this conventional way is not clear. The deaths in question are not related precisely to the population at risk, for some infants dying in a given year were born in the previous year, and some born in the year under consideration will die in the following year. This becomes a particular problem if there are sharp fluctuations in the number of births between and within years. The measure is not, therefore, a rate in any normal understanding of the term and comes closer to being a probability of infant death, although it is not exactly this because of the lack of the correspondence between numerator and denominator. In recognition of these drawbacks in the conventional measure various adjusted rates are used to provide measures closer to true probabilities. Where information on deaths classified by both age and cohort is available (double classification) it is a relatively simple matter to reconstruct cohort probabilities. In the absence of such data demographers fall back on the use of separation factors, which are weights, allowing an appropriate importance to be given to the births of different years in contributing to the population of infants at risk. Unfortunately, the detailed tabulations of infant death by age needed to estimate the separation factors correctly are often lacking, so general factors based on the level of infant mortality are used. In many cases, given the uncertainties sometimes involved in the use of separation factors, researchers prefer simply to calculate average infant mortality rates for periods of several years, which often serves just as well if exact annual estimates are not required.

The values found for the infant mortality rate vary greatly. Certain European historical populations show rates of well over 300 per 1000, a figure paralleled until recently in some developing countries. Today, while some of the poorest countries continue to experience rates of 200 per 1000 or above, most areas have seen large improvements. Many developing countries show values of less than 100, and in the developed world values of below 30 are virtually universal, with some countries below 10. Detailed assessment of levels and trends in developing countries is made difficult by problems with data, for better registration of deaths may suggest increases in mortality which in fact only reflect better coverage. In general, declines similar to those of developed countries have been seen, though often with less smooth changes over time (the consequence of the greater susceptibility of developing countries to economic, social or natural disturbances). The lack of reliable time-series data makes analysis of trends particularly hazardous, though some commentators have seen recent evidence as pointing to the stabilising of rates at relatively high levels (Gwatkin 1980). The ultimate scope for improvement is limited by the existence of endogenous mortality (for infants, congenital malformations and birth trauma) which is less susceptible to improvement than exogenous mortality (infections and accidents). The relative importance of the two can be estimated with the BIOMETRIC ANALYSIS OF INFANT MORTALITY.   RP, CW

Reference

Gwatkin, D.R. 1980: Indications of change in developing country mortality trends: the end of an era. *Population and development review* 6, pp. 615–44.

Reading

Gwatkin 1980.
McNamara, R. 1982: Infant and child mortality. In J.A. Ross, ed. *International encyclopaedia of population.* New York: Free Press. Pp 339–43.
Shryock, H.S., Siegel, J.S. et al. 1976: *The methods and materials of demography.* Condensed edition by E.G. Stockwell. London and New York: Academic Press. Pp. 235–41.
Vallin, J. 1976: World trends in infant mortality since 1950. *World health statistics report* 29, pp. 646–58.

infanticide The practice of killing infants at birth or soon afterwards. Infanticide has been a feature of many societies though its significance for overall population growth is rarely quantifiable.

The reasons for it are diverse: sex-preference for offspring, multiple births, illegitimate and deformed infants, protection of older children from competition and many others. The mechanisms of killing have varied greatly. In Europe, where explicit killing was rarely acceptable, the smothering of infants who shared a bed with their parents (overlaying) and the use of wet-nurses, whose care of infants was often poor, both represent 'quasi-infanticidal' arrangements. The abandoning of children in streets or church doorways may have been similarly motivated. The general importance of such tendencies for the population at large, as opposed to specific socially and economically marginal groups, is doubtful, and the concern expressed over such phenomena may well indicate their relative rarity rather than their ubiquity.   CW

Reading

Langer, W.L. 1974: Infanticide: a historical survey. *Journal of psychohistory* 1, pp. 353–65.

infectious diseases Diseases caused by various micro-organisms, bacteria or viruses. The host's immune system (humoral or cellular responses) has the task of preventing the spread of infection internally, and immunological control of infection can be preventively stimulated by vaccines. Successful vaccines have been developed for many important human viral infections such as smallpox, rabies, measles, and some forms of acute respiratory diseases.

Another type of control of infection widely available is chemotherapy: antimicrobial agents such as penicillin and the sulfa drugs have been responsible for the significant control of many bacterial infections though comparable successes have not been achieved in the field of viral infections.

Adequate nutrition and good sanitation probably play a major role in the control of infectious diseases. Quality control of drinking water, adequate sewage facilities, and the use of antibacterial substances (such as soap) have been active in eliminating or drastically reducing the incidence of most infectious diseases in the developed nations. (See also MORBIDITY).   GW

Reading

Black, F.L. 1975: Infectious diseases in primitive societies. *Science* 187, pp. 515–8.

Hilleman, M.R. 1969: Toward control of viral infections of man. *Science* 164, pp. 506–14.

Lopez, C. 1979: Immune response to viruses. In S.B. Day, ed. *A companion to the life sciences.* New York: Van Nostrand Reinhold.

McKeown, T. 1977: *The modern rise of population.* London: Edward Arnold.

Wehrle, P.F. and Top, F.H., eds. 1981: *Communicable and infectious diseases.* Ninth edition. St Louis, Misssouri: C.V. Mosby.

infecundity See STERILITY.

infertility See STERILITY.

injectable contraceptive Long-acting synthetic hormones (progestins) which act in a similar way to the natural female hormone progesterone to prevent pregnancy.

The injectable contraceptive is one of a variety of long-acting contraceptive methods based on progestins now available, including hormone releasing IUDs, implants under the skin, vaginal rings and monthly oral pills. Injectable contraceptives involve injections every two or three months, depending on the compound, or in some cases every six months. They have the advantage, of ease of use and high effectiveness, but have the disadvantage of disrupting the normal menstrual cycle causing irregular bleeding or amenorrhoea. A further effect is that their contraceptive action may last somewhat longer than the specified number of months, leading to a longer wait before conception after discontinuation of use. There is no evidence that they are a risk to women's health, though experiments with beagle dogs have suggested a possible risk of cancer.

Use of injectable contraceptives is most widespread in Jamaica, New Zealand, Sri Lanka and Thailand, and in 1982 it was estimated that over 2.5 million women worldwide were using them (Liskin 1983). In many countries, however, they remain controversial. In the UK they were approved for use in 1984 after several inquiries; approval has not been granted by the United States Food and Drug Administration.   RP, CW

Reference

Liskin, L.S. 1983: Long acting progestins – promise and prospects. *Population reports,* series K, 2.

in-migration Movement into a given area from a different part of the same country. In-migration is one of the components of INTERNAL MIGRATION whereas immigration refers to entry into an area from a foreign country.   CW

instantaneous death rate Also termed the force of mortality and conventionally represented by the Greek letter μ, the instantaneous death rate represents the limiting value of the age-specific death rate when the age interval to which the rate refers becomes infinitessimally short. The rate is a form of HAZARD FUNCTION analogous to any other non-renewable failure rate and terms such as the instantaneous birth rate or marriage rate are also used. The expression of the death rate in this form facilitates algebraic manipulation of the life table and the development of HAZARDS MODELS.   CW

Reading

Elandt-Johnson, R.C. and Johnson, N.M. 1980: *Survival models and data analysis.* New York and Chichester: Wiley.

instantaneous growth rate The limit of the growth rate of a population as the interval to which the rate refers becomes infinitesimally short. The rate is used in mathematical formulations of growth, mainly in stable population theory.   RP

institutional population Persons not living in conventional family or single-person households and who, in consequence, are often enumerated separately in censuses.

Typical persons in this category are military personnel in barracks, children at boarding school, patients in hospitals and prisoners. The precise specification of those included varies between countries, though the general distinction between household and institutional or non-household population is invariably made. Institutions containing non-household populations are sometimes termed collective households, though internationally recommended definitions restrict the term household to private households. In some cases further distinctions are made. In the United States, for example, 'institutional inmate' is a term reserved for persons in the care or custody of public or private institutions and the term 'other residents of group quarters' is applied to students, soldiers, etc.   CW

insurance effect The hypothesized result of parents choosing to have more births than their desired number of surviving children owing to a fear that some of their children will die.

This factor is only likely to have a significant impact on fertility levels in certain societies – in particular in those with a level of mortality high enough to be of major concern to parents, in those with economic systems in which large numbers of surviving children are perceived as constituting a heavy burden, and in those with populations which have access to effective means of birth control.

Although the idea of such an effect is intuitively very satisfying, experience has proved that it is very difficult to demonstrate its existence. This is partly due to the difficulty of finding societies which meet the above criteria. It is also associated with the awkwardness of asking questions about potential deaths in societies where death in infancy is a common occurrence. Furthermore, if parents are aware that most deaths of children occur in infancy, it is to be expected that the insurance effect would be extremely hard to discern since parents could produce the desired number of children early in marriage and replace infant deaths only as they occurred. (See also REPLACEMENT EFFECT.)   HW

Reading

Cain, M.T. 1981: Risk and insurance: perspectives on fertility and agrarian change in India and Bangladesh. *Population and development review* 7, pp. 435–74.
Preston, S.H., ed. 1978: *The effects of infant and child mortality on fertility*. New York and London: Academic Press.
Ware, H. 1977: The relationship between infant mortality and fertility: replacement and insurance effects. In International Union for the Scientific Study of Population, *International Population Conference, Mexico, 1977*. Liège: IUSSP.

intensity See QUANTUM.

intercensal A qualifier applied to the period between two censuses, and to measures and phenomena occurring in this period.   RP

intergenesic interval See BIRTH INTERVAL.

intermediate fertility variables A term introduced by Davis and Blake (1956) to describe the range of physiological and social factors which directly influence the process of reproduction: coital rate, contraception, abortion, separation, abstinence, etc. The term has been replaced in most current work by the alternative, the PROXIMATE DETERMINANTS OF FERTILITY.   RP

Reference

Davis, K. and Blake, J. 1956: Social structure and fertility: an analytic framework. *Economic development and cultural change* 4, pp. 211–35.

internal migration Migration within a specified country or territory. The terms in-migration and out-migration are used to refer to moves into or out of an area when both origin and destination are parts of the same country. In contrast, immigration and emigration are conventionally taken to be the components of international migration.

Internal mobility is normally considerably greater than international migration, and different countries display very different absolute levels. The movement of persons is facilitated by improvements in transport, communication and other infrastructural factors, but even at similar levels of socio-economic development pronounced differences exist. Many countries ask census questions on the place of residence one year previously, providing an elementary comparative measure. In North America and Australia over 19 per cent of persons moved in the year before recent censuses, whereas the values for Japan and Britain were around 12 per cent, Hungary 11 per cent, France 10 per cent and Ireland 5 per cent (Long 1982). These figures confirm many long-held notions about the spatial mobility of different societies, but throw little light on the reasons for such differences. Size alone is seemingly irrelevant, since Hong Kong, one of the smallest and most densely populated of countries, has turnover rates little below those of the United States and above European nations.

As internal migration embraces both long-distance migration, in some countries involving moves of hundreds or thousands of miles, and short-distance local migration, it is not surprising that several different techniques are employed in its estimation and analysis. A number of simple measures have considerable currency. Simple crude or age-specific rates of in- and out-migration relating to the whole population studied are common, as are the addition and subtraction of them: gross and net migration rates. Estimates based on intercensal survival ratios are also commonly used. A more sophisti-cated approach, using information on both mortality and fertility to place the migration rates in their full demographic setting, is MULTIREGIONAL DEMOGRAPHY. Whatever the level of study, one particular point which is invariably in evidence is the highly age-specific nature of migration, young adults and their pre-school children often dominating the pattern of migration.

The study of internal migration has long involved discussion of its economic and social determinants. RAVENSTEIN'S LAWS, outlined in the nineteenth century, specified economic causes to be of primary importance. Much subsequent work has been based on this assumption, though in recent years more stress has been placed on the perceived economic benefits of migrating as an incentive to potential migrants (Todaro 1976; Findley 1982), and on life cycle patterns related to marriage and household formation and dissolution. (Short 1978; Quigley and Weinberg 1977).

CW

References

Findley, S.E. 1982: *Internal migration: determinants*. In J.A. Ross, ed. *International encyclopaedia of population*. New York: Free Press. Pp. 344–51.

Long, L.H. 1982: *Internal migration: The United States* In J.A. Ross, ed. *International encyclopaedia of population*. New York: Free Press. Pp. 360–5.

Quigley, J. and Weinberg, D. 1977: Intra-urban residential mobility: a review and synthesis. *International regional science review* 2, pp. 41–66.

Short, J. 1978: Residential mobility. *Progress in human geography* 2, pp. 419–47.

Todaro, M.P. 1976: *Internal migration in developing countries: a review of theory, evidence, methodology and research priorities*. Geneva: International Labour Office.

Reading

Brown, A.A. and Neuberger, E. 1977: *Internal migration: a comparative perspective*. London: Academic Press.

Findley 1982.

Todaro 1976.

International Classification of Diseases (ICD) A list of diseases and causes of death established by the World Health Organization, and adopted by its member states for VITAL REGISTRATION purposes.

The first attempts to draw up a list of diseases for classification purposes date from the eighteenth century (de Sauvages, Linne, Cullen). Following an initiative of William Farr (1807–1883), the Registrar General of England and Wales, the first international statistical conference (Brussels 1853) agreed to the need for an international classification of diseases. Both Farr and d'Espine presented their views at the international conference held in Paris in 1855, Farr's classification being based partly on the anatomical location of the disease while d'Espine's considered its 'nature'. The international conference held in 1864 adopted a classification which mostly followed Farr's views, and this list was subsequently revised during the latter half of the nineteenth century, though no country seems to have adopted it. The next major step was taken at the end of the century when the international statistical conference held in Vienna in 1891 put a committee headed by the French statistician Jacques Bertillon (1851–1922) in charge of drawing up a new classification of causes of death. Once again the classification which resulted followed Farr's views more or less, stressing even more strongly the anatomical location of the disease. Furthermore three lists were prepared this time (the first classification, abridged, contained 44 causes, the second 99 causes, and the third 161 causes). Since then the Bertillon classification has been periodically revised (in 1900, 1910, 1920, 1929, 1938, 1946, 1955, 1965 and 1975). The fourth and fifth revisions were conducted jointly by the International Statistical Institute and the League of Nations; subsequent revisions have been carried out under the auspices of the World Health Organisation.

The ninth (1975) revision is divided into 17 chapters. Once again the classification is based mainly on the anatomical location of the disease. A multiple-digit coding system is used, the main headings receiving a 3-digit code and subclassifications a 4-digit code. In some instances (e.g. NEOPLASM), an optional 5–digit code is suggested. Special lists are provided for tabulation purposes: a basic list of 307 items classified under 57 headings, a list of 50 causes of mortality and another of 50 causes of morbidity. Before the ninth revision different special lists were proposed, among others an A list of 150 items, a B list of 50 items for cause of death, and a C list of 70 items for morbidity statistics.

These successive revisions of the ICD make a time series analysis of mortality by cause of death difficult to achieve because of the changes in definitions. Bridge tables have been established in various countries to derive comparable groupings over time, either by dually coding deaths according to two successive ICDs, or by regrouping items in one classification in order to make them more or less comparable to another. (See also CAUSE OF DEATH, MORBIDITY.)

GW

Reference

World Health Organisation 1968 and 1977: *International Classification of Diseases*. Eighth revision (1965) and ninth revision (1975). Geneva: WHO.

Reading

Office of Population Censuses and Surveys: 1983: *Mortality statistics: comparison of the 8th and 9th revisions of the International Classification of Diseases*. London: OPCS.

Siener, C.H. 1982: International Classification of Diseases. In J.A. Ross, ed. *International encyclopaedia of population*. New York: Free Press. Pp. 365.

United States, National Center for Health Statistics 1975: *Comparability of mortality statistics for the seventh and eighth revisions of the International Classification of Diseases, United States*. Vital and health statistics. Data evaluation and methods research, series 2, number 6.

international migration Migration across national boundaries. It is termed emigration from the point of view of the nation from which the move takes place and immigration in the receiving nation. The terms in- and out-migration are conventionally reserved for moves within a country.

The sources of information on international migration are varied: statistics collected as people cross international borders; lists of passengers on international flights or sea crossings; statistics on passport and visa applications; data from population registers; and questions on place of previous residence in a census or survey. Because of their varied nature it is rare for these sources to agree exactly on the scale of international migration, though it is usually of a much smaller scale than internal mobility. The range of data sources also leads to variety in types of analysis for different countries, making comparative studies problematic.

The scale of international migration is influenced by many factors. Economic causes are often fundamental, as with internal mobility, but movement across borders also reflects the laws governing entry and departure. In some cases these may be so strictly enforced as to effectively prohibit migration. Politics is another factor, affecting individual motivation or causing mass movements, e.g. such as caused by war, political disturbance or decolonisation.

Changes in the relative liberality of laws controlling immigration provide governments with a ready mechanism for the implementation of policy (often economically inspired). For example a broadly positive official attitude to immigration in the countries of western Europe from 1945 to 1973 was rapidly replaced by restrictive policies in the 1970s when the previous labour shortage was replaced by unemployment. The scope for government action on immigration, however, is often constrained (e.g. the protracted debate over illegal migrants in the United States).

The economic bases of international migration are highlighted in the so-called brain drain, the exodus of skilled workers from poor countries to others offering a higher standard of living. Although often

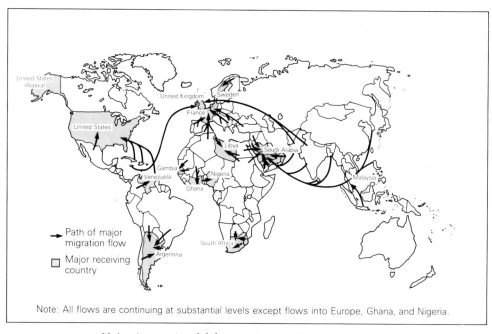

Note: All flows are continuing at substantial levels except flows into Europe, Ghana, and Nigeria.

Major international labour migration flows 1960 to 1980.
Source: Population reports 1983.

slight in terms of number the loss of these skilled individuals can have significant effects on their countries of origin. International moves have in the past been a significant factor in the settlement of thinly-populated areas (the European migration to the Americas is the most striking example). Such features are rare today (though internal development of frontier zones still occurs) and are not generally seen as a plausible means of achieving a more equal population distribution.   RP

Reading

Heisel, D.F. 1982: International migration. In J.A. Ross, ed. *International encyclopaedia of population*. New York: Free Press. Pp. 366–73

United Nations 1979: *Trends and characteristics of international migration since 1950*. Series A, 69. New York: Department of Economic and Social Affairs.

interpolation The estimation of the values of a particular series of numbers at points intermediate between given values using either graphical or mathematical techniques.

The need for interpolation arises frequently in demographic work at a variety of levels of sophistication. It may suffice to run a straight line through a series of points, though at times the use of elaborate mathematical formulae is appropriate. Many forms of mathematical interpolation have been suggested for various purposes, ranging from straightforward linear interpolation and prorating to polynomial functions and difference formulae.   CW

Reading

Shryock, H.S., Siegel, J.S. et al. 1976: *The methods and materials of demography*. Condensed edition by E.G. Stockwell. London and New York: Academic Press. Appendix C.

intervening opportunities A concept proposed by the American social psychologist S. A. Stouffer (1940) to explain the spatial pattern of migration. Stouffer suggested that conventional measurements of distance gave little indication of the economic and social opportunities which

might lie between two locations. Since migration is both financially and socially costly mobile persons may refrain from moving when they encounter an appropriate opportunity. The number of migrants from one place to another will be proportional to the number of opportunities at the destination and inversely proportional to the opportunities between the origin and the destination. The concept has been widely used in studies of migration and other forms of flow and interaction.   CW

Reference

Stouffer, S.A. 1940: Intervening opportunities: a theory relating mobility to distance. *American sociological review* 5, pp. 845–67.

Reading

Jones, H.R. 1981: *A population geography*. London and New York: Harper and Row. Pp. 218–21.

intra-uterine device (IUD) Foreign body placed in the uterus with a contraceptive purpose; also known as the coil or loop.

The forerunners of contemporary IUDs, particularly Graefenberg's ring introduced in Germany at the end of the 1920s, were not made widely available, largely because of uncertainty over medical complications. It was not until the end of the 1950s, with the development of IUDs made from plastics or stainless steel which could be left in place indefinitely, that there was a resumption of interest. IUDs vary greatly in both shape and composition, though most may be classified in two groups: the original plastic and metal devices (such as the Lippes Loop), and the newer so-called medicated devices. The latter include 7–shaped or T-shaped IUDs containing copper or progesterone. No significant differences have been detected between the IUDs in terms of complications, though the World Health Organisation has suggested that copper-bearing devices may be more effective. The exact way in which IUDs work remains problematical, the contraceptive effect appearing to depend essentially on a local inflammatory effect which, because of the reactions it provokes, stops implantation. This has prompted those who believe that conception occurs the moment the ovum is fertilised to regard the IUD as an abortive method. Without being total, the CONTRACEPTIVE EFFECTIVENESS achieved, though it varies from model to model, is always of a very high order, with only oral and injectable contraceptives being more effective reversible methods.

The most noticeable minor side effects relate to problems with bleeding, often at the time of menstrual periods. This can lead to a fairly high failure rate due to intolerance. Finally, expulsion of the IUD by the uterus sometimes takes place, and often goes unnoticed so that the woman runs the risk of becoming pregnant. A potentially more serious complication comes from the possible introduction of infection into the uterus. However, recent analysis indicates that the health risks associated with IUDs are modest and much less than the risks attendant on pregnancy. Because of the risk of pelvic inflammatory disease and scarring which could result in sterility, other forms of contraception are sometimes preferred by women who have not had any children.

RP, CW

Reading

Rosenfield, A. 1982: Contraceptive methods: oral contraceptives and intrauterine devices. In J.A. Ross, ed. *International encyclopaedia of population*. New York: Free Press. Pp. 109–13.

intra-uterine mortality See FOETAL MORTALITY.

intrinsic growth rate See INTRINSIC RATE OF NATURAL INCREASE.

intrinsic rate of natural increase The rate of natural increase in a closed population which has been subject to constant age-specific schedules of fertility and mortality for many years and has converged to be a STABLE POPULATION. First defined by Dublin and Lotka (1925), as the true

rate of natural increase, it is also termed the intrinsic growth rate.

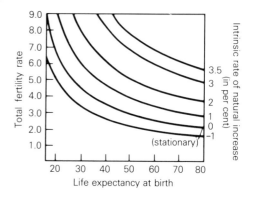

Each combination of life expectancy at birth and total fertility rate defines a value of the intrinsic rate of natural increase in an associated stable population. Curves join points with the same intrinsic rates.

The rate indicates the long-run growth rate implied by a particular combination of fertility and mortality independent of any impact of the current age structure. It is therefore a purely hypothetical measure, but one which illustrates the long-term consequences of maintaining current behaviour. Since the fundamental assumption of unchanging fertility and mortality is never met in real populations the rate has to be interpreted with caution.   RP

Reference

Dublin, L.I. and Lotka, A.J. 1925: On the true rate of natural increase. *Journal of the American Statistical Association* 20, pp. 305–39.

Reading

Shryock, H.S., Siegel, J.S. et al. 1976: *The methods and materials of demography*. Condensed edition by E. G. Stockwell. London and New York: Academic Press. Chapter 18.

isolate A population with low numbers whose members marry only each other.

An isolate is a group in which strict ENDOGAMY prevails. This may be geographical in nature (in the case of populations isolated by distance or the nature of the terrain), but it can also be related to religious and social barriers. Because of its low numbers and the impossibility of marriage outside the group, the isolate is frequently a site for consanguineous marriages. This may lead to genetic impoverishment, a qualitative weakening of the population, and even to various genetic anomalies and malformations. In the end strict endogamy can lead to the disappearance of the isolate, thus relating this concept to that of a MINIMUM POPULATION. With the development of means of communication and the weakening of social and religious barriers, most countries have witnessed a breaking-up of isolates.

RP

E

K

KAP survey 'KAP' is an acronym in demographic terminology standing for 'knowledge, attitude and practice' with regard to contraceptive use. It is associated with a whole series of surveys begun in the 1950s which aimed at measuring the spread of FAMILY PLANNING throughout the world.

While many KAP surveys were well-executed and of lasting scientific value the term has acquired unfortunate connotations because of the weakness of the theoretical premises on which some of them were based. The population establishment up to the 1970s believed that the provision of cheap family planning and abortion services would quickly reduce fertility in poor countries. Many KAP surveys set out to demonstrate this 'unmet need for family planning' and became the hallmark of the intervention of the rich countries and the international agencies in the population affairs of the developing world. Many of the early KAP surveys were supported and organised by the Population Council. Summary results are to be found in the *Studies in family planning* published by this organisation. The KAP survey was usually a single-round RETROSPECTIVE SURVEY containing a MATERNITY HISTORY and a number of questions on desired family size as well as the core questions on family planning knowledge, attitudes to its use, and actual practice (or, more often, lack of it).   AH

Reading

Hauser, P.M. 1983: The limitations of KAP surveys. In M. Bulmer and D.P. Warwick, eds. *Social research in developing countries.* Chichester and New York: Wiley. Pp. 65–70.

Mauldin, W.P. 1965: Fertility studies: know-ledge, attitude and practice. *Studies in family planning* 7, pp. 1–10.

Population Council 1970: *A manual for surveys of fertility and family planning: knowledge, attitude and practice.* New York: Population Council.

United Nations 1971: *Methodology of demographic sample surveys.* Series M, statistical papers 51. New York: Department of Economic and Social Affairs.

Warwick, D.P. 1983: The KAP survey: dictates of mission versus demands of science. In M. Bulmer and D.P. Warwick, eds. *Social research in developing countries.* Chichester and New York: Wiley. Pp. 349–64.

Kersseboom, Willem (c.1690–1771) A Dutch financial expert whose work led him to an interest in demography, above all to the analysis of mortality. He is principally remembered as the author of a LIFE TABLE based on the mortality of holders of life annuities in the provinces of Holland and West Friesland. In using these data relating to groups of individuals over a long period of time Kersseboom made a significant methodological advance over the earlier life tables constructed by Graunt and Halley. Moreover Kersseboom saw his life table as merely a tool which enabled him to carry out further work on the duration of marriage, the mortality of widows, and (in conjunction with the annual number of births) estimates of population size.   RP

Reading

Pearson, K. 1978: *The history of statistics in the seventeenth and eighteenth centuries*, edited by E.S. Pearson. London: Charles Griffin. Pp. 329–47.

kinship The relationship based on real, putative or fictive consanguinity. In all societies it forms an important element of the social system, and forms the basis of simpler societies. It is precisely in societies where a full range of kinship relationships is necessary that such relations are most likely to be created artificially (i.e. by adoption) if they chance to be naturally absent. Strictly, the term kinship refers to blood relationships (or relationships so defined) among whom those in the patrilineal line are described as agnates, and those with a common ancestor cognates, but it is frequently employed more loosely to include relatives by marriage, i.e. affines, the total sometimes being termed kindred.

The sum of all such relationships can be described as the kinship network. The kinship system is a jural one in simpler societies and determines most social relations and roles. It may determine the form of descent or succession (patrilateral, matrilateral or bilateral), of inheritance (patrilineal or matrilineal), and the residence of the younger couples (patrilocal, matrilocal or neolocal). It is not the genetic association which is important but its socially ascribed significance.

In all societies the kinship system helps to determine the nature of marriage, sexual relations, family residence, the circle of social intimacy, the exercise of authority in the smallest social units, and the rearing and socialisation of children; while in pre-industrial societies it also embraced the corporate possession of property, economic production, occupational training, religious practice and the treatment of illness. Demographers have a range of interest in kinship. The kinship network is built, dissolved or residentially modified by demographic processes: marriage, birth, death and migration. Furthermore the kinship system has a significant impact on deciding when most demographic processes should take place and thus influences the levels of demographic rates. Some demographers are becoming more interested in kinship systems because of the demonstration that different levels of intergenerational and other intrafamilial economic and social obligations may influence the cost and VALUE OF CHILDREN and hence the level of fertility. Demographers, especially when carrying out surveys, often use the residential family as a sampling or interviewing unit, frequently distinguishing between that consisting of only husband, wife and unmarried children, or the nuclear family, and larger groupings of relatives described as stem, joint, joint-stem or extended families.   JCC, PQ

Reading

Eggan, F. 1968: Kinship: introduction. In D.L. Sills, ed. *International encyclopedia of the social sciences*. New York: Macmillan and the Free Press.

Fox, R. 1967: *Kinship and marriage*. Harmondsworth: Penguin.

Keesing, R.M. 1975: *Kin groups and social structure*. New York: Holt, Rinehart and Winston.

Mitchell, D.G., ed. 1975: *A dictionary of sociology*. London: Routledge and Kegan Paul.

L

labour force Also known as the economically active population, the labour force is conventionally defined as the total number of persons who supply labour for the production of economic goods and services. Precise definitions of the labour force are difficult, sometimes impossible, and almost always open to controversy since the activities carried out by individuals rarely conform to the convenient categorisation of the definitions.

The conventional approach to the topic is seen in the United Nations recommendations for classification of the population according to economic activity. A fundamental contrast is made between the economically active and 'inactive' populations. The former is composed both of persons in gainful employment and of those not currently employed but looking for work. The rest of the population is classified as not economically active. This includes housewives (termed homemakers in the United States), students, pensioners and other groups receiving private or public support without engaging in 'economic' activity. Further distinctions are made within the labour force according to industry or brand of economic activity. For the convenience of comparing these various categories the International Labour Organisation has produced a standard classification of occupations (ILO 1968).

In spite of its ubiquity this approach has several drawbacks, many of which derive from the notion that a distinction can be made between economic and non-economic uses of time. Such a distinction is often unjustified, and even where appropriate may lead to illogicalities. For example, the domestic activities of a homemaker or housewife are not usually classified as economic, whereas a domestic servant performing identical tasks would normally be regarded as part of the labour force. Similarly, although domestic labour is not classified as economic, unpaid work in an economic enterprise operated by a related person living in the same household is. The usefulness of the conventional approach is particularly low in rural areas of low-income countries: in areas dominated by subsistence agriculture the concepts of economic and non-economic work are effectively meaningless since work, leisure and consumption are often intermingled. A further drawback with traditional approaches is their inability adequately to measure underemployment. An attempt is usually made to identify a reference period (commonly the week before the interview) within which a person must have worked or have actively sought work to be included in the labour force. There is no particular justification, however, for using a week or any other period as the reference.

The most widely used measures of economic activity are labour force PARTICIPATION RATES, the ratio of the active population in an age-sex category to the total population in the category. Particular attention is paid to female participation rates since these vary much more than rates for men and have increased significantly in many developed countries in recent decades.

Given the limitation of the conventional approach, a number of alternative strategies have been proposed. particularly valuable are studies of TIME BUDGETS, giving in detail the time spent on different activities, enabling a much more detailed examination of labour force participation to be made.   RP, CW

Reference

International Labour Organisation 1968: *The international standard classification of occupations*. Geneva: ILO.

Reading

Standing, G. 1982: Labor Force. In J.A. Ross, ed. *International encyclopaedia of population*. New York: Free Press. Pp. 391–8.

labour force life table   See WORKING LIFE TABLE.

labour force participation rate   See PARTICIPATION RATE.

lactation   See BREASTFEEDING.

legal abortion   INDUCED ABORTION carried out in accordance with the laws of the country in which it takes place. These laws vary, from some countries prohibiting induced abortion under any circumstances to others providing for abortion on demand.

The legal framework of induced abortion generally deals with two areas: the reasons regarded as acceptable for performing an abortion and the conditions under which the operation is carried out. The reasons may normally be defined on medical grounds (permitted only in order to save the mother's life), or on eugenic grounds (known genetic impairment of the foetus). Legal or juridical circumstances may also be taken into account in, for example, pregnancies following rape or incest. These reasons enable abortions to be legally performed in only a small proportion of cases. However, if medical justification of a wider scope is countenanced (i.e. averting a threat to health, physical or mental, rather than to life) greater opportunity exists for legal termination of pregnancy. Even more important are social or economic grounds for abortion which lead to the widest availability. Abortion laws invariably specify a specific duration of pregnancy within which termination may take place, this is most commonly set at within the first 12 weeks when risk of complications is lowest, though sometiimes it can be up to as late as 28 weeks. Additionally, the kind of establishment permitted to carry out the abortion is normally specified by law.

It is important to realise that in many countries statutory provision does not correspond with availability. In some countries (e.g. Taiwan, South Korea and the Netherlands before 1981) restrictive laws are widely ignored and abortion is openly available from private clinics. On the other hand the existence of a liberal abortion law does not guarantee that the service is in fact available. Lack of medical facilities or conservative attitudes among doctors and administrators may greatly limit access to abortion, especially for economically or socially deprived women.

The traditional legal position of abortion varied widely. In some countries hostility to abortion was intense, but in English common law, which also formed the basis of the US legal system, abortion was not an indictable offence until 1803, and even then was not severely punished if it took place before the foetus quickened. During the nineteenth century, however, statutes outlawing abortion came into effect in many countries, and in some have not yet been overturned. The first country to make legal abortion widely available was the Soviet Union in 1920, although this was reversed between 1936 and 1955. Japan undertook liberalisation in the Eugenic Protection Law of 1948, which has been interpreted as sanctioning abortion on request, and from the late 1960s most developed nations have introduced more liberal abortion laws. In contrast, a number of Eastern European countries, where liberal abortion laws were introduced in the 1950s, have made their statutes more restrictive in recent years in an attempt to increase population growth. In most Third World countries abortion remains either illegal or only sanctioned on narrow medical grounds, a consequ-

122   legitimacy

ence, in part at least, of the scarcity of doctors and medical facilities.   RP

Reading

International Planned Parenthood Federation 1979: *The human problem of abortion: the medico-legal dimensions*. London: IPPF.
Tietze, C. 1983: *Induced abortion: a world review 1983*. New York: Population Council.

legitimacy   See ILLEGITIMACY.

Leslie matrix   A matrix formulation of the technique of cohort-component PROJECTION developed by P.H. Leslie (see Leslie 1945, 1948). It is also referred to as the projection matrix.

The matrix combines the effects of fertility and mortality in producing population change. The first row contains factors which reflect the levels of fertility and child survival while the principal subdiagonal contains SURVIVORSHIP RATIOS indicating the chances of survival from one age group to the next. All other elements in the matrix are zero. If the age structure of a population is given in a vector, each element being the number in a particular age group x to $x + n$, premultiplication of the vector by the Leslie matrix will produce another vector representing the projected population n years ahead.

The matrix facilitates the expression of STABLE POPULATION theory in discrete terms and its properties have been extensively analysed by mathematical demographers, particularly in connection with work on ERGODICITY. The basic matrix has been extended into multistate models in which projections are made for several states or regions (see MULTISTATE DEMOGRAPHY.   CW

References

Leslie, P.H. 1945: On the use of matrices in certain population mathematics. *Biometrika* 33, pp. 183–212.
— 1948: Some further notes on the use of matrices in population mathematics. *Biometrika* 35, pp. 213–45.

Reading

Keyfitz, N. 1977: *Introduction to the mathematics of populations, with revisions*. London and Reading, Mass.: Addison-Wesley. Part 2.
Rogers, A. 1968: *Matrix analysis of interregional population growth and distribution*. Berkeley, California: University of California Press.
Woods, R. 1979: *Population analysis in geography*. London: Longman. Pp. 221–5.

Lexis diagram   A diagram first devised by the German statistician Wilhelm Lexis

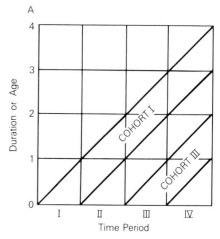

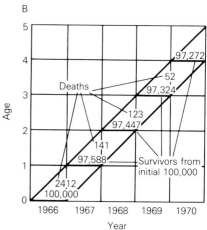

Mortality in Ireland: 1966 life table deaths applied to 1966 birth cohort.
Source: G. Wunsch and M. Termote 1978: *Introduction to demographic analysis*. New York and London: Plenum Press. P. 108.

in 1875. It provides a convenient way of displaying data with the aim of demonstrating the relationship between periods and COHORTS. It is widely used, especially in works drawing on the French tradition of analysis.

The diagram is composed of a grid marking out units of calendar time on the horizontal axis and age (or some other measure of duration) on the vertical. Diagonal lines running upwards from the horizontal axis separate particular cohorts. By locating data within the appropriate square, parallelogram or triangle of the diagram it is possible to give a more immediate representation of the way in which information on periods and cohorts are related. The diagram was first suggested as a means of analysing mortality, but it is applicable to any data. In Lexis's original formulation, the diagonals ran downwards, but modern convention reverses this.   RP

Reading

Lexis, W. 1977: Formal treatment of aggregate mortality data (1875). In D. Smith and N. Keyfitz, eds. 1977: *Mathematical demography: selected papers*. Berlin and New York: Springer-Verlag. Pp. 39–41.

Pressat, R. 1972: *Demographic analysis: methods, results, applications*. London: Edward Arnold; Chicago: Aldine Atherton. Chapter 2.

life cycle   The sequence of stages through which individuals or families pass beginning with birth and ending in death (for individuals) or beginning with formation and ending in dissolution (for families).

Analysis of the life cycle typically concerns the timing of particular life-cycle events (e.g. marriage), the frequency of persons in particular life-cycle stages (e.g. unmarried) in a population cross-section, or the time spent in particular states.

Although the concept of the life cycle is clearly related to the process of ageing, it is the social and economic significance of the events and states which mark the life cycle, independent of age, from which the

concept derives its analytic utility. For example, in the comparative analysis of fertility, a statistical control for duration of marriage (a life-cycle variable) is often preferred to age. Another important application of the concept is in the study of female labour force participation, where life-cycle stage, defined with reference to a woman's marital and reproductive history, is often used as an explanatory or control variable.   MTC

Reading

Cain, M.T. 1978: The household life cycle and economic mobility in rural Bangladesh. *Population and development review* 4, pp. 421–38.

Elder, G. 1981: History and the family: the discovery of complexity. *Journal of marriage and the family* 43, pp. 489–519.

Preston, S.H. 1982: Relations between individual life cycles and population characteristics. *American sociological review* 47, pp. 253–64.

Ryder, N.B. 1975: Reproductive bahavior and the family life cycle. In United Nations, *The population debate: dimensions and perspectives*. Volume 2, population studies 57. New York: Department of Economic and Social Affairs. Pp. 278–88.

life expectancy   The average number of additional years a person would live if the mortality conditions implied by a particular life table applied. Life expectancy at age x is represented by $\overset{\circ}{e}_x$ and life expectancy at birth by $\overset{\circ}{e}_o$.

Although life tables normally present values of $\overset{\circ}{e}_x$ for all ages, life expectancy at birth is by far the most quoted value, so that where life expectancy is referred to without further qualification the value at birth is normally assumed. In actuarial notation a distinction is made between $\overset{\circ}{e}_x$ and e_x the latter being the curate life expectancy (the number of whole years lived after age x). Since the latter statistic is scarcely ever used in demography some authors have adopted e_x as a synonym for $\overset{\circ}{e}_x$. This is especially true for less technical works.

Life expectancy at birth is very widely

used as an indicator of mortality conditions. It is well suited to this role, being a measure based on mortality experience at all ages and independent of the effects of age structure. It is noteworthy, however, that in many cases $\overset{\circ}{e}_o$ is less than some other values of $\overset{\circ}{e}_x$. In populations with high infant and early childhood mortality the highest values are found for $\overset{\circ}{e}_5$ and even in developed countries with low infant mortality $\overset{\circ}{e}_1$ is often greater than $\overset{\circ}{e}_0$.

The range of values of life expectancy at birth observed for human populations is considerable: from around 20 years in particularly poor historical populations to close to, or even beyond, 80 in modern developed countries. In common with other indices of mortality, $\overset{\circ}{e}_0$ has improved markedly in most parts of the world in the twentieth century: values below 40 are very rare for national populations. In general women enjoy life expectancies of between 2 and 8 years greater than men in the same population, although this is not universal (see SEX DIFFERENTIAL MORTALITY). (See also LIFE TABLE FUNCTIONS.)   RP, CW

life history   A detailed account of a person's experience of one or more demographic processes. The term event history is used synonymously. These data are often collected in retrospective surveys and may refer to the lifetime up to the time of the survey. Complete information on all aspects of a person's life is rarely collected, most histories being limited to data on a single phenomenon. This leads to the terms maternity history, migration history and so on.   RP, CW

life table   A detailed description of the mortality of a population giving the probability of dying and various other statistics at each age. The life table is a powerful tool for the analysis of mortality or any other NON-RENEWABLE PROCESS and is the most important analytical technique for such phenomena.

The life table is composed of the values of various functions for persons of each age or age group. When information on each year of age is present the life table is referred to as complete or unabridged; more commonly age groups are used to produce an abridged life table. A further distinction is between COHORT LIFE TABLES, expressing the occurrence of deaths within a cohort of individuals born in the same year or group of years, and period life tables which are based on the age-specific death rates of a particular period, often one year. While cohort life tables have several theoretical advantages the longevity of human beings is such that the more readily calculable period life tables, which are based on the idea of a HYPOTHETICAL COHORT, are normally used. Life tables provide the most complete and exact way of comparing the mortality of different populations or groups. Their great advantage is that they provide measures which are not affected by differences in age structure and also avoid the arbitrary adoption of some 'standard' as do measures derived from STANDARDISATION.

Whatever the type of life table, the definitions of the LIFE TABLE FUNCTIONS are the same. The basis of the table is a set of probabilities of dying, $_nq_x$, which give the proportion of individuals alive at age x who die before reaching age $x + n$. Given this set of probabilities a second set of values is presented for the probability of survival from birth to each age, the l_x column. The first value of this, l_0, is termed the radix of the life table and usually set at 1000 or 100,000 to facilitate interpretation. The number of persons dying in each age interval of the table, $_nd_x$ is also commonly given. The number of PERSON-YEARS lived in each age-group appears in the values of $_nL_x$ and the number of person-years lived by the population beyond age x is given as T_x. The final function which is generally given is $\overset{\circ}{e}_x$, the additional LIFE EXPECTANCY at age x. The most widely quoted value of this function is $\overset{\circ}{e}_0$, the life expectancy at birth. In some sources only the values for $_nq_x$, l_x and $\overset{\circ}{e}_x$ are produced for the sake of brevity. This leads to little loss of information since the other major functions can be calculated from them.

An alternative interpretation of the life table functions is as a description of a STATIONARY POPULATION, a population whose total numbers and age distribution do not alter, and in which exactly as many births occur each year as are needed to

in the eighteenth century, notably by KERSSEBOOM, DEPARCIEUX and DUVILLARD. The first scientifically correct life table was calculated by MILNE based on data from Carlisle in 1779 to 1787 and published in 1815. In the 1840s the Registrar General William FARR established an official English life table, and similar work

Abridged life table for females, Hong Kong 1976.

Age interval	Death rate	Probability of dying	Of 100,000 live births Survivors	Deaths	Stationary Population		Life expectancy	Years lived before dying
Period of life between two exact ages in years x to $x+n$	Central death rate per person aged x to $x+n$ $_nm_x$	Proportion of persons alive at beginning of age interval who die during interval $_nq_x$	Number of persons alive at beginning of age interval l_x	Number dying during age interval $_nd_x$	Person– years lived in this age interval $_nL_x$	Person– years lived in this and all subsequent age intervals T_x	Average number of years of life remaining at beginning of age interval $\mathring{e}_x$	Average number of years lived in age interval by persons who die in interval $_na_x$
0–1	.01229	.01215	100,000	1215	98,890	7,656,843	76.568	0.086
1–5	.00084	.00336	98,785	332	394,312	7,557,953	76.509	1.504
5–10	.00034	.00171	98,453	168	491,845	7,163,641	72.762	2.500
10–15	.00029	.00143	98,285	141	491,072	6,671,796	67.882	2.500
15–20	.00041	.00207	98,144	203	490,243	6,180,724	62.976	2.649
20–25	.00059	.00294	97,941	288	489,022	5,690,481	58.101	2.628
25–30	.00077	.00384	97,653	375	487,373	5,201,459	53.265	2.621
30–35	.00106	.00528	97,278	514	485,163	4,714,086	48.460	2.611
35–40	.00133	.00661	96,764	640	482,308	4,228,922	43.703	2.632
40–45	.00202	.01006	96,125	967	478,367	3,746,615	38.977	2.666
45–50	.00300	.01488	95,158	1416	472,495	3,268,248	34.346	2.673
50–55	.00479	.02367	93,742	2219	463,564	2,795,753	29.824	2.681
55–60	.00750	.03686	91,523	3374	449,778	2,332,189	25.482	2.677
60–65	.01206	.05865	88,149	5170	428,614	1,882,411	21.355	2.653
65–70	.01764	.08469	82,980	7028	398,300	1,453,797	17.520	2.638
70–75	.02794	.13112	75,952	9959	356,419	1,055,497	13.897	2.656
75–80	.04939	.22105	65,993	14,588	295,349	699,078	10.593	2.627
80–85	.08424	.34925	51,405	17,953	213,120	403,729	7.854	2.554
85 and over	.17550	1.00000	33,452	33,452	190,608	190,608	5.698	5.698

Source: United Nations 1982: *Model life tables for developing countries.* Population Studies 77. New York: Department of International Social and Economic Affairs. P. 311.

balance the deaths indicated by the life table. In this context the total number of births and deaths is equal to the radix of the life table, the $_nL_x$ values indicate the number of persons in each age group, and the T_x values the size of the population in a given age group or older.

Two further functions, which are not always given in life tables, but are of consequence in LIFE TABLE CONSTRUCTION are $_nm_x$, the life table central death rate and $_na_x$, the average length of time lived between x and $x + n$ by persons who die between those ages.

The work of GRAUNT in the seventeenth century was a precursor of the modern life table, though a more systematic approach was taken by HALLEY. Several further attempts to produce a life table were made

was carried out in a number of other European countries in the later nineteenth century. The first official complete life tables for the United States were prepared in 1900–02. With the spread of data collection and analysis since the second world war life tables have been produced for most countries, although the accuracy of many from the Third World is questionable. On the basis of the more reliable life tables several series of MODEL LIFE TABLES have been developed. These are particularly useful in the estimation of mortality and other processes for populations for which reliable data are unavailable.

LIFE TABLE METHODS are applicable to any phenomenon which can only occur once, and they have been employed in many branches of demography. For example, first marriages are often analysed in a nuptiality table and entry into and departure from the labour force in working life tables. As an extension of life tables with only one factor leading to the attrition of individuals (single decrement tables) demographers also use MULTIPLE DECREMENT LIFE TABLES which allow for several causes of loss. The impact of various causes of death is sometimes analysed in this way, or by means of CAUSE-DELETED LIFE TABLES which enable the researcher to extract the effects of one cause of death from overall death rates and examine the resultant gain in life expectancy. An added sophistication comes from the use of IN-CREMENT-DECREMENT LIFE TABLES and MULTISTATE DEMOGRAPHY which describe the phenomena under study using the sophisticated mathematics of a TRANSITION MATRIX.   RP, CW

Reading

Pressat, R. 1972: *Demographic analysis: methods, results, applications.* London: Edward Arnold; Chicago: Aldine Atherton. Chapter 6.

Ross, J.A. 1982: Life tables. In J.A. Ross, ed. *International encyclopaedia of population.* New York: Free Press. Pp. 420–5.

Shryock, H.S., Siegel, J.S. et al. 1976: *The methods and materials of demography.* Condensed edition by E.G. Stockwell. London and New York: Academic Press. Chapter 15.

Smith, D.P. 1980: *Life table analysis.* World Fertility Survey, technical bulletin 6. Voorburg, The Netherlands: International Statistical Institute.

life table construction The techniques used to calculate the functions of a life table from observed data. In most cases this takes the form of methods of estimating the probability of dying in each age group, $_nq_x$, since the remaining functions may be generated from this series.

Early life tables, such as those produced by Graunt, Halley and others, were based simply on the observed distribution of ages at death. This only provides correct information if dealing with a STATIONARY POPULATION, a point sometimes noted by the authors but unlikely to be true for the

populations they studied. The first correct use of classical life table construction, using information on both the population at risk and deaths at each age, was by MILNE in 1815. Modern life tables are usually based on the same two types of data; normally using censuses for the population at risk and vital registration for the deaths. The classical method is based on the exact relationship between $_nq_x$ and the other life table function $_nm_x$, the life table central death rate and $_na_x$ the average number of years between ages x and $x + n$ by those dying in the interval:

$$_nq_x = \frac{n \times {}_nm_x}{1 + (n - {}_na_x) \times {}_nm_x}$$

If it is further assumed that the observed age-specific central death rate, $_nM_x$, is equal to the life table value, the probability may be estimated from observed data. The values of $_na_x$ are often unavailable but, if the assumption is made that deaths occur evenly throughout an age interval, it can be replaced with $0.5n$. This assumption is reasonable except for very young and very old ages. If it is used the following simpler relation holds:

$$_nq_x = \frac{2 \times n \times {}_nm_x}{2 + (n \times {}_nm_x)}$$

Deaths at ages for which this simplifying assumption is not acceptable, especially infant mortality, receive particular attention. Infant mortality is normally estimated by relating observed deaths to the number of births in a year and calculating the $_1q_0$ value directly.

A different approach uses the REED-MERRELL TABLES, devised by two American demographers, which provide $_nq_x$ values equivalent to each $_nM_x$ value. In some types of analysis using INDIRECT ESTIMATION TECHNIQUES certain values of the $_nq_x$ function, or the survival function, l_x, are calculated for responses to questions on the survival of relatives (infants, parents, spouses or siblings). In these cases classical construction methods are

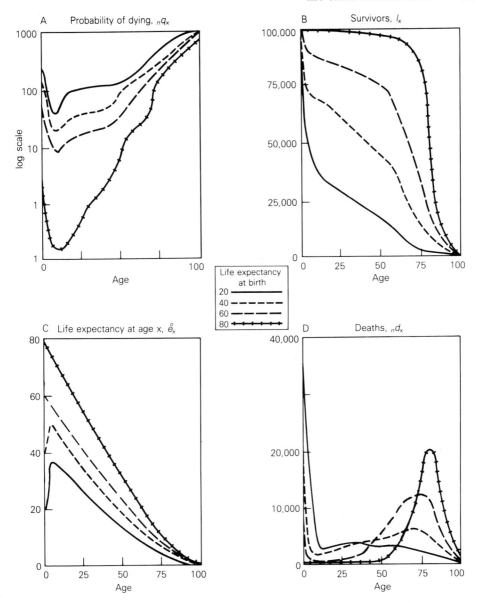

A Probability of dying, $_nq_x$

B Survivors, l_x

C Life expectancy at age x, $\overset{o}{e}_x$

D Deaths, $_nd_x$

Life expectancy at birth
20 ——————
40 ------------
60 – – – – –
80 +–+–+–+–+

Values are plotted for four life tables from the Coale-Demeny series (region West) for females with life expectancies at birth of 20, 40, 60 and 80 years.

circumvented and much attention is paid to the linking together of estimates of adult and child mortality (derived from different questions) to produce consistent and plausible life tables. The use of MODEL LIFE TABLES is often invaluable in such work.   MM

Reading

Keyfitz, N. 1977: *Applied mathematical demography.* New York and London: Wiley. Chapter 2.

— and Flieger, W. 1971: *Population: facts and methods of demography.* San Francisco: Freeman.

Pressat, R. 1972: *Demographic analysis: methods, results, applications*. London: Edward Arnold; Chicago: Aldine Atherton. Chapter 6.

Shryock, H.S., Siegel, J.S. et al. 1976: *The methods and materials of demography*. Condensed edition by E.G. Stockwell. London and New York: Academic Press. Chapter 15.

Smith, D.P. 1980: *Life table analysis*. World Fertility Survey, technical bulletin 6. Voorburg, The Netherlands: International Statistical Institute.

life table functions   The functions which make up the life table and express the various aspects of the mortality conditions prevailing in a population. The commonly used functions in simple decrement life tables and the relationships between them can be defined in the following way for an abridged life table:

l_x The number of persons surviving to exact age x out of the original number at age zero, l_0, termed the radix of the life table. The l_x function is sometimes termed the survival function.

$_np_x$ The probability that a person alive at exact age x will survive for a further n years. (Equal to l_{x+n}/l_x.)

$_nq_x$ The probability that a person alive at exact age x will die before reaching age $x + n$. (Equal to $1-_np_x$.)

$_nd_x$ The number of deaths occurring between ages x and $x + n$. (Equal to $l_x - l_{x+n}$.)

$_na_x$ The average number of years lived in the interval between ages x and $x + n$ by those who die in the interval. If this information is not available it will often be assumed that deaths are spread evenly over the interval. In such a case the values of $_na_x$ will be taken as $0.5n$. This is normally reasonable except for very young and old ages.

$_nL_x$ The total number of PERSON-YEARS lived in the interval between ages x and $x + n$. It is also the number of people in this age group which would be found in a STATIONARY POPULATION experiencing the mortality implied by the life table and with the number of

births per year equal to l_0. (Equal to $n.l_x - _nd_x._na_x$ or $0.5n(l_x + l_{x+n})$ if $_na_x$ is taken to be $0.5n$.)

T_x The total number of person-years lived beyond age x. Also the size of the stationary population at ages x and above. (Equal to the sum of the $_nL_x$ values for all values above x.)

$\overset{\circ}{e}_o$ The LIFE EXPECTANCY at age x., i.e. the average additional number of years lived beyond age x by those who reach x. (Equal to T_x/l_x). The most often quoted value of this function is $\overset{\circ}{e}_0$, the life expectancy at birth. In actuarial notation a distinction is made between $\overset{\circ}{e}_x$, the complete life expectancy, and e_x, the curate life expectancy which gives the average number of whole years lived beyond age x. However, there is a tendency for recent work, especially that of a less technical nature to use e_x in place of $\overset{\circ}{e}_o$.

$_nm_x$ The CENTRAL DEATH RATE in the life table. (Equal to $_nd_x/_nL_x$.)

In a COMPLETE LIFE TABLE, where each individual years of age are used, the size of the age group is 1, and by convention the left-hand subscript is deleted.

RP, MM

life table methods   The application of the analytic techniques of the LIFE TABLE to a particular problem. The term embraces both single and MULTIPLE DECREMENT LIFE TABLES.

Any process which involves the removal of individuals from an initial COHORT (or HYPOTHETICAL COHORT) may be analysed by life table methods, although whether this is the most efficient form of analysis will depend on the circumstances of the study (Smith 1980). For example, marriage removes an individual from the group of single persons and can be studied with a nuptiality table. Similarly the entry and departure of persons from the labour force can be analysed with WORKING LIFE TABLES. Both these examples ideally use multiple decrement life tables since death is an additional way of leaving the cohort and needs to be taken into account. In practice mortality is sometimes ignored either because of its assumed unimportance to the problem in hand or because of lack of suitable data. Conventional single-decrement approaches are also widely used in the analysis of fertility – the analysis of BIRTH INTERVALS and POST-PARTUM VARIABLES for example. Much of this work has been stimulated by the availability of MATERNITY HISTORIES collected in sample surveys and the techniques of SURVIVAL ANALYSIS (see Rodriguez and Hobcraft 1980, Bracher and Santow 1982). In recent years work on MULTI-STATE DEMOGRAPHY together with INCREMENT-DECREMENT LIFE TABLES has provided ways to cope with re-entrants into the cohort, so that, for example, divorce and remarriage or repeated departure from and re-entry into the labour force can be analysed correctly. These methods have been particularly important in the study of migration using MULTIREGIONAL DEMOGRAPHY.

One potentially significant problem is that of HETEROGENEITY within the population. Traditionally demographers have attempted to deal with this by producing separate life tables for subpopulations, each assumed to be homogeneous. This approach is not always practical, for example when dealing with small numbers of cases (usually true with survey data). A technique which allows to some extent for observable heterogeneity is the use of HAZARDS MODELS with appropriate covariates. Unmeasured heterogeneity remains a potential difficulty, however (Heckman and Singer 1982).   MM

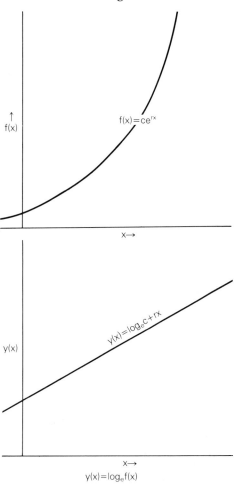

$y(x) = \log_e f(x)$

References

Bracher, M. and Santow, G. 1982: Breastfeeding in Central Java. *Population studies* 36, pp. 413–29.

Heckman, J.J. and Singer, B. 1982: Population heterogeneity in demographic models. In K.C. Land and A. Rodgers, eds. *Multidimensional mathematical demography*. New York and London: Academic Press.

Rodriguez, G. and Hobcraft, J.N. 1980: *Illustrative analysis: life table analysis of birth intervals in Colombia*. World Fertility Survey, scientific reports 16. Voorburg, The Netherlands: International Statistical Institute.

Smith, D.P. 1980: *Life table analysis*. World Fertility Survey, technical bulletins 6. Voorburg, The Netherlands: International Statistical Institute.

Reading

Ross, J.A. 1982: Life tables. In J.A. Ross, ed. *International encyclopaedia of population*. New York: Free Press. Pp. 420–5.

linearising transform A transform which converts a non-linear function to a linear one. For example, the logarithmic transformation linearises an exponential function, as illustrated in the figure above.

In demographic work the term is sometimes loosely used, i.e. the transformed function may not be strictly linear, just closer to a straight line than the original function.

The importance of such transformations in statistical work is that linear functions are often mathematically more tractable than the curvilinear functions from which they were derived. Also, it is easier to smooth data points on a graph (to get rid of random errors or small biases) if they approximate to a straight line.   BZ

Reading

Brass, W. 1971: Disciplining demographic data. In *Proceedings of International Population Conference, London, 1969.* Volume 1. Liège: International Union for the Scientific Study of Population. Pp. 183–204.

listing   See NOMINATIVE LISTING.

literacy   The ability to read and/or write. UNESCO (1957, 1961) has distinguished three levels:

(1) Absolute minimum: the ability to read and write one's own name, or 'yes' or 'no', or a few numerals.
(2) Relative minimum: the ability to read or write a 'simple message', a 'letter to a friend' or 'a simple statement on everyday life'. This corresponds to census data based on questions such as 'Can you read?', 'Can you write?'.
(3) Functional: sufficient knowledge and skill in reading and writing to be able to participate actively in all activities for which literacy is normally assumed in a culture or group.   RSS

References

UNESCO 1957: *World illiteracy at mid-century.* Paris: UNESCO.
— 1961: *Manual of educational statistics.* Paris: UNESCO.

Reading

Goody, J. 1968: *Literacy in traditional societies.* Cambridge: Cambridge University Press.
Graff, H.J. 1979: *The literacy myth.* New York: Academic Press.
— 1981: *Literacy in history: an interdisciplin-*

ary research bibliography. New York: Garland.

live birth   See BIRTH.

logistic population growth   Population growth which conforms to the mathematical form of the logistic curve. This makes the rate of growth a linearly decreasing function of population size, producing an S-shaped curve with population size gradually approaching an asymptotic value. If P_{max} is this asymptote and a and b are constants, the population at time t, P_t, is given by:

$$P_t = \frac{P_{max}}{1 + e^{a-bt}}$$

The application of the logistic curve as a model of population growth was first suggested in 1838 by Verhulst, but taken up again and popularised by Pearl and Reed in 1920. A considerable literature has developed in biostatistics using the logistic for the description and projection of the growth of many species. In the 1920s and 1930s it enjoyed popularity in demographic projections, but has largely been replaced by more sophisticated techniques.   RP, CW

Reading

Smith, D. and Keyfitz, N., eds. 1977: *Mathematical demography: selected papers.* Berlin and New York: Springer-Verlag. Pp. 333–47. Reproduction of papers by Verhulst and Pearl and Reed.

logit   A type of LINEARISING TRANSFORM widely employed in biostatistics and demography especially in INDIRECT ESTIMATION TECHNIQUES. As used by demographers the logit, y, of a proportion, p, is given by:

$$y = \frac{1}{2} \log_e \left(\frac{1-p}{p} \right)$$

The logit transformation converts a proportion into a number between minus infinity and plus infinity. The reverse of the transformation is:

$$p = \frac{1}{1 + e^{2y}}$$

A slightly different form of the definition is generally found in statistical works. (See also LOGIT LIFE TABLE SYSTEM.).   BZ

Reading
Ashton, W.P. 1972: *The logit transformation*. London: Charles Griffin.

logit life table system A RELATIONAL MODEL of the age pattern of mortality developed by Brass (1971).

The basic assumption underlying the model system is that a linear relationship exists between the logits, y_x, of the survivorship values, l_x, of any two life tables at all ages, x. Denoting the two life tables by the superscripts a and b, we have:

$$y_x^a = \alpha + \beta y_x^b$$

By defining a standard life table (denoted by the superscript s) it is possible to derive a whole range of MODEL LIFE TABLES by varying α and β using the following equations:

$$y_x = \alpha + \beta y_x^s$$

$$l_x = \frac{1}{1 + e^{2y_x}}$$

In this two-parameter model α represents the overall level of mortality (positive values of α indicate worse mortality than the standard, negative values lower mortality), while β governs the age-pattern of mortality, in particular the relationship between adult and child mortality (Carrier and Gom 1972). More elaborate versions of the system have been suggested using four parameters to give further flexibility at young and very old ages (Zaba 1979, Ewbank et al. 1983).   BZ

References
Brass, W. 1971: On the scale of mortality. In W. Brass, ed. *Biological aspects of demography*. London: Taylor and Francis. Pp. 69–110.

Carrier, N.H. and Gom, T.J. 1972: The validation of Brass's model life table system. *Population studies* 26, pp. 29–52.
Ewbank, D.C., Gomez de Leon, J.C. and Stoto, M.A. 1983: A reducible four-parameter system of life tables. *Population studies* 37, pp. 105–27.
Zaba, B. 1979: The four parameter logit life table system. *Population studies* 33, pp. 79–100.

Reading
Brass, W. 1975. *Methods for estimating fertility and mortality from limited and defective data*. Chapel Hill, N. Carolina: Laboratories for Population Statistics. Chapters 12–15.
Ewbank et al. 1983.

longevity The length of life, often measured at a population level by LIFE EXPECTANCY.

Although average life expectancy has increased greatly since pre-industrial times the maximum length of life seems to be little altered and to be somewhat over 100 years. Reports of special populations with high proportions of centenarians have all proved to be based on poor data with considerable age over-statement. If the upper limit to life is, therefore, broadly fixed it is natural to think of a minimum life table representing the best mortality conditions to which societies could aspire. Such a life table was produced in 1952 by Bourgeois-Pichat giving a life expectancy of 78 years for women and 76 for men. The female value has already been exceeded in several countries, though the slower improvement in male mortality in developed countries leaves the male figure on the upper boundary of current experience. Benjamin (1982) has more recently examined the consequences of rapid mortality improvement in Britain. The theoretical basis for a minimum level of mortality comes from genetics and biology. It is generally accepted that genetic factors play a major role in determining the potential life span of an individual and that after reaching sexual maturity many physiological functions begin to decline, gradually increasing the individual's susceptibility to death. This 'biological clock' concept of ageing has been well described by Hayflick (1981).

Genetic inheritance, life-style and environment all cause individuals to age biologically at different rates. Most attempts to predict biological age use multivariate techniques, and Tobin (1977) has suggested four clinically important variables. Although medical intervention is an essential component of improved average life span the scope for improvement based on changes in life-style, diet and behaviour seems to be larger.   cw

References

Benjamin, B. 1982: The span of life. *Journal of the Institute of Actuaries* 109, pp. 319–40; discussion pp. 341–57.

Hayflick, L. 1981: Biological aspects of ageing. In S.H. Preston, ed. *Biological and social aspects of mortality and the length of life*. Liège: Ordina Editions.

Tobin, J.D. 1977: Physiological indices of aging. In *Proceedings of the Vichy Conference*. Paris: Institut de la Vie.

Reading

Benjamin 1982.

Hayflick 1981.

Pollard, J.H. 1982: Morbidity and longevity. In J.A. Ross, ed. *International encyclopaedia of population*. New York: Free Press. Pp. 452–9.

longitudinal analysis   See COHORT ANALYSIS.

longitudinal observation   A form of observation in which events relating to cohorts are studied. A contrast can be made between genuine PROSPECTIVE OBSERVATION, in which individuals are identified and the events occurring to them recorded as they happen, and other methods, based on RECORD LINKAGE, which enable cohort experience to be reconstructed after the fact. A prime example of this latter approach is FAMILY RECONSTITUTION which uses records of vital events in parish registers to piece together life histories.   RP

Lotka, Alfred (1880–1949)   An American mathematical demographer whose work formed the basis of STABLE POPULATION analysis. In a series of articles Lotka devised and solved the renewal equation, specifying the way in which populations replace themselves, and demonstrated the links between theoretical constructs and actual populations. In particular, he showed that populations would always achieve a constant age-structure and growth rate if subjected to unchanging patterns of fertility and mortality, defined the INTRINSIC RATE OF NATURAL INCREASE, and elaborated many interrelationships among the parameters of the stable population. In addition Lotka used the insights gained from these theoretical studies to analyse a wide variety of practical problems. The importance of Lotka's work has led to Smith and Keyfitz (1977) describing it as 'a singular achievement in demography'.   RP

Reference

Smith, D. and Keyfitz, N. 1977: *Mathematical demography: selected papers*. Berlin and New York: Springer-Verlag.

Reading

Lotka, A. 1939: *Théorie analytique des associations biologiques*. Paris: Hermann.

Smith and Keyfitz 1977. Pp. 75–7 and 93–107.

M

macrosimulation   See SIMULATION.

Makeham formula   A mathematical expression devised by W.M. Makeham in 1860 and 1867 to provide a better model of the age-specific pattern of the INSTANTANEOUS DEATH RATE than the GOMPERTZ FORMULA. By examining cause-specific death rates Makeham found that mortality levels could be better represented if, in addition to the exponential increase in death with age suggested by Gompertz, a constant term to represent causes of death which were not dependent on age were added to the probability of dying. If q_x is the probability of dying at age x, and A, B and C are constants we have:

$$q_x = A + BC^x$$

For ages beyond childhood Makeham's equation combines both intuitive plausibility and a close fit to observed patterns.

RP

Reading
Makeham, W.M. 1977: On the law of mortality (1867). In D. Smith and N. Keyfitz, eds. 1977: *Mathematical demography: selected papers*. Berlin and New York: Springer-Verlag. Pp. 283–8.

male reproduction   See REPRODUCTIVITY.

Malthus, Thomas Robert (1766–1834) English clergyman and teacher and author of *An essay on the principle of population*. A controversial figure since the first publication of his work in 1798, Malthus's reputation has fluctuated greatly and his ideas have frequently been misunderstood. Nevertheless, he was unquestionably one of the most influential figures in the development of population studies as well as an economist of the first rank and (through his influence on Darwin) possibly the only social scientist to have played a crucial role in the development of a major natural science.

In brief outline Malthus's central thesis is remarkably simple: human beings are able to reproduce at a rate which economic growth can rarely match; therefore population growth must be restrained, either by the 'preventive check' of late marriage (and abstinence before it) or by the 'positive check' of high mortality from disease, war or famine. Malthus saw postponement of marriage as the only acceptable means of preventing births, regarding contraception or any other form of birth control as a 'vice'.

As a demonstration of the human capacity to reproduce Malthus cited the experience of the British colonies in North America and the youthful United States which had consistently doubled in size every twenty-five years since the earliest settlement. This rate of growth could only be sustained until the land became fully occupied at which point population growth would be constrained by the limits to economic growth. To dramatise the different capacities for growth of the population and the economy, Malthus characterised the former as being potentially subject to geometric increase while the latter grew in arithmetic sequence.

The manner in which Malthus discussed this central observation of the tension between reproduction and production changed considerably in the different editions of his *essay*, particularly between the first edition of 1798 and the second of

1803. Malthus's chief aims in the first edition were to refute the views of Condorcet and Godwin about the perfectability of human society and to demonstrate the unfortunate effects of the English Poor Law. His aims are well expressed in the essay's full title *An essay on the principle of population as it affects the future improvement of society*. The work was little more than a polemical pamphlet with a limited exposition of theory and little supporting evidence. When he first wrote it Malthus was largely ignorant of even the most basic facts about the English population (his estimate of the size of the population, seven million, was well below the true figure of 10.9 million indicated by the 1801 census). But by the time he prepared the second edition he had at his disposal both the census returns and a large body of information drawn from parish registers as part of the same operation, and he incorporated his responses to these data, along with comparable information from other countries into this edition. In particular the data caused him to stress the preventive, rather than the positive, check as the key element in the restraint of population growth in England, and more generally in Europe. Unfortunately the more scholarly and dull nature of the second and subsequent editions has tended to focus attention on the first edition to the detriment of Malthus's mature work.

As a description of the relation between population and economics in a pre-industrial society Malthus's work is astute and detailed. He failed, however, along with near-contemporaries such as Adam Smith and Ricardo, to anticipate the industrial revolution, though he was writing at the very time when sustained economic growth was beginning to alter the fundamental bases of economic-demographic relations. A man of liberal and humane intentions (he favoured universal education, medical assistance for the poor and wider democracy), Malthus cuts an unlikely figure as one of the most controversial social theorists of all time. That he has

become this is testimony partly to the penetration of his ideas, but mainly to their misinterpretation. The term Malthusianism has passed into all the Western languages with a variety of meanings, almost all incorrect.   RP, CW

Reading

Dupâquier, J. and Fauve-Chamoux, A., eds. 1983: *Malthus past and present*. London and New York: Academic Press.

James, P. 1979: *Population Malthus: his life and times*. London and Boston: Routledge and Kegan Paul.

Petersen, W. 1979: *Malthus*. London: Heinemann; Cambridge, Mass.: Harvard University Press.

Malthusianism   A theory of population based on, or drawing inspiration from, the writings of Malthus. It is often used to denote the doctrine that a check in the rate of population increase is desirable.

Although originally used in a way closely related to the theories of Malthus, the term has taken on several different meanings, some of them completely contradictory to his ideas. For example, although Malthus explicitly discouraged any form of contraception or induced abortion, recommending instead delayed marriage and abstinence before marriage as the appropriate way to limit population growth, Malthusianism (or more commonly NEO-MALTHUSIANISM) is sometimes used to refer to the advocacy of family planning to solve economic problems. In some countries the term is used more generally to refer to any form of birth control or to denote a narrow, pessimistic view of the availability of resources and future economic growth.   RP

manpower   See LABOUR FORCE.

marital dissolution   See DIVORCE.

marital fertility   The childbearing prodctiveness of married women (also referred to as legitimate fertility).

Marital fertility is commonly analysed through the calculation of marital fertility rates for specific age groups of women or according to the duration of marriage. The most revealing analyses are those which examine age and duration together. In doing so demographers decompose overall fertility into the separate effects of marriage patterns and childbearing within and outside marriage. The separate treatment of married and unmarried women has been based on the observation that fertility rates for the two groups are usually very different, and that in most societies marriage is a virtual pre-requisite for socially acceptable reproduction. In societies where this is not the case the value of concentration on married women is questionable. In particular, it may lead to analysis where marriage and fertility within marriage are studied as separate phenomena, rather than as two aspects of the same reproductive process.   RP, CW

marital status   The status of individuals with regard to marriage is a fundamental aspect of the composition of a population and is widely presented in information derived from censuses, surveys and registration systems.

The most common method of categorising individuals, and that recommended by the United Nations, is to distinguish five categories:

(1) single persons (never-married)
(2) the currently married population
(3) persons divorced and not re-married
(4) persons widowed and not re-married
(5) persons married but legally separated.

All groups other than (1) are often combined to form the category of ever-married. In theory it would be desirable to know the number and order of a person's marriages, so as to separate first marriages from remarriages. In practice this is rarely possible from census material, though special surveys and registration data sometimes permit it.

In societies where extra-legal CONSENSUAL UNIONS are common it is usual for there to be one or more extra categories reflecting this. For example Caribbean data on marital status often include visiting and common-law unions as well as the conventional categories.   RP, CW

Markov chain models   Stochastic or probabilistic models of the evolution of a process (here a demographic process). Markovian models are distinguished from other stochastic models by the special characteristic that, given the present state of the process, the probability distribution of future states is assumed to be the same regardless of the previous history of the process. The Markovian property is summarised by saying that the future is conditionally independent of the past, given the present.

A Markovian model is often said to be a Markov chain model when the number of states used to describe the process is finite or countably infinite and time is treated as progressing in discrete steps. In these cases the Markov chain can be completely described by the probabilities that the system is in each state when the process is first observed (these probabilities constitute the initial probability distribution) and by the TRANSITION MATRIX.

A concrete example of a Markov chain model in demography is a model for the reproductive history of a woman. In a simple version the states of the woman could be: susceptible to conception, pregnant, post-partum lactating but non-susceptible, and amenorrheic after a miscarriage or abortion. The time step might be the duration of one normal menstrual cycle. The transition probability matrix would specify, say, the probability that a woman susceptible to conception at one menstrual cycle would remain susceptible at the time of the next; the complement of that probability would be the probability that she would become pregnant. The equilibrium fraction of time that a woman would spend (during her fertile years) in each state and the mean inter-birth interval could be examined as a function of the conditional probability of remaining susceptible from one cycle to the next, which in turn would be affected by contraceptive practice. The Markovian assumption in this model implies that the woman's probability of conception during her next cycle, given that she is susceptible to conception now, is independent of her entire past: in particular, independent of how long she has been susceptible and how often she has been pregnant previously. Thus the Markovian assumption may limit the empirical relevance of the model.

Even in Markovian models that are more sophisticated than this simple example it is important to use longitudinal data on the history of the process being modelled to check the Markovian assumption as directly as possible.

Markov chain models fall between the extreme of dependence, or complete memory, in which the probability distribution of a future state depends on the entire present and past history of the process, and the extreme of independence, or no memory, in which the probability distribution of a future state is entirely independent of present and past states.

Markov chain models have been extensively developed for reproduction, multiregional migration, intergenerational and intraorganisational mobility, population genetics, morbidity and health.   JEC

Reading

Bartholomew,D.J. 1982: *Stochastic models for social processes*. Third edition. New York and Chichester: Wiley.

Coleman, J.S. 1964: *Introduction to mathematical sociology*. New York: Free Press of Glencoe.

Feichtinger, G. 1971: *Stochastic Modelle demographischer Prozesse*. Berlin: Springer-Verlag.

Pollard, J.H. 1973: *Mathematical models for the growth of human populations*. Cambridge: Cambridge University Press.

Sheps, M.C. and Menken, J.A. 1973: *Mathematical models of conception and birth*. Chicago: University of Chicago Press.

marriage   The legal union of persons of opposite sex, the legality being established by civil, religious or other means according to the custom and laws of each country.

In virtually all societies socially sanctioned childbearing is limited to women in relatively stable sexual unions which are in most cases termed marriage. It is this connection to the fundamental process of reproduction that leads to marriage being regarded as a basic demographic phenomenon. Some societies recognise a variety of other forms of stable sexual union in addition to legal marriage, and in some analyses marriage is used as an omnibus word to cover all such unions. Many demographic measures and research strategies have been based on the assumption that marriage is a necessary and sufficient condition for childbearing, and these do not adapt well to more complex situations. Similarly, legal forms and statistical concepts sometimes fail to keep pace with reality when extra-marital cohabitation and reproduction are increasing, as is the case in many developed countries.

Demographic techniques are generally better developed for the study of the formation of marriage rather than its dissolution; methods of analysis of first marriages are particularly elaborate, with less attention given to remarriages. In all societies first marriage is a highly age-specific phenomenon, concentrated largely in the early adult years between the ages of fifteen and thirty. Because of this concentration demographers pay great attention to differentials or changes in the mean age at first marriage.   RP, CW

Reading

Sweet, J.A. 1982: Marriage and divorce. In J.A. Ross, ed. *International encyclopaedia of population*. New York: Free Press. Pp. 429–36.

marriage cohort   Individuals who marry during the same period (often one calendar year) and who are identified as a group in subsequent analysis.

Patterns of marital fertility are often best studied in terms of the experience of different marriage cohorts, particularly in countries with relatively low fertility where the impact of age on fertility rates may be less that that of marriage duration. Although normally referring to all marriages in a given period, more detailed specification of the marriage cohort is sometimes made, for example, first marriages only or marriages to women of certain ages.   RP, CW

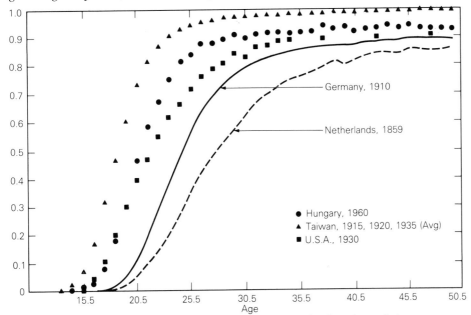

Marriage models: 1. Proportions ever-married, selected populations.

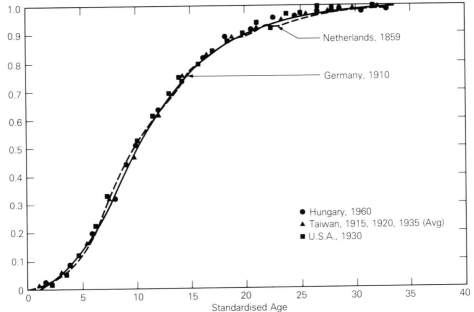

Marriage models: 2. Proportions ever-married, adjusted scale and origin using Coale model, selected populations.
Source: Coale 1977.

marriage models Mathematical constructs aimed at providing a description or explanation of marriage patterns, or, more generally, patterns of cohabitation in stable sexual unions.

Marriage models are often used to smooth irregularities in observed data and interpolate between or extrapolate beyond a limited set of values. One very widely employed model was devised by A.J. Coale (1971), who observed that the variation in the age-specific pattern of proportions of persons ever-married could be represented by variation in just three parameters: a_0 the lowest age at which a consequential number of persons marry, C the ultimate proportion of persons who do marry and k the speed with which marriage becomes a general phenomenon. By varying these factors any age pattern of first marriage can be related to a standard schedule of first marriages based on Swedish data of the nineteenth century. (See diagrams on p. 137.)

Most models of marriage describe the behaviour of each sex separately. A potentially more rewarding approach, however, is to analyse them simultaneously. One attempt to do this has been made by Henry (1972) who proposed that the matrix of marriages cross-classified by the age at marriage of both husband and wife could be disaggregated into submatrices within which marriage was a random phenomenon (termed panmictic circles by Henry). Similar decompositions based on other characteristics could also be made with the intention of identifying more clearly the social and geographical determinants of choice of partners. In spite of its potential Henry's model has been little used in English or American work RP, CW

References and Reading

Coale, A.J. 1971: Age patterns of marriage. *Population studies* 25, pp. 193–214.

Henry, L. 1972: Nuptiality. *Theoretical population biology* 3, pp. 135–52.

marriage rates Rates calculated to describe the occurrence of marriage in a population.

Crude marriage rates, giving the ratio of the total number of marriages to the total population during a specified period, are of little value in analysis since they are the product of many factors. Rates which specify marriage order, notably first marriage rates are more revealing. Above all, given the highly age-specific nature of marriages, rates classified by age are needed for full analysis. With age-specific first marriage rates it is possible to compute a NUPTIALITY TABLE in which lifetable techniques are employed to give a detailed probabilistic description of marriage. In view of the particular importance of the timing of first marriage and its relatively narrow age range, demographers often cite the SINGULATE MEAN AGE AT MARRIAGE, rather than marriage rates, as an indicator of nuptiality patterns.   CW

Reading

Shryock, H.S., Siegel, J.S. et al. 1976: *The methods and materials of demography.* Condensed edition by E.G. Stockwell. London and New York: Academic Press. Chapter 19.

Smith, P.C. 1982: Nuptiality indexes. In J.A. Ross, ed. *International encyclopaedia of population.* New York: Free Press. Pp. 492–8.

marriage squeeze An imbalance in the relative numbers of males and females available for marriage, caused by, for example, excess male mortality in war, sex-specific migration to some areas such as frontiers or cities, or fluctuating population growth rates (since men usually have a different mean age at marriage than women).   RDL

Reading

Ermisch, J.F. 1981: Economic opportunities, marriage squeezes and the propensity to marry: an economic analysis of period marriage rates in England and Wales. *Population studies* 35, pp. 347–56.

Schoen, R. 1983: Measuring the tightness of a marriage squeeze. *Demography* 20, pp. 61–78.

Marx, Karl. (1818–1883) The writings on population form only a tiny fraction of the corpus of Marx's works, but his stature has ensured that his analysis has been widely influential. In Marx's view many of the demographic characteristics of a population were determined by the fundamental economic constitution of the society in question, just as class relationships or political structure were similarly determined. Marx therefore postulated 'laws' of population peculiar to feudal or capitalist societies whose character stemmed from the economic circumstances produced by the relationships of ownership and production in such societies.

Industrial capitalist societies, for example, were characterised by what Marx termed relative surplus population, a condition brought about by the steady fall in variable capital as a proportion of total capital. Since employment opportunities depended upon the rate of growth of variable capital only, this tended to restrict progressively the rate of growth or even the absolute level of demand for labour.

'The labouring population therefore produces, along with the accumulation of capital produced by it, the means by which it itself is made relatively superfluous, is turned into relative surplus population; and it does this to an always increasing extent. This is a law of population peculiar to the capitalist mode of production; and in fact every special historic mode of production has its own special law of population, historically valid within its limits alone. An abstract law of population exists for plants and animals only, and only in so far as man has not interfered with them' (Marx 1887).

The progressive immiseration of the working classes came about in this way. Labour was incapable of commanding a wage higher than the minimum necessary to secure its own reproduction, a variant of the 'iron law of wages' of Ricardo.

Empirical demographic material does not figure very largely in Marx's works, though he was well informed about the very high levels of mortality found in many of the new industrial towns, and sometimes used mortality rates as a surrogate measure of poor living standards, bad environmental conditions, and the pres-

sures stemming from the existence of relative surplus population. This was to be expected because the capitalist mode of production 'extends the labourer's time of production during a given period by shortening his actual life time' (Marx 1887).

Marx's bitter condemnation of MALTHUS is well known. He took exception to what he saw as an attempt to justify the misery of working people by an appeal to a necessary feature of all societies when it should more justly have been seen as an evil associated with one type of society.   EAW

Reference
Marx, K. 1887: *Capital: a critical analysis of capitalist production.* Translated from the third German edition by S. Moore and E. Aveling. Two volumes. London: Swan, Sonnenschein, Lowry. Vol. i, p. 251 and vol. ii, p. 645.

Reading
Daly, H.E. 1971: A Marx-Malthus view of poverty and development. *Population studies* 25, pp. 25–37.
Hoselitz, B.F. 1964: Karl Marx on secular economic and social development. *Comparative studies in society and history* 8, pp. 42–61.
Keyfitz, N. 1982: Population theory. In J.A. Ross, ed. *International encyclopaedia of population.* New York: Free Press. Pp. 536–44.
Secombe, W. 1983: Marxism and demography. *New left review* 137, pp. 22–47.

matching   A form of RECORD LINKAGE defined in a DUAL RECORD SYSTEM as the process of identifying whether or not two reports on vital events, each obtained from two separate investigations, refer to the same individual or event.

A set of matching criteria, such as agreements on name, age and sex of the person involved, names of the parents, date of the event, etc., is applied to determine whether two reports match or do not match. Usually a tolerance limit and/or a weight, is prescribed for each matching criterion before the process begins. The purpose of matching is to classify events into groups of (1) those reported by both agencies, (2) those caught in the first operation but missed by the latter, and (3) those caught in the second operation but missed by the former. Application of matching procedures may give rise to erroneous matches or non-matches. To minimise these as well as to control for the possibility of events that are extraneous to the system being included in one of two operations, some dual record systems classify events into a fourth category of doubtful matches which are later re-verified in the field. Occasionally, as in the evaluation of the completeness of civil registration based on census returns, matching may be only one-way (i.e. the quality of only one of the sources of data is determined); but usually, as in PGE surveys, matching is two-way.   PNM-B

Reading

Madigan, F.C. and Wells, H.B. 1976: Report on matching procedures of a dual record system in the southern Philippines. *Demography* 13, pp. 381–95.

Marks, E.S., Seltzer, W. and Krotki, K.J. 1974: *Population growth estimation. A handbook of vital statistics measurement.* New York: Population Council.

Thomlinson, R. 1976: Matching experimentation in a dual record system for births and deaths in Morocco. *Population studies* 30, pp. 153–64.

Wagner, G. and Newcombe, H.B. 1970: Record linkage – its methodology and application in medical data processing. *Methods of information in medicine* 9, pp. 121–38.

maternal mortality Mortality from causes connected with pregnancy, labour or the puerperium (lying-in period).

A commonly calculated measure of the phenomenon is the maternal mortality rate which is usually taken to be the number of deaths from these causes divided by the number of live births and expressed per 10,000 or per 100,000. Although somewhat imprecise, since the denominator does not correspond exactly with the populaion at risk, the rate is normally the best choice given the available data. In developed countries the rate is very low (less than 1 death per 10,000 births), while

in historical populations values as high as two or three deaths per 100 births have been observed. Alternative measures, relating maternal deaths to the number of women of childbearing age, or to all pregnancies (including stillbirths and abortions) are also encountered.   RP

maternity history A term used to refer to a detailed account of the childbearing experience of a woman (or, less commonly, of a couple). The alternative terms birth history and reproductive history are also used.

The data are often collected in sample surveys and may refer to the experience up to the time of the survey. In contrast, histories assembled by record linkage from registration data more commonly involve a complete record of the reproductive years. The minimum information for detailed analysis is the woman's date of birth (or age at survey) and the dates of the various significant events in the history: marriage and the birth of each child. Beyond this most attempts to collect maternity histories ask for details of other relevant events (e.g. abortions, stillbirths or divorce) and for information on factors such as contraception or breastfeeding which also directly influence fertility. Less direct determinants such as education, economic status or religion are also commonly included.

The analysis of maternity histories has been the subject of considerable debate among demographers. The measures calculated from surveys are often the same as those conventionally used for registration data (e.g. age-specific fertility rates). Given the origins and nature of survey-based histories this is a dubious procedure, more illuminating analyses being based on the use of life table techniques to describe each segment of the history, i.e. each birth interval. Similarly, detailed analysis of maternity histories has provided new insights into the questions of selectivity and bias in many calculations.

RP, CW

mathematical demography The presentation in mathematical terms of the measures of demographic analysis and of the relations between them.

Mathematical formulations provide an increased precision in reasoning and results and have a long history in demography. The term 'incipient mathematical demography' has been used (Keyfitz 1982) for the work of GRAUNT, De Wit, and other seventeenth-century actuaries, and in particular for the work of EULER, whose devising of the fundamental bases of STABLE POPULATION theory (a life table and a constant rate of growth) made him a forerunner of modern mathematical demography. Work in the nineteenth century by GOMPERTZ and MAKEHAM who put forward mathematical models of mortality, has also been of continued relevance.

Probably the most fruitful branch of the subject, in terms both of theoretical insights and of practical applications, has been stable population theory which was reformulated in this century by Lotka, apparently unaware of Euler's 1760 work. Lotka's model enables the age distribution and vital rates of a stable population to be calculated given any combination of fertility and mortality. Although no population has ever been truly stable, the approximation to stability of many populations and the relative insensitivity of some features to violations of the stable assumption have enabled the theory to be widely used in demography and many other disciplines. The model has also served as a stimulus to further work. For example, Preston and Coale (1982) have generalised Lotka's equations so that they apply to any population, and many scholars have attempted to tackle the failure of stable theory to relate simultaneously to both sexes, the so-called two-sex problem.

The development of high-speed computers and matrix algebra have led mathematical demographers to an increased use of matrix models, one of the best known being the LESLIE MATRIX which formulates population dynamics in a discrete, rather than a continuous manner. The recent extension of matrix notation into MULTISTATE DEMOGRAPHY has been of considerable value, especially in the study of migration where MULTIREGIONAL DEMOGRAPHY has provided a way of integrating all aspects of population change. In principle, however, such MARKOV CHAIN MODELS are applicable to many processes. Computers have become invaluable aids to the mathematical demographer and much work now leans heavily on numerical analysis similar to that seen in engineering or physics. Two further areas where computers have made a particular impact are SIMULATION, especially using STOCHASTIC MODELS, and the use of elaborate statistical methods such as log-linear modelling.

A good example of the way in which mathematical reasoning can illuminate a problem and make it amenable to solution is the development of models of the PROXIMATE DETERMINANTS of fertility. Early discussion of the social and biological determinants of fertility was marked by an awareness of their complexity. Mathematical modelling of the reproductive process, combined with more data on the variation in these factors seen in real populations, enabled simpler and more informative models to be developed. The well-known BONGAARTS' DECOMPOSITION, for example, involves only four factors.

An important area in which mathematical demography has implications for wider analysis is the question of bias and selectivity in the data. These cause problems at present since demographic processes do not take place in isolation, and mortality (and migration) are liable to disturb the phenomena under study (see DISTURBING PROCESS). Mathematical demographers have been able to show that the calculated indices will only truly reflect actual behaviour if these disturbances are independent of the studied process (see NON-SELECTIVITY).   RP, CW

142   **maximum population**

References

Keyfitz, N. 1982: Mathematical demography. In J.A. Ross, ed. *International encyclopaedia of population*. New York: Free Press. Pp. 437–43.

Preston, S.H. and Coale, A.J. 1982: Age structure, growth, attrition and accession: a new synthesis. *Population index* 48, pp. 217–59.

Reading

Keyfitz, N. 1977: *Applied mathematical demography*. London and New York: Wiley.
— 1982.

Preston and Coale 1982.

Smith, D. and Keyfitz, N. eds. 1977: *Mathematical demography: selected papers*. New York and Berlin: Springer Verlag.

maximum population The maximum size which may be reached by a population, living in isolation, in a given environment and with a given level of technological development. The term carrying capacity is used synonymously.

This absolute maximum may be seen as the result of an egalitarian distribution of resources satisfying minimum physiological needs. A ceiling would be reached, and any subsequent pursuit of population growth would quickly be blocked by a lack of per capita resources bringing about an increase in mortality. The population figure would thus be brought back to the possible maximum value. On to this principle of maximum population may be grafted other concepts dealing with wider needs in relation to living standards, defined according to the frameworks of different social systems introducing greater or lesser degrees of inequality between individuals.

All else being equal, it is technological development, with the increase in the means for subsistence and the more effective action against mortality which it makes possible, that is the most significant factor in the raising of the maximum population level. In the past, populations may have reached the maximum levels then possible, levels which, incidentally, fluctuated with the unpredictability of agricultural production. Wars and, more importantly, epidemics were other factors regulating population size and may have kept numbers below the limits of the available means of subsistence. Current speculation as to the maximum world population have given rise to wide variations in estimates going up to several tens of billions. The uncertainty of these calculations is related to the lack of precision with which it is possible to specify future living conditions and technological advance.   RP

Reading

Sauvy, A. 1969: *General theory of population*. London: Weidenfeld and Nicholson. Chapter 2.

mean age at childbearing The mean age of mothers at the birth of their children. The measure is referred to in many different ways: mean age of mothers, mean age at reproduction, mean age of fertility and so on.

There are two differing definitions. Most commonly the age referred to is calculated as a weighted average of the set of AGE-SPECIFIC FERTILITY RATES or of AGE-SPECIFIC MARITAL FERTILITY RATES, the weights being the mid-point of each age group (17.5 for the 15–19 age group, 22.5 for 20–24 and so on). This definition eliminates the effects of differences in the age-sex structure of populations and may be interpreted as the mean for a hypothetical cohort of women experiencing the given rates over their lifetimes. In order to draw attention to the fact that the measure ignores the age structure, it is sometimes referred to as the mean age of the fertility schedule. In contrast, the actual mean age of mothers in any population reflects the age structure as well as the age pattern of fertility. In some circumstances this measure is also calculated and termed the mean age of childbearing in the population, to indicate the difference between it and the conventional definition.

A further measure is the mean age of net reproduction, (or mean age at net maternity) in which the age pattern of both fertility and mortality are taken into account. It is normally only employed with reference to the NET REPRODUCTION RATE. RP, CW

mean age at first marriage The average age at which individuals marry for the first time.

The age is quoted for cohorts and for periods, using the concept of a hypothetical cohort. The mean is most precisely specified within a NUPTIALITY TABLE.

A widely used variant is the SINGULATE MEAN AGE AT MARRIAGE (SMAM) which employs census information on the proportions never-married in each age group to create a synthetic estimate of the mean. Interpretation of the SMAM is complicated, however, when marriage patterns are changing. A variety of other measures of the TEMPO of marriage are also used, the median age being the most often quoted. CW

Reading
Shryock, H.S., Siegel, J.S. et al. 1976: *The methods and materials of demography*. Condensed edition by E. G. Stockwell. London and New York: Academic Press. Pp. 165–8 and 340–2.

mean age at marriage The average age at which individuals marry. An essential distinction is that between remarriages and the MEAN AGE AT FIRST MARRIAGE. More attention is paid by demographers to the latter. (See also MARRIAGE and SINGULATE MEAN AGE AT MARRIAGE.) CW

mean length of generation See GENERATION.

mean population See MID-YEAR POPULATION.

median age at death The age at which, in terms of a LIFE TABLE, the initial number of survivors (the radix, l_0) is reduced to half its initial value (i.e. with a radix of 10,000, when 5000 persons are still alive). This rarely corresponds to an exact age, so interpolation between the two values on either side of the median is normally required. Except in populations with very high infant and child mortality the median age at death usually exceeds the life expectancy at birth. RP

menarche The first menstruation in a woman's life. Menarche marks the potential beginning of the childbearing years, but full FECUNDITY is not established until several years later. During the transition period the girl experiences ADOLESCENT SUBFECUNDITY. Menarche usually takes place in the early or mid-teens. The mean age at menarche is near 13 in modern developed countries and slightly higher in poor, malnourished populations. JB

Reading
Hafez, E.S.E. and Evans, T.N., eds. 1980: *Human reproduction: conception and contraception*. Hagerstown, Maryland: Harper and Row.
Wyshak, G. and Frish, R.E. 1982: Evidence for a secular decline in age of menarche. *New England journal of medicine* 306, pp. 1033–5.

menopause The permanent cessation of menstruation at the end of the reproductive years. Menopause marks the end point of a transition period of up to several years during which female FECUNDITY gradually approaches zero. This impairment of fecundity is the result of a decline in the regularity of menstruation, and increase in the incidence of anovulatory cycles and a rise in intrauterine mortality.

The mean age at menopause of most populations for which measurements exist falls between ages 45 and 50, but the age of menopause of individual women ranges from less than 40 to near 60. JB

Reading
Beard, R.J., ed. 1976: *The menopause*. London: MTP Press.
Hafez, E.S.E. and Evans, T.N., eds. 1980: *Human reproduction: conception and contraception*. Hagerstown, Maryland: Harper and Row.

menstrual regulation Aspiration of the uterus in the two weeks following the absence of menses. The operation is sometimes termed 'mini-suction'.

Menstrual regulation is a fairly painless practice which serves either to trigger the menses, in cases where their absence is not related to a pregnancy, or else as an abortion. Proponents of this practice justify it as being reassuring for women worried about pregnancy and without the means of ending it later. One of the major disadvantages of the operation is its indiscriminate nature, linked to the impossibility of ascertaining whether there is a pregnancy or not, which leads to the carrying out of unnecessary surgery. On the other hand it is this indiscriminate and therefore ambiguous nature which makes menstrual regulation admissible in countries where possibilities for the interruption of pregnancy are very limited. A recently-developed method of menstrual regulation makes use of prostaglandins which act to release the physiological mechanism for the evacuation of the uterus, and may constitute an important improvement on methods of a surgical nature.   RP

Reading
Plaskon, V. 1982: Abortion: medical techniques. In J.A. Ross, ed. *International encyclopaedia of population*. New York: Free Press. Pp. 8–11.

metropolitan area A term first used in the United States to describe a very large urban settlement. Definitions vary between countries, but a population of at least 100,000 and containing one or more centres with 50,000 inhabitants is typical. Areas bordering the city which are socially and economically integrated with it are included. In the 1910 US census various Metropolitan districts were defined, and in 1950 the concept of a Standard Metropolitan Statistical Area (SMSA) was introduced in America. In view of the close links, especially through commuting, between cities and their hinterlands, some studies employ the concept of a Metropolitan Labour Area.   CW

Reading
Murphy, R.E. 1974: *The American city: an urban geography*. Second edition. New York: McGraw-Hill.

microcensus A large-scale sample survey conducted at regular intervals with the aim of obtaining a fuller understanding of particular issues and following trends over time in ways not possible in a full CENSUS. The term is most frequently used to refer to data collection operations in parts of Europe, most notably in the Federal Republic of Germany, though recurrent large-scale surveys are undertaken in many countries.   RP

microsimulation See SIMULATION.

mid-year population The size of a population (or any specified group within the population) at the mid-point of a calendar year, often calculated as the arithmetic mean of the size at the beginning and the end of the year. Assuming a linear variation over time the mid-year population can be taken to be the mean value for the year and used in the denominator of various rates. It is equivalent to the number of PERSON-YEARS lived during the year. The concept is often extended to cover periods of more than one year when the term mid-interval population is employed.   RP

migration Movement of individuals or groups which involves a permanent or semi-permanent change of usual residence. In contrast the term mobility is used for all forms of spatial mobility, whether permanent or temporary.

The precise definition of a migratory move varies with the analysis in hand, though three dimensions are normally considered. The first is the permanence of a move: tourist trips (over no matter what distance), commuting and nomadic movements are not part of migration, though they may be classified as CIRCULATION. The second dimension is that of distance, or more precisely the crossing of some administrative boundary. Whatever the spatial level of the study a 'migration-defining area' is always used as a reference. Third, a consideration of the time within which moves have taken place will be needed, leading to the concept (either explicit or implicit) of a 'migration-defining period'. A broad distinction is made between internal and international migration, the former almost always being the more common phenomenon. Many qualifiers are applied to migration to specify its nature or causes.

Migration is enormously influential in determining the size and composition of population, especially at a local level, and in many countries regional differentials in net migration are significantly greater than analogous differences in fertility and mortality.

Data on migration are drawn from several sources. POPULATION REGISTERS potentially provide the most complete information, though the time-consuming nature of the record-linkage needed to exploit them reduces their practical usefulness in many cases. International moves are sometimes studied through analysis of statistics on border crossings or air and sea passenger movements, but these are often difficult to deal with. The most general source of data is the census, which commonly includes questions on place of birth and residence at earlier dates. The detail obtained in this way is limited, however, and special surveys producing a MIGRATION HISTORY for each person questioned offer more scope for analysis.

Partly because of the variety of source material and partly because much spatial analysis has been conducted by geographers, the techniques of migration analysis have developed along somewhat different lines from other areas of demography. In recent years, however, the increased use of MULTIREGIONAL DEMOGRAPHY and concern over the analysis of migration histories have produced a greater convergence.   RP, CW

Reading
Brown, A. A. and Neuberger. E., eds. 1977: *Internal migration: a comparative perspective.* London and New York: Academic Press.

Haenszel, W. 1967: Concept, measurement and data in migration analysis. *Demography* 4, pp. 253–61.
Lee, E.S. 1966: A theory of migration. *Demography*, 3, pp. 47–57.
Shryock, H.S., Siegel, J.S. et al. 1976: *The methods and materials of demography.* London and New York: Academic Press. Chapters 20 and 21.

migration field   An area in which well-established migration paths and institutions operate; or an area encompassing the origins of migrants to a particular destination. Such areas are usually perpetuated by 'positive feedback'. Although often small-scale, describing movement within a localised labour or marriage market, a migration field may encompass long-range movement in a CIRCULAR MIGRATION system.   DCS

Reading
Hägerstrand, T. 1957: Migration and area. In D. Hanneberg et al., eds. *Migration in Sweden.* Lund studies in geography. Lund, Sweden: Gleerup.

migration history   A form of LIFE HISTORY giving data on previous residences of an individual or family with dates of moving.

Migration histories are sometimes compiled from POPULATION REGISTERS, but they are more commonly derived from retrospective questions in a census or survey. Surveys do not usually attempt to record all the moves an individual has made, but concentrate on moves within a specified period before the survey and the place of birth. In addition to information on moves, histories frequently also ask about reasons for moving. Migration histories are a potentially rich source of data on mobility, but the lack of standardised questions and definitions, with attendant methodological problems, makes comparative analysis difficult.   RP, CW

migration matrix   A two-dimensional table containing the GROSS MIGRATION flows from origin areas (rows of the table) to destination areas (columns of the table).

Migration is defined as a change of permanent residence by a person. Some four principal types of migration matrix can be distinguished: *lifetime migration* tables with areas of birth as rows and areas of current residence as columns; *fixed period migration* tables with areas of residence a specified number of years previously as rows and areas of current residence as columns; *last residence migration* tables with areas of last residence as rows and areas of current residence as columns; *movement migration* tables with areas of residence prior to the move as rows and areas of residence after the move as columns. Migration matrices for different age groups are essential inputs in MULTIREGIONAL DEMOGRAPHY and in multiregional demographic accounting. A major body of literature has been devoted to the explanation of the patterns of gross migration flows in terms of origin characteristics, destination conditions, and the channels of communication between them.   PR

Reading

Courgeau, D. 1980: *L'analyse quantitative des migrations humaines*. Paris: Masson.

Hägerstrand, T. 1957: Migration and area. In D. Hannersberg et al., eds. *Migration in Sweden*. Lund studies in human geography series. Lund, Sweden: Gleerup.

Rees, P.H. 1977: The measurement of migration from census data and other sources. *Environment and planning A* 9, pp. 247–72.

migration models A theoretical construct, often expressed mathematically, which attempts to explain observed patterns of migration.

Although not formulated mathematically RAVENSTEIN'S 'LAWS' OF MIGRATION of the nineteenth century contained the implicit basis of the size-distance rule, which states that the migration between two places is proportional to their size and inversely proportional to thre distance between them. This idea, known as the GRAVITY MODEL was formalized by George Zipf as:

$$M_{12} = k \frac{P_1 P_2}{D}$$

where M_{12} is the migration between two populations P_1 and P_2 separated by distance D and k is a constant. Variation in k and raising D to different powers n gives the model added flexibility.

The simple gravity model was modified by S.A. Stouffer who introduced the concept of INTERVENING OPPORTUNITIES which stated that the number of migrants over a certain distance is proportional to the opportunities (broadly defined) at that distance and inversely related to the opportunities in between. This modification lends further flexibility to the gravity formulation.

A number of recent models are expressed in terms of individual decisions and perceptions. Many of these explicitly use the concept of COST-BENEFIT ANALYSIS, although increasingly emphasis has been placed on the expectations of migrants, rather than real economic benefits, as an impetus to migrate. A recognition of the role of variation within a population has led to the elaboration of mover-stayer models which distinguish frequent 'movers' from the relatively static 'stayers'. These models use matrix algebra to give mathematical form to their ideas, as do the models underlying MULTIREGIONAL DEMOGRAPHY.   RP, CW

Reading

McNamara, R. 1982: Internal migration: models. In J.A. Ross, ed. *International encyclopaedia of population*. New York: Free Press. Pp. 351–3.

Shaw, R.P. 1975: *Migration theory and fact: a review and bibliography of current literature*. Philadelphia: Regional Science Research Institute.

migration probability See MIGRATION RATES.

migration rates The measures used in migration analysis have developed somewhat differently from other demographic analysis. In part this reflects differences in the source data and in part it reflects the fact that migration has only recently been generally integrated in demographic models and theories.

The most basic indications of migration relate it to the total population. The in-migration rate IR (immigration rate for international migration) is defined as:

$$IR = \frac{I}{P} \times k$$

where I is the number of migrants into an area, P is the area's population and k is a constant, often 1000. Analogously the out-migration rate (emigration rate), OR, is taken to be:

$$OR = \frac{O}{P} \times k$$

where O is the number of outmigrants. The rate of NET MIGRATION, NR, follows from these definitions as:

$$NR = \frac{I - O}{P} \times k$$

Only the out-migration rate corresponds to the concept of a rate as a number of events divided by a population at risk. Nevertheless the other rates are widely cited despite their logical ambiguities. Net migration is also commonly estimated from census data using forward or reverse survival techniques. Gross migration has hitherto received less attention because of the greater difficulty which often exists in estimating it, though the development of MULTIREGIONAL DEMOGRAPHY, which requires gross migration flows as an input, has made it the subject of more frequent study.

More specific rates for age groups, socio-economic categories and regions, are also calculated, and the rates for each age group are combined to form a migration schedule. A major step forward in recent years has been the development of model migration schedules with uses simi-lar to those of model life tables. Probabilities of migration are often calculated in the context of age-specific measures which make possible the use of life-table methods.   RP, CW

Reading

Haenszel, W. 1967: Concept, measurement and data in migration analysis. *Demography* 4, pp. 253–61.

Land, K.C. and Rogers, A., eds. 1982: *Multidimensional mathematical demography*. New York and London: Academic Press.

Shryock, H.S., Siegel, J.S. et al. 1976: *The methods and materials of demography*. New York and London: Academic Press. Chapters 20 and 21.

migration schedule See MIGRATION RATES.

Milne, Joshua (1776–1851) English actuary and author of the first scientifically correct LIFE TABLE. Published in 1815 Milne's life table was based on data for Carlisle during the period 1779–87 and used information classified by age at death and the population at risk of dying. This method of construction is closely related to modern methods, unlike previous life tables, which could only be regarded as accurate given unrealistic assumptions. CW

Reading

Milne, J. 1977: A treatise on the valuation of annuities and assurances on lives and survivors (1815). In D. Smith and N. Keyfitz, eds. *Mathematical demography: selected papers.* Berlin and New York: Springer Verlag. Pp. 27–34.

minimum life table See LONGEVITY.

minimum population The minimum number of members necessary for a population living in isolation to ensure its survival.

Obstacles to the survival of a small group are manifold. First, there are those encountered by all ISOLATES, which relate to the dangers inherent in the frequent practice of consanguineous marriages. There are also the dangers in having very few members: the increased risk of being wiped out in a single epidemic; the possibility of a chance drop in the sex ratio leading to an imbalance between the sexes which will later be prejudicial to universal nuptiality. This may both encourage consanguineous marriages and reduce the birth rate. However, the influence of this last factor may be modified through polygamy. In addition to these problems, there are those caused by the absolute physical isolation of the population, which may be economic (unsatisfactory distribution between producers and non-producers) or else related to the physical environment (as being more or less favourable). It is impossible to fix minimum population membership in any final, uniform way. It was suggested by the Italian demographer Livio Livi that demographic stability and continuity are ensured only when a population numbers over 500, and that isolated groups of between 300 and 500 are often in a state of imbalance, leading either to stability or to their rapid disappearance.

RP

Reading

Sauvy, A. 1969: *General theory of population.* London: Weidenfeld and Nicholson. Chapter 3.

mobility   All phenomena involving the displacement of individuals. The term MIGRATION is used only for movement involving a permanent or semi-permanent change of usual residence. The term mobility is also used when dealing with SOCIAL MOBILITY and occupational mobility. Its use without one of these qualifiers usually implies spatial movement.   RP

modal age at death   The age or age-group at which the largest number of deaths occurs in a LIFE TABLE.

Given that risks of dying are highest in infancy and old age, the modal age at death is either zero (where infant mortality is high) or some age towards the end of life, often the final age-group (e.g. 85 plus) in low-mortality populations. The particular value of the mode is of little signifi-

cance, and the statistic is only rarely quoted.   RP

model   A theoretical construct representing a demographic phenomenon or a population.

Models are used in the study of most aspects of demography and can be divided into those which attempt accurately to describe the process or population studied, those used to demonstrate underlying relationships between demographic variables which may not be immediately apparent, and those linking demographic phenomena to outside factors, particularly economic and social characteristics.

The earliest demographic models aimed at describing mortality and were constructed by Gompertz and Makeham. Advances in the field of modelling mortality have led to the development of MODEL LIFE TABLES based on increasingly sophisticated descriptions of observed age patterns. Similar work in other areas has produced age-specific models of other processes: fertility, nuptiality and migration. Many of these models are used in the analysis of data from statistically underdeveloped areas or historical sources where they provide a basis for the calculation of detailed results from limited data.

In addition to acting as an aid to description, models are widely used in demography to identify variables which play a critical role in population change, to demonstrate the interrelationships between variables and to clarify the implications of demographic trends. Without doubt the most influential model of population dynamics is the STABLE POPULATION, first devised by Euler in 1760, but deriving its modern form from the work of Lotka. Assuming constant rates of mortality and fertility over time, a population will ultimatley assume a fixed age structure whatever its initial characteristics. The stable population model also produces relatively simple expressions of the interdependence of demographic variables and throws light on problems which may otherwise remain intractable. For example it proves that fertility change has a greater impact on the age structure than does mortality change.

Another topic in which models have been used to demonstrate underlying relationships is fertility, where models demonstrating the roles of the various PROXIMATE DETERMINANTS: contraception, abortion, breastfeeding, etc. have been highly influential.

Models linking demographic characteristics to other variables are also in wide use, economic models of fertility and migration being particularly common. The acceptance of such models, however, has been less universal than those restricted to purely demographic interrelations, partly because no economic or social models can realistically aspire to the generality of models such as the stable population. The most pervasive model linking economic and social variables with population trends is that of the DEMOGRAPHIC TRANSITION, though much recent analysis casts doubt on the utility of even this general model.   RP, CW

Reading

Coale, A.J. 1977: The development of new models of nuptiality and fertility. *Population* 32, special number, pp. 131–54.

Keyfitz, N. 1977: *Applied mathematical demography*. London and New York: Wiley.

Ryder, N.B. 1975: Notes on stationary populations. *Population index* 41, pp.3–27.

model life tables Systems of hypothetical schedules describing variations in mortality by sex and age, normally in terms of a limited number of constants (parameters). The resulting frameworks of the possible structure of LIFE TABLES have many uses.

The demographic applications of model life tables are varied but can be broadly classified into two areas: the estimation of life tables from limited or deficient data and the projection of future trends. Estimation from limited information is necessary because for most of the world's

population this is all that is available. The function of models here is to enable disparate and biased pieces of information to be interpreted and made to yield more conventional and useful indices of mortality. Projection of future population can also be described in some ways as a problem of inevitably limited information.

The search for mathematical representations of mortality is almost as old as demography, but it is only in the last 30 years that convenient and detailed model life tables have been developed, often using RELATIONAL MODELS. These concentrate on variation in mortality between populations, (or between levels of mortality), taking the age pattern of death to be determined by general regular patterns. The first such system constructed was constructed by the United Nations (1955) and used the averaging of empirical data to produce a 'typical' age pattern at each level of mortality. This pioneering work was largely superseded by the publication of the COALE-DEMENY MODEL LIFE TABLES in 1966. These allowed greater flexibility by providing four families or 'regions' of age-specific mortality patterns at each level of mortality. They were based principally on life tables from Europe and North America in the nineteenth and twentieth centuries, from which a series of regression equations were derived to provide the mortality model. The ease of use and compendious detail of Coale and Demeny's tabulations has led to them being the most widely used model life tables. A slightly revised version was published in 1983.

An alternative approach was made by Ledermann (1969) who estimated that five parameters (or degrees of freedom) were needed accurately to reflect the observed variation in mortality. His system of model life tables based on five parameters, however, was less workable than others and the apparent gains over simpler arrangements were modest. In spite of its theoretical advantages, Ledermann's system is rarely employed. In wider use is the

LOGIT LIFE TABLE SYSTEM constructed by Brass (1971). This is based on the assumption that, once the probabilities of surviving to each age are transformed by the LOGIT function, a linear relation exists between different populations. The system has great flexibility and, although so far mainly used for work on developing countries, is applicable to any population.

One irony about many of the model life table systems is that whereas they are most frequently employed to analyse Third World data, the models are largely or entirely based on mortality patterns from developed countries. In an attempt to overcome this a second set of United Nations model life tables was produced in 1982, based on life tables from 22 developing countries. The development of the system led to the classification of data into different groups (Latin America, South Asia, etc.), and to the explicit consideration of the different relationships between male and female mortality in the various areas.   RP, CW

References

Brass, W. 1971: On the scale of mortality. In W. Brass, ed. *Biological aspects of demography*. London: Taylor and Francis. Pp. 69–110.

Coale, A.J. and Demeny, P. 1966: *Regional model life tables and stable populations*. Princeton, NJ: Princeton University Press.

— with Vaughan, B. 1983: *Regional model life tables and stable populations*. Second edition. New York and London: Academic Press.

Ledermann, S. 1969: *Nouvelles tables-types de mortalité*. Institut National d'Études Démographiques. Cahier 53. Paris: Presses Universitaires de France.

United Nations 1955: *Age and sex patterns of mortality: model life-tables for under-developed countries*. Population studies 22. New York: Department of Social Affairs.

— 1982: *Model life tables for developing countries*. Population studies 77. New York: Department of International Social and Economic Affairs.

Reading

Brass 1971.
Coale et al. 1983.
United Nations 1982.

momentum The increase (or decrease) in population size which would occur if the fertility of a population changed immediately to the level which would just ensure the replacement of each generation.

Because growing populations have large proportions of children the growth rate will not fall to zero at once, even if replacement level fertility is achieved, since the large cohorts born at a time of high fertility will still have more children than earlier smaller cohorts. Keyfitz (1971) has shown that the amount of growth 'built-in' to a population's age structure can be estimated on the basis of its current birth rate, the level of mortality (as represented by its LIFE EXPECTANCY) and the NET REPRODUCTION RATE. In certain circumstances a doubling of present numbers could be expected and in many countries an increase of 50 per cent or more would occur. In countries with low growth rates, however, the momentum of present age structures is minimal.

The theory of demographic momentum is based on Lotka's STABLE POPULATION model. In one sense the momentum of a population can be regarded as the opposite of the INTRINSIC RATE OF NATURAL INCREASE. This rate indicates the growth rate implicit in current fertility and mortality patterns ignoring the age structure, while the momentum shows the growth potential implied by the age structure alone. The large momentum of most countries in the developing world ensures that they will continue to grow, even if fertility falls rapidly. Given a more realistic trend in fertility than an immediate fall to replacement levels it is reasonable to expect most countries to at least more than double their present populations.   RP

Reference

Keyfitz, N. 1971: On the momentum of population growth. *Demography* 8, pp. 71–80.

Reading

Keyfitz 1971.
Ryder, N.B. 1975: Notes on stationary populations. *Population index* 41, pp. 3–27.

morbidity The state of illness and disability in a population (from Latin *morbus*, disease). Morbidity statistics are based on causes of death drawn from death certificates, on data from hospital and other institutional records, and on data obtained by special health or morbidity surveys, either cross-sectional or longitudinal. Moreover in many countries the occurrence of certain diseases (e.g. several infectious diseases, cancer and mental illness) has to be reported to the health authorities.

Morbidity data are usually classified according to the INTERNATIONAL CLASSIFICATION OF DISEASES, and are broken down according to such variables as age, sex, place of residence, and socio-economic characteristics. These tabulations can be useful in determining the etiology (or causes) of a disease. EPIDEMIOLOGY distinguishes between the incidence of disease, i.e. the number of new cases observed during a specified period, and its prevalence, the number of persons ill at a given moment (point prevalence) or during a given period (period prevalence). Duration of illness is measured as the length of time elapsed between onset and termination of disease. The PREVALENCE RATE varies with the product of the incidence rate and the average duration of a disease. In particular, when incidence and duration remain constant the prevalence rate will equal the product of incidence rate and duration.   GW

Reading
Biraben, J.N. 1982: Morbidity and the major processes culminating in death. In S. H. Preston, ed. *Biological and social aspects of mortality and the length of life*. Liège: Ordina Editions.
Chaire Quetelet 1982: *Morbidité et mortalité aux âges adultes dans les pays développés*. Louvain-la-Neuve, Belgium: Cabay.
Freeman, J. and Hutchison, G.B. 1980: Prevalence: incidence and duration. *American journal of epidemiology* 112, pp. 707–23.
Holland, W.W., Ipsen, J. and Kostrzewski, J., eds. 1979: *Measurement of levels of health*. World Health Organisation, regional publications, European series 7. Copenhagen: WHO.

MacMahon, B. and Pugh, T.E. 1970: *Epidemiology, principles and methods*. Boston: Little, Brown and Company.
Pollard, A.H. 1980: The interactions between morbidity and mortality. *Journal of the Institute of Actuaries* 107, pp. 233–302.
Ware, J.E., Brook, R.H., Davies, A.R. and Lohr, K.L. 1981: Choosing measures of health status for individuals in general populations. *American journal of public health* 71, pp. 620–25.

morning-after pill See POST-COITAL CONTRACEPTION.

mortality The process whereby deaths occur in a population.

The statistical study of death was the origin of demography, and mortality forms one of the principal foci of modern research.

The word mortality refers implicitly to the underlying conditions with regard to death, rather than to specific measures which may be affected by other factors. For example the CRUDE DEATH RATE reflects a population's age structure as well as the prevailing patterns of mortality. Other measures, such as LIFE EXPECTANCY, are more revealing and are normally understood when phrases such as 'high mortality' are employed. The age at which death is likely to occur and its cause vary greatly from country to country and according to such factors as age, sex, social class and occupation within each country. The two classifications which form the basis of analysis are age and CAUSE OF DEATH.

In the general population age is by far the most significant determinant of death rates. For example, for females in Japan in 1965 the death rate for the 10–14 age group was 4.8 per 10,000 whereas it was 2607 per 10,000 for those over 85. The importance of age-specific variation in mortality has long been clear, leading to the development of the LIFE TABLE as the main tool of analysis. In comparison, when examining whole populations the variations are less extreme; virtually the entire range of variation between populations is covered by life expectancies of between 20 and 80 years.

The cause of death also varies greatly; EXOGENOUS MORTALITY from such infectious diseases as plague, smallpox and tuberculosis is a principal cause of high mortality, whereas deaths from endogenous causes (above all cancer and cardiovascular disease) predominate in developed countries. (See also DIFFERENTIAL MORTALITY.)   RP, CW

mortality crisis   See CRISIS.

mother tongue   The language spoken at home in earliest childhood. A distinction is made between the mother tongue and the usual language, which is the one customarily spoken, though this distinction is not always easy among bilingual or multilingual persons. Censuses often collect statistics according to one or other of these definitions, often with the intention of acquiring information on ethnic status when direct questions on the matter may be regarded as controversial. In some countries, however, language is itself regarded as a sensitive issue, especially where it is closely linked to significant ethnic differences. In these circumstances questions on language may be omitted from census schedules.   RP

multigravida   See PREGNANCY ORDER.

multiparous   See PARITY.

multiple births   In all human populations a proportion of confinements results in more than one birth, most commonly twins. A fundamental distinction is that between monozygotic (MZ) twins resulting from the ovum splitting after fertilisation and dizygotic (DZ) multiple births, which are the result of multiple ovulation and the simultaneous fertilisation of more than one ovum. MZ twins are identical in their genetic make-up; DZ twins are no more alike than any two siblings.

The proportion of confinements which

result in the birth of MZ twins is largely invariant in all populations, and at all ages of mothers (around 4 per 1000 confinements). The rate of DZ twinning is variable, however, both by age of mother and in different populations. In most populations the rate rises steadily up to about age 40 then declines steeply, though in some cases high rates are observed up to age 45. The highest recorded frequencies of DZ twinning are in black populations in Africa and America (over 20 per 1000 confinements in some areas), whereas the lowest rates are observed in East Asia (2 to 3 per 1000 confinements in Japan, for example). Evidence from couples of different races suggests that the mother's genetic make-up is of primary importance in determining these differences (Khoury and Erickson 1983). In most developed countries the DZ twinning rate declined significantly during the 1960s and 1970s. The causes of this decline are still not entirely clear. The overall result of both forms of twinning is that about one person in 80 is a twin in populations of European origin. Triplets and larger groups of multiple births are much rarer. A broadly accurate empirical rule (Hellin's rule) states that the frequency of triplets is approximately the square of the twinning rate, and the frequency of quadruplets approximately the cube.

Because they are genetically identical MZ twins have been widely studied by psychologists and geneticists in attempts to ascertain the relative importance of genetic inheritance and environment in various aspects of life. Twins, especially second-born twins, have a much higher risk of dying in infancy or of being stillborn. In Belgium, for example, throughout the period from 1920 to 1972 the infant mortality and stillbirth rates for twins were around three times those of singletons.   CW

Reference

Khoury, M.J. and Erickson, J.D. 1983: Maternal factors in dizygotic twinning: evidence from interracial crosses. *Annals of human biology* 10, pp. 409–16.

Reading

Bulmer, M.G. 1970: *The biology of twinning in man*. Oxford: Oxford University Press.

Cavalli-Sforza, L.L. and Bodmer, W.F. 1971: *The genetics of human populations*. San Francisco: W.H. Freeman. Pp. 565–97.

multiple decrement life table   A life table in which an initial population is subject to more than one risk of attrition. Double or triple decrement tables, with two and three risks respectively, are particular examples.

Multiple decrement life tables are a straightforward extension of the conventional single-decrement variety and enable the effects of several competing risks to be examined simultaneously. They have been used to study mortality from several causes of death (Preston et al. 1972) and to construct nuptiality tables in which the single population is reduced through both marriage and mortality.

Although potentially very useful, multiple decrement approaches have not been widely used in demography. Indeed, as Keyfitz (1982) has pointed out, the methodology is more widely employed in studies of reliability engineering (i.e. where several parts of a machine may break down) than in demography where the technique originated. The development of MULTISTATE DEMOGRAPHY, with its emphasis on multiple INCREMENT-DECREMENT LIFE TABLES seems likely to lead to a wider use of multidimensional approaches.   RP, CW

References

Keyfitz, N. 1982: Mathematical demography. In J.A. Ross, ed. *International encyclopaedia of population*. New York: Free Press. Pp. 437–43.

Preston, S.H., Keyfitz, N. and Schoen, R. 1972: *Cause of death: life tables for national populations*. New York: Seminar Press. Chapter 2.

Reading

Shryock, H.S., Siegel, J.S. et al. 1976: *The methods and materials of demography*. Condensed edition by E.G. Stockwell. London and New York: Academic Press. Chapter 15.

multiregional demography   The branch of demography devoted to the study of the population dynamics of many regions simultaneously. It is the version of MULTI-STATE DEMOGRAPHY in which the states of principal interest are geographical regions. Three models in conventional demography have been generalised from single region into multiregional form.

> The 'national' demographic accounts model developed by Stone (1971) has been converted into a multiregional accounts model by Rees and Wilson (1977).
>
> The matrix cohort survival model of Leslie (1945) and others has been converted into a multiregional cohort survival model by Rogers (1968).
>
> The single population LIFE TABLE model has been generalised in multiregional matrix form, also by Rogers (1975).

Methods and computer programs for multiregional life table analysis and projection are elegantly outlined in Willekens and Rogers (1978). Both the multiregional cohort survival model and the multiregional life table model can be most consistently derived from the multiregional accounts model.

The multiregional forms of these demographic models have a key advantage over their conventional equivalents. Population change in one region is affected by the number of migrations from other regions and hence is dependent on the population size of those origin regions and the propensity of people to migrate out of them. Only multiregional models incorporate such interactions. Single region models, even with net migration components, fail to reflect these relations. The disadvantage of multiregional models is their need for input data, namely MIGRATION MATRICES for each age group used in the model.

These models have many uses. Multiregional accounts models have demonstrated the sensitivity of any projection of the population of a set of regions to the way in which the system is 'closed' (Rees 1979), and the findings of the multiregional cohort survival model and the multiregional life table model have been used extensively in the Migration and Settlement Project at the International Institute for Applied Systems Analysis to study the population dynamics of many countries. Rogers (1983) gives a summary of the results of the project in the course of which estimates were made, for the first time, of the distribution of the expected life of a regional birth cohort across other regions of residence for some seventeen countries. The process of migration was shown, under certain assumptions, to be instrumental in evening out the disparities in life expectancy among regions within a country.   PR

References

Leslie, P.H. 1945: On the use of matrices in certain population mathematics. *Biometrika* 33, pp. 183–212.

Rees, P.H. 1979: Regional population projection models and accounting methods. *Journal of the Royal Statistical Society*, series A, 142, pp. 223–55.

— and Wilson, A.G. 1977: *Spatial population analysis*. London: Edward Arnold.

Rogers, A. 1968: *Matrix analysis of interregional population growth and distribution*. Berkeley and Los Angeles: University of California Press.

— 1975: *Introduction to multiregional mathematical demography*. New York: Wiley.

— 1983: Migration and settlement. *Options* 1983/1, pp. 1–5.

Stone, R. 1971: *Demographic accounting and model-building*. Paris: OECD.

Willekens, F. and Rogers, A. 1978: *Spatial population analysis; methods and computer programs*. Research report RR-78–18. Laxenburg, Austria: International Institute for Applied Systems Analysis.

multi-round survey A SURVEY design involving more than one visit to the same respondents or, alternatively, the same or matched study areas. If the same respondents are re-interviewed, it can be called a FOLLOW-UP SURVEY or a 'panel' survey.

The French demographic tradition leans towards multi-round surveys, which when carefully done, can be more illuminating than the single-round variety. There are many practical difficulties, however, especially in countries where addresses are poorly known or where the population is highly mobile.   AH

multi-stage sampling A form of SAMPLING, also called CLUSTER SAMPLING, implying a hierarchical SAMPLE DESIGN. After the selection of a sample of first stage units (primary sampling units, or PSUs) a further stage of sampling is conducted within the selected PSUs, yielding a sample of secondary sampling units (SSUs). The process may be continued for as many stages as desired, the essential feature being that at each stage the sampling is carried out only within the units selected at the preceding stage. The overall probability of selection of a unit at the last stage is the product of the selection probabilities of the units at each stage.

The objectives of multi-stage sampling are twofold: (1) to reduce data collection costs by clustering the sample, and (2) to reduce the costs of sampling frame construction (the frame for stage n need be constructed only within the units selected in stage $n - 1$).   CS

multistate demography The study of population movement between the different states into which the population can be classified and which can both import and export population. Among the systems of interest that have been studied are the populations of different regions (by Rees and Liaw, see Rogers 1980), the populations of different marital conditions (Espenshade 1983), population classified by labour force states (by Willekens, see Rogers 1980), and population classified by educational grade (Stone 1971).

The principal tool of multistate demography is still the increment-decrement life table model which has been developed in a variety of forms by different authors (e.g. Ledent, see Rogers 1980). The traditional life table model allows populations only to lose as they age: in the increment-decrement formulation populations may also gain. For example, the population of married persons may lose members through divorce, widowhood and death, but will gain members through marriage from single persons and remarriage from divorced and widowed persons.   PR

References

Espenshade, T.J. 1983: Marriage, divorce and remarriage from the retrospective data: a multiregional approach. *Environment and planning A* 15.

Land, K.C. and Rogers, A., eds. 1982: *Multidimensional mathematical demography*. New York and London: Academic Press.

Rogers, A., ed. 1980: Essays in multistate mathematical demography. Special issue of *Environment and planning A* 12, containing articles by Ledent, Liaw, Rees, and Willekens referred to above.

Stone, R. 1971: *Demographic accounting and model building*. Paris: OECD.

multivariate analysis   A statistical technique used to assess the relationships between several variables, more precisely to measure the association between several independent variables and one dependent variable.

Many multivariate methods require such extensive and elaborate calculation that they can only feasibly be performed on a computer; the use of multivariate techniques has accordingly increased greatly with the wider availablity of computers. Varieties of multiple REGRESSION are probably the most widely used in demographic work. The underlying principles of these techniques are the same as simpler statistical procedures, though it is often harder with multivariate models to verify that the data used meet the various requirements needed for meaningful interpretation, and that the model is correctly specified.   CW

Reading

Namboodiri, N., Carter, L.F. and Blalock, H.M. 1975: *Applied multivariate analysis and experimental designs*. New York and London: McGraw-Hill.

Myers index   An index of age misreporting that results in overreporting of ages which end in particular digits (see DIGIT PREFERENCE). The index is equal to half of the sum of the absolute deviations from an expected value of the number of persons reported at ages ending with each digit. The expected distribution of final digits is based on a distribution which takes into account the effects of mortality and differences in cohort size.   DE

N

natality A word used as an approximate synonym of fertility. It is normally given the general meaning of the occurrence of births in relation to overall population change, while fertility is restricted to more precise measures. The terms are, however, widely used interchangeably and fertility is now generally taken to embrace the wider concept.   CW

nationality Characteristic of an individual indicating his or her citizenship of a particular nation.

Citizenship and nationality are usually synonymous, though a distinction is sometimes drawn between political or legal nationality and ethnic nationality. This arises particularly in multi-ethnic states such as China and the USSR where individuals are classified according to various ethnic nationalities, while all remain citizens of the one state. Nationality is normally acquired through being born within a state (or elsewhere with parents of the given nationality), but may also be gained through naturalisation or marriage. In all these respects the legal situation varies between countries. Moreover, the presentation of statistical data on nationality is highly variable, making international comparisons very difficult.   RP

natural fertility Marital fertility where couples do not alter their reproductive behaviour according to the number of children already born. In practice, this can be taken to mean the fertility of populations whose members do not use contraception or induced abortion.

The concept of natural fertility was introduced by Henry (1961) and has subsequently been widely influential both in demographic analysis and in the development of mathematical models of the process of reproduction. The adjective 'natural' is an unfortunate choice since it seems to imply that only one level of fertility is natural to humanity (and possibly universal in the past). In fact natural fertility populations have wide variations in the level of fertility: Leridon (1977) found that the TOTAL FERTILITY RATE varied between 3.7 and 9.5 in a group of 23 populations with natural fertility. Even allowing for the impact on these values of different marriage patterns some populations had fertility close to double that of others. These differences arise from differences in the various PROXIMATE DETERMINANTS, above all from variation in the postpartum NON-SUSCEPTIBLE PERIOD owing to different patterns of breastfeeding. This, along with such factors as sexual taboos, physiological sterility and foetal mortality, produces the great variation in levels. Natural fertility is not, therefore, a specific level of fertility; it is a reproductive strategy: births may be spaced at long or short intervals, but couples do not make extra efforts to reduce fertility after reaching any particular family size or parity. The term 'parity-independent' fertility is thus sometimes employed.

Although the overall level of fertility is a poor indicator of fertility regime, a number of other measures show consistency between natural fertility populations. The fact that no effort is made to reduce fertility at older ages leads to high mean age of mothers at the birth of their last child (often around 40) and to a characteristic AGE PATTERN OF FERTILITY. Henry and later Coale and Trussell (1974) have provided quantitative estimates of

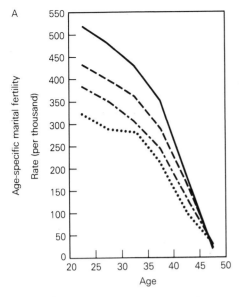

A

550
500
450
400
350
300
250
200
150
100
50
0

Age-specific marital fertility
Rate (per thousand)

20 25 30 35 40 45 50
Age

——— Blankenberghe, Belgium, 1650–1849
– – – 4 Waldeck villages, Germany, 1662–1849
–·–·– 14 English parishes, 1550–1849
······· Bengal, 1945–46

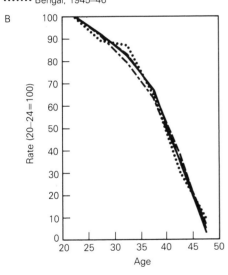

B

100
90
80
70
60
50
40
30
20
10
0

Rate (20–24 = 100)

20 25 30 35 40 45 50
Age

Populations with natural fertility have different levels of age specific marital fertility rates (a) but show a common pattern when the rates are indexed to the rate for women aged 20–24 (b). Source: Wilson 1984.

this age-specific profile which shows a convex pattern in contrast to the concave pattern of rates in a population whose members practise family limitation (see graph). The COALE-TRUSSELL FERTILITY MODEL, based on this variation in age pattern provides a convenient summary of the extent to which a particular set of rates diverges from natural fertility in the parameter *m*. A considerable range of other tests for the presence of natural fertility has been suggested by various authors, and the view that most (possibly all) societies experienced natural fertility before the onset of the DEMOGRAPHIC TRANSITION has become widespread.   RP, CW

References

Coale, A.J. and Trussell, T.J. 1974: Model fertility schedules: variations in the age structure of childbearing in human populations. *Population index* 40, pp. 185–258 and Erratum, *Population index* 41, p. 572.

Henry, L. 1961: Some data on natural fertility. *Eugenics quarterly* 8, pp. 81–91.

Leridon, H. 1977: *Human fertility: the basic components.* Chicago: University of Chicago Press.

Reading

Bongaarts, J. and Potter, R.G. 1983: *Fertility, biology and behavior: an analysis of the proximate determinants.* New York and London: Academic Press. Chapter 2.

natural increase   Change in the size of a population produced by the surplus (or deficit) of births over deaths in a given period. Where net migration is zero the rate of natural increase is identical to the growth rate of the population.   RP

neo-Malthusianism   A doctrine which, following MALTHUS, posits the need for the control of population growth but which, unlike Malthus, advocates contraception and induced abortion to this end.

While Malthus recommended only late marriage, and strict continence before it, as a way of avoiding births, handbills distributed in 1823 by one of his earliest followers, the trade unionist and social reformer Francis Place, advocated contraception (coitus interruptus and vaginal sponge). Other early advocates in England were Joseph Townsend, a Methodist utilitarian author, and the radical publisher Richard Carlile. In an 1825 article entitled *What is love?* Carlile put forward several reasons for favouring contraception which have remained tenets of birth control advocates to this day: couples need have no more children than they want, no woman need endanger her health and life, no unwanted illegitimate children need be born, and intercourse could be made independent of the risk of conception (Fryer 1965).

Advocacy of birth control spread to the United States in 1831 with Robert Dale Owen's book *Moral physiology, or a brief and plain treatise on the population question*, in which both social and eugenic arguments were made in support of contraception. The next year Charles Knowlton, a Massachusetts physician published his treatise *Fruits of philosophy*. In spite of great opposition (including several legal prosecutions, fines and a sentence of three months hard labour for Knowlton) his inexpensive booklet became widely circulated and remained in print for 40 years. Among the influential writers of the mid-nineteenth century stand out the Scottish physician George Drysdale with his work *The elements of social science* (1854) and the reformist publisher Charles Bradlaugh. It was Bradlaugh who proposed the first Malthusian League in 1861, which adopted the title neo-Malthusian in the 1870s.

Bradlaugh was also involved in a crucial legal battle in the late 1870s when he and Annie Besant, the social reformer and trade union leader, reprinted Knowlton's *Fruits of philosophy* amid attempts to suppress birth control literature (Chandrasekhar 1981). Their victory in the highly publicised case marked a major liberalisation of the legal position of the neo-Malthusians in England, and one not matched in the United States until 1936, although the legal battles of Margaret Sanger earlier in the century served a similar purpose of publicising the neo-Malthusian case. The 1920s and 1930s saw significant developments, both in the United States with the work of Sanger and in Britain with the work of Marie Stopes, towards means of improving women's control over their own bodies. Moreover the growth of an institutional framework for the birth control movement in various leagues and centres provided the basis of longer-term influence. They led to the creation of the Planned Parenthood Federation of America in 1942 and the Family Planning Association of Great Britain in 1930. A liberal attitude was taken by the Anglican church in the Lambeth Declaration of 1930, further strengthening the position of the birth control movement in England.

Development in other countries was more sporadic, indeed in some parts of Europe non-existent. In France, for example, in spite of the early and widespread adoption of family limitation by large sections of the population, official hostility to antinatalist propaganda was intense. The formation by Dr Paul Robin of a neo-Malthusian league in 1896 had isolated support until the law of 1930 which outlawed all birth control propaganda and associations. Since the second world war, however, family planning has taken on a world-wide perspective, signified by the creation in 1952 of the International Planned Parenthood Federation. Moreover the virtually universal governmental hostility of earlier eras has been replaced by official advocacy of many family planning programmes as rapid population growth has added new elements of economic necessity to the long-standing rationales of improved health, family life and equality.

RP, CW

References

Chandrasekhar, S. 1981: '*A dirty, filthy book*': *the writings of Charles Knowlton and Annie Besant on reproductive physiology and birth control and an account of the Bradlaugh-Besant trial*. Berkeley: University of California Press.

Fryer, P. 1965: *The birth controllers*. London: Secker and Warburg; New York: Stein and Day (1966).

Reading

Soloway, R.A. 1982: *Birth control and the population question in England, 1877–1930.* London and Chapel Hill, NC: University of North Carolina Press.

neonatal mortality Mortality of live-born infants during the first 4 weeks (28 days) of life or, less commonly, during the first month. Deaths occurring after 28 days are termed post-neonatal deaths, and deaths in the first 7 days of life are referred to as early neonatal deaths.

Deaths attributable to congenital defects, birth trauma or similar conditions (ENDOGENOUS MORTALITY) form the main group of neonatal deaths, and, as infant mortality rates have declined, neonatal mortality has become proportionately more important since these causes of death have proved less amenable to reduction than EXOGENOUS MORTALITY. The neonatal mortality rate is conventionally taken as the number of neonatal deaths during a year divided by the number of live births in the same period. Although not strictly accurate, the measure has fewer problems than estimates of later infant mortality and comes close to being the probability of dying in the first 28 days of life.   RP

neoplasm Synonym of tumour, i.e. an abnormal growth of cells. A distinction is made between 'benign' tumours, which do not invade other parts of the body, and 'malignant' tumours (see CANCER) which not only continue to grow in a disorderly way but can also spread from the primary site to other organs. This dissemination is known as metastasis. 'Malignant' tumours may remain dormant for years: rapid growth occurs when the tumour becomes vascularised, i.e. once the tumour induces the host to provide it with a network of blood vessels.

'Benign' tumours can be distinguished from 'malignant' tumours by recourse to a biopsy, i.e. by using a fragment of tumour for histological examination.

Three major forms of treatment currently exist: surgery, radiation, and chemotherapy (drug treatment). Early detection of malignant tumours is often a condition of successful treatment in many forms of cancer: population screening programmes, for example for breast or cervical cancer, have therefore been established in several countries.   GW

Reading

Currie, G.A. and Currie, A.P. 1982: *Cancer: the biology of malignant disease.* London: Edward Arnold.

Folkman, J. 1976: The vascularisation of tumours. *Scientific American* 234, pp. 58–73.

Marx, J.L. 1978: Tumour promoters: carcinogenesis gets more complicated. *Science* 201, pp. 515–8.

Wilber, J.A. 1979: Cancer. In S.B. Day, ed. *A companion to the life sciences.* New York: Van Nostrand Reinhold.

net A qualifier applied to measures of phenomena in two distinct ways. (1) It indicates that mortality or some other disturbance has been taken into account in analysis, as in, for example, the NET REPRODUCTION RATE. (2) It is used in a more restricted sense in studies of migration, where the balance of flows into and out of a population is termed NET MIGRATION.

In the Anglo-American tradition of demographic analysis the first use of the word net, to indicate that a correction for disturbances has been made, is less common than it is in French demography where net values are often calculated, expressing the effect of mortality in altering patterns of marriage, fertility or migration. Where adjustments of this sort are made in English language works terminology is not consistent; terms such as adjusted rate or corrected probability are used in an ad hoc fashion to cover particular circumstances.   RP, CW

net migration The difference between the number of persons moving into a specified area and the number leaving. When internal migration is under consideration net migration is the difference between in- and out-migration; when international movements are being studied it is the difference between immigration and emigration.

Net migration and NATURAL INCREASE (the balance of births and deaths) are the two components of population growth, and the logical connections between these three aspects of demographic change are represented in the BALANCING EQUATION

$$P_2 = P_1 + B - D + I - O$$

where P_1 and P_2 stand for the population size at two dates and D, B, I and O are deaths, births, in-migrants, and out-migrants between the dates. This can be re-expressed in terms of natural increase, $NT(B - D)$, and net migration, NM $(I - O)$:

$$P_2 = P_1 + NT + NM$$

Estimates of net migration may be made directly from comparison of gross flows into and out of an area or indirectly by comparing a population at two points (often at two censuses) determining what change would be expected on the basis of fertility and mortality, and attributing any differences from the expected values to net migration. Where accurate statistics on births and deaths are available these may be used to assess natural increase and make an estimate of migration. An alternative approach is to combine survivorship probabilities from a LIFE TABLE with the census data to estimate expected intercensal deaths in each age and sex category. Applying the survivorship probabilities to each age group in the first census provides an estimate of the size of each age group at the second date. Differences between these estimates and actual enumerated population are attributed to net migration. The technique is commonly referred to as forward survival. Analogously, combining the life table values with the population at the second date permits reverse survival estimates to be made. Because of differing

assumptions in the estimation these two procedures result in different estimates of net migration (although the differences are small when mortality rates are low). To overcome this discrepancy, the average of forward and reverse survival estimates is usually taken.   RP

Reading

Shryock, H.S., Siegel, J.S. et al. 1976: *The methods and materials of demography*. Condensed edition by E.G. Stockwell. London and New York: Academic Press. Chapter 21.

net rate A rate calculated taking into account the effects of mortality or some other disturbance of the phenomena under consideration. The qualifier is sometimes extended to other measures such as net probabilities. The alternative terms corrected rate and adjusted rate are also used. Except for particular measures, such as the net reproduction rate, the use of net measures and the names given to them vary, and ad hoc terminology is often employed.   RP, CW

net reproduction rate (NRR) The average number of daughters that would be born to a birth cohort of women during their lifetime if they experienced a fixed pattern of age-specific fertility and mortality rates.

The NRR was popularised by R.R. Kuczynski (1935), though originally calculated by the English Registrar General William Farr as early as 1880 and also used by LOTKA (Lewes 1984). It provides a measure of the way in which a generation of women replaces itself, given a particular combination of fertility and mortality. Although the measure is sometimes calculated for cohorts it is much more commonly used to refer to a particular period, indicating what the long-term effects would be if current fertility and mortality persisted for many years. A value of 1.0 for the NRR indicates that a population's fertility and mortality are such as to ensure that the population exactly replaces itself, while higher values indicate a growing population and lower values show declining numbers. Since the NRR is usually estimated on the basis of period measures of fertility, which may fluctuate considerably, it should be interpreted with due caution. The NRR is closely related to the GROSS REPRODUCTION RATE (GRR), employing the same data on fertility, but also indicating the effects of mortality. In developed countries, where mortality before the end of the reproductive period is low, the difference between the two measures is minimal; but in conditions of high mortality the GRR may be double the NRR.

Although the most widely quoted, the NRR is only one of many indices of replacement that have been suggested. The NRR compares the number of females born in one generation with the number born in the next; an alternative measure is the comparison of the numbers reaching a given age in one generation with those who do so in the next. If mortality is falling rapidly this latter measure may be a more informative guide to replacement. For example, for several French birth cohorts in the nineteenth century the NRR was below 1.0, yet modest population growth continued because the survival chances of women were improving steadily, leading to values of above 1.0 for replacement assessed at age 15 rather than at birth.   RP

References

Kuczynski, R.R. 1935: *The measurement of population growth*. London: Sidgwick and Jackson.

Lewes, F.M.M. 1984: A note on the net reproduction ratio. *Population studies* 38, pp. 321–4.

Reading

Hajnal, J. 1959: The study of fertility and reproduction – a survey of thirty years. In *Thirty years of research in human fertility – retrospect and prospect*. New York: Milbank Memorial Fund. Pp. 11–37.

Pressat, R. 1972: *Demographic analysis: methods, results, applications*. London: Edward Arnold; Chicago: Aldine Atherton. Chapter 11.

Shryock, H.S., Siegel, J.S. et al. 1976: *The methods and materials of demography*. Condensed edition by E.G. Stockwell. London and New York: Academic Press. Chapter 18.

nominative listing   Listings of persons whose identification by fore and surname, at the very least, is given. These lists were produced for a variety of purposes: administrative, electoral, poor relief, taxation, the monitoring of religious allegiances and military recruitment. They are particularly important sources of demographic information for European countries before the era of national censuses.

For Roman Catholic countries of Europe the promulgation of the *Ritulae Romanum* in 1614 formalised a longstanding tradition laying down a procedure for the priest to follow in maintaining a *Liber Status Animarum*, a register of souls. For demographic purposes the most useful of such lists are those recording all the inhabitants of any one locality by age, sex and marital status, and divided by household with the occupation of its head listed along with the relations of household members to the head.

These listings have found their most widespread use in the analysis of household or CO-RESIDENT GROUP structure. Most of the pre-nineteenth century European listings provide no explicit criteria concerning what was used to define a household. For instance, the purpose of the listing could strongly influence the way in which the enumerator made his divisions. These biases can best be identified if a series of lists for the same locality prepared for different administrative purposes survive. Hajnal (1982) has suggested that the effects of different definitions are probably greater in north-west Europe than in societies with joint-family household systems because in the latter, households consist almost entirely of members who have a permanent right to belong by virtue of relationship. In north-west European agricultural communities groups of individuals not sharing fully in the integrated household were frequently to be found living in the same farm, house or group of buildings; these could either have been treated as separate from or part of the main household. (See also CENSUS.)

RMS

Reference

Hajnal, J. 1982: Two kinds of pre-industrial household formation systems. *Population and development review* 8, pp. 449–94.

Reading

Berkener, L.K. 1975: The use and misuse of census data for the historical analysis of family structure. *Journal of interdisciplinary history* 5, pp. 721–38.

Hajnal 1982.

Henry, L. 1980: *Techniques d'analyse en démographie historique*. Paris: Institut National d'Études Démographiques.

Wrigley, E.A., ed. 1966: *An introduction to English historical demography*. London: Weidenfeld and Nicolson.

non-marital fertility   See ILLEGITIMACY.

non-renewable process   A demographic process in which the constituent events cannot be repeated.

Mortality is clearly not repeatable, but other phenomena can be similarly defined: first marriage or the birth of a first child, for example. This makes it possible to use LIFE TABLE METHODS in analysis by specifying the order of events in a RENEWABLE PROCESS and examining the constituent non-renewable parts. Fertility, for example, can be specified by birth order, and life table methods used for each birth interval.

RP, CW

Reading

Wunsch, G. and Termote, M. 1978: *Introduction to demographic analysis*. New York and London: Plenum. Chapter 1.

non-selectivity   A fundamental condition which must be satisfied if observed demographic measures are to be interpreted as being true reflections of actual behaviour.

Since most demographic processes take place in the presence of other processes which could disturb their occurrence it is essential that a DISTURBING PROCESS (e.g. mortality preventing marriage) should act in the same way for all individuals. If all persons have the same chance of experiencing the disturbance (i.e. it does not act selectively on particular individuals) non-selectivity is said to apply. If the disturbance acts in a selective manner the values observed for a particular measure will not exactly reflect the underlying behaviour in the population and a correction factor indicating the size of the bias involved will be needed. Hoem (1972, 1983) has shown that these correction factors can be ignored if and only if the disturbance is non-selective in its occurrence.

Many types of selectivity arise in demographic studies; they are often attributable to aspects of data collection or to the way in which data are organised. The most pervasive and possibly the most insidious type is that introduced by mortality. Since measures of demographic processes can normally only be calculated for people who are still alive, mortality always has the potential for introducing bias. This has been termed 'selection by virtue of survival' by Ryder (1965), and it will be apparent if mortality strikes individuals differentially according to their status in terms of other demographic processes. For example, if married and single persons experience different death rates any estimates of proportions marrying will be biased. In practice explicit correction for biases introduced by a lack of non-selectivity in survival chances is rarely undertaken, either because of the lack of the necessary data on the scale of biases or because where data do exist (mostly in developed countries) biases are usually small. In populations with higher mortality, however, where scope for selectivity is greater, few data exist so accurate corrections cannot be made.

While selectivity by virtue of survival is an underlying feature of demography and always potentially present, other forms of selectivity arise from inappropriate choices of analyses or from poor data collection. Hoem (1983) has provided examples of bias being introduced by the way in which data are organised, in particular with reference to retrospective surveys. He notes that it is always dangerous to group life histories according to their final outcome (e.g. final family size in the case of maternity histories) since this outcome is itself the result of the process being studied. Similarly, concentrating on the most recent event or two is also open to massive biases. The scope for introducing selectivity at the stage of data collection is also large. If misreporting, underreporting or non-response is related to particular characteristics of the respondents, selectivity results.

In general, demographic analysis is presented without explicit correction for biases arising from selectivity. An awareness of the possibility of its occurrence and a sensitivity to its nature are, however, invaluable assets in all demographic studies.   CW

References

Hoem, J. 1972: Inhomogeneous semi-Markov processes, select actuarial tables and duration dependence in demography. In T.N.E. Greville, ed. *Population dynamics*. New York: Academic Press. Pp. 251–96.

— 1983:*Weighting, misclassification and other issues in the analysis of survey samples of life histories*. Stockholm research reports in demography 11. Stockholm: Department of Statistics, University of Stockholm.

Ryder, N.B. 1965: The measurement of fertility patterns. In M.S. Sheps and J.C. Ridley, eds. *Public health and population change*. Pittsburgh: University of Pittsburgh Press. Pp. 287–306.

non-susceptible period (NSP)   The period immediately following a birth or an abortion (either spontaneous or induced) during which a woman does not ovulate or during which she is not sexually active and hence cannot conceive again. The terms post-partum infecundability and the infecundable interval are also used. The duration of the pregnancy which precedes

the anovulatory period is sometimes also included in the NSP.

After a live birth an average of about two months of non-susceptibility occurs if BREASTFEEDING is not undertaken. Prolonged and intensive lactation, however, can lengthen the NSP considerably (populations with up to two years of non-susceptibility have been reported). In some populations, especially in parts of sub-Saharan Africa, a further lengthening of the NSP occurs as a consequence of prolonged sexual abstinence. The variation in the length of birth intervals which results from variation in the NSP is a very important source of differences in overall fertility, especially for populations where contraception is not widely used (see BONGAARTS' DECOMPOSITION). After a stillbirth or an abortion, whether spontaneous or induced, the duration of the NSP is usually much shorter than it is after a live birth.   RP

Reading

Bongaarts, J. and Potter, R.G. 1983: *Fertility, biology and behavior: an analysis of the proximate determinants*. New York and London: Academic Press.

normal distribution   A theoretical FREQUENCY DISTRIBUTION whose identifying characteristic is its bell-shaped symmetry around the three measures of central tendency (mean, median and modal class): (fig. 1). It has properties which allow precise statements concerning the poportion of all observations lying to the left and right of any point on the horizontal scale.

The theoretical normal distribution refers to a histogram for an infinitely large population. It is used as the bases for many SIGNIFICANCE TESTS.

1 The theoretical normal distribution

Common deviations from the theoretical distribution involve skewness. A positively skewed distribution has a longer right-hand than left-hand tail (fig. 2), with the reverse for a negatively skewed distribution (fig. 3); a truncated skewed distribution lacks the shorter tail (fig. 4).

RJJ

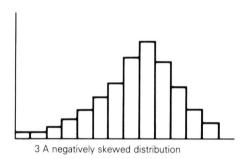

2 A positively skewed distribution

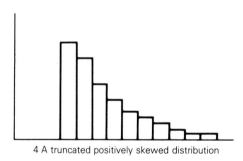

3 A negatively skewed distribution

4 A truncated positively skewed distribution

Source: R. J. Johnston, *ed.* 1981: *The dictionary of human geography.* Oxford: Basil Blackwell; New York: Free Press. P. 243.

Reading

Gardner, V. and Gardner, G. 1978: *Analysis of frequency distributions.* Concepts and techniques in modern geography 19. Norwich: Geo Abstracts.

nuclear family   The unit consisting of one husband (father) one wife (mother) and their sons and/or daughters if any (brothers and sisters). The relationships involved are those basic to KINSHIP reckoning: husband-wife, parent-child and inter-sibling (see BIOLOGICAL FAMILY). The terms elementary family, immediate family and conjugal family are also used to refer to this basic grouping of kin relations. A conjugal family unit (CFU) consists of a married couple, or a married couple with offspring or a widowed person with offspring.

In the Hammel-Laslett (1974) scheme of CO-RESIDENT GROUP structures when a conjugal family unit is found on its own it is called a simple family HOUSEHOLD, even if an unrelated person is part of the group.

RMS

Reference

Hammel, E.A. and Laslett, P. 1974: Comparing household structures over time and between cultures. *Comparative studies in society and history* 16, pp. 73–109.

Reading

Harris, C.C. 1969: *The family.* London: Allen and Unwin. Especially chapter 6.

Laslett, P. 1972: Introduction to P. Laslett and R. Wall, eds. *Household and family in past time.* London and New York: Cambridge University Press.

nulligravida   See PREGNANCY ORDER.

nullipara   See PARITY.

nuptiality   The frequency, characteristics and dissolution of MARRIAGES in a population (or, more generally, of all sexual unions involving rights and obligations fixed by law or custom).

Although nuptiality is not strictly a demographic phenomenon (in that it does not directly affect the number of persons in a population as do mortality, fertility and migration), the close link between nuptiality and fertility has meant that the study of marriage has long been part of demographic analysis. Most attention focuses on the formation of unions, with particular emphasis on first marriages, since DIVORCE and remarriage have been relatively rare in most societies and have much less impact on childbearing. In the examination of first marriages two measures are of particular importance: the mean age at first marriage and the proportion of people never married or permanently single at the end of the reproductive years. The importance of first marriage leads to nuptiality in general being termed high or low, depending on the age at first marriage and the proportion never married.

A variety of MARRIAGE RATES are used to measure nuptiality. The most general is the CRUDE MARRIAGE RATE relating the number of marriages to the total population, while more precise age-specific rates, distinguished according to the order of marriages permit more penetrating analysis, the most detailed approach being that of the NUPTIALITY TABLE.   RP, CW

nuptiality table   A detailed probabilistic description of the occurrence of marriages of a specified order, calculated through the use of LIFE TABLE METHODS.

The nuptiality table is the most refined device for investigating marriage patterns, and can be used to study any aspect of nuptiality which can occur only once, although it is most commonly used to examine first marriages. The basis of the nuptiality table is the calculation of a set of probabilities of marrying for each age group. Since first marriage is rare in old age, the schedule of probabilities usually stops at 50, or sometimes 60, years of age. From these probabilities it is possible to calculate the number of persons still single at each age, given an initial number at birth (or at the age at which marriages first take place). All the remaining life table functions may be calculated from this information.

A distinction is made between *gross* nuptiality tables, which assume that no one dies before passing through all the ages of the table, and *net* nuptiality tables, which explicitly take into account probabilities of dying at each age. Thus net tables are an example of MULTIPLE DECREMENT LIFE TABLES with the population of single persons subject to two risks, marriage and death. Both types of table provide detailed descriptions of marriage, including measures of the mean age at first marriage and the proportion of the population that has never married.   RP, CW

Reading
Pressat, R. 1972: *Demographic analysis: methods, results, applications*. London: Edward Arnold; Chicago: Aldine Atherton. Chapter 7.
Shryock, H.S., Siegel, J.S. et al. 1976: *The methods and materials of demography*. Condensed edition by E.G. Stockwell. London and New York: Academic Press. Pp. 338–42.

O

occupational mortality Mortality among different occupational groups, or, more specifically, mortality arising from the pursuit of a particular occupation.

In developed countries deaths caused directly by the circumstances of a given occupation are relatively rare and hard to distinguish from those caused by the life style or other environmental conditions of individuals. Only very specific illnesses such as pneumoconiosis among miners or the results of exposure to toxic chemicals are readily identifiable. For this reason most studies consider principally the broader definition of the topic. Methodological problems also exist, especially with female mortality. It has been pointed out, for example, that the recording of occupation on the death certificates of women is often relatively poor, and sometimes significantly less complete than the reporting of occupation in the census. Analysis is therefore hampered by varying biases in the two sources. These points were noted as long ago as 1851 by William Farr, the Registrar General of England and Wales, in an innovative study of occupational mortality. His basic methodology has been followed in all the Decennial Supplements produced by his successors. One way of overcoming many of the problems in assessing occupational mortality is the use of prospective or longitudinal studies.

RP, CW

Reading

Fox, A.J. and Goldblatt, P.D. 1982: *Longitudinal study: socio-demographic mortality differentials 1971–75.* London: Office of Population Censuses and Surveys.

Kitagawa, E.M. and Hauser, P.M. 1973: *Differential mortality in the United States: a study in socio-economic epidemiology.* Cambridge, Mass.: Harvard University Press.

McDowall, M. 1983: William Farr and the study of occupational mortality. *Population trends* 31, pp. 12–4.

— 1983: Measuring women's occupational mortality. *Population trends* 34, pp. 25–9.

ogive A version of graphical INTERPOLATION used to smooth irregular data, especially age structures with marked AGE HEAPING. The graph plots the cumulated population up to a particular age on the vertical axis against the age on the horizontal to produce a smoother curve than the uncumulated data. A logarithmic vertical scale is often employed as are other elaborations of technique which accentuate irregularities or make smoothing easier.

RP

open interval A term most frequently used in the context of the analysis of fertility by means of BIRTH INTERVALS. The interval between the birth of a woman's most recent child and a fixed date, such as a census or survey, is termed an open interval (the event which will close the interval, the next birth, having not yet occurred). In contrast, intervals between successive births before the most recent one are called closed. Open intervals are subject to different biases from those that affect closed intervals and considerable attention has been paid to the question of their interpretation.

RP

open population A population which is open to the effects of migration. It is the opposite of a CLOSED POPULATION.

RP

optimum population The population size which makes possible the achievement of a particular objective or set of objectives.

There are theoretically as many optimum populations as there are objectives. Economic aims, especially those related to the maximum per capita income or welfare, are most commonly cited. Objectives concerning the community as a whole rather than individuals, for example political or military goals, are also sometimes invoked. Although the notion of an optimum population is appealing, and has long been discussed, it remains a largely academic one, and concern has increasingly focused on particular aspects of a population, such as its growth rate or age structure. Certain authors have questioned the very concept of an optimum population, suggesting that increased population simply produces new social and economic solutions to cope with the greater density of population (Boserup 1965).   RP

Reference

Boserup, E. 1965: *The conditions of agricultural growth: the economics of agrarian change under population pressure*. London: Allen and Unwin; Chicago: Aldine Atherton.

Reading

Boserup 1965.
Sauvy, A. 1969: *General theory of population*. London: Weidenfeld and Nicolson; New York: Basic Books. Chapter 4.

optimum rate of growth   The growth rate of the population which makes possible the attainment of certain objectives, such as economic growth.

A given rate of population growth affects not only total numbers, but also age structure, in particular the AGEING of the population and the ratio of the population in the labour force to the dependent population. Because of its impact on these areas the dynamic relations between population and economic growth are now emphasized by economists, rather than the static concept of an optimum size of population. The whole area remains controversial since no single model of economic-demographic relations has gained universal acceptance.   RP

oral contraceptive   A hormone-based tablet commonly termed the contraceptive pill, or just 'the pill', which is taken orally to halt ovulation.

First introduced in 1960, oral contraception rapidly became one of the main contraceptive methods and is now the most common in many countries. By the 1980s as many as 60 million women were estimated to be using the pill at any one time. Initial enthusiasm for the method has been somewhat moderated by reports of complications in long-term use and the percentage of women using it has declined in developed countries since the mid 1970s.

Oral contraception is the most effective reversible means of preventing pregnancy. In addition it appears to confer on its users enhanced protection against several forms of cancer and other conditions. On the other hand results from the latest and most thorough cohort studies indicate that deaths from circulatory disease are higher among users of oral contraceptives in some circumstances. The increased risk is only statistically significant, however, for users over age 45, and for those over age 35 who also smoke. Overall the risks associated with the pill appear to be much less than the risks attendant on pregnancy. In addition to these major risks a number of side effects are often noted, among them nausea and weight gain.   RP, CW

Reading

Kols, A. et al. 1982: Oral contraceptives in the 1980s. *Population reports*, series A, 6.
Rosenfield, A. 1982: Contraceptive methods: oral contraceptives and intrauterine devices. In J.A. Ross, ed. *International encyclopaedia of population*. New York: Free Press. Pp. 109–13.

orphanhood techniques   A set of IN-DIRECT ESTIMATION TECHNIQUES somewhat loosely qualified by orphanhood though in fact based on information on the death of one specified parent rather than both.

The methods were developed for the estimation of adult mortality using information collected by questions on the survival of the mother of a respondent (to estimate female mortality) or of the father (to estimate male mortality). Such questions are often included in single-round surveys in areas where conventional sources of information on mortality are deficient.

For the theoretical development, see Brass and Hill (1973) and Hill (1977). The original methodology assumed constant fertility and mortality over an extended period, though Brass and Bamgboye (1981) have developed procedures for locating the time reference of the estimates obtained under conditions of steady mortality change.

Numerous applications (see Blacker 1977) suggest the following conclusions: the results obtained for female mortality (survival of mother) are more reliable than those for male mortality; the data for young respondents are systematically biased, probably by the reporting of adoptive parents for biological parents; the data from respondents aged 30 to 45 provide reasonably reliable estimates of mortality conditions 10 to 15 years before the survey, though apparent trends must be interpreted with caution. Problems of selectivity (only parents with surviving children are reported) and response weight (a particular parent is reported by the number of interviewed surviving children) seem to be of minor importance; attempts to eliminate the response weight problem by limiting analysis to one respondent, either the first-born or eldest surviving, per parent, have not proved successful because of problems in collecting the necessary data.   KH

References

Blacker,J.G.C. 1977: The estimation of adult mortality in Africa from data on orphanhood. *Population studies* 31, pp. 107–28.

Brass, W. and Bamgboye, E.A. 1981: The time location of reports of survivorship: estimates for maternal and paternal orphanhood and the ever-widowed. Working paper 81–1. London: Centre for Population Studies, London School of Hygiene and Tropical Medicine.

Brass, W. and Hill, K. 1973: Estimating adult mortality from orphanhood. *Proceedings of the International Population Conference, Liège, 1973*. Liège: International Union for the Scientific Study of Population. Volume 3.

Hill, K. 1977: Estimating adult mortality levels from information on widowhood. *Population studies* 31, pp. 75–84.

— and Trussell, T.J. 1977: Further developments in indirect mortality estimation. *Population studies* 31, pp. 313–33.

United Nations 1983: *Manual X: indirect techniques for demographic estimation*. New York: Department of International Economic and Social Affairs.

Reading

Blacker 1977.

Brass, W. 1975: *Methods for estimating fertility and mortality from limited and defective data*. Chapel Hill, North Carolina: University of North Carolina, Laboratories for Population Statistics.

Hill, K. and Zlotnik, H. 1982. Indirect estimation of fertility and mortality. In J.A. Ross, ed. *International encyclopaedia of population*. New York: Free Press. Pp. 324–34.

United Nations 1983.

out-migration Movement from a given area into another part of the same country. Out-migration is one of the components of INTERNAL MIGRATION whereas emigration refers to migration to a foreign country.   CW

overcount Overcounting of persons or events in censuses or surveys is caused by double counting or by counting of observations which should not be included. Overcounting in censuses frequently results from inadvertent double counting of persons with more than one residence or of those in transit, double processing of forms, and confusions between de jure and de facto definitions of residence. Overcounting of the number of persons with especially desirable characteristics (for example certain marital statuses or education categories) can result from inaccurate attribution of characteristics. Overcounting of vital events for a period can be caused by inclusion of late registrations, events to non-residents or events occurring elsewhere to residents. Net overcounting occurs when the number overcounted exceeds the number undercounted.   DE

overpopulation An excess of population in an area in relation to the resources available or to broader economic or social goals.

The concept of overpopulation is vague and open to considerable criticism. Reference is sometimes made to the notion of an OPTIMUM POPULATION, but this too is far from easy to define. Overpopulation is almost always a relative term in the sense that improved exploitation of a country's resources would permit the current population to be maintained at a higher standard of living. The concept of overpopulation, therefore, is only meaningful in conjunction with the specification of a certain level of technological advance. Some demographers dispute the validity of the concept in any circumstances, maintaining instead that apparent overpopulation is a stimulus to the evolution of new economic and social structures capable of sustaining the higher density of population.   RP, CW

own children method A method of estimating past fertility trends based solely on census information.

The method, proposed by Lee-Jay Cho (1973), consists of linking the children of a household to their mothers using the data on the relationship to the head of the household. Once this has been done RE-VERSE SURVIVAL methods are used to estimate the initial size of the birth cohort from which the children still alive at the time of the census came. Reverse survival of the mothers is also undertaken so that estimates of the number of births and the number of mothers are available at various points, usually each of the ten or 15 years preceding the census.

The method enables the analyst to calculate AGE SPECIFIC FERTILITY RATES as well as more overall statistics. Moreover since the socio-economic characteristics of the mother at the time of the census are known, it is possible to calculate rates for subgroups of the population and thus examine differentials more easily than with other forms of INDIRECT ESTIMATION TECHNIQUES. However, since the correct specification of the ages of children and mothers is essential, the method is potentially vulnerable to age errors. In societies where age is well reported, such as those of East Asia, the method is particularly informative.   CW

Reference

Cho, L.-J. 1973: The own-children approach to fertility estimation: an elaboration. In *International population conference, Liège, 1973.* Liège: International Union for the Scientific Study of Population. Volume 3, pp. 111–23.

Reading

Cho 1973.

Hill, K. and Zlotnick, H. 1982: Indirect estimation of fertility and mortality. In J.A. Ross, ed. *International encyclopaedia of population.* New York: Free Press. Pp. 324–34.

P

palaeodemography The study of past populations for which no conventional written sources of data exist. Palaeodemography is closely related to archaeology and physical anthropology and is distinguished by its specific techniques of data collection and analysis rather than by reference to any particular period. Epitaphs on tombs, skeletal remains and archaeological materials are the sources most used by palaeodemographers, though evidence of place names, climatic conditions and ethnographic data are also used to piece together the demographic history of populations which would otherwise remain completely obscure. In spite of the inherent problems of limited source material and the difficulties of interpretation, palaeodemographic research has thrown considerable light upon the distant past, an era which comprises by far the greatest part of human history.   CW

Reading

Acsadi, G.T. 1982: *Paleodemography*. In J.A. Ross, ed. *International encyclopaedia of population*. New York: Free Press. Pp. 512–19.
Brothwell, D.R. 1971: Palaeodemography. In W.Brass, ed. *Biological aspects of demography*. London: Taylor and Francis. Pp. 111–30.

pandemic An EPIDEMIC occurring over a very wide area; more strictly, over the whole of an area. For example, the influenza pandemic of 1918 and 1919.   RSS

panmictic circle See MARRIAGE MODEL.

parish registers Registers of baptisms, marriages and burials kept by the ecclesiastical authorities in many European countries and in their overseas colonies, and now a primary source of data for HISTORICAL DEMOGRAPHY.

Although certain Italian city states had effective registration systems as early as the late Middle Ages, it was only in the later sixteenth century (on the instructions of Thomas Cromwell in 1538) that a registration system functioning on a nationwide scale came into existence in England. In France, registration of a reliable quality did not become widespread until the late seventeenth century in spite of the edict of Villers-Cotterets (1539) prescribing the registering of events. By the eighteenth century registration of some kind was found in virtually all Western European countries and in many of their colonies, especially those in North America.

Historical demographers have mainly used two approaches to extract information from parish registers: aggregative analysis, in which simple counts of vital events are made to produce time series data, and FAMILY RECONSTITUTION, in which records of vital events are linked together to produce family histories.
          RP, CW

Reading

Hollingsworth, T.H. 1969: *Historical demography*. London and Ithaca, NY: Hodder and Stoughton and Cornell University Press.
Willigan, J.D. and Lynch, K.A. 1983: *Sources and methods of historical demography*. London and New York: Academic Press.

parity The number of children previously born alive to a woman (or to a couple). Parity is also sometimes used to mean the number of previous CONFINEMENTS experienced by a woman.

Parity is used as a means of categorizing women, whereas BIRTH ORDER is conventionally used when referring to births: 'two-parity women' have had two live births while 'zero-parity women' have had none. An alternative terminology refers to women with no children as nullipara, women with one child as primipara, and those with several children as multipara. Information on parity is widely used in the analysis of fertility, especially in measures such as the parity progression ratio, parity-specific fertility rates and P/F ratio methods.   RP

parity progression ratio The proportion of women (or couples) with at least *n* children who go on to have at least one more child.

The ratio is normally calculated for marriage or birth cohorts which have completed their childbearing and is conventionally represented by a_n. Alternative uses for period analysis based on the number of births of each order in a given year are also possible. The parity progression ratio is a particularly sensitive indicator of family building patterns since it reflects the sequential nature of fertility decisions, i.e. women (or couples) are able to have a second child only if they already have one, a third only if they already have two, and so on. In this way the ratio is a very useful indicator of the reproductive strategies followed in a population.   RP, CW

Reading
Henry, L. 1976: *Population: analysis and models.* London: Edward Arnold. Pp. 86–9.
Pressat, R. 1972: *Demographic analysis: methods, results, applications.* London: Edward Arnold; Chicago: Aldine Atherton. Pp. 218–43.

parity-specific A term used to refer to behaviour or measures which depend on PARITY. For example, when dealing with family limitation, demographers often refer to parity-specific control of fertility, indicating that it comes into use only after a certain family size is reached.   CW

parity-specific fertility rates Rates relating births of a given order to women of a particular PARITY, e.g. third births, divi-

ded by the number of women who have already had two children, 'two-parity women'. These rates are usually age-specific or specific to the duration of marriage. Closely related calculations, parity-specific birth probabilities are also often quoted. Since the births are specified by order it is possible to use LIFE TABLE METHODS to analyse them. This is frequently done in the context of birth interval analysis of cohort data, though period data may also be analysed in this way.   CW

participation rate The proportion of the population (usually in a specific age and sex category) in the LABOUR FORCE. The synonym activity rate is also commonly used.

The conventional approach to the study of economic activity is to multiply the participation rate by the 'working-age' population to provide an estimate of aggregate labour supply. The utility of this approach has been questioned since definitions of economic and non-economic activity are often largely arbitrary. When combined with data on mortality, age-specific participation rates are used to construct WORKING LIFE TABLES. Most attention is given to female participation rates since these vary more between countries and over the course of a working life. In most developed countries, female rates have risen substantially in recent decades, though the level and age-pattern vary considerably. See figure on p. 172.   RP, CW

Reading
Standing, G. 1982: *Labor force.* In J.A. Ross, ed. *International encyclopaedia of population.* New York: Free Press. Pp. 391–8.

Pearl rate A measure of CONTRACEPTIVE EFFECTIVENESS which divides the number of undesired conceptions (UC) in a given period by the number of months of EXPOSURE TO RISK of conceiving (EXP). The result of this division is conventionally multiplied by 1200 so that the rate is expressed per 100 women-years of exposure:

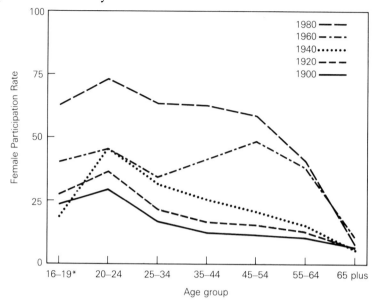

Labour force participation rates of US women 1900, 1920, 1940, 1960, 1980.
Source: L. J. Waite 1981: US women at work
Population bulletin 36.2, p. 7. *14–19 1900, 1920 and 1940.*

$$PR = \frac{UC}{EXP} \times 1200$$

The rate, first proposed by Pearl (1939), has a major drawback: it fails to take into account the fact that contraceptive failure rates decrease with the duration of use. Initial contraceptive effectiveness may be relatively low, whereas once the women for whom the method was unacceptable have stopped using it, only effective contraceptors remain and low failure rates are apparent. A further complication is heterogeneity in coital frequency, and hence in FECUNDABILITY. A hundred woman-years of exposure within the first year of using a contraceptive will usually produce a higher failure rate than 100 woman-years spread over several years for each woman. This can lead to erroneous assessment of effectiveness. In an attempt to overcome this difficulty Henry (1968) proposed an 'improved' Pearl rate in which only periods of exposure within the first year of use would be considered.

Although still widely quoted, the Pearl rate and its improved version are being increasingly replaced by more elaborate LIFE TABLE METHODS. The improved rate is closely related to one of the indices produced by the life table approach, the one-year cumulative failure rate.   RP, CW

References

Henry, L. 1968: Essai de calcul de l'efficacité de la contraception. *Population* 23, pp. 265–78.
Pearl, R. 1939: *The natural history of population.* London: Oxford University Press.

Reading

Bongaarts, J. and Potter, R.G. 1983: *Fertility, biology and behavior: an analysis of the proximate determinants.* New York and London: Academic Press. Chapter 3.

perinatal mortality The sum of FOETAL MORTALITY after 28 weeks of pregnancy and mortality in the first week of life. Slightly different definitions of the age limits are sometimes found, but all measures of perinatal mortality include both late foetal deaths and deaths of live-born infants.

The justification for considering perinatal death rates rather than separate measures of late foetal mortality and early neonatal mortality is twofold. First, the causes of mortality are similar in the two cases, and second, errors arising from misclassification of births, stillbirths and neonatal deaths are minimised. One measure frequently presented is the perinatal mortality rate. This is defined as the number of deaths in the first week of life plus foetal deaths after 28 weeks of pregnancy, divided by the number of live births plus the late foetal deaths. An alternative, the perinatal mortality ratio, uses the same numerator divided by the number of births. The ratio has the disadvantage of not being a true probability, but is sometimes preferred for international comparisons.   RP, CW

period analysis Demographic analysis which focuses on occurrences within a specified period, often one year. The synonyms current analysis and cross-sectional analysis are also used.

Period analysis, which studies the behaviour of many cohorts within a given period (or year), stands in contrast to COHORT ANALYSIS which involves the study of particular groups of individuals over a number of years. Several strategies are used in period analysis. STANDARDISATION attempts to remove the effects of age structure on overall measures, while TRANSLATION attempts to clarify the relationships between period and cohort measures. The most common approach is to use the idea of a HYPOTHETICAL COHORT in which the age-specific or duration-specific rates of a given period are combined in the same way as data from real cohorts to yield summary measures of the phenomenon under study. This method can produce problems in interpretation since period rates for many processes are more volatile than cohort indices and past experience may influence current behaviour.   RP, CW

Reading
Hobcraft, J., Menken, J. and Preston, S. 1982: Age, period and cohort effects in demography: a review. *Population index*, 48, pp. 4–43.
Shryock, H.S., Siegel, J.S. et al. 1976: *The methods and materials of demography*. Condensed edition by E.G. Stockwell. London and New York: Academic Press. Pp. 550–3.

period life table A LIFE TABLE constructed on the basis of the death rates in each age group during a specific period, often a year.

Since human beings are long-lived complete COHORT LIFE TABLES cannot be constructed until many years after the births of the individuals studied (in fact only after the death of the last member of a cohort). For this reason period life tables are much more common. By using the notion of a HYPOTHETICAL COHORT period life tables provide summary indicators of the mortality conditions prevailing in a specific period, notably the LIFE EXPECTANCY at birth. However, the value of life expectancy estimated in this fashion does not relate to any particular cohort, certainly not to the birth cohort of the period. A further point of concern is whether or not the period in question is one of unusual and unrepresentative conditions. This is particularly important if mortality rates in a population fluctuate considerably over time, but in most modern populations the relatively smooth evolution of mortality patterns minimizes these difficulties of interpretation.   RP

Reading
Shryock, H.S., Siegel, J.S. et al. 1976: *The methods and materials of demography*. Condensed edition by E.G. Stockwell. London and New York: Academic Press. Chapter 15.

period net reproduction rate (NRR) See NET REPRODUCTION RATE.

period total fertility rate (TFR) See TOTAL FERTILITY RATE.

periodic abstinence The avoidance of sexual intercourse at certain times during each menstrual cycle, usually with the intention of avoiding the fertile period and hence conception. The terms natural family planning and rhythm method are used synonymously.

Periodic abstinence depends on the identification of the fertile period of around two days which occurs at the time of ovulation and during which a woman is able to conceive. To avoid intercourse during that period involves abstinence for about seven to 18 days on account of the variation in precise timing of ovulation within each cycle and imprecision in its identification. The method dates from the 1930s when K. Ogino in Japan and H. Knaus in Austria identified the time of ovulation and its relation to the other aspects of the menstrual cycle. They suggested basing the period of abstinence on the number of days since the last bleeding (the calendar method). Variation in the precise day of ovulation has led recent advocates of periodic abstinence to base their methods on physiological observations such as the woman's temperature or the nature of her cervical mucus. A combination of these factors and the calendar method predicts ovulation more accurately.

Periodic abstinence is not a very effective contraceptive method. This is partly because of the inherent imprecision and partly because of difficulties in application, both in motivation and in understanding. Studies in several countries have shown that less than half the users of periodic abstinence know that the fertile period occurred at approximately midcycle. In spite of these difficulties, however, the fact that periodic abstinence is the only form of deliberate birth control sanctioned by the Roman Catholic Church has led to its widespread advocacy in Catholic countries.   CW

Reading

Liskin, L.L. 1981: Periodic abstinence: how well do new approaches work? *Population reports*, series I, 3.

Segal, S.J. et al. 1982: Contraceptive methods: overview. In J.A. Ross, ed. *International encyclopaedia of population.* New York: Free Press. Pp. 103–9.

permanent sterility   See STERILITY.

permanently single   See MARRIAGE.

personal history   See LIFE HISTORY.

person-years   The sum, expressed in years, of the time spent in a given category by all the individuals comprising the population. The concept allows the different periods lived by individuals to be taken into account proportionately when calculating rates.

The calculation of person-years can be illustrated by considering the example below in which individuals enter and leave observation at different dates in a particular year. The sum of person-years indicates the amount of time spent in observation, and can be used as the average population in a given category or exposed to a certain risk.

Entry date	Exit date	Duration (days)	Person years
1.1.85	1. 1.86	365	1.000
1.1.85	19. 8.85	230	0.630
5.3.85	1. 1.86	302	0.827
3.5.85	15.11.86	196	0.537
		Total	2.994

When dealing with aggregate data, where individual years of exposure are not given, the mid-year population is used. In analysing information on individuals, however, the calculation of person-years is usually necessary. This is the case when analysing LIFE HISTORIES. A very important consideration is the question of HETEROGENEITY. In many circumstances the chance of experiencing a demographic event is closely related to the length of time at risk. Thus the person-years contributed to the total by individuals with differing durations of EXPOSURE TO RISK are not equivalent, and misleading estimates may result from treating them as though they are. To overcome this limitation demographers use measures disaggregated by age or duration of exposure.

The concept of person-years is general and many different units of exposure are calculated: contraceptive effectiveness is often related to couple-years or couple-months, fertility to woman-years and so on.   RP

Reading
Elandt-Johnson, R.C. and Johnson, N.L. 1980: *Survival models and data analysis*. New York and Chichester: Wiley. Chapters 1 and 2.
Sheps, M.C. 1966: On the person-years concept in epidemiology and demography. *Milbank Memorial Fund quarterly* 44, pp. 69–91.

P/F ratio methods Techniques used to estimate fertility through the comparison of a measure of cohort or lifetime fertility, PARITY, P, with a measure of cumulative current fertility, F.

Initially devised by Brass to analyse data from African censuses, the method has been widely used and the basic concept of the ratio has been extended in several ways, including estimating parity-specific fertility.

The method involves comparing the mean number of children ever born to women in a given age group with the cumulation up to that age of current age-specific fertility rates. When computed for each of the conventional five-year age groups this produces a series of ratios. If the age pattern and level of fertility have not changed over the last 30 years or so and if both parity and current fertility are correctly reported, the ratios should all be unity. Deviations from unity indicate the extent and nature of biases in the data. If independent checks show that both the P and F values are accurate then a pattern of rising ratios with age could be taken as an indication of falling fertility.   BZ

Reading
Hill, K. and Zlotnik, H. 1982: Indirect estimation of fertility and mortality. In J.A. Ross, ed. *International encyclopaedia of population*. New York: Free Press. Pp. 324–34.

PGE survey See CHANDRASEKAR-DEMING TECHNIQUE.

pill, contraceptive See ORAL CONTRACEPTIVE.

pilot survey A trial SURVEY, usually small, undertaken to test the practicability of proposed field procedures, QUESTIONNAIRES and other techniques of information collection. The pilot survey is often used for training interviewers and other survey staff. All well-run surveys pass through a pilot stage: the field experience gained usually has (or should have) a major impact on the wording, scope, structure and possibly the aims of the questionnaire. Pilot surveys generally lead to shorter and simpler final questionnaires and clearer instructions for field procedures.   AH

Reading
United Nations 1971: *Methodology of demographic sample surveys*. Series M, statistical papers 51. New York: Department of Economic and Social Affairs.

polygamy Marriage in which a person of one sex is married simultaneously to several members of the other sex. Polyandry occurs when a woman has more than one husband, polygyny when a man has several wives. The latter is more common than the former, and polygamy is sometimes used solely in the sense of polygyny.

Even in societies where polygamy is accepted it is rare for a majority of marriages to be polygamous; economic and demographic constraints often restrict it to specific groups, usually those of higher status. Polygamy (polygyny) is most widespread in sub-Saharan Africa and it has been suggested that this is related to traditionally long periods of post-partum ABSTINENCE (Page and Lesthaeghe 1981).

A number of measures of polygamy are used. The polygamy rate is conventionally defined as the number of wives per married man (polygyny) or husbands per married woman (polyandry). The same term is also sometimes used for the proportion of marriages which are polygamous.   RP, CW

Reference

Page, H.J. and Lesthaeghe, R. 1981: *Child-spacing in tropical Africa; traditions and change*. New York and London: Academic Press.

population   A group of individuals co-existing at a given moment and defined according to various criteria.

The term population usually denotes all the inhabitants of a specified area (state, province, city, etc.), but is also used to refer to subpopulations within this (for example, female population or school population). In an even more restricted sense the term is used to refer to any group under study, the employees of a company, patients in a hospital, and so on, where entry into and exit from the population can be seen as determining its size and structure, in the same way that birth, death and migration affect the population at large. Population is also used adjectivally as a synonym for demographic, as in population studies, population policy, etc.

                                            RP

Reading

Ryder, N.B. 1964: Notes on the concept of a population. *American journal of sociology* 69, pp. 447–63.

population at risk   See EXPOSURE TO RISK.

population dynamics   The study of changes in population size and structure brought about by mortality, migration and fertility. The term is sometimes used more generally to indicate the study of any demographic process susceptible to change.

Population dynamics involve the analysis of the flow of vital events over time in contrast to population statics, where the state of a population at a particular moment is the focus of attention. Although referring in principle to many aspects of demographic analysis, the term population dynamics is most often used to connote integrated studies which analyse all the components of demographic change. Mathematical formulations of these changes are especially likely to be called dynamics.   CW

population forecast   See FORECAST.

population genetics   The subject concerned with the transmission of characteristics from one generation to the next at the level of populations rather than of individuals. It has several points of contact with demography. In theory, since detailed demographic statistics are an invaluable aid to population genetics, and since genetic structure is fundamental to any population, the scope for convergence in the two disciplines should be great, but in practice genetics has made only a very limited impact on the mainstream of demographic study.

One highly significant demographic development for genetics has been the great reduction in the role of natural selection in human populations. The decline in the variation of both fertility and mortality among the members of a population has meant (in developed societies and increasingly elsewhere), that virtually all individuals survive to reproductive age and that family size is concentrated in a narrow range around two children per couple. This has enormously reduced the role of natural selection, since competition between individuals is largely irrelevant to the number of offspring they produce. This in turn has the result of increasing the number of genes in the population (the genetic load). The long-run implications of the development of such a feature, which is very different from the circumstances in which our species evolved, are uncertain.

One area of demography in which genetic theory has been generally taken up is the study of ISOLATE populations, especially research into the effects of inbreeding. This has led to some branching-out into the analysis of migration (Boyce 1984). There has also been overlap between genetics and demography in the field of mathematical model building.   RP, CW

Reference

Boyce, A.J., ed. 1984: *Migration and mobility: biosocial aspects of human movement*. London and Philadelphia: Taylor and Francis.

Reading

Cavalli-Sforza, L.L. 1974: The genetics of human populations. *Scientific American* 231, pp. 81–9. (Also published in the Scientific American book *The human population*. San Francisco: Freeman.)
— and Bodmer, W.F. 1971: *The genetics of human populations*. San Francisco: Freeman.

population ogive   See OGIVE.

population policy   Explicit measures taken by a government to influence population size, growth and composition.

The idea of a population policy is clear, the reality is not. Most countries have never had explicit and coherent policies on population, although all aspects of demographic change are affected by many government actions, usually taken for other reasons. The range of policies affecting population characteristics is so large that full consideration would include virtually all aspects of social and economic policy. Policies which have implicit rather than explicit demographic effects cannot be regarded as population policy.

As J.M. Stycos (1982) has pointed out, a policy is a guide to controlling the world rather than understanding it. To this end a population policy requires a clear, explicit statement of aims and a plan, backed by a theoretical framework, of how to achieve these aims. Most policies contain problems in both formulation and operation. The goals set by political leaders frequently refer to isolated targets with little apparent awareness of the interrelationship between factors. In part this results from the fact that demographic change is rarely so rapid as to form the forefront of political concern. (An exception is large-scale migration such as that from Indo-China in the early 1980s, which usually leads to considerable political action in receiving countries.) The lack of universally applicable population theories encourages an *ad hoc*

approach. Even where clear and coherent statements of policy are made they are frequently qualified by admissions that government policy should not impinge on human rights or individual freedom of action. At times, practical policy and population theory may also evolve in apparently different directions. For example, although Marxist theory generally denies the possibility of overpopulation in a socialist state, both the USSR and China have at times pursued active antinatalist policies.

The aims of policy usually relate to specific attributes of the population: commonly its size, but also its growth rate or geographical distribution and, sometimes, its age structure. Many long-term policies aim at achieving a stationary population or zero population growth. To attain these goals policies must affect the three components of change: mortality, fertility and migration. The most notable population policies in European countries have been pronatalist attempts to increase fertility at periods of slow or negative growth (1930s and 1970s). The success of these policies has been limited. In many parts of the world, however, rapid population growth has induced policies aimed at reducing fertility, especially through the adoption of family planning. As Nortmann and Hofstatter (1980) have pointed out, however, in 1979 only 35 out of 132 developing countries had an official policy to reduce the growth rate, though these included most of the largest nations and accounted for more than three-quarters of the population in the 132 countries. The motivation for improving health and mortality conditions has rarely been explicitly demographic, the lengthening of human lives being taken as an end in itself. Indeed in many cases the increased growth attributable to mortality reduction conflicts with policies of reducing fertility to slow growth. In an analogous way, the impact of policy on fertility has often been indirect. In particular, in Western countries increased provision of facilities for family planning and easier access to abortion may have played a role in reducing fertility, but the declared aim of these policies was to give couples better means of deciding their own family size rather than to reduce the birth rate. While most antinatalist policies concentrate on family planning, some also encourage delayed marriage. In China, for example, late marriage has been a significant factor in the dramatic fall in fertility over recent years.

Unlike fertility and mortality, which usually change slowly, migration is susceptible to rapid fluctuations and is often a politically sensitive issue. This is especially true of international migration in which the effects of government policies are most visible. Most countries have controls on persons entering and leaving their territories, sometimes so stringent as to make frontiers virtually uncrossable. Changes in these controls, frequently in response to prevailing economic conditions, provide a ready mechanism for the implementation of policy. In western Europe, for example, a positive attitude to immigration in the years from 1945 to 1973 encouraged considerable movement from poorer countries to northern Europe. The labour shortage which led to this policy disappeared after 1973 when unemployment grew, producing a reversal of policies. A more dramatic example of the relation between economic conditions and migration is the expulsion of over a million illegal immigrants from Nigeria in 1983 after a downturn in the country's economy. Although international migration provides some of the clearest evidence of government intervention, constraints on action are strong even in this area, as evidenced by the continued debate in the United States about the levels of legal and illegal immigration. Official attempts to control internal migration are rarely so successful as controls over international moves. This is attributable both to the much greater scale of internal mobility and to the lack of effective means of enforcing residence in specific areas. Although policies encouraging the development of specific areas are common,

especially with regard to the control of urbanization and the depopulation of remote areas, policy initiatives are usually restricted to economic incentives.   RP, CW

References

Nortmann, D.L. and Hofstatter, E. 1980: *Population and family planning programs: a compendium of data through 1978.* New York: Population Council.

Stycos, J.M. 1982: Population policy: overview. In J.A. Ross, ed. *International encyclopaedia of population.* New York: Free Press. Pp. 530–3.

Reading

Berelson, B. 1974: *Population policy in developed countries.* New York: McGraw-Hill.

Stycos 1982.

population pressure The situation in which there is a tension between the size of a population and the resources at its disposal.

An imprecise but widely used concept, population pressure may conveniently be related to the concept of OPTIMUM POPULATION. Wherever numbers exceed an optimum level (or in a more sophisticated analysis when the rate of population growth exceeds an optimum level) population pressure may be said to exist and to grow more severe if population growth continues (or the rate of growth fails to decline). The term is usually employed in relation to the living standards of the population. Population pressure exists because excess numbers cause living standards to be lower than would be attainable with reduced numbers.   EAW, RP

Reading

Sauvy, A. 1969: *General theory of population.* London: Weidenfeld and Nicolson; New York: Basic books.

population projection See PROJECTION.

population psychology The application of approaches, methodologies, concepts and theories developed within the discipline of psychology in order to explain human behaviour with a demographic outcome: fertility, mortality, migration, etc.

During the first decade of the use of the term writings described as being in the area of population psychology have been devoted almost solely to fertility and birth control, and within this area to the reasons for valuing children (see VALUE OF CHILDREN) and to the processes of choice involved in deciding whether or not to control fertility and how to do so. The field of interest can also embrace the attempt to distinguish individual psychological traits which may help to determine attitudes to family size and the likelihood of limiting fertility, as, for instance, in the Indianapolis study of 1941 (Whelpton and Kiser 1946–58).   JCC, PQ

Reference

Whelpton, P.K. and Kiser, C.V., eds. 1946–58: *Social and psychological factors affecting fertility*. Five volumes. New York: Milbank Memorial Fund.

Reading

Burch, T.K., ed. 1980: *Demographic behavior:* *interdisciplinary perspectives on decision-making*. AAAS selected symposium 45. Boulder, Colorado: Westview Press for the American Association for the Advancement of Science.

Fawcett, J.T. 1970: *Psychology and population: behavioral research issues in fertility and family planning*. New York: Population Council.

— ed. 1973: *Psychological perspectives on population*. New York: Basic Books.

Newman, S.H. and Thompson, V.D., eds. 1976: *Population psychology: research and educational issues*. Center for Population Research monograph. Bethesda, Maryland: United States Department of Health, Education and Welfare.

Pohlman, E. with Pohlman, J.M. 1969: *The psychology of birth planning*. Cambridge, Mass.: Schenkman.

population pyramid   A double bar-chart showing the AGE-SEX STRUCTURE of a population. See fig. below.

The pyramid consists of two sets of horizontal bar graphs, one for each sex,

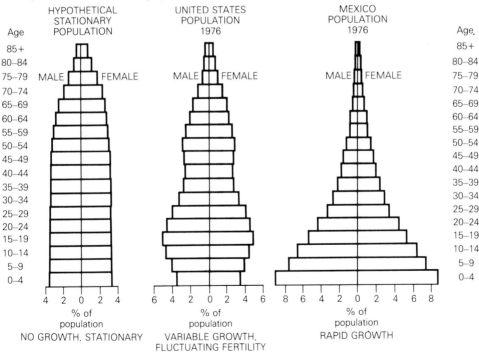

Source: L. H. Day 1979: What will a ZPG society be like? *Population bulletin* 33.3, p. 5.

which indiate either the number or the proportion of persons in each age group, or each single year of age. For convenience of comparison the graphs for each sex are placed on either side of a central axis which has the youngest ages at the bottom and the oldest at the top. The figure narrows at the top, hence the term pyramid, though not all age structures have a strictly pyramidal profile. Fast-growing populations, with each birth cohort larger than the one before, do resemble pyramids, but populations with low growth rates have more even age structures. In a STATIONARY POPULATION the age structure corresponds exactly to the SURVIVAL CURVE. In general, fertility has a greater impact on the age structure than does mortality, and countries with marked fluctuations, in fertility have irregular pyramids. This is true for most European countries and North America. Similarly, large migratory movements can lead to highly distorted pyramids.

A problem sometimes occurs when representing the oldest age-group since this is normally open-ended and not strictly comparable to younger ones. Pyramids are highly effective and widely used in demography to illustrate age structures. They are frequently produced for sub-populations and are sometimes shaded, or otherwise divided, to show more detail on the same graph.   RP

Reading

Lauro, D. 1982: Composition. In J. A. Ross, ed. *International encyclopaedia of population.* New York: Free Press. Pp. 98–102.

Shryock, H.S., Siegel, J.S. et. al. 1976: *The methods and materials of demography.* Condensed edition by Stockwell, E.G. London and New York: Academic Press. Pp. 134–9.

population register A system of data collection in which the demographic and socio-economic characteristics of the population are continuously recorded. A distinction is made between universal registers, which attempt to include the whole population, and partial registers, limited to specific groups, for example, voter registration.

When complete a population register combines some of the functions of a census and vital registration in providing information on both the stock of population and the flow of events. In practice, since the census can provide information not contained in the registers, the two sources are complementary and serve as checks on each other.

Although population registers have been used at certain times in many countries, for example for the rationing of food and consumer goods in wartime, their permanent use is rare. Only in parts of Europe, especially Scandinavia, in parts of eastern Asia and in Israel are more or less complete registers maintained. Where records of vital statistics are complete the only extra information provided by population registers is on changes of residence. This makes them particularly valuable sources of data on internal migration.   RP

Reading

Shryock, H.S., Siegel, J.S. et. al. 1976: *The methods and materials of demography.* Condensed edition by E. G. Stockwell. London and New York: Academic Press. Pp. 23–5.

population studies Whereas the term DEMOGRAPHY connotes principally the study of FERTILITY, MORTALITY, NUPTIAL-ITY and MIGRATION and their interrelationships, population studies embraces a wider area. The demographic characteristics of a population are strongly influenced by its economic and social constitution, and may in turn profoundly affect that constitution. Other elements of both the social and the physical environment of a population may also influence and be influenced by its demographic characteristics. Population studies covers all these aspects of population behaviour. As an area of study it has benefited in recent years from the recognition that attempts to understand and explain a community's demography in terms, say, of its economic characteristics (so that its fertility, mortality and nuptiality lie 'downstream' from some other aspect of its constitution) have seldom proved successful.

Accordingly, increased attention has been devoted to describing and attempting to model the complexity and contingency of the mutual relationships between economic, social and demographic variables.

EAW

population theory Theoretical frameworks which attempt to explain or predict demographic trends, in particular the relationship between population and economic, social and psychological factors.

All branches of demography involve theorizing of some kind, but the term population theory usually refers to overall models of demographic change in relation to economics. Many discussions of population theory begin with the opposing contributions of MALTHUS and MARX, though the earliest theories are much older. Ideas on the desirable characteristics for a population and the demographic processes which condition it were in existence well before the avilability of precise numerical knowledge, for they existed in classical Greece in the views of Plato and Aristotle, and in China with the Confucian school. In both traditions the concept of an OPTIMUM POPULATION was given a central role.

PRONATALISM prevailed for the most part during the Christian Middle Ages, with emphasis placed at least as much on a respect for fertility and for the importance of life as on explicit statements of the advantages of population growth. Sixteenth and seventeenth-century mercantilism and eighteenth-century physiocracy, while being primarily economic doctrines, nonetheless paid great attention to demography. Mercantilist authors largely wrote in favour of demographic expansion, seeing men as the source of wealth, while the physiocrats' emphasis on the tendency for population to put pressure on resources prefigured Malthus. But it was with Malthus and the neo-Malthusian movement which followed him, that the populationist tendencies which had been expressed earlier found themselves under the most sustained attack. Propagandists

of NEO-MALTHUSIANISM saw in birth control the prime method of alleviating working-class poverty. In this they echoed the propositions put forward by contemporary economists (Ricardo and John Stuart Mill in England, Jean-Baptiste Say in France) who justified the new doctrine on the basis of extensive socio-economic analyses. Opposed by utopian socialists, and to an even greater extent by Marx and his disciples, Malthus's population law is seen by the latter as being linked to the conditions of capitalist production and irrelevant to the communist society of the future.

In the contemporary world antagonistic doctrinal positions are taken up in relation to Third World problems. While some believe that these problems will solve themselves once a sufficient level of development has been reached, others stress the need to limit population growth in order to attain economic expansion. The argument is particularly vehement between proponents of ZERO POPULATION GROWTH and those who regard people as, in Julian Simon's words, 'the ultimate resource'.

RP

Reading

Keyfitz, N. 1982: Population theory. In J. A. Ross, ed. *International encyclopaedia of population.* New York: Free Press. Pp. 536–44.

Overbeek, J. 1974: *History of population theories.* Rotterdam: Rotterdam University Press.

Sauvy, A. 1969: *General theory of population.* London: Weidenfeld and Nicolson; New York: Basic Books.

Simon, J. 1981: *The ultimate resource.* Princeton, NJ: Princeton University Press.

postcoital contraception Intervention, a short time after sexual intercourse, aimed at avoiding conception.

Since fertilisation occurs shortly after sexual intercourse postcoital contraception can only be effective in stopping implantation. It can therefore only be called contraception if conception is defined as taking place after implantation. One form of intervention is based on the

G

hormones that are used in other forms of ORAL CONTRACEPTIVES. A pill containing a synthetic oestrogen is taken within 72 hours of coitus and for a period of 5 days (hence the name morning-after pill). Alternatively an intra-uterine device of copper is inserted within the same period of time. Although highly effective in preventing implantation, current post-coital oestrogens produce serious side effects (nausea, disruption of subsequent cycles and potential carcinogenesis) and cannot be used routinely. A further method, the postcoital douche, is the least effective of all forms of contraception because the sperm enter the cervix before the douche can be administered.   RP

Reading
Segal, S.J. et al. 1982: Contraceptive methods: overview. In J.A. Ross, ed. *International encyclopaedia of population.* New York: Free Press. Pp. 103–9.

post-enumeration survey A sample survey conducted after a CENSUS primarily to estimate completeness of enumeration. Subsidiary aims can include evaluation of the quality of responses by re-interview of the same respondents using different interviewers but the same questionnaires; also the asking of additional questions too complex for the main census form.

The results of the post-enumeration survey are often used to adjust the census results for under- or over-enumeration. Groups which are difficult to enumerate – nomads, immigrants or young single people in cities – are frequently under-counted in censuses, and specially designed searches may be necessary to arrive at appropriate inflation factors for these groups. The smaller more carefully controlled post-enumeration survey is designed for just these purposes.   AH

post-partum non-susceptibility See NON-SUSCEPTIBLE PERIOD.

post-partum variables A term referring to a series of temporary behavioural and biological conditions that both start at and

occur as a result of childbirth. It is used in particular to refer to those conditions that play a significant role in determining the duration of the post-partum NON-SUSCEPTIBLE PERIOD. The most important are BREASTFEEDING, the post-partum period of ANOVULATION and AMENOR-RHOEA, and post-partum ABSTINENCE from sexual relations. For some of these the incidence is variable (not every woman breastfeeds, for example). For all of them the length of time a woman remains in the condition is highly variable, with durations ranging from zero or nearly zero to periods of as long as 18 months or more (post-partum amenorrhoea) or three or more years (breastfeeding and post-partum abstinence).   HP

Reading
Bongaarts, J. and Potter, R.G. 1983: *Fertility, biology and behavior: an analysis of the proximate determinants.* New York and London: Academic Press.
Leridon, H. 1977: *Human fertility: the basic components.* Chicago: University of Chicago Press.
Lesthaeghe, R. and Page, H.J. 1980: The post-partum non-susceptible period: development and application of model schedules. *Population studies* 34, pp. 143–69.

pregnancy The period between CON-CEPTION and the CONFINEMENT or ABOR-TION which follows. Pregnancy is sometimes defined as beginning at implantation or nidation, about a week after fertilization.

The product of conception is successively termed an embryo and then a foetus though there is no general agreement about the point at which the terminology changes, and the term foetus is often employed throughout the pregnancy.   RP

pregnancy history A type of LIFE HISTORY which records details of all the pregnancies a woman has experienced, including the date at which each began and ended and the outcome.

Pregnancy histories are usually collected in retrospective surveys and potentially provide data on every aspect of a woman's childbearing experience. They frequently include socio-economic information which opens up the scope for analysis of fertility differentials. In practice, pregnancy histories encounter considerable problems. Many persons, particularly in societies with low literacy, are unfamiliar with notions of precise chronological age or the calendar and are unable to locate past events with precision. Even in completely literate societies, lapse of memory poses severe problems, especially when an exact month-by-month reconstruction of the reproductive ages is being attempted, so that the collection of usable pregnancy histories is both difficult and expensive. As a consequence most surveys prefer to concentrate on gathering MATERNITY HISTORIES which relate only to births.   RP, CW

pregnancy order   The number of previous pregnancies a woman has had. The word gravidity, drawn from medical usage, is used synonymously: a woman is termed a nulligravida if she has never been pregnant, a primigravida during her first pregnancy, and a multigravida if she has had at least one previous pregnancy.   CW

pregnancy rate   See CONCEPTION RATE.

pre-marital pregnancy   A pregnancy in which conception occurs before marriage and the birth after marriage.

Many studies of pre-marital sexual activity are based upon the study of pregnancies which result in a birth (usually a live birth) after marriage. This excludes pregnancies which end in an induced or spontaneous abortion, a factor of increasing importance in many societies. The detailed analysis of pre-marital pregnancies is often difficult. There are two main sources of information. The first is MATERNITY HISTORIES in which women are asked retrospectively for the dates of their marriages and the births of their children (sometimes a PREGNANCY HISTORY in which all pregnancies are detailed is avail-

able). The second source is RECORD LINKAGE studies based on vital registration. In general the latter provide more accurate information. In one study in the United States a significant proportion of women who had been identified by record linkage as having had a pre-marital birth adjusted the date of the first birth in the reported maternity history to make it appear the outcome of a post-marital conception.

A further complication is that the duration of pregnancy varies and a simple, unambiguous demarcation of pre-marital pregnancies cannot therefore be made. Although subject to a slight uncertainty, births occurring before eight months' duration of marriage are often taken as representing the number of pre-marital pregnancies.

The factors influencing the prevalence of pre-marital conceptions are numerous: access and information about contraception and abortion, the frequency of sexual relations before marriage and the extent of social pressure exerted towards marriage are all important. In many western countries pre-marital conceptions are most likely among teenage brides and in groups of lower socio-economic status, though this is not universal. Long-standing regional patterns are also clear, indicating distinct socio-cultural variations. In France, for example, the north and east of the country have long had significantly higher proportions of bridal pregnancies than have Brittany and the south.   RP

pre-testing   See PILOT SURVEY.

prevalence rate   A measure of MORBIDITY during a specified period of time (period prevalence) or at a specified point in time (point prevalence). These can be defined as follows:

$$\text{Point Prevalence Rate} = \frac{N}{P_{point}} \times k$$

where N stands for the number of persons with a disease at a point in time, P_{point} is the number of persons in the population at that point in time and k is a constant (usually 1000, but sometimes 100,000 for rare diseases).

$$\begin{array}{c} Period \\ Prevalence \\ Rate \end{array} = \frac{N_{cases}}{P_{period}} \times k$$

where N_{cases} represents the number of cases of disease occurring during a specified time period, P_{period} is the average number of persons exposed to the risk of contracting the disease during the period and k is a constant (commonly 1000 or 100,000).

The numerator of a period prevalence rate can either be the total number of persons with the disease or the total number of spells of disease. The number of persons exposed to risk (denominator) is often estimated by the total mid-period population. A better estimate can, however, be obtained from longitudinal or follow-up studies where person-years (or, if appropriate, person-weeks, etc.) of exposure to risk can be calculated.

Even though it takes time to ascertain all the cases of disease within a population, point prevalence is frequently estimated. Point prevalence and incidence are related as follows:

$$PPR = Dur \times IR$$

where PPR is the point prevalence rate, IR is the incidence rate and Dur is the mean duration of disease per sick person. RP, ER

Reading
Bradford Hill, A. 1977: *A short textbook of medical statistics*. London: Hodder and Stoughton Educational.

Lilienfeld, A.M. and Lilienfeld, D.E. 1980: *Foundations of epidemiology*. Second edition. Oxford: Oxford University Press.

primary sterility See STERILITY.

primagravida See PREGNANCY ORDER.

primipara See PARITY.

principal components analysis A multivariate statistical technique consisting of finding new variables, composed of linear combinations of the original variables, that have the property of being orthogonal (i.e. uncorrelated) to each other, but are correlated with the original variables. The linear transformations are chosen in such a way that the first principal component represents the maximum variance in the data, the second principal component represents the second largest variance subject to being uncorrelated with the first component, and so on. In precise technical terms the linear combinations are obtained by finding the eigenvalues and eigenvectors of either the covariance matrix (original variables) or the correlation matrix (standardised variables).

There are usually as many different principal components (eigenvectors) as there are variables. However, eigenvectors corresponding to low eigenvalues may be neglected, thereby reducing the dimensionality of the data matrix. GW

Reading
Kim, J.O. 1975: Factor analysis. In N.H. Nie et al., eds. *Statistical package for the social sciences*. Second edition. New York: McGraw Hill.

Ledermann, S. and Bréas, J. 1959: Les dimensions de la mortalité. *Population* 14, pp. 637-82.

Van de Geer, J.P. 1971: *Introduction to multivariate analysis for the social sciences*. San Francisco: W.H. Freeman.

probability The relative frequency with which a demographic event occurs within a COHORT, given that the event is a NON-RENEWABLE PROCESS and that the individuals all have a chance of experiencing it (see EXPOSURE TO RISK). Probabilities are also calculated for period data, making use of the concept of a HYPOTHETICAL COHORT.

Probabilities are usually calculated either for different age groups or according to duration since some previous event; they thus represent the chance of an event occurring between two ages (or durations) among people who have not previously experienced it. Examples are the probability of marrying between ages 25 and 30 for those still single at 25, and the probability of dying between ages 50 and 55 among those alive at 50.

Probabilities can be defined only for non-renewable events. Where an event can be experienced several times it is possible for more than one occurrence per person to be observed, rendering the calculation of probabilities impossible.

The calculation of probabilities is closely linked to the idea of the LIFE TABLE, and forms a constituent of all LIFE TABLE METHODS. When using MULTIPLE DECREMENT LIFE TABLES, in which several sets of probabilities are taken into account simultaneously, the term net probability is used to indicate that the effects of one phenomenon have been taken into account when calculating the probability that a second phenomenon will occur. For example, net marriage probabilities take into account the impact of mortality in disturbing marriage patterns. In most circumstances probabilities refer to the chance of an event occurring between two exact ages or durations, e.g. death between exactly age 50 and exactly 55. At times, however, probabilities are calculated that refer to chances between two points, e.g. survival from one census to the next. These are called PROJECTIVE PROBABILITIES.   CW

Reading
Pressat, R. 1972: *Demographic analysis: methods, results, applications.* London: Edward Arnold; Chicago: Aldine Atherton. Chapters 2 and 3.
Wunsch, G. and Termote, M. 1978: *Introduction to demographic analysis.* New York and London: Plenum. Chapters 1 to 3.

probability of dying The probability that a person aged exactly x years will die before reaching the age $x + n$ and conventionally given as $_nq_x$ or simply q_x when n is one.

The measure is related to other LIFE TABLE FUNCTIONS by the following equations, where l_x stands for the number of survivors in the life table at exactly age x, and $_np_x$ is the probability of survival from x to $x + n$.

$$_nq_x = 1 - \left(\frac{l_{x+n}}{l_x}\right)$$

$$_nq_x = 1 - {}_np_x$$

The probability of dying usually declines with age up to about 12 or 13 years, then increases steadily to the highest ages.
                                                      RP

Reading
Shryock, H.S., Siegel, J.S. et al. 1976: *The methods and materials of demography.* Condensed edition by E.G. Stockwell. London and New York: Academic Press. Chapter 15.

probability of survival See PROBABILITY OF DYING.

probability sampling Also known as 'scientific sampling'. Any sampling process in which the (relative) selection probabilities of the sample units are *non-zero* and *known in principle*.   CS

projection The computation of future population size and characteristics based on assumptions about future trends in fertility, mortality and migration.

A distinction is made between a projection and a FORECAST, the latter implying an element of prediction while the former simply represents the working out of various hypothetical assumptions. Demographers have in theory insisted that, given the inherent unpredictability of human behaviour, they can make only projections, but in practice the distinction between forecasts and projections is often artificial. Most projections made by official bodies are treated as forecasts, since many business and government decisions have to be based on a 'best guess' of future population size and composition.

In the most widely used methodology for projection, COMPONENT METHODS, each of the components of change (birth, death, migration) is estimated. Attempts to improve on the accuracy of this approach have involved various time-series and econometric methods, which offer potentially greater reliability by which are harder to relate to basic demographic processes (see Lee in United Nations 1979). The use of theoretical models of demographic behaviour as a guide to projections has had little impact, possibly because the fundamental causes of population change are poorly understood (Keyfitz 1982). Whatever their sophistication, no projection techniques can predict future population with great accuracy. Figure 1 indicates the extent to which UK government projections varied over the 20 years 1955–1975, a period of rapidly increasing then sharply falling fertility. In an attempt to cope with this unpredictability projections are frequently made under several sets of assumptions, see fig. 2. Keyfitz (1981) has suggested that a better approach would be to make estimates of a confidence interval, or likely error associated with the main projection.

RP, CW

References

Keyfitz, N. 1981: The limits of population forecasting. *Population and development review*, pp. 579–93.

— 1982: Can knowledge improve forecasts? *Population and development review* 8, pp. 729–51.

United Nations 1979: *Prospects of population: methodology and assumptions*. New York: Department of International Economic and Social Affairs.

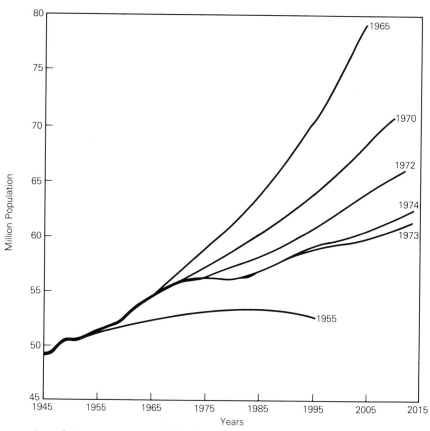

1.   Population projections for the United Kingdom, made 1955 to 1974.

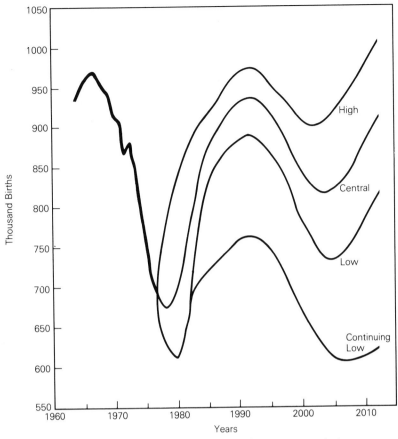

2. Variant birth projections for Great Britain.

Sources: OPCS Population projections 1974–2014 (1976) (fig. 1) and *1974–2011* (1975) (fig.2). After Woods 1977: *Population analysis in geography.* London and New York: Longman. Crown copyright: reproduced with the permission of the controller of Her Majesty's Stationary Office.

Reading

Brass, W. 1974: Perspectives in population prediction: illustrated by the statistics of England and Wales. *Journal of the Royal Statistical Society* series A, 137, pp. 532–70; and discussion, pp. 571–83.
Keyfitz 1981, 1982.

projection matrix   See LESLIE MATRIX.

projective probability   The probability that a given demographic event will occur in the interval between two dates (often between two censuses). It is also called a probability between completed ages or durations.

Projective probabilities are related to changes within groups classified by age in completed years, rather than exact age. For example the proportion of individuals aged 20 to 24 in one census who are still alive (aged 30 to 34) at the time of the next census 10 years later is the projective probability of survival. Such measures are often termed census survival rates or survivorship ratios and are widely used in population PROJECTIONS and in migration analysis.   RP, CW

pronatalism   A theory or policy which aims at increasing the growth rate of the population by raising fertility. The term populationism is used synonymously. The opposite is ANTINATALISM.

Pronatalist theories have a long history, especially in the Christian tradition, and above all in the work of Catholic theorists. In addition to religious motivations proponents of pronatalism often cite social and economic changes which they see as advantages arising from an increased birth rate: reduced ageing of the population, and stronger family ties in larger families with a better developmental environment for children. Other theorists dispute the existence or value of all these points.

RP, CW

proportional hazards models See HAZARDS MODELS.

prospective observation A method of data collection in which events are recorded as and when they occur. Although this is the case with conventional vital registration systems, the use of the term is usually limited to special PROSPECTIVE SURVEYS. RP

prospective survey A SURVEY which involves repeated observations through interviews or postal questionnaires of the same subjects or the residents of a fixed geographical area or areas. The object is to examine the relationship at different times between events, status or responses which are difficult or impossible to measure using the retrospective method.

The series of interviews normally begins with a lengthy baseline survey followed by a number of shorter inquiries at fixed intervals (ranging from one month to several years apart) which are designed to capture vital events or migrations which may have occurred between two survey rounds. Prospective surveys can either: (1) repeatedly interview the same respondents, when they are called 'panel' or 'follow up' surveys; or (2) they can use a rotating sample of respondents.

Examples of major surveys which have employed the prospective approach involving repeated interviews with the same individuals are the 1970 US National Fertility Study (Ryder 1973; Westoff 1975) and cohort inquiries such as the National Survey of Health and Development in the UK (Atkins et al. 1980). Prospective surveys sometimes use a rotating sample of individuals to minimise interference: here representativeness is retained by selecting sample areas at the outset by the usual methods of probability sampling, but between rounds areas and individuals are changed within the overall sample frame. Examples of these kinds of surveys are the UK General Household Survey and the US Current Population Survey.

AH

References

Atkins, E., Cherry, N., Douglas, J.W.B., Kiernan, K.E. and Wadsworth, M.E.J. 1980: The 1946 British birth cohort: an account of the origins, progress and results of the National Survey of Health and Development. In J.A. Medwick and A.E. Baert, eds. *An empirical basis for primary prevention in prospective longitudinal research in Europe*. Oxford: Oxford University Press.
Ryder, N.B. 1973: A critique of the National Fertility Study. *Demography* 10, pp. 495–503.
Westoff, C.F. 1975: The yield of the imperfect: the 1970 National Fertility Study. *Demography* 12, pp. 573–80.

Reading

Douglas, J.W.B. 1976: The use and abuse of national cohorts. In M. Shipman, ed. *The organization and impact of social research*. London: Routledge and Kegan Paul.
Moser, K. and Kalton, G., eds. 1971: *Survey methods in social investigation*. Second edition. London: Heinemann; New York: Basic Books (1972).
United States, National Academy of Sciences 1981: *Collecting data for the estimation of fertility and mortality*. Committee on Population and Demography, report 6. Washington DC: National Academy Press.

protogenesic interval See BIRTH INTERVAL.

proximate determinants of fertility Biological and behavioural factors which directly influence fertility, and through which social, economic and other factors come to influence childbearing. The alternative term intermediate fertility variables is also used.

The distinguishing feature of proximate determinants is their direct effect on fertility. If a proximate determinant changes, fertility will also change (assuming that other proximate determinants remain the same). Thus differentials and trends in childbearing can be related to the prevailing values of the proximate determinants.

A variety of frameworks has been used to describe the relation between fertility and its determinants. In the 1950s Louis Henry constructed mathematical models of the reproductive process but, although highly illuminating, their relative complexity meant that few applications were possible. A different approach was made by Davis and Blake (1956) who defined a comprehensive set of determinants grouped into three categories: factors which influenced the frequency of sexual relations (e.g. the prevalence of MARRIAGE and coital rates), factors which affected the chance of conception (e.g. CONTRACEPTION), and factors related to the outcome of a pregnancy (e.g. spontaneous and INDUCED ABORTION). The development of reproductive models continued during the 1960s, notably in the work of Sheps and Potter, but relatively straightforward and more easily applicable models were not developed until the 1970s. The most influential of these is the BONGAARTS DECOMPOSITION model which focuses on four things: marriage (or other sexual unions), contraception, induced abortion and post-partum non-susceptibility, which is mainly influenced by BREAST-FEEDING. These four appear to account for most of the observed variation in fertility throughout the world. A recent extension of the use of proximate determinants is the development of techniques which enable their influence to be assessed at the individual level (Hobcraft and Little 1984).

RP, CW

References
Davis, K. and Blake, J. 1956: Social structure and fertility: an analytic framework. *Economic development and cultural change* 4, pp. 211–35.

Hobcraft, J..and Little, R.J.A. 1984: Fertility exposure analysis: a new method for assessing the contribution of proximate determinants to fertility differentials. *Population studies* 38, pp. 21–45.

Reading
Bongaarts, J. 1982: Fertility determinants: proximate determinants. In J.A. Ross, ed. *International encyclopaedia of population.* New York: Free Press.
— and Potter, R.G. 1983: *Fertility, biology and behavior: an analysis of the proximate determinants.* New York and London: Academic Press.
Hobcraft and Little 1984.

puberty The period of physical and sexual maturation that transforms a child into a young adult. During puberty rapid growth in body weight and height takes place and the reproductive organs mature. The developments in the female include the onset of menstruation and ovulation (see MENARCHE), the enlargement of the breasts and the appearance of pubic hair. In the male semen production begins, first ejaculation occurs, the voice deepens and body hair appears. JB

Reading
Hafez, E.S.E. and Evans, T.N., eds 1980: *Human reproduction: conception and contraception.* Hagerstown, Maryland: Harper and Row.

push-pull hypothesis The production of a MIGRATION flow through factors at both the origin and destination. The hypothesis assumes that at each end there are factors promoting and retarding migration and that the balance of these factors determines the size and strength of the flow. Hence, for example, migration from a low-income to a high-income area is assumed to be the result of the predominance of *pull* factors while movement from areas hit by famine would be the result of *push* factors predominating.

DCS

Reading

Lee, E.S. 1969: A theory of migration. In J. A. Jackson, ed. *Migration*. Cambridge: Cambridge University Press.

Q

quantum The ultimate frequency with which a given event occurs to the members of a COHORT. The term intensity is used synonymously, and both are contrasted with measures of the timing of events or TEMPO.

The terms quantum and tempo were introduced by Ryder and have been used by him in several valuable studies of fertility (see Ryder 1980). The quantum can best be thought of as the mean number of events per person at the end of a cohort's experience. Thus for mortality the quantum is always one (everyone dies), while for other processes a variety of values are found. Events which cannot be experienced more than once (see NON-RENEWABLE PROCESS) have a maximum value of one, but may fall below it. For example the proportion of persons who marry for the first time has been as low as 70 per cent in some populations, but is virtually 100 per cent in others. When studying fertility the quantum is usually the COMPLETED FERTILITY of a cohort, i.e. the average births per woman, or per couple. When analysing births of each order separately, however, the quantum indicates the proportion of the women who reach a given family size or PARITY who go on to have another child (i.e. the PARITY PROGRESSION RATIO for the order in question). Occasionally the disturbing effects of mortality or migration in preventing other events are taken into account, leading to a distinction between net and gross quantum.   RP

References

Ryder, N.B. 1980: Components of temporal variation in American fertility. In R.W. Hiorns, ed. *Demographic patterns in developed societies*. London: Taylor and Francis.

Reading

Ryder 1980.
Wunsch, G. and Termote, M. 1978: *Introduction to demographic analysis*. New York and London: Plenum. Chapters 1 and 2.

quasi-stable population A population which is closed to migration and has constant fertility but regularly changing mortality. It can most conveniently be regarded as a formerly STABLE POPULATION which has undergone destabilisation through a smooth alteration (usually a fall) in mortality.

Originally formulated by Bourgeois-Pichat (1958), the theory and techniques of quasi-stability were developed to enable stable population methods, which assume unchanging fertility and mortality, to be applied more widely. In the 1950s and 1960s every country showed improved mortality while in many parts of the Third World fertility remained largely constant. Since these conditions closely approximated quasi-stability, techniques for analysing census age distributions to estimate mortality levels which assumed this were often used (Coale 1971). Accurate adjustments for quasi-stability require detailed information which is rarely available for the countries being studied. In the absence of such data it is generally assumed that mortality change is smooth and regular and that only the level is changing, not the age-specific pattern. These assumptions are unlikely to be exact and some biases are therefore introduced.   RP, CW

Reference

Bourgeois-Pichat, J. 1958: Utilisation de la notion de population stable pour mésurer la mortalité et la fécondité des populations des pays sous-développés. *Bulletin de l'Institut International de Statistique* 36, pp. 94–121. (Proceedings of 30th session, Stockholm 1957.)

Coale, A.J. 1971: Constructing the age distribution of a population recently subject to declining mortality. *Population index* 37, pp. 75–82.

questionnaire   A written series of questions designed to elicit information from an informant on a given topic. It may be administered by an enumerator or interviewer or self-administered. Answers are usually recorded on the questionnaire form itself.

The nature of the questions is decided in relation to the subject of the survey and the type of answers required. The questions may be designed to educe opinion, factual, or knowledge responses and are set in a standardised form in order to increase comparability across respondents. The questions are arranged in a logical order and the questionnaire may have printed on it definitions and instructions to the interviewer or to the informant. The layout of the questionnaire is designed primarily to facilitate the task of this interviewer and/or respondent but also to help further processing such as CODING and data entry. Questionnaires vary greatly in their structural complexity. The questions are generally phrased in everyday language with a special effort to achieve unambiguous wording. The construction of a questionnaire is often preceded by an exploratory pilot investigation and its efficacy may be ascertained by means of a field pre-test. (See also INDIVIDUAL QUESTIONNAIRE and HOUSEHOLD QUESTIONNAIRE).

JGC

Reading

Moser, C.A. and Kalton, G. 1971: *Survey methods in social investigation.* Second edition. London: Heinemann; New York: Basic Books (1972).

Oppenheim, A.N. 1966: *Questionnaire design and attitude measurement.* London: Heinemann; New York: Basic Books.

Payne, S.L.B. 1951: *The art of asking questions.* Princeton, NJ: Princeton University Press.

Population Council 1970: *A manual for surveys of fertility and family planning: knowledge, attitudes and practice.* New York: Population Council.

United Nations 1970: *Variables and questionnaire for comparative fertility surveys.* New York: Department of Economic and Social Affairs.

World Fertility Survey 1975: *Core questionnaires.* Basic documentation number 1. Voorburg, The Netherlands: International Statistical Institute.

R

radix (of a life table) The arbitrary number of births at the start of a LIFE TABLE against which the survivors at each age may be compared. More generally it is the initial size of any cohort subjected to a particular chance or 'risk' of experiencing an event as represented in a life table. A power of 10 is conventionally taken as the radix: 1000, 10,000, 100,000 or 1 million are common, depending on the accuracy with which data are presented.   RP, CW

random sampling This term strictly refers to a selection process within one sampling stage and within one stratum, rather than to a complete SAMPLE DESIGN, and means a sample in which each unit has an equal and independent chance of selection. This is usually achieved by using random numbers to determine selection.

Two variants can be distinguished. (1) Random sampling *with replacement*, in which a unit selected is replaced immediately in the list and can be selected again. (2) Random sampling *without replacement*, in which no unit can be selected more than once. The latter has minor practical advantages and is generally preferred. Random sampling should be distinguished from SIMPLE RANDOM SAMPLING. Moreover the term random sampling is often misused where PROBABILITY SAMPLING is intended.   CS

randomised response technique (RRT) A form of data collection which allows respondents to give information on 'sensitive' subjects, such as induced abortion, without directly revealing the facts to the interviewer.

As originally devised RRT involved the use of a box containing beads of two col-ours. Through a window in the box the respondent sees only one bead, which is invisible to the interviewer. The respondent is asked to answer a question on either a sensitive or an innocuous issue according to the colour of the visible bead (e.g. blue – Have you ever had an abortion? Red – Were you born in the month of January?). The interviewer records the answer but does not know which question is being replied to (Warner 1965). From this data it is easy to estimate the proportion of respondents answering each question, and thus the number who have had an abortion is calculable.

RRT usually indicates a greater prevalence of the sensitive factor under consideration than is suggested by direct questioning. However, in spite of, or perhaps because of, its elaboration the technique does not completely overcome the respondents' reluctance to reply truthfully to sensitive questions. For example, when women in Taiwan who were known to have had abortions were asked whether this was the case using RRT, the estimated result was only 40 per cent (Rider et al. 1976).   CW

References

Rider, R.V. et al. 1976: A comparison of four methods for determining prevalence of induced abortion, Taiwan 1970–1971. *American journal of epidemiology* 103, pp. 137–50.

Warner, S.L. 1965: Randomised response: a survey technique for eliminating evasive answer bias. *Journal of the American Statistical Association* 60, 309, pp. 63–9.

rate A term used in many ways in demographic studies, but most appropriately applied to the number of events in a given period of time divided by the average population (or appropriate sub-population) during the period.

The word is also used more loosely to refer to the ratio between a sub-population and the total: for example, the school enrolment rate or the literacy rate. In many other uses of rate, the measure in question would be better termed a RATIO, proportion, or PROBABILITY. The term can be justified only when a dynamic process is being measured, not a static description of a population at a given date, although its use in the latter sense is widespread. In general the word ratio is preferable to rate when the measure is not one relating events to a population at risk.

Various qualifiers are used to indicate the nature of the rate in question. A CRUDE RATE is one in which the total number of events is divided by the average population, whereas various specific rates provide more detailed information. Rates which are age-specific are widely used, as are rates specified by duration since a particular BASELINE EVENT. Any adjustment or correction to the rate is reflected in the terminology. For example, rates which take into account the disturbance of mortality in preventing other processes are called NET RATES. In contrast GROSS rates ignore the effects of all disturbing processes. Most rates refer to the occurrence of events over a year, though monthly or quarterly rates are sometimes given. The definition of the average population forming the denominator of a rate is commonly that of the MID-YEAR POPULATION, although when individual-level data are used it is necessary to calculate the PERSON-YEARS of EXPOSURE TO RISK. Using person-years in the denominator automatically gives the rate an annual dimension.

A fundamental difference exists between rates where the occurrence of an event leads to the removal of an individual from the population at risk, ATTRITION RATES (which are calculable only for a NON-RENEWABLE PROCESS, e.g. mortality), and rates where the denominator is composed of both those who have experienced the event in question and those who have not. The latter rates may be termed INCIDENCE RATES and are calculated for both renewable and non-renewable events.   RP

Reading

Elandt-Johnson, R.C. 1975: Definition of rates: some remarks on their use and misuse. *American journal of epidemiology* 102, pp. 267–71.

— and Johnson, N.L. 1980: *Survival models and data analysis.* New York and Chichester: Wiley. Chapter 2.

Pressat, R. 1972: *Demographic analysis: methods, results, applications.* London: Edward Arnold; Chicago: Aldine Atherton. Chapter 3.

Ross, J.A. 1982: Rates and ratios. In J.A. Ross, ed. *International encyclopaedia of population.* New York: Free Press, pp. 575–8.

Shryock, H.S., Siegel, J.S. et al. 1976: *The methods and materials of demography.* Condensed edition by E.G. Stockwell. London and New York: Academic Press. Chapter 1.

ratio   The result of dividing one number by another when the two quantities are not related in the way necessary for the calculation of a RATE.

While rates are a measure of change over time, ratios are appropriate to the description of a population at a particular moment. The DEPENDENCY RATIO, for example, indicates the relative sizes of the working age population and the dependent population while the SEX RATIO gives the number of males relative to the number of females. Ratios are also used to relate phenomena which are mutually exclusive: for example, the number of foetal deaths occurring in a year divided by the number of live births during the same period is termed the foetal death ratio.   RP

ratio methods   Methods of calculating population PROJECTIONS for subpopulations through the application of the proportion of the total population in each subgroup. A variety of methods exists based on this central idea. Ratio methods are capable of extension to cover an entire hierarchy of projections; for a nation, for provinces, for communities and so on, each level related to the one above. Ratios for factors other than geographical location are also used to provide projections for different socio-economic or ethnic groups. RP

Reading
Shryock, H.S., Siegel, J.S. et al. 1976: *The methods and materials of demography*. Condensed edition by E.G. Stockwell. London and New York: Academic Press. Chapter 23.

Ravenstein's 'laws' of migration Statements on MIGRATION propensities propounded by Ernst George Ravenstein (1834–1913). In a pioneering use of the published British census statistics (of 1861, 1871 and 1881) Ravenstein argued that migration was not random but was governed by general laws. In three publications (1876, 1885 and 1889) he put forward eleven laws:

(1) the majority of migrants go only a short distance
(2) migration proceeds step-by-step, in that the places of outmigrants are filled by inmigrants from more remote areas
(3) each migration current produces a compensating counter-current
(4) longer distance migrants tend to go to larger towns
(5) the urban-born are less migratory than the rural-born
(6) females are more migratory over shorter distances, males over longer
(7) most migrants are adults
(8) large towns grow by migration more than by natural increase
(9) migration increases in volume with economic and transport improvement
(10) the major migration flow is from agricultural areas to large towns
(11) the major causes of migration are economic.

Ravenstein's laws have been widely used, and have been reformulated by recent demographers (e.g. Lee 1969) though this early success has tended to place greater emphasis on testing laws rather than on wider empirical research.

Grigg has recently demonstrated that the applicability of Ravenstein's laws to nineteenth-century England has been largely confirmed by subsequent research (Grigg 1977). DCS

References
Grigg, D.B. 1977: E.G. Ravenstein on the laws of migration. *Journal of historical geography* 3, pp. 41–54.
Lee, E.S. 1969: A theory of migration. In J.A. Jackson, ed. *Migration*. Cambridge: Cambridge University Press.
Ravenstein, E.G. 1876: Census of the British Isles 1871; birthplaces and migration. *Geographical magazine* 3.
— 1885: The laws of migration. *Journal of the Statistical Society* 48.
— 1889: The laws of migration. *Journal of the Statistical Society* 52.

Reading
Grigg 1977.
Lee 1969.

recall error Responses to retrospective questions are subject to error owing to omission of events, incorrect sequencing of events and misreporting of dates and ages at events. The term recall error is used to refer to all such deficiencies. Examples include underreporting of children everborn, and incorrect reporting of age at first marriage and of past changes of residence. DE

record linkage The compilation of a variety of information, often coming from several different sources, relating to a person or a marriage.

The various events marking the life of an individual or of a couple are recorded in many sources of information. Vital events in the past were recorded in PARISH REGISTERS and are now the concern of VITAL REGISTRATION; most of the episodes of illness in a person's life will appear in the dossiers of health or social insurance bodies; legal transactions and contracts appear in legal records, and so on. Elsewhere CENSUSES provide, at more or less regular intervals, an inventory of a population with details of the current status and histories of the subjects of the census. By bringing together the information scattered through these documents record linkage offers considerable scope for detailed analysis. In particular it often makes possible cohort studies when only period information would otherwise be available. The exploitation of traditional demographic sources in this way can be invaluable for particular studies. A good case is the study of differential mortality, where the benefit of being able to use both census and registration data is considerable. Even using only one source of data such as vital registration the advantages of using linkage to create life histories is often great. For example, FAMILY RECONSTITUTION of historical records provides insights which would be unobtainable in any other way.   RP

Reading

Wrigley, E.A. ed. 1973: *Identifying people in the past.* London: Edward Arnold.

reduced events   See INCIDENCE RATE.

Reed-Merrell tables   Tables calculated by the American demographers Lowell J. Reed and Margaret Merrell (1939) to facilitate the construction of ABRIDGED LIFE TABLES by allowing central death rates to be converted into probabilities of dying.

The conversion tables are based on empirical data for the United States from which Reed and Merrell derived equations linking death rates and probabilities. In spite of this limited database the equations have proved useful in many situations although the development of MODEL LIFE TABLES has in many ways reduced the importance of the Reed-Merrell approach. (See also LIFE TABLE CONSTRUCTION.)   RP

Reference

Reed, L.J. and Merrell, M. 1939: A short method for constructing an abridged life table. *American journal of hygiene* 30, pp. 33–62.

Reading

Shryock, H.S., Siegel, J.S. et al. 1976: *The methods and materials of demography.* Condensed edition by E.G. Stockwell. London and New York: Academic Press. Pp. 253–7 and 513–20.

reference period errors   Errors in response to retrospective survey questions caused by a failure to place the timing of an event in correct relation to a reference period. For example, data from questions about births or deaths in a household during the previous twelve months or change of residence since the previous census are subject to inclusion of events outside the reference period or to omission of events during the reference period.   DE

regime, demographic   The particular combination of interrelated demographic characteristics that pertains in a given population. For example a situation in which fertility and mortality are in balance and where social arrangements maintain this balance is sometimes referred to as a HOMEOSTATIC REGIME.   CW

regional analysis   A region is a geographic area with some measure of internal homogeneity with respect to the characteristic, functions or interconnections of its constituent parts. Regional analysis is the investigation of the structure and behaviour of the populations, resources and environments of regions.

The analysis begins with the delineation of the boundaries of the regions then being studied using selected taxonomic techniques. A part of the man-environment regional system is then usually selected for study. For example, the population subsystem, the settlement subsystem, the economic subsystem, or the land-use-transport subsystem, are studied using techniques such as demographic accounting and cohort survival modelling, central place modelling, input-output modelling, spatial interaction modelling and location-allocation modelling. More occasionally attempts are made to construct semi-comprehensive models of a regional system.   PR

Reading

Abler, R., Adams, J. and Gould, P. 1971: *Spatial organisation: the geographer's view of the world.* Englewood Cliffs, NJ: Prentice Hall.

Haggett, P., Cliff, A.D. and Frey, A. 1977: *Locational analysis in human geography.* Second edition. London: Edward Arnold.

Isard, W. et al. 1960: *Methods of regional analysis: an introduction to regional science.* Cambridge, Mass.: MIT Press.

Wilson, A.G. 1974: *Urban and regional models in geography and planning.* Chichester and New York: Wiley.

— Rees, P.H. and Leigh, C.M., eds. 1977: *Models of cities and regions.* Chichester: Wiley.

registration system A system for the continuous recording of events for legal or statistical purposes. Registration systems such as VITAL REGISTRATION, or POPULATION REGISTERS are permanent, and exist primarily for their value as legal documents. Hence registration in these is mandatory by law. On the other hand, a system such as the SAMPLE VITAL REGISTRATION is usually temporary, and exists in underdeveloped areas solely because of its usefulness as a source of statistics. The hallmark of any registration system is its 'continuous' nature. VITAL EVENTS occurring in a geographical area are registered regularly more or less as they take place, whereas other sources of demographic data, such as the CENSUS or SURVEYS, are periodic and elicit information by retrospective questioning.   PNM-B

Reading

United Nations 1953: *Principles for a vital statistics system.* Series M, 19. New York: Department of Economic and Social Affairs.

United Nations 1955: *Handbook of vital statistics methods.* Series F, 7. New York: Department of Economic and Social Affairs.

regression A statistical technique used to model or test the association between variables.

The regression model assumes that a dependent (response) variable, Y, may be expressed as the sum of a deterministic term, $f(x)$, which depends on a vector, $\underline{x}$,

of p independent (explanatory) variables, and on a disturbance (error or residual) term, ε, which has an expected value of zero. In most applications the term, $f(x)$, is taken to be a linear sum of the individual explanatory variables weighted by a value β, indicating the degree of association:

$$\dot{Y} = \sum_{i=1}^{p} \beta_i x_i + \varepsilon$$

The β values (regression coefficients) are usually estimated by minimising the sums of squares of the residual terms (ordinary least squares). They may be interpreted as the average change in the dependent variable associated with a unit change in the corresponding independent variable.

Because of its apparent simplicity regression is widely used in demographic studies on both aggregate and individual-level data. Correct interpretation, however, depends on several pre-conditions. These include: that the process under study conforms with the proposed model (e.g. omitted independent variables may lead to serious biases in the estimated coefficients), that the explanatory variables are measured without error, and that the residual terms are uncorrelated with each other and have the same variance. It is very rare for all the necessary conditions to be met in any demographic or social research.

It is sometimes possible to interpret regression results as showing causation as well as simply association. In most cases, however, the best use of regression is to provide a convenient way of summarising multivariate data, especially when used in conjunction with EXPLORATORY DATA ANALYSIS.   MM

Reading

Bibby, J. 1977: The general linear model – a cautionary tale. In C. O'Muircheartaigh and C. Payne, eds. *The analysis of survey data.* Volume II Model fitting. New York: Wiley.

Draper, N.R. and Smith, H. 1981: *Applied regression analysis.* Second edition. New York and Chichester: Wiley.

Mosteller, F. and Tukey, J.W. 1977: *Data analysis and regression: a second course in statistics.* Reading, Mass. and London: Addison-Wesley.

rejuvenation of the population See AGEING (OF THE POPULATION).

relational model A type of mathematical model commonly used to represent FREQUENCY DISTRIBUTIONS and other sets of data. A mathematical relationship is postulated to exist between two sets of data of some kind – e.g. two distributions of migration probabilities by age – so that if the exact form of one of the data sets is known the other can be derived from it. The variables in the relationship are the parameters of the model.

By defining a particular data set to be a standard, and varying the parameters, a whole family of model data sets can be generated from the standard. Among the most commonly used relational models in demography are the LOGIT LIFE TABLE SYSTEM, the GOMPERTZ FERTILITY MODEL and the COALE-TRUSSEL FERTILITY MODEL. All these relational models are particularly useful in population projections (Brass 1974), since future variations in fertility and mortality rates can be described very simply in terms of changes in model parameters, taking the base-line fertility and mortality rates as standards. The term is used in a different sense in computer science to describe a form of database management system.   BZ

Reference and Reading

Brass, W. 1974: Perspectives in population prediction. *Journal of the Royal Statistical Society* series A, 137, pp. 532–70. Also discussion, pp. 571–83.

relative risk A measure of the effect of a given factor in making the occurrence of a demographic event more or less likely. If p_1 is the probability of occurrence when the factor is present, and p_2 the probability when it is absent, the relative risk, r, is defined as:

$$r = \frac{p_1}{p_2}$$

CW

remarriage Marriage in which one or both partners has been married previously.

The prevalence of remarriage depends on the occurrence of widowhood and divorce, and also on social customs concerning the acceptibility of remarrying. In many societies attitudes have differed with regard to the two sexes, remarriage being more acceptable and therefore more widespread for men than it is for women. In many developed countries remarriage has become more common in recent years as a result of increased divorce. In the UK, for example, about one marriage in three is now remarriage for one or both partners.

RP, CW

renewable process A demographic event or process which can be experienced more than once (e.g. fertility), in contrast with NON-RENEWABLE PROCESSES. The distinction has important implications for analysis since only non-renewable processes can be studied using LIFE TABLE METHODS. However, a renewable process can be broken down into its non-renewable components: e.g. fertility can be analysed according to birth order or parity, each birth being a non-renewable event.

RP, CW

renewal (of the populations) The process by which individuals entering the population at birth replace those leaving it through death, producing constant change in a population's make-up.

It takes a century or more for all the members of a population alive at a given moment to die and for the population thus to be renewed entirely. In contrast the time taken for it to change by a given amount varies widely according to the growth rate. For example in a population growing at 3 per cent a year it takes 16 years from an initial date to reach a state at which half the population then alive was not present at the start. Whereas in a population declining in total size at 2 per cent a year it takes 44 years to reach the same point. These large differences in the speed with which a population renews itself are reflected in its various age groups, particularly in the labour force, leading to differences in the flexibility of different populations to adapt to changing social and economic conditions.

The detailed study of renewal is based on the well-known renewal equation produced by Lotka (1939);

$$B(t) = \int_{\alpha}^{\beta} B(t-a)\, l(a)\, m(a)\, da + G(t)$$

This states that the births at time t, $B(t)$ are determined by the summation from α to β (the lower and upper limits of the reproductive ages) of the births a years previously multiplied by the probability of these individuals surviving, $l(a)$, and the probability of them giving birth, $m(a)$, in the interval from a to $a + da$. In addition births to women already born at the start of the process need to be taken into account, $G(t)$, until the time when these women cease childbearing. This equation has been fundamental to the development of STABLE POPULATION theory, and makes it possible to examine the consequences for renewal of any combination of fertility and mortality.   RP, CW

Reference

Lotka, A. 1939: *Théorie analytique des associations biologiques*. Paris: Hermann.

Reading

Keyfitz, N. 1977: *Applied mathematical demography*. New York and London: Wiley.
Ryder, N.B. 1975: Notes on stationary populations. *Population index* 41, pp. 3–27.
Smith, D. and Keyfitz, N. 1977: *Mathematical demography: selected papers*. Berlin and New York: Springer-Verlag. Pp. 75–172.

replacement effect   The replacement of dead children by subsequent births. It can be consequent upon either biological or volitional factors.

As a result of the physiological relationship between the extent of BREASTFEEDING and the duration of postnatal ANOVULATION it is possible to have a substantial replacement effect in populations which practise no form of fertility regulation within marriage. More common however are societies where lactation, child survival and patterns of acceptable sexual intercourse all interact. In many traditional societies it is contrary to custom for lactating women to engage in sexual intercourse, but intercourse follows rapidly upon the death of a still-suckling child in order to provide for its replacement. Thus in Gambia in the year following a fatal measles epidemic among young children the birth rate reached 87 per thousand, demonstrating the efficiency of this replacement mechanism. In populations where contraception is widespread levels of infant and child mortality are generally sufficiently low to make replacement an insignificant factor in determining fertility levels. Indeed, in highly sophisticated populations a negative replacement effect may occur where parents whose children have died as a result of genetic defects may decide not to have children planned before the death.

It should be noted that it is very difficult to prove the existence of a volitional replacement effect in the absence of prospective data about hoped for fertility. Studies of biologically determined replacement effects are also complicated by the existence of a two-way relationship between mortality and fertility.   HW

Reading

Chowdhury, A., Khan, A. and Chen, L. 1976: The effect of child mortality experience on subsequent fertility in Pakistan and Bangladesh. *Population studies* 30, pp. 249–61.
Hashimoto, M.H. 1981: Effects of child mortality on fertility in Thailand. *Economic development and cultural change* 29, pp. 781–94.
Thompson, B. 1975: Some demographic factors illustrated in a Gambian village. In J. Cald-

well, ed. *Population growth and socio-economic change in West Africa.* New York: Population Council and Colombia University Press.

Ware, H. 1977: The relationship between infant mortality and fertility: replacement and insurance effects. In International Union for the Scientific Study of Population *International Population Conference, Mexico, 1977.* Liège, Belgium: IUSSP.

replacement level fertility See next entry.

replacement (of generations) The way in which a population replaces one generation with another.

The term is used principally to indicate a type of fertility analysis. If the level of childbearing is such that each woman will, on average, be succeeded by at least one daughter the population is said to be replacing itself. Replacement level fertility occurs when the combination of fertility and mortality leads to a NET REPRODUCTION RATE of one. The fertility needed to ensure this varies according to the mortality conditions, but in developed countries it is commonly taken to be 2.1. In order to be a strictly accurate guide to replacement, these measures should also take migration into account, but this is rarely done, and the measures are used as general indicators of current fertility levels rather than as predications of long-term replacement (see also RENEWAL).   RP, CW

reproductive ages The ages at which individuals are capable of becoming parents. The term is used most frequently with regard to women but can also apply to men. The synonyms childbearing ages and fertile ages are also used.

For women the age range 15 to 49 is widely employed though some women are able to bear children at ages outside these limits. Rates of childbearing at older ages are so low in countries with low fertility that 15 to 44 is sometimes used instead. For men the exact range is less clear, relatively few statistics being available on paternal age at the birth of offspring. The upper limit appears to be higher for males,

however. In addition to physiological constraints, social factors sometimes play a role in determining the effective span. In some countries, for example, it is socially unacceptable for a woman to continue to bear children once her own children have become parents (the grandmother effect). Similarly in most developed countries the awareness of the increased risks associated with childbearing at older ages effectively curtails fertility after 40.   RP

Reading

Gray , R.H. 1979: Biological factors other than nutrition and lactation which may effect natural fertility. In H. Leridon and J. Menken, eds. *Natural fertility.* Liège: Ordina editions. Pp. 217–51.

Rindfuss, R.R. and Bumpass, L.L. 1978: Age and the sociology of fertility: how old is too old? In K. Taeuber, L.L. Bumpass and J.A. Sweet, eds. *Social demography.* New York and London: Academic Press. Pp. 43–56.

reproductivity The quantitative study of the way in which populations replace themselves through natural processes (see RENEWAL).

Reproductivity is usually studied by means of a set of measures derived from the work of Lotka on STABLE POPULATION models. The overall level of REPLACEMENT is indicated by the gross and net reproduction rates, the former measuring just fertility and the latter measuring both fertility and mortality. The mean length of GENERATION and the INTRINSIC RATE OF NATURAL INCREASE are also principal indices of reproductivity. Although attempts are made to study male reproductivity, most analyses relate only to women. When male and female measures are calculated for the same population they frequently indicate different levels and trends in replacement, and attempts to construct two-sex models have not as yet proved entirely satisfactory.

The measures of reproductivity indicate the long-run consequences of a particular combination of fertility and mortality, with no concern for current age structure.

They should be regarded not so much as predictive tools, but rather as illustrative indicators of current patterns. In particular, fluctuations in fertility lead to commensurate variation in estimated reproductivity and estimates based on period measures of fertility must be interpreted with great caution.   RP

Reading

Shryock, H.S., Siegel, J.S. et al. 1975: *The methods and materials of demography*. Condensed edition by E.G. Stockwell. London and New York: Academic Press. Chapter 18.

retrospective observation   Methods of data collection in which events are recorded after they occur by questioning those who experienced them. Retrospective questions are widely used in CENSUS operations and in RETROSPECTIVE SURVEYS, often to collect LIFE HISTORIES.

Since only those present at the time of the survey or census are questioned data relating to persons who have died or migrated are excluded. This opens up the possibility of biases and misinterpretation unless migration and mortality are independent of the events being asked about. (see NON-SELECTIVITY).   RP

retrospective survey   A SURVEY which asks respondents about events, experiences or views with reference to any period of interest before the interview date. In practice the reference period is usually restricted in some way: for example, in fertility surveys women are generally only asked about the period between their first union and the survey date.

The core of many retrospective demographic surveys is a LIFE HISTORY, often a MATERNITY HISTORY, in which a complete timetable of demographic events is compiled for each woman. The surveys organised by the World Fertility Survey added a number of questions on contraception and abortion to this core and in many cases marriage histories and data on other PROXIMATE DETERMINANTS OF FERTILITY are also collected restrospectively.

Retrospective data on both fertility and mortality can be analysed in two principal ways: on the one hand, all the experience (lifetime or part thereof) can be cumulated giving summary measures such as total children ever born alive (parities) or total children born alive but dead at survey. Data in this form are the most common in demography. As a result the methodology for analysis is well developed. Data from developing countries often contain errors and omissions, and a whole body of work now exists on the correction and analysis of such results. (See INDIRECT ESTIMATION TECHNIQUES.) On the other hand retrospective surveys which collect full maternity, marriage or migration histories in which all events are dated, can be analysed by dissecting parts of the pre-survey experience in a variety of ways. Rates for birth or marriage cohorts can be calculated or, alternatively, the data can be treated as a series of cross-sections of the population's experience by slicing up their experience into blocks of years before the survey (0–4, 5–9, 10–14, etc.).   AH

Reading

United Nations 1971: *Methodology of demographic sample surveys*. Series M, statistical papers 51. New York: Department of Economic and Social Affairs.

United States, National Academy of Sciences 1981: *Collecting data for the estimation of fertility and mortality*. Committee on Population and Demography, report 6. Washington DC: National Academy Press.

World Fertility Survey 1981: *Proceedings of the World Fertility Survey Conference 1980*. Voorburg, The Netherlands: International Statistical Institute.

return migration   Migration in which an individual returns to a previous area of residence.

The previous area may be variously defined according to the nature of the analysis. If lifetime migration is studied it will be the area of birth; if a particular period is the focus of study it will be the area of residence at the start of the period. Not all return migration is identified in estimations based on census information since a return migrant who makes the outward and return moves between two censuses will appear to have been immobile.

RP

reverse survival   Also known as reverse projection, it is the reconstruction of a population's age structure at an earlier date on the basis of its current age structure and given assumptions about the prevailing level of mortality.

Reverse survival is the opposite of a conventional PROJECTION, and uses the inverse of the probability of survival to 'project' a population backwards and determine the size of each age group at the earlier date.

One common use for countries with deficient vital registration, is to estimate the level of the CRUDE BIRTH RATE in the years immediately preceding a census. With accurate information on the level of early age mortality during the period, the number of births occurring x years before the census (where x is usually 5 or 10) can be estimated. Dividing the estimated average annual number of births occurring during the period by the mid-period population gives an estimate of the crude birth rate. If the population growth rate is available the BALANCING EQUATION can be used to estimate the corresponding CRUDE DEATH RATE. Unfortunately, birth rate estimates so ordered will be underestimates to the extent that young age groups suffer differentially from under-registration. (See also OWN CHILDREN METHOD.) A variation of this technique is also used to estimate net migration.   RP, TD

Reading

Shryock, H.S., Siegel, J.S. et al. 1976: *The methods and materials of demography*. Condensed edition by E.G. Stockwell. London and New York: Academic Press. Chapter 4.

United Nations 1967: *Manual IV: methods of estimating demographic measures from incomplete data*. Population studies 42. New York: Department of Economic and Social Affairs.

rhythm method   See PERIODIC ABSTINENCE.

risk   See EXPOSURE TO RISK.

robustness   A measure of the sensitivity of a measure to violation of the assumptions made in calculation.

Many demographic measures and statistical procedures involve probability theory and depend for their exactitude upon various assumptions about such features as unmeasured variation in the population (see HETEROGENEITY) or the validity of the sampling techniques used. A measure is said to be robust if violation of these assumptions does not significantly affect it.   CW

rural population   The population living in areas defined as rural in the census of a particular country. Various criteria are used and it is not possible to give a single definition of the term.

The underlying concepts used in definitions are fivefold:

(1) national administrative divisions, based on historical, political or administrative, rather than statistical concepts
(2) population size
(3) local administrative areas
(4) specific rural characteristics
(5) predominant economic activities.

Most censuses employ combinations of all five. Even with elaborate definitions it is often necessary to use a three-way distinction of rural, urban and semi-urban or suburban areas, in order accurately to reflect the range of settlement patterns.

CW

Reading

Lewis, G.J. 1979: *Rural communities: a social geography*. Newton Abbot and North Pomfret, Vt: David and Charles.

Shryock, H.S., Siegel, J.S. et al. 1976: *The methods and materials of demography*. Condensed edition by E.G. Stockwell. London and New York: Academic Press. Chapter 6.

S

'safe' period See PERIODIC ABSTINENCE.

sample design The complete sampling plan, covering sampling frames, sampling stages, stratification, choice of selection probabilities, and the type of selection procedures used (random, systematic, etc.). An important concern of sampling statisticians is the *optimization* of sample design in terms of minimal sampling error for given cost, often with some account taken of non-sampling error.   CS

sample vital registration Intensive registration of VITAL EVENTS occurring in a representative sample of households.

Originally at least it was conceived as an interim measure for providing much needed information on vital statistics in areas where the conventional civil registration system is deficient, with a long-term objective of gradually increasing the coverage to the whole nation. As it operates on a much smaller scale than civil registration, more effort is made to include all events occurring in the sample area. Instead of waiting for people to come for registration a locally resident registrar takes active steps to find out what vital events are occurring in his sample area. Sample registration is usually part of a wider DUAL RECORD SYSTEM in which events recorded under sample registration are cross-checked against the events enumerated in an independent survey.

PNM-B

Reading

Cavanaugh, J.A. 1961: Sample vital registration experiment. *International Population Conference, New York*. Volume 2. London: International Union for the Scientific Study of Population.

Hauser, P.M. 1954: The use of sampling for vital records and vital statistics. *Bulletin of the World Health Organization* 11, pp. 5–24.

India, Registrar General 1972: *Sample registration of births and deaths in India, 1969–70*. New Delhi: Manager of Publications.

United Nations 1955: *Handbook of vital statistics methods*. Series F, 7. New York: Department of Economic and Social Affairs.

sampling The research strategy of collecting data from a part of a population with a view to drawing inferences about the whole. The 'population' in this sense is often termed the 'universe'.

The term 'representative sample' is generally avoided in modern writings, although it is broadly true that the sample is selected to represent the population. In a narrow sense sampling means sample selection, but it is often used in a broader sense to cover the whole range of associated processes: SAMPLE DESIGN, sample selection and estimation, and the computation of SAMPLING ERROR.   CS

Reading

Cohran, W.G. 1977: *Sampling techniques*. Third edition. Chichester and New York: Wiley.

Kish, L. 1975: *Survey sampling*. Chichester and New York: Wiley.

Kish, L. 1982: Sampling methods. In J.A. Ross, ed. *International encyclopaedia of population*. New York: Free Press. Pp. 601–5.

Verma, V., Scott, C. and O'Muircheartaigh, C. 1980: Sample designs and sampling errors for the World Fertility Survey. *Journal of the Royal Statistical Society*, series A, pp. 431–73.

sampling error In broad terms error caused by the fact that only part of the population is studied and not the whole.

The term sampling error refers not to the error of a particular sample but to the *distribution* of errors from all possible samples. More precisely, the researcher considers the set of estimates that would be obtained from all samples consistent with the given sample design, each weighted by its probability of being selected. The variance of this set is called the 'sampling variance' while the difference between the mean of the set and the population estimate is called the 'sampling bias'. Strictly speaking, the term sampling error includes both sampling variance and sampling bias. The sampling variance can, in general, be estimated from the particular sample used and it is this estimate, or more often its square root, that is generally reported as the sampling error for the particular study undertaken. This estimate should strictly be termed the estimated sampling variance, and its square root the estimated sampling standard error. In practice the latter is often abbreviated to the 'sampling error'. It is thus a measure of the uncertainty due to sampling and is a function of the sample design, the particular formula used for estimation, and the variability of the population.   CS

sampling frame   The list, or other representation, from which the sampling units are selected in the process of sampling. Examples are: a map showing area units, a list of areas by name, a list of households, a register of persons.   CS

school-age population   The population within the range of ages during which education normally takes place. Schooling is usually compulsory for a specified number of years but the availability of optional schooling at either end of the age range makes it preferable to consider wider limits. The number of children enrolled at schools divided by the school age population provides the school enrolment rate.   CW

school enrolment rate   The proportion of a population (usually specified accord-ing to age and sex) enrolled in an educational establishment at a given date.

The school-age population is often used as the base population, distinction being made between various types of schooling, especially between part- and full-time enrolment, the former sometimes not being counted in the rate. Although the enrolment records of schools are some-times used, it is usual to calculate these rates from census data from which it is possible to establish rates of entry into and departure from the school population, and to use LIFE TABLE METHODS to refine analysis further. The transition from school to the labour force is often of parti-cular interest to sociologists and econo-mists.   RP

Reading
Shryock, H.S., Siegel, J.S. et al. 1976: *The methods and materials of demography*. Con-densed edition by E.G. Stockwell. London and New York: Academic Press. Pp. 178–80 and 268–9.

seasonal migration   A particular form of CIRCULAR MIGRATION in which indi-viduals or groups move from the original point and return within an agricultural cycle. Seasonal migration usually occurs either because of agricultural tasks – trans-humance, pasturing, harvesting – which take place in a variety of locations, or because of seasonal variation in labour needs which enable surplus individuals to seek work temporarily elsewhere.   DCS

seasonality, demographic   Regular re-curring patterns of variation by season in demographic processes.

All demographic events are potentially subject to seasonality. Climate exerts the most fundamental influence, producing, for example, peaks in the death rate at the least favourable times of the year (e.g. in winter in temperature regions). Climatic changes also have an effect on various economic and social factors and the sea-sonal pattern of work may have a more direct bearing on demographic variation than do more basic climatic changes. The agricultural cycle is clearly a case in point. In pre-industrial England, for example, marriages most frequently took place during the period after the harvest (October and November), a time of slack demand for labour and one marking the end of the annual contracts for servants in husbandry (mostly young, marriageable persons). Social and religious norms also play a part in seasonality. The traditional proscription by the Catholic church of marriage during Lent and Advent was once strictly observed, and the number of marriages during those periods has sometimes been used as an index of secularisation. In modern industrial societies demographic seasonality is generally less noticeable though it is always present to a certain extent.

In addition to forming a topic of research in itself seasonality is often investigated by those wanting to remove its effects from a time-series of data in order to assess certain trends more accurately.

RP

Reading

Chambers, R., Longhurst, R. and Pacey, A. eds. 1981: *Seasonal dimensions to rural poverty*. London: Frances Pinter; Totowa, New Jersey: Allanheld, Osmun.

Sakamoto-Momiyama, M. 1977: *Seasonality in human mortality: a medico-geographical study*. Tokyo: University of Tokyo Press.

secondary sterility   See STERILITY.

self-enumeration   See ENUMERATION.

self-weighting sample   A sample in which all individuals (units of analysis) have the same overall selection probability. The data from such a sample can be processed as in a census, without weighting.   CS

serial monogamy   Marriage to more than one person in a lifetime, each new marriage taking place after the dissolution of the previous marriage by divorce or death. The need for such a term arises from an ambiguity in the definition of

monogamy: one of the two meanings (and the older) being one marriage in a lifetime, in contrast to one marriage at a time. In early English society the distinction was made between two successive marriages or digamy and parallel marriages or bigamy.

The term serial monogamy is invariably employed to describe the situation in societies which do not legally allow polygamy, and is sometimes used pejoratively by defenders of polygamy to suggest that a practice akin to polygamy (usually achieved by divorce and remarriage) exists in societies described as monogamous (hence serial polygamy or sequential polygamy – while the more rigorous serial polygyny might be anticipated, it does not seem to have been used). No society has yet recorded the majority of the population as practising serial monogamy, although those marrying for the first time during the 1970s in the United States may approach this situation. The term serial monogamy has also been used to describe the sequential relationships between unmarried persons of the opposite sex and of the same sex.   JCC, PQ

Reading

Alpenfels, E.J. 1970: Progressive monogamy: an alternate pattern? In H. A. Otto, ed. *The family in search of a future*. New York: Appleton-Century-Crofts.

Hajnal, J. 1965: European marriage patterns in perspective. In D. V. Glass and D. E. C. Eversley, eds. *Population in history* London: Edward Arnold.

Landis, P.H. 1950: Sequential marriage. *Journal of home economics* 42, pp. 625–9.

Savells, J. and Cross, L.J. 1978: *The changing family: making way for tomorrow*. New York: Holt, Rinehart and Winston.

Shorter, E. 1976: *The making of the modern family*. London: Collins.

sex differential mortality   Differences in the mortality rates experienced by males and females.

In developed countries male mortality is at present higher than female in every age group and mean LIFE EXPECTANCY at birth $(\overset{\circ}{e}_o)$ is typically 5–8 years shorter for men than for women. This has not always been the case: in the nineteenth century it was common for female death rates to exceed those for males in some age groups, notably in childhood and adolescence and in the childbearing years. This situation persisted in some countries well into the twentieth century (Stolnitz 1956). Even then, however, $\overset{\circ}{e}_o$ was higher for females than males, though the difference was much less than it is today.

The case of the Third World is less clear because of a shortage of reliable data. The situation in many countries is probably similar to that found historically in the developed world, each sex being disadvantaged in some age groups (Stolnitz 1956, 1975). Excess female mortality in early childhood (after infancy) seems to be quite common (Heligman 1983, Rutstein 1983). In some populations, notably in the Indian subcontinent, excess female mortality is so marked and extends over such a wide range of ages that life expectancy at birth is (or was until recently) lower for women than for men. A LIFE TABLE for India for 1970–72, for example, shows higher death

rates for females at all ages up to 40, excess male mortality between 40 and 70, and excess female rates at later ages. The overall result is that female $\overset{\circ}{e}_o$ was 46.2 years against 49.1 years for males (United Nations 1982).

Excess female mortality in the first year of life (as in India 1970–72) is very rare, and in the first month probably unknown. This is thought to reflect a greater constitutional robustness on the part of females.

Interpretations of sex differential mortality vary: the most common view is that women are more resilient than men in most environmental circumstances. Excess female mortality other than during the childbearing years tends therefore to be seen, at the very least, as indicating differences of environment or life style between the sexes which happen to be disadvantageous to women, and is taken by many writers as evidence of neglect. Differences in levels of nutrition, medical attention and general care (among others) have been suggested as possible causes. Among the factors suggested as contributing to the

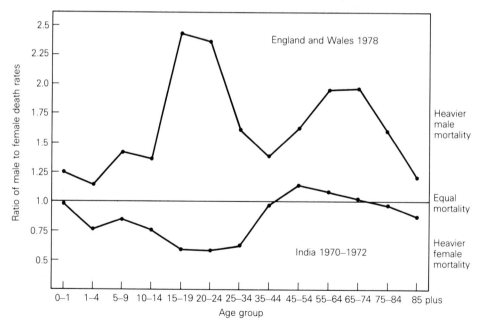

Sources: England and Wales: Office of Population Censuses and Surveys 1980: *Mortality statistics.* London: HMSO. Pp. 6–7. India: United Nations 1982. P. 314.

widening difference in life expectancy between men and women in developed societies are differences in smoking habits, in alcohol consumption, in obesity, and in exposure to stress, as well as occupational and bio-physical differences.   CML

References

Heligman, L. 1983: Patterns of sex differentials in mortality in less developed countries. In A.D. Lopez and L.T. Ruzicka, eds. *Sex differentials in mortality*. Canberra: Australian National University.

Rutstein, S.O. 1983: *Infant and child mortality: levels, trends and demographic differentials*. World Fertility Survey, comparative studies 24. Voorburg, The Netherlands: International Statistical Institute.

Stolnitz, G.J. 1956: A century of international mortality trends: II *Population studies* 10, pp. 17–42.

— 1975: International mortality trends: some main facts and implications. In United Nations *The population debate: dimensions and perspectives*. Population studies 57. New York: Department of Economic and Social Affairs. Volume 1.

United Nations 1982: *Model life tables for developing countries*. Population studies 77. New York: Department of International Economic and Social Affairs.

Reading

Chen, L.C., Huq, E. and D'Souza, S. 1981: Sex bias in the family allocation of food and health care in rural Bangladesh. *Population and development review* 7, pp. 55–70.

Lopez, A.D. and Ruzicka, L.T., eds. 1983: *Sex differentials in mortality*. Canberra: Australian National University.

Retherford, R.D. 1975: *The changing sex differential in mortality*. Westport, Conn.: Greenwood.

Ware, H. 1981: *Women, demography and development*. Canberra: Australian National University.

sex ratio   The ratio, within a population, of the number of males to the number of females, or the ratio of events occurring to males divided by the number occurring to females.

The most often quoted ratio is the sex ratio at birth, though, in a more general way, ratios can be calculated for any events attributable to one or other of the sexes (sex ratio of conceptions, sex ratio of deaths, etc.). As well as the sex ratio of the whole population, measurements are usually counted for each age group in order to study how the ratio varies with age. In most populations SEX DIFFERENTIAL MORTALITY causes the ratio to decline consistently, going from about 1.05 at birth to a value of about 0.30 at 100 years of age. Discrepancies will appear in this profile when the birth cohort is affected by sex-specific migratory movements. Since males tend to be more mobile than females countries of immigration usually have a higher sex ratio than countries of emigration. A notable exception to the general pattern of sex ratios is the Indian subcontinent, where heavy female mortality has traditionally led to an excess of males at almost all ages.   RP

Reading

Shryock, H.S., Siegel, J.S. et al. 1976: *The methods and materials of demography*. Condensed edition by E.G. Stockwell. London and New York: Academic Press. Chapter 7.

significance test   A test to indicate the probability that a characteristic observed in a sample is representative of the overall population and not a chance result of the sampling process or some other source of random error.

Theoretical distributions used in hypothesis testing vary according to the problem to be solved, but the BINOMIAL DISTRIBUTION is widely used. When interpreting significance tests it is important to realise that the test is purely statistical and does not necessarily indicate substantive significance. Where the data used do not meet the assumptions of the test, for example, or where a research design is badly specified, statistically significant results may be of no substantive importance.   CW

Reading

Blalock, H.M. 1979. *Social statistics*. Revised second edition. Chapter 10.

simple random sampling (SRS) Selection by random sampling of a single stage unstratified sample.   cs

simulation An approach to solving problems which are too complex for conventional mathematical methods. A simulation attempts to replicate actual circumstances or to investigate circumstances and conditions which are relevant to an understanding of past, present or future demographic behaviour.

In this broad sense any population PROJECTION can be regarded as a simulation. The term is more commonly reserved, however, for techniques developed specifically for use with computers and impractical without rapid computational facilities. A major distinction is made between macro- and micro-simulation. Macro models normally have a mathematical base consisting of a set of equations that cannot be solved analytically but which can provide numerical results when programmed on a computer. These models are referred to as deterministic or 'expected value' models and provide results for the population as a whole or for groups within it. Microsimulation replicates the exprience of individuals, with the probability of experiencing a given event determined by random chance. This stochastic nature leads to these models being termed 'Monte Carlo' simulation. The process of passing through a complete life course, or whatever section is under study, is repeated many times to produce a collection of LIFE HISTORIES.

The use of simulation models has grown with the increased availability and sophistication of computing facilities. Fertility has been a particular focus. Macro models of the reproductive process have been constructed in order to measure the effects of family planning (Nortmann et al. 1978) and to examine the impact of the PROXIMATE DETERMINANTS (Bongaarts and Potter 1983). Analogous micro-simulation models have also been proposed (Barrett 1971). A large and controversial area is that of modelling economic-demographic relationships. Numerous macrosimulations have been made, though their relevance has been debated (Arthur and McNicoll 1975). Most of these models employ SYSTEMS ANALYSIS and a variety of econometric techniques. Microsimulation has also been fruitfully used in studies of household and family composition (Wachter et al. 1978).   RP/CW

References

Arthur, W.B. and McNicholl, G. 1975: Large-scale simulation in population and development: what use to planners? *Population and development review* 1, pp. 251–65.

Barrett, J. 1971: Use of a fertility simulation model to refine measurement techniques. *Demography* 8, pp. 481–90.

Bongaarts, J. and Potter, R.G. 1983: *Fertility, biology and behaviour: an analysis of the proximate determinants.* New York and London: Academic Press. Chapter 6.

Nortman, D. et al. 1978: *Birth rates and birth control practices: relations based on the computer models TABRAP and CONVERSE.* New York: Population Council.

Wachter, K.W., with Hammel, E.A. and Laslett, P. 1978: *Statistical studies of historical social structure.* New York and London: Academic Press.

Reading

Bongaarts and Potter 1983.

Srikantan, K.S. 1982: Population models. In J.A. Ross, ed. *International encyclopaedia of population.* New York: Free Press. Pp. 526–9.

Wachter et al. 1978.

single decrement life table See LIFE TABLE.

singulate mean age at marriage (SMAM) An estimate of the mean age at first marriage, derived from the proportion of each age group not yet married, as shown by a census or survey.

First proposed by Hajnal (1953), the SMAM is easy to compute but can only be interpreted as indicating the true mean age at first marriage at the time of the census under stringent (often unrealistic) assumptions. It is nevertheless one of the most widely cited indices of nuptiality.

The logic of the calculation is straightforward. In a true cohort the difference between the proportion single at different ages clearly indicates the marriages which have taken place between those ages. It is also possible to calculate the number of PERSON-YEARS lived by persons before they marry. The average number of person-years lived as a single person among those who marry is the mean age at first marriage. When calculating the SMAM the proportions single from one census or survey are used as a HYPOTHETICAL COHORT instead of proportions from a true cohort. This provides a measure of nuptiality at the time of the census only if there are no differentials in mortality and migration according to marital status, and, more importantly, if marriage patterns have not changed in the recent past. If these conditions are not met, the interpretation is somewhat conjectural, although they are rarely violated to so great an extent as to undermine analysis.

The SMAM is defined as the following where S_x is the proportion single (never married) at age x and S_{50} the proportion single at 50:

$$SMAM = \frac{\sum_{x=0}^{50} S_x - (50 \times S_{50})}{1 - S_{50}}$$

Using conventional five-year age groups this becomes:

$$SMAM = \frac{5 \times \sum_{x=0-4}^{45-49} S_x - (50 \times S_{50})}{1 - S_{50}}$$

The summation of the S_x values indicates the number of person-years lived as single persons before age 50, and the second term in the numerator indicates the person-years lived by those who were still unmarried at age 50. Subtraction of $50.S_{50}$ removes the unmarrieds from consideration, and division by the proportion of those married before age 50 yields the SMAM. In practice, the summation of proportions single usually starts at the earliest age at which marriage occurs (i.e. 10–14 or 15–19).   RP, CW

Reference

Hajnal, J. 1953: Age at marriage and proportions marrying. *Population studies* 7, pp. 111–36.

Reading

Smith, P.C. 1982: Nuptiality indexes. In J.A. Ross, ed. *International encyclopaedia of population*. New York: Free Press. Pp. 492–8.

smoothing   See GRADUATION.

social demography   The branch of demography dealing with the interaction of population and the wider life of societies.

In an area where disciplines overlap social demography places population measures in their proper context as causes and consequences of various social processes. Specifically demographic processes such as the AGEING OF THE POPULATION, increased human life expectancy, DIFFERENTIAL MORTALITY, changes in the FAMILY CYCLE, and DIFFERENTIAL FERTILITY lie at the origin of social concerns; examination of the general context in which these specific processes appear (the mode of social organization, the value system, the physical environment) provides insights into their occurrence. This interplay benefits from the combination of social variables and the rigorously quantitative measures of demography.   RP

Reading

Taeuber, K.E., Bumpass, L.L., and Sweet, J.A., eds. 1978: *Social demography*. New York and London: Academic Press.

social mobility   Change over time in the socio-economic status of an individual or between generations of a family.

The study of social mobility presupposes that an identifiable system of social stratification exists in a society. The measurement of this stratification can be made either according to socio-economic groupings specified by official bodies, or according to wealth, educational attainment and other criteria. Difficulties in determining the most appropriate measures of stratification and complexities brought about by life-cycle effects make analysis of social mobility far from simple. Many researchers into social mobility regard it as a sociological rather than a demographic phenomenon and therefore one that cannot be studied properly by demographic techniques.   RP, CW

Reading

McFarland, D.D. 1978: Mobility and stratification: an overview. In K.E. Taeuber et al., eds. *Social demography*. New York and London: Academic Press, pp. 181–96.

socio-economic class   See next entry.

socio-economic status   A classification of an individual, household or family according to occupation, income, education or some other indicator of economic or social status.

All studies of social stratication and mobility, and most detailed analysis of labour force patterns, use some system of categorising the subjects of the study. The term social class has a sociological connotation which many researchers prefer to avoid by use of the more neutral term status. Occupation is the most widely used indicator of status though it entails the grouping of many diverse occupations into a smaller number of broad categories for the purpose of analysis. One of the earliest and best known attempts to group occupations is the system of five social classes introduced in Britain by the Registrar General in 1911. The system was designed primarily for use in the study of infant mortality and has subsequently been used in the analysis of many phenomena.

Many systems of stratification classify all the members of a household according to the status of the HEAD OF HOUSEHOLD. This is likely to cause problems in the accurate categorisation of other household members, especially women. Moreover, the changing occupational and social structure of a population sometimes leads to a system of classification becoming obsolete. In spite of all these drawbacks the convenience of some rough and ready classification is considerable and the continued use of such systems certain.   CW

Reading

Bendix, R. and Lipset, S.M., eds. 1966: *Class, status and power: social stratification in comparative perspective*. Second edition. London: Collier-Macmillan; New York: Free Press.

Leete, R. and Fox, J. 1977: Registrar General's social classes: origins and uses. *Population trends* 8, pp. 1–7.

Powers, M.G., ed. 1982: *Measures of socioeconomic status: Current issues*. Boulder, Colorado: Westview Press for the American Association for the Advancement of Science.

spacing behaviour   See BIRTH SPACING.

spontaneous abortion   An ABORTION which occurs without the deliberate intervention of the mother or any other person. It is also termed a miscarriage, and is contrasted with INDUCED ABORTION. (See also FOETAL MORTALITY.)   RP

stable equivalent population   The STABLE POPULATION which is implied by a particular combination of fertility and mortality rates. The term is often used to refer to the stable population defined by the rates observed in a particular period. Just as the INTRINSIC RATE OF GROWTH indicates the growth rate which would ultimately apply if current vital rates were maintained, the stable equivalent indicates the implied long-run age structure.   RP

stable population   A population which is closed to migration and has an unchanging age-sex structure that increases (or decreases) in size at a constant rate.

A stable population is the outcome of the maintenance over many decades of fixed rates of fertility and mortality. Although its overall size changes its characteristics do not; the proportion of the population in each age group, the age patterns of childbearing and death and any other features are all constant. A STATIONARY POPULATION is a special case of a stable one, with a growth rate of zero. It is a mathematical abstraction to which no actual population corresponds. Nevertheless, the stable model has been widely influential in demographic work and its development is unquestionably one of the main achievements of mathematical demography with many applications.

EULER formulated the fundamental bases of stable population theory (a fixed life table and growth rate) as early as 1760. It was not until the twentieth century, however, that the idea came to prominence in the work of LOTKA who proposed the fundamental equation:

$$\int_0^\infty e^{-rx} f(x)\, p(x)\, dx = 1$$

where e is the exponential function, r is the INTRINSIC RATE OF NATURAL INCREASE, $f(x)$ is the number of live female births to each women aged x and $p(x)$ is the probability of survival from birth to age x. Lotka solved this equation for r, providing a way of estimating the growth rate implied by any combination of fertility and mortality. He was also able to provide equations to define the age structure of a stable population.

Although not met by any real population, the simplifying assumptions of stable population theory have provided a useful and illuminating model of population dynamics. One area of particular value is that of demonstrating the interdependence of demographic characteristics and clarifying the determinants of the age structure. For example, it can be shown that change in fertility has a greater impact on the age structure than change in mortality (see AGEING). The capacity of the stable model for illuminating theoretical relations has been exhausitvely demonstrated by Coale (1972). Another immensely valuable role for stable theory is in IN-

DIRECT ESTIMATION TECHNIQUES where a stable population is often used as a benchmark against which to judge observed, potentially flawed, data. Since a stable population's age structure can be calculated easily from the LIFE TABLE which defines the mortality conditions, model stable populations are often presented in conjunction with MODEL LIFE TABLES.

Extensions of the stable model have also been made. For example, a QUASI-STABLE POPULATION is one with constant fertility and linearly changing mortality. More importantly, the stable model has provided the basis for a set of equations which replicate its functions but apply to any population (Preston and Coale 1982). These more general relations, known as variable -r methods, are likely to replace stable population theory in may of its uses.   RP

References

Coale, A.J. 1972: *The growth and structure of human populations*. Princeton, NJ: Princeton University Press.

Preston, S.H. and Coale, A.J. 1982: Age structure, growth, attrition and accession: a new synthesis. *Population index* 48, pp. 217-59.

Reading

Coale 1972.

Preston and Coale 1982.

Shryock, H.S., Siegel, J.S. et al. 1976: *The methods and materials of demography*. Condensed edition by E.G. Stockwell. London and New York: Academic Press. Chapter 18.

Woods, R. 1979: *Population analysis in geography*. London: Longman. Chapter 8.

standard life table See MODEL LIFE TABLE.

standardisation A technique used to enhance the comparability of data from different populations, or different subpopulations, by making adjustments for the effects of compositional differences, above all different AGE-SEX STRUCTURES.

Any aspect of composition can be controlled but age is the most common. Two forms of the technique are mostly used,

DIRECT STANDARDISATION and INDIRECT STANDARDISATION, though they are sometimes combined (double standardisation). In the direct form an arbitrary age structure is combined with the observed age-specific rates for each population to estimate comparable overall rates. In the indirect, the actual age structure of each population is combined with an arbitrary set of age-specific rates to estimate an 'expected' number of events, which is compared with the observed number to provide a standard index for each population. Although computationally simple, and certainly better than a comparison of CRUDE RATES, standardisation has many potential drawbacks. The choice of a standard can have a significant impact on the resulting indices, and the standardised rates are purely comparative and have no intrinsic meaning. Some analysts noting these points have questioned the use of standardisation in any circumstances. As Elandt-Johnson and Johnson (1980) have put it 'standardisations are not often very helpful and are very often misleading'.

Standardisation techniques are an inheritance from an era before the availability of more statistically sophisticated methods using computers, and their prevalence in demographic analysis must be seen as somewhat anachronistic.   CW

Reference
Elandt-Johnson, R.C., and Johnson, N.L. 1980: *Survival models and data analysis*. New York and Chichester: Wiley.

Reading
Fleiss, J.L. 1981: *Statistical methods for rates and proportions*. New York and Chichester: Wiley. Chapter 14.

stationary population A population closed to migration with unchanging age structure and mortality in which the annual number of births is equal to the number of deaths, producing a zero growth rate. A stationary population, therefore, is a special case of a STABLE POPULATION with no growth in numbers.

A stationary population, sometimes also termed a life table population, is a construct based on the age-specific death rates of a given LIFE TABLE. The SURVIVAL CURVE defines the population in continuous terms while the number of person-years lived in each age group, L_x, can be interpreted as the number of persons in that age group in the stationary population. Because the population size is constant, a variety of relationships can be identified. For example, the total population is equal to the annual number of births multiplied by the LIFE EXPECTANCY at birth and the crude birth and death rates are equal to the inverse of the life expectancy.

Although no real population has ever been stationary in this strict sense the simplifying assumptions enable underlying relationships between phenomena to be studied more readily (Ryder 1975). (See also AGEING.)   RP, CW

Reference
Ryder, N.B. 1975: Notes on stationary populations. *Population index* 41, pp. 3–27.

Reading
Ryder 1975.

Shryock, H.S., Siegel, J.S. et al. 1976: *The methods and materials of demography*. Condensed edition by E.G. Stockwell. London and New York: Academic Press. Chapter 15.

stem family A concept associated for a long time with the work of Frederic le Play (Brooke 1970) who had identified it as one of three fundamental domestic groups. For le Play *la famille souche*, like the patriarchal family, was marked by being stable in structure and faithful to the family line (patriline) but different from it in permitting only one rather than all the children to marry and remain within the domestic group. Le Play therefore thought of the stem family as both a domestic group and a patriline (a succession of male heads of household directly descended from each other).

The stem family has been associated with sociological theories relating to the evolution of the family; an evolution from the EXTENDED FAMILY to the nuclear one with the stem family as an intermediary stage. It has also been seen as responsible for late age at marriage and high celibacy rates (Hajnal 1965). In fact most sociologists and historians have seen an equation between the stem family and impartible inheritance (Homans 1941; Berkner 1972, 1977). The passage from the patriarchal-joint family to the stem has been explained in terms of land scarcity with the concomitant transition from partible to impartible inheritance. These views have been criticised, with the suggestion that stem families are better understood as nuclear families which reluctantly co-reside because of specific economic circumstances (Verdon 1979).

Debates using data on LIFE CYCLE patterns of residence have been pursued over whether CO-RESIDENT GROUP structures when calculated for whole communities can still indicate a pervasive stem family ideal even though stem or extended family households are relatively rare. This focus of discussion has provided an important seeding-ground for the development of micro-simulation techniques for the analysis of co-resident group structures, thereby helping to establish the variance of outcomes observed at the community level, given an adherence to clearly defined houshold formation rules and the operation of specific demographic rates (Wachter et al. 1978). Evidence suggests that many of the observed levels of extended family households in west European communities could clearly have been produced by chance rather than through adherence to a community-wide stem family ideal. (See also NUCLEAR FAMILY.)   RMS

References

Berkner, L. 1972: The stem family and the developmental cycle of the peasant household: an eighteenth-century Austrian example. *American historical review* 77, pp. 398–418.

— 1977: Peasant household organization and demographic change in Lower Saxony (1686–1766). In R.D. Lee, ed. *Population patterns in the past*. London and New York: Academic Press. Pp. 53–69.

Brooke, M.Z. 1970: *Le Play: Engineer and social scientist*. London: Longman.

Hajnal, J. 1965: European marriage patterns in perspective. In D.V. Glass and D.E.C. Eversley, eds. *Population in history*. London: Edward Arnold.

Homans, G.C. 1941: *English villagers in the thirteenth century*. Cambridge, Mass.: Harvard University Press.

Wachter, K.W. et al. 1978: *Statistical studies of historical social structure*. London and New York: Academic Press.

Verdon, M. 1979: The stem family: towards a general theory. *Journal of interdisciplinary history* 10, pp. 87–105.

Reading

Berkner 1972.

Wachter et al. 1978.

Verdon 1979.

sterilisation An operation carried out on either a man or a woman with the aim of ensuring sterility.

Apart from intervention carried out for therapeutic purposes, which may involve various organs which have a role in reproduction, sterilisation is usually carried out on men, as a vasectomy, which entails tying or cutting the sperm duct (vas deferens) and on women, as a tubectomy, which entails the blocking or cutting of the Fallopian tubes. Vasectomy is a painless operation, rapidly performed, and not requiring a general anaesthetic; tubectomy is a more delicate operation, despite recent improvements in the modes of access and the operative procedures employed. Both operations are considered as irreversible and virtually perfect in their contraceptive effect, though it is sometimes possible to reverse them (especially vasectomy). Sterilisation has become a major form of contraception in developed countries (e.g. in the United States in 1982 12 per cent of couples relied on female sterilisation and nine per cent on vasectomy) and is increasing in importance in most parts of the Third World. In developing countries female sterilisation is predominant (only in India does vasectomy play a major role in birth control), but male and female

214   sterility

methods are used approximately equally in those developed countries where sterilisation is common.   RF

Reading

Green, C.P. 1978: Voluntary sterilization: world's leading contraceptive method. *Population reports* Series M, 2.

Liskin, L. 1983: Vasectomy – safe and simple. *Population reports*. Series D, 4.

Plaskon, V. 1982: Sterilization techniques. In J.A. Ross, ed. *International encyclopaedia of population*. New York: Free Press. Pp. 622–5.

sterility The inability to produce a live birth. The term usually refers to women, but men or couples can be the focus of attention.

Used without qualification sterility implies irreversibility, but the term temporary sterility is sometimes used. A distinction is made between *primary* sterility where a woman has never been able to have a child and *secondary* sterility which occurs after the birth of at least one offspring. A further contrast is that between voluntary and involuntary or physiological sterility.

The inability to bear children may be

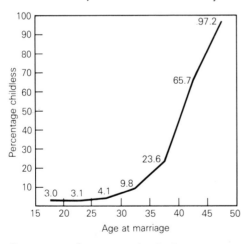

Percentage of women who had no children according to age at marriage, 14 German villages 1750–1899. Sterility has a similar profile in most populations.
Source: J. Knodel and C. Wilson 1981: The secular increase in fecundity in German village populations. *Population studies* 35, p. 64.

due to several distinct problems either in conceiving or in bringing a pregnancy to term. In the analysis of couples modern studies have found the cause in the male in a third to a half of all cases (McFalls 1979).

The most detailed data on sterility come from historical populations in Europe where voluntary childlessness can be assumed to be absent. These suggest that about 3–6 per cent of women around age 20 were sterile, with this percentage rising slowly to the mid-thirties and sharply thereafter; the average age at ceasing childbearing was close to 40 in most populations studied. Similar low values of sterility among young women are found in many societies, but parts of Sub-Saharan Africa are characterised by much higher values. In some populations more than half of all women remained childless (Retel-Laurentin 1979). There may well be several causes for these high values, but the simultaneously high incidence of a number of diseases which impair the ability to conceive or which produce high FOETAL MORTALITY is certainly important. Among these diseases are gonorrhoea, syphilis, ricketsiae, toxoplasmosis, goitre and malaria. Where these have been treated medically marked increases in fertility have occurred.   RP, CW

References

McFalls, J. 1979: Frustrated fertility: a population paradox. *Population bulletin* 34, 2.

Retel-Laurentin, A. 1979: Quelques éléments de la fecondité naturelle dans deux populations africaines à faible fecondité. In H. Leridon and J. Menken, eds. *Natural fertility*. Liège: Ordina Editions.

Reading

Bongaarts, J. and Potter, R.G. 1983: *Fertility, biology and behavior: an analysis of the proximate determinants*. New York and London: Academic Press. Chapter 2.

Leridon, H. 1977: *Human fertility: the basic components*. Chicago: University of Chicago Press.

stillbirth The expulsion or extraction from the mother of a dead foetus after the time at which it would normally be presumed capable of independent extrauterine existence. This is commonly taken to be after 28 weeks duration of pregnancy. The term late foetal death is used synonymously.

Since the exact distinction between stillbirths and early neonatal deaths is often far from simple, demographers sometimes combine the two and use the term PERINATAL MORTALITY. The ratio of stillbirths to total live and stillbirths is termed the stillbirth rate, whereas the ratio of stillbirths divided by live births is referred to as the stillbirth ratio. (See also FOETAL MORTALITY.)   RP

stochastic model   A mathematical model of a physical or social process in which a number of states are defined between which individuals or elements move according to probabilistic laws.

Most demographic processes are inherently stochastic (i.e. unpredictable at the individual level) rather than deterministic, although this may often be ignored, for example in the construction of life tables based on large samples. Stochastic models have been applied to diverse areas in demography: the properties of the stochastic LESLIE MATRIX; models of conception and birth (Sheps and Menken 1973); household structure (Wachter et al. 1978); and the extinction of surnames. These studies emphasise the importance of variability in demographic parameters as well as their mean values. In many cases the complexity of the underlying stochastic process has required a SIMULATION or Monte Carlo approach rather than a purely analytic treatment.   MM

References
Sheps, M.C. and Menken, J.A. 1973: *Mathematical models of conception and birth*. Chicago: University of Chicago Press.
Wachter, K.W. with Hammel, E.A. and Laslett, P., eds. 1978: *Statistical studies of historical social structure*. New York and London: Academic Press.

Reading
Bartholomew, D.J. 1983: *Stochastic models for social processes*. Third edition. New York and Chichester: Wiley.
Wachter et al. 1978.

stopping behaviour   The use of FAMILY LIMITATION to end childbearing. It is contrasted with BIRTH SPACING where couples use birth control to space the births of their children at particular points.   CW

straddling interval   A term used most frequently in the analysis of BIRTH INTERVALS, referring to an interval which begins before a specified reference date (usually the date of a census or survey) and ends after it.   RP

stratified sampling   A form of SAMPLING in which the SAMPLING FRAME is subdivided into strata and sampling is carried out independently in each stratum.

In unstratified sampling the overall sampling fraction is specified, but within any particular division of the population the proportion actually selected may differ by chance from this fraction. In stratified sampling this source of chance variation is controlled and each stratum receives the exact sample planned. In general this reduces SAMPLING ERROR by an amount that depends on the internal homogeneity of the strata. Stratification may be used either to maintain the same sampling fraction in all the strata or deliberately to vary it in different strata. Such variations may be introduced to increase sampling efficiency, taking account of differences between the strata in operational costs and in population variability. Similarly, stratification is often used to permit oversampling of identified small but significant subpopulations in order to ensure their representation by a sample of adequate size within the planned total sample; the strategy reduces the sample error for the subgroup in question, while increasing it for the population as a whole. Where sampling fractions are deliberately varied between strata the biasing effect is corrected in the estimation process by appropriate weighting. Stratification may sometimes be imposed on the sample designer by the fact that the sampling frames for different parts of the population are different in character, or are available in different places.

Sampling strata should not be confused with domains of study; the latter are sub-populations of analytic concern. It is not necessarily appropriate to use such domains as sampling strata.   CS

Reading
Cohran, W.G. 1977: *Sampling techniques.* Third edition. Chichester and New York: Wiley.
Kish, L. 1975: *Survey sampling.* Chichester and New York: Wiley.
— 1982: Sampling methods. In J.A. Ross, ed. *International encyclopaedia of population.* New York: Free Press. Pp. 601–5.

subfecundity The diminished capacity to reproduce. Subfecundity may refer to the male, female or couple. It occurs most frequently at the beginning and end of the reproductive years (see ADOLESCENT SUB-FECUNDITY). In the female it may be caused by irregular ovulation, abnormalities in ova, structural and functional abnormalities of the Fallopian tubes, uterus or cervix, and by repeated spontaneous foetal deaths. In the male, low quantity and quality of sperm and impotence can cause subfecundity. Couples are subfecund if either partner has a diminished capacity to reproduce, but also in some instances when both the male and the female are fully fecund with other partners. This is the case, for example, when the female produces antibodies against the sperm of her partner.   JB

Reading
McFalls, J.A. 1979: Frustrated fertility: a population paradox. *Population bulletin* 34, pp. 1–43.
Speroff, L., Glass, R.H. and Kase, N.G. 1978: *Clinical gynecologic endocrinology and infertility.* Baltimore: Williams and Wilkins.

survey The purposes and methods of demographic surveys are extraordinarily wide but the principal aim is always to *describe* as accurately as possible some aspects of the demography of a population. This can include fertility, mortality and migration as well as the circumstances in which these events occur. A second and occasionally more important aim of most demographic surveys is to *explain* some aspect of these demographic events by searching for associations between the variables measured by the survey.

In the investigator's mind there may be a hypothesis about the way in which demographic parameters are affected by one or more variables or, more grandly, the survey may be designed to examine the validity of a whole series of theoretical constructs. In all cases even the simplest ideas or aspirations for the product of a survey are dependent on the ability of respondents to give unequivocal answers to direct questions. It is the ability of the survey to express the usually complex reasons for its undertaking into a clear interview schedule which, more than any other feature, distinguishes good surveys from bad ones.

There is little point in trying to describe in full the diverse purposes which demographic surveys have been designed to serve; in Britain social reformers such as Charles Booth in the nineteenth century and B.W. Rowntree in the early twentieth conducted surveys with a demographic component. One of the major inquiries into British and Irish fertility was contained within the 1911 census and since that time there has been a multitude of surveys into health (e.g. the UK National Survey of Health and Development begun in 1946), fertility and birth control practice (Langford 1976) and migration organised and paid for by a mixture of public and private bodies. In the United States the Growth of the American Families study and the succeeding four national studies of US fertility are classics in that they were, and remain, the prime source for the interpretation of US fertility trends from the 1950s to the 1970s (see Ryder 1973 for a critique of the national survey and Westoff 1975 for a defence).

Demographic surveys are also diverse in

design as well as in aims but two main types of survey are worth distinguishing:

(1) The single-round survey which involves only one interview with the respondents. This design permits the use of larger samples and is especially suitable for use in countries where addresses are not well defined or where the population is highly mobile. Internationally, the largest survey of this kind is the series of studies of over 60 countries conducted by the World Fertility Survey.

(2) The multi-round survey which encompasses a great variety of survey designs, among which we can distinguish: (a) Surveys which re-interview the same respondent several times. These are sometimes referred to as 'follow-up' or 'panel' surveys. Good examples of this kind of survey are the UK National Survey of Health and Development and the US National Fertility Survey of 1975. (b) Surveys which re-interview similar respondents to produce indications of trends over time. The UK General Household Survey and the US Current Population Survey use a rotating sample of households which nonetheless remains a nationally representative sample of the total population. Some multi-round surveys use fixed geographical areas as residential sampling units and interview all residents at each round, regardless of whether the people were resident in the unit during the previous round.

Multi-round designs are sometimes referred to as 'prospective' surveys, especially when they trace the experience of individuals over two or more rounds. This is confusing, especially when used to distinguish the survey from a 'retrospective' design. All surveys, single-round or multi-round, collect information for the immediate pre-survey period and are therefore 'retrospective'.

All surveys question only a fraction of the total population for which data are sought. The task of relating the survey findings to the larger population is a complex one. SAMPLE DESIGN is therefore of major importance to all surveys and has become a well-developed field of applied mathematics in its own right. In most field situations, however, the strict rules of scientific probability sampling are impossible to follow exactly and some pragmatism is required.

Survey questionnaires are as diverse as surveys themselves but it is again worthwhile to distinguish two main types:

(1) Pre-coded forms with 'closed' questions, i.e. a respondent's answers must conform to some pre-set range of acceptable responses.
(2) Forms with 'open-ended' questions which do not constrain the respondent in any way. These are quite rare in most demographic surveys.

Most modern surveys are analysed by computer and for this reason special care is needed to ensure ease of handling during the data entry and checking phases.

As a final note it is worth indicating that, however factual a survey sets out to be, the choice of questions, the sequence in which they are posed, the words in which they are expressed and even the comportment and attitude of the interviewer may have a powerful effect on the offered responses. Re-survey of the same respondents with the same questionnaire and quite 'factual' questions often produces two different sets of results.   AH

References

Langford, C.M. 1976: *Birth control practice and marital fertility in Great Britain.* London: Population Investigation Committee.

Ryder, N.B. 1973: A critique of the National Fertility Study. *Demography* 10, pp. 495–503.

Westoff, C.F. 1975: The yield of the imperfect: the 1970 National Fertility Study. *Demography* 12, pp. 573–80.

Reading

Atkins, E., Cherry, N., Douglas, J.W.B., Kiernan, K.E. and Wadsworth, M.E.J. 1980: The 1946 British birth cohort: an account of the origins, progress and results of the National Survey of Health and Development. In J.A. Medwick and A.E. Baert, eds. *An empirical basis for primary prevention in prospective lon-*

218   **survival analysis**

gitudinal research in Europe. Oxford: Oxford University Press.

Douglas, J.W.B. 1976: The use and abuse of national cohorts. In M. Shipman, ed. *The organisation and impact of social research.* London: Routledge and Kegan Paul.

Moser, K. and Kalton, G., eds. 1971: *Survey methods in social investigation.* Second edition. London: Heinemann; New York: Basic Books (1972).

Shryock, H.S., Siegel, J.S. et al. 1976: *The methods and materials of demography.* Condensed edition by E.G. Stockwell. London and New York: Academic Press.

United Nations 1971: *Methodology of demographic sample surveys.* Series M, statistical papers 51. New York: Department of Economic and Social Affairs.

United States, National Academy of Sciences 1981: *Collecting data for the estimation of fertility and mortality.* Committee on Population and Demography, report 6. Washington DC: National Academy Press.

survival analysis   A branch of statistical theory concerned with the analysis of non-renewable phenomena or failures, including mortality.

In contrast with traditional demographic procedures, in which special attention is given to the problems of constructing measures from large-scale data sources and aggregate level data, survival analysis has stressed the problems involved in the estimation and statistical properties of models, often parametric, based on relatively smallscale studies using individual level data. Such techniques are particularly relevant to the analysis of sample survey data (see also HAZARD MODELS.)   MM

Reading

Bracher, M. and Santow, G. 1982: Breastfeeding in Central Java. *Population studies* 36, 3, pp. 413–29.

Elandt-Johnson, R.C. and Johnson, N.L. 1980: *Survival models and data analysis.* New York and Chichester: Wiley.

Kalbfleisch, J.D. and Prentice, R.L. 1980: *The statistical analysis of failure time data.* New York and Chichester: Wiley.

survival curve   A curve indicating the number of survivors at each age in a cohort. It corresponds to the l_x column of a LIFE TABLE and defines the age structure of the STATIONARY POPULATION.   CW

survivorship ratio   Also referred to as the survival ratio or the survival rate, the ratio $_nS_x$ is the number of persons alive in an age group x to $x+n+k$, divided by the number in the younger age group x to $x+n$, k years earlier. If the persons alive in these two cases are represented by the life table person-years, L, this is:

$$_nS_x = \frac{_nL_{x+k}}{_nL_x}$$

The simplicity of the data required, just two age structures (often from two censuses) k years apart means that the ratio is one of the most easily calculable indicators of mortality. It can be used to compute inter-censal estimates of mortality and as input to forward or REVERSE SURVIVAL methods of estimating population size, birth rate trends or NET MIGRATION. Although extremely useful when accurate, the ratio is open to considerable distortion from misreporting of the age structure, and in particular by differential under-reporting by age and age misstatement.   CW

Süssmilch, Johann (1707–1767)   A Lutheran pastor born in Berlin, the author of *The Divine Order*, first published in 1741, and then in a considerably expanded edition in 1761.

Following the influence of GRAUNT, Süssmilch tried to establish statistical constants within the variation of demographic processes. These constants he regarded as manifestations of the Divine Order, though this reference to the supernatural did not lead him to depart from the most stringent scientific rigour. Making use of the statistical material available at the time, drawn from England, Sweden and the Netherlands, he put forward several series of indices in relation to the dynamics and age-patterns of deaths, marriages and births and the sex ratio at birth. He calculated several LIFE TABLES, the first of which, relating to the whole of Prussia, he used as the basis for an estimate of the total world population (1 billion). As a whole, *The Divine Order* can be seen as the first comprehensive demographic study. Süssmilch's contribution was not limited to a rich harvest of statistics; he also provided sophisticated analyses of the causes and consequences of the processes which he brought to light.   RP

synthetic cohort See HYPOTHETICAL COHORT.

systematic sampling A selection process within one sampling stage and stratum rather than a complete SAMPLE DESIGN. Selection is made from a list at a fixed interval, taking a randomly determined starting point. Systematic sampling is generally preferred to RANDOM SAMPLING both because it is easier to implement and check and because it ensures a sample spread evenly through the list, so providing 'implicit stratification'.   CS

systems analysis A system is a set of phenomena of which the structure and behaviour is largely determined by their mutual interconnections and interactions. Systems analysis consists of methods of investigating the structure and behaviour of systems of interest which recognise the interdependence of system components. Systems analysis has been applied most successfully to systems in which clearly defined stocks of phenomena and flows into and out of these stocks can be defined. The methods used involve the construction of a model of the behaviour of the elements of the system. Elements recognised usually include level or stock variables, flows into or out of stock variables, influencing variables that determine flows, the couplings or relationships between the elements, regulators or control variables, and the inputs and outputs between the system and the environment.
                PR

Reading
Meadows, D.L. et al. 1974: *Dynamics of growth in a finite world.* Cambridge, Mass.: Wright-Allen Press.
Wilson, A.G. 1980: *Geography and the environment: systems analytical methods.* Chichester: Wiley.

T

target family size See DESIRED FAMILY SIZE.

tempo (of a process) The timing of events within a particular COHORT.

The term was introduced by Norman Ryder and is contrasted with the QUANTUM or overall intensity of a phenomenon within a cohort. The two concepts have been used by him in a series of revealing studies (see Ryder 1980). Tempo is sometimes used in period analysis when the concept of a HYPOTHETICAL COHORT is employed to combine rates for different cohorts.

The most common measure of tempo is the mean age or duration at which the members of a cohort experience an event (e.g. mean age at childbearing). Alternative indicators are also used, particularly the median age or duration. The tempo and quantum of a process are not independent. For example, a slow tempo of marriage will often lead to a higher proportion who never marry. Similarly, low fertility is usually associated with a higher proportion of childbearing taking place at younger ages than is found when fertility is high. A distinction is sometimes made between gross and net measures of timing, the latter explicitly taking into account the effects of DISTURBING PROCESSES such as mortality.   RP

Reference

Ryder, N.B. 1980: Components of temporal variation in American fertility. In R. W. Hiorns, ed. *Demographic patterns in developed societies*. London: Taylor and Francis.

Reading

Wunsch, G. and Termote, M. 1978: *Introduction to demographic analysis*. New York and London: Plenum. Chapter 1.

termination of pregnancy See ABORTION.

time budget An accounting of how people spend their time. Time budget, or time use, studies collect data on how much time people allocate to different activities. Methods of data collection include direct observation, diary keeping, and retrospective recall; data may be recorded sequentially or non-sequentially, and studies vary greatly in detail of activities recorded and precision of time estimates.

Time budgets have been used in the measurement and analysis of labour force participation and employment. Distinctive applications of time use data in social and economic demography are the estimation of the labour contributions and productivity of children in less developed countries and investigation of the trade-off for women between work in the labour market and work in the home (including childrearing) and its implications for reproductive behaviour.   MTC

Reading

Birdsall, N. 1980: Measuring time use and non-market exchange. In W.P. McGreevy, ed. *Third world poverty: new strategies for measuring development progress*. Lexington, Mass.: Lexington Books.

Cain, M.T. 1977: The economic activities of children in a village in Bangladesh. *Population and development review* 3, pp. 201–28.

Evenson, R.E., Popkin, B.M. and Quizon, E.K. 1980: Nutrition, work and demographic behavior in rural Philippine households. In H.P. Binswanger et al., eds. *Rural household studies in Asia*. Singapore: University of Singapore Press.

time series analysis The statistical analysis of a series of repeated observations of the same variable, or, in the case of multiple time series analysis, set of variables. The term refers to a general methodology in statistics which takes explicit account of the ordering of the data and of the interdependence of the observations. Analysis can be done either in the frequency domain (spectral analysis) or in the time domain. Univariate time series analysis has been used in demography for forecasting, and to study seasonality and other periodic tendencies. Multivariate time series analysis is used to study causes and correlates of fluctuations in vital rates. RDL

Reading

Box, G. and Jenkins, G. 1970: *Time series analysis: forecasting and control*. San Francisco: Holden-Day.

Lee, R. 1977: Methods and models for analyzing historical series of births, deaths and marriages. In R.D. Lee, ed. *Population patterns in the past*. London and New York: Academic Press. Pp. 337–70.

total abortion rate   The average number of induced abortions which a cohort of women would have by the end of their reproductive years if they were to experience the age-specific abortion rates of a given period.

The total abortion rate uses the concept of a HYPOTHETICAL COHORT to provide a convenient indicator of the prevalence of abortion in a given period, often one year. Recent estimates suggest that the rate is above 1.0 in five countries in Eastern Europe, in Cuba and in South Korea, between 0.5 and 1.0 in several other developed countries including the United States (0.69), and below 0.5 elsewhere. Completely reliable statistics are far from universally available.   CW

Reading

Tietze, C. 1983: *Induced abortion: a world review*. New York: Population Council.

total fertility rate (TFR)   The sum of the AGE-SPECIFIC FERTILITY RATES over the whole range of reproductive ages for a particular period (usually a year). It can be interpreted as the number of children a woman would have during her lifetime if she were to experience the fertility rates of the period at each age.

The TFR is a widely-cited period measure which uses the idea of a HYPO-

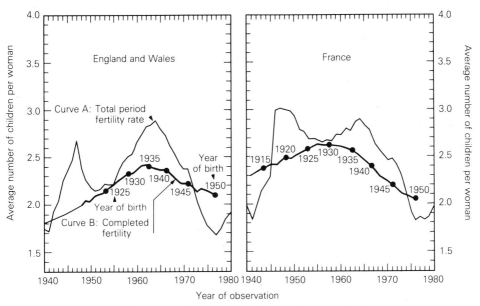

Period TFR may be a poor indicator of cohort fertility.
Source: Calot and Blayo 1982, p. 361.

THETICAL COHORT to provide an overall summary of the fertility level unaffected by age structure. It is analogous to COMPLETED FERTILITY which indicates family size in a true cohort. If f_a is the age-specific fertility rate at age a, the TFR is defined as:

$$TFR = \sum_{a=15}^{49} f_a$$

With five-year age groups this becomes:

$$TFR = 5 \times \sum_{a=15-19}^{45-49} f_a$$

Although one of the most frequently quoted measures of fertility, the TFR sometimes requires a certain caution in interpretation. It is a hypothetical measure, not necesarily applicable to any true cohort, and may be a dubious value when the QUANTUM or level and timing or TEMPO of fertility are changing.   RP, CW

total marital fertility rate (TMFR)   The sum of the AGE-SPECIFIC MARITAL FERTILITY RATES of a particular period (often a year) over the whole range of reproductive ages. It represents the number of children a woman would have if she experienced the average marital fertility at every age.

Normally defined as referring to a period, the TMFR is also sometimes quoted for a COHORT in the absence of a generally accepted alternative term for cohort fertility. The TMFR is defined, where mf_a is the age-specific marital fertility rate at age a, as follows:

$$TMFR = \sum_{a=15}^{49} mf_a$$

With five-year age groups this becomes

$$TMFR = 5 \times \sum_{a=15-19}^{45-49} mf_a$$

RP, CW

total rate   A rate calculated by summing the age-specific rates of a particular phenomenon in a given period.

Total rates are widely cited period measures and use the idea of the HYPOTHETICAL COHORT to enable an overall summing of the level of a process to be made. Examples of total rates are the total abortion rate and the total fertility rate. Although they have the advantage of being unaffected by the age structure of a population, total rates can give a misleading impression of a phenomenon when its overall level (QUANTUM) and timing (TEMPO) are changing. The terminology is sometimes also employed for cohort measures calculated on a similar basis, though it is usually better to restrict it to period indices.   RP

traditional birth attendant   The term (frequently abbreviated to TBA) encompasses the entire category of indigenous midwives, that is people – almost always women – whose prime job is to help mothers in childbirth. Local terms, such as in parts of Asia 'dai', or 'dunkun' are often used.

It has been estimated that between 60 per cent and 80 per cent of births in the developing world are attended by TBAs (WHO 1979). The practices of the trade tend to be handed from one generation of TBAs to another and sometimes – as in the widespread use in northern India of cow dung after severance of the umbilical cord – these can be dangerous for the lives of both mother and child. However governments of developing countries are to an increasing extent training TBAs so that they can propagate modern ideas and methods of both family planning and infant and childcare. This reflects the fact that in many cultures, in addition to supervising at the delivery itself, traditional birth attendants advise and assist women throughout their pregnancy and for some time after the birth.   TD

Reference

World Health Organisation 1979: *Traditional birth attendants.* Geneva: WHO.

Reading

Bayoumi, A. 1976: The training and activity of village midwives in the Sudan. *Tropical doctor* 6, pp. 118–25.

Gordon, J.E., Gideon, H. and Wyon, J.B. 1965: Midwifery practice in rural Punjab, India. *American journal of obstetrics and gynaecology* 93, pp. 734–42.

Rogers, E.M. and Solomon, D.S. 1975: *Traditional midwives as family planning communicators in Asia.* Honolulu: East-West Population Institute.

Simpson-Hebert, M., Piotrow, P.T., Christie, L.J. and Streich, J. 1980: Traditional midwives and family planning. *Population reports*, series J, 22.

World Health Organisation 1979.

transition matrix A tabular summary of the absolute or relative frequencies with which individuals move among states within a certain time period. ('Individual' may refer to a family or other unit.) For example, in studies of intergenerational mobility a transition matrix may tabulate the social class of a son as a function of the social class of the father. In this example, 'state' refers to a social class.

Assuming that individuals can occupy only one state at any given instant, one row of a transition matrix and one column of the matrix is assigned to each state. In the intersection of the row for state i and the column for state j is recorded the number of individuals who were in state i at an initial time and in state j at a final time.

Such a transition matrix of absolute frequencies may be converted to a transition matrix of relative frequencies by dividing each number in row i by the sum of the numbers in row i. The fraction in row i and column j then describes the proportion of individuals initially in state i who were finally in state j.

Transition matrices of absolute and relative frequencies are descriptive statistics. Theoretical transition matrices that specify probabilities in place of relative frequencies are frequently derived from MARKOV CHAIN MODELS.   JEC

translation A term introduced by the American demographer Norman Ryder (1964) to designate models and formulae which make it possible to establish the relations between cohort and period measurements of demographic processes.

The simplest models are based on linear variations in the overall level, the QUANTUM, and the timing or TEMPO of a particular phenomenon. Period measures are sometimes poor indicators of the underlying cohort experience, especially when the quantum and tempo are changing. The bias in period measures brought about by such changes has been termed distributional distortion by Ryder. Translation models potentially offer the chance of overcoming this problem. In practice, however, even elaborate translation models can rarely fully replicate true cohort behaviour, and analysts usually prefer to use cohort data when available.   RP, CW

Reference

Ryder, N.B. 1964: The process of demographic translation. *Demography* 1, 74–82.

Reading

Ryder 1964.

Wunsch.G. and Termote, M. 1978: *Introduction to demographic analysis.* New York and London: Plenum. Chapter 2.

transversal analysis See PERIOD ANALYSIS.

triplets See MULTIPLE BIRTHS.

truncation A term used to indicate the lack of information on a part of a distribution.

Truncation can impose limits on analysis and is always a potential source of bias. Discussion of the problem within demography has mostly taken place in connection with LIFE HISTORIES collected by RETROSPECTIVE OBSERVATION, often in conjunction with comments on the related problem of censoring. Truncation implies a total lack of information on a section of the population or group in question. For example, it is often possible to study the height and weight of young men over long periods from records of entry into military service, but since minimum requirements were set no information is available for persons below the minima. The distribution is thus truncated and interpretation made more difficult. Contemporary data collection sometimes creates similar problems. The World Fertility Survey provides detailed marriage and maternity histories for married women, but since single women were not interviewed it does not indicate the proportion of the whole population married at each age, only the proportion among those who do marry. Truncation can only be overcome with reference to a model of the process involved or to information from another source.

Censoring is a related problem, though somewhat more amenable to adjustment and correction. It derives from the nature of data gathering in a survey or census. Since individuals have reached a certain age, or a certain duration since a given event, at the time of the survey they cannot provide information of events at older ages or longer durations. Their experience is said to be censored at the point of the survey. However, although each individual is censored at some age or duration,

so long as persons in all age or duration groups are questioned information is available on the whole distribution. A much cited example occurs in the analysis of BIRTH INTERVALS. In the analysis of, say, the interval between second and third births the survey will capture some women who have had a second child but there is no way of knowing whether they will have a third. All that is known is that the interval from the second to third births will be at least as long as the gap from the second birth to the interview. Simple cross-tabulation and descriptive statistics on such data are inevitably biased. However, since women at all durations since a second birth are available for analysis, LIFE TABLE METHODS can be used to handle the censored information provided that the phenomenon is not marked by strong selectivity (see NON-SELECTIVITY).   CW

tubectomy   See STERILISATION.

twins   See MULTIPLE BIRTHS.

U

undercount Failure to enumerate all the persons or events which should be counted in CENSUS or SURVEY. In a census undercounting of complete households is frequently distinguished from under-counting of individuals in enumerated households. Undercounting is generally more frequent among young adults, especially those not living in households with other family members. The word is sometimes used to mean net undercounting, the difference between the number of events overcounted and the number under-counted. DE

underenumeration See UNDERCOUNT.

urban population The population living in areas with a census definition as urban.

The criteria used to specify what is an urban area vary and it is not possible to give a single definition. The underlying concepts are fivefold:

(1) national administrative divisions based on historical, political or administrative, rather than statistical concepts
(2) population size
(3) local administrative areas
(4) specific urban characteristics
(5) predominant economic activities.

Most censuses use combinations of these five aspects. Even with elaborate definitions, however, a three-way distinction of rural, urban and semi-urban or suburban is often necessary in order accurately to reflect the range of settlement patterns. Although the density of population is implicitly involved in most definitions it is rarely mentioned explicitly.

The whole range of definitions in use makes comparative studies of URBANISA-TION very difficult. While geographers have made extensive studies of urban populations (it is possibly the most popular subfield within human geography), demographers have largely concentrated on general studies of urbanisation, with relatively few attempts at detailed analysis of the social and ecological aspects of urban areas. RP, CW

Reading
Carter, H. 1981: *The study of urban geography*. Third edition. London: Edward Arnold; New York: Wiley.
Shryock, H.S., Siegel, J.S. et al. 1976: *The methods and materials of demography*. Condensed edition by E.G. Stockwell. London and New York: Academic Press. Chapter 6.

urbanisation An increase in the proportion of a population living in urban areas. The term is sometimes also used to mean the level of population concentration rather than its change.

Urbanisation in this definition only takes place when the URBAN POPULATION is growing more rapidly than the population as a whole. In a country with rapid population growth cities could expand rapidly without urbanisation in the strict sense. Urbanisation may be the result of migration from rural areas or of differences in fertility and mortality between the different areas. Most studies of the phenomenon are based on census data and comparative analysis is complicated by the lack of homogeneity in the definition of what constitutes an urban area. It is estimated that by the year 2000 half the world's population will live in cities (in 1980 the figure was around 40 per cent). Urbanisation is one of the most significant of current demographic phenomena. CW

Reading

Berry, B.J.L. 1973: *The human consequences of urbanisation*. London: Macmillan; New York: St Martin's Press.

Chandler, T. and Fox, G. 1974: *Three thousand years of urban growth*. New York and London: Academic Press.

Ross, J.A. 1982: *International encyclopaedia of population*. New York: Free Press. Section on urbanisation with entries by R. McNamara, S.H. Preston, P. Korcelli and E.E. Arriaga, pp. 649–64.

use-effectiveness (of contraception) A measure of CONTRACEPTIVE EFFECTIVE-NESS which takes into account accidental pregnancies attributable both to method and user failure.

Traditionally failure rates were expressed using the formulation suggested by Pearl (1932) where the number of accidental pregnancies is divided by the number of woman-years of exposure and the result expressed per 100 woman-years. Since failure rates usually decline with duration of use the PEARL RATE can only realistically be used when the time period to which it applies is specified. Recognition of the fact that contraceptive effectiveness varies over time has led to the widespread application of LIFE TABLE METHODS as a technique of analysis. Life tables allow the investigator to take account of the pro-portion of users who discontinue use of the contraceptive (continuation rates) as well as the specific risk of accidental pregnancy.   ER

Reference

Pearl, R. 1932: Contraception and fertility in 2000 women. *Human biology* IV, pp. 363–407.

Reading

Bone, M. 1975: *Measures of contraceptive effectiveness and their uses*. Studies on medical and population subjects 28. London: Office of Population Censuses and Surveys.

Tietze, C. and Lewit, S. 1968: Statistical evaluation of contraceptive methods: use-effectiveness and extended use-effectiveness. *Demography* 5, pp. 931–40.

Vaughan, B., Trussell, J., Menken, J. and Jones, E.F. 1977: Contraceptive failure among married women in the United States, 1970–1973. *Family planning perspectives* 9, pp. 251–8.

Vessey, M., Lawless, M. and Yeates, D. 1982: Efficacy of different contraceptive methods. *Lancet* 1, pp. 841–2.

usual language The language customarily used by an individual. A contrast is made with a person's mother tongue, though the distinction for bilingual or multilingual persons is not always easy. A further distinction between the language spoken at home and at work is sometimes also make.   RP

V

value of children A phrase that has many synonyms or near-synonyms; it is often encountered in discussion of the impact of fertility. The word value can be replaced by benefits, satisfactions, rewards, advantages, utilities, gratifications, gains, functions, or positive values. Children can also be considered as a source of happiness or as fulfilling personal and social needs.

In order to strike a balance or a measure of the net value (even though value can be regarded as quantitatively negative) these terms are often employed with their antonyms: value and cost (or, occasionally, disvalue) of children, utilities and disutilities, satisfactions and dissatisfactions, advantages and disadvantages, positive values and negative values, etc.

In terms of exchanges or flows the value of children to the older generation has been described as an upward wealth flow (or, negatively, a downward wealth flow) or benefit flow or resource flow, and the net value as the net intergenerational wealth flow which may approach a point of reversal where it is zero or in equilibrium. The value of children is usually discussed solely in terms of the value to their parents, although sometimes reference is made to a broader group of relatives (including grandparents) or to the clan, tribe or society. When the cost of children is emphasised the implied burden may be on other dependent siblings as well as on parents.

There is considerable debate as to what the value of children means: it has been defined as the sum of the material and psychological gratifications received by parents or as the functions children serve and the needs they fulfil for parents. Reference is sometimes made to economic and non-economic benefits. The economic benefits can be described as the returns from children and may be measured in absolute terms or may be the discounted returns according to the period elapsing before they are received. There has been some debate as to the extent to which some of the psychological satisfaction arises from material satisfaction and hence to whether double-counting is involved. There is agreement that the economic benefits include all kinds of work, services and earnings provided by children, together with expected returns at maturity including work, financial and other assistance, guarantees of protection from danger and of help in crises (or, alternatively, the advantage of numbers), and support in old age. There is some debate about the extent to which this can be regarded as an investment and about the discounting factors that should be employed.

For the purpose of measurement the value of children has been defined only to a limited extent, most effort having been exerted in terms of measuring work inputs, usually by the duration of activities or a TIME BUDGET although the imputation of the market value of labour has also been used. The costs of children are the various negative values, particularly parental expenditure of resources and effort, although the new household economists have emphasised the alternative options foregone by mothers not only as measured by income but also by leisure. JCC, PQ

Reading

Cain, M.T. 1977: The economic activities of children in a village in Bangladesh. *Population and development review* 3, pp. 207–28.

Caldwell, J.C. 1982: *Theory of fertility decline*. New York and London: Academic Press. Chapter 11.

Espenshade, R. 1977: The value and cost of children. *Population bulletin* 32.

Fawcett, J.T. 1982: Value of children. In J.A. Ross, ed. *International encyclopaedia of population*. New York: Free Press. Pp. 665–71.

Hoffman, L.W. and Hoffman, M.L. 1973: The value of children to parents. In J.T. Fawcett, ed. *Psychological perspectives on population*. New York: Basic Books.

Shultz, T.W. 1973: The value of children: an economic perspective. *Journal of political economy* 81, 2, part 2, pp. S2–S13.

variable-r methods   See STABLE POPULATION.

vasectomy   See STERILISATION.

visiting unions   Sexual and reproductive unions in which the partners do not live in the same houshold.

Visiting unions are common in many Caribbean and Latin American countries, often as part of a complex process of union formation. A contrast is made between these and other non-marital unions such as common-law marriages which usually involve cohabitation.   CW

vital event   A major change in an individual's status which leads to a change in composition of the population. Birth, stillbirth and death are clearly vital events, and the term can also embrace marriage, adoption, annulment, legitimisation, separation, divorce and migration, which are not strictly speaking vital. Vital registration is a system for collecting data on these events though not all countries collect all of these and some do not publish them all, even though they are collected. The data are produced as vital statistics which have long been a crucial source for demographic analysis, providing information on the dynamics of the situation to com-plement the static data collected in a census or survey.   RP

vital registration   The registration of the demographic events occurring in a population and the basic source of information on its dynamics.

The origins of vital registration lay in the need for official documents confirming the birth, marriages and death of each individual. This requirement remains but it has been supplemented by the increasing demand for quantitative information for various purposes of forward planning.

Although a tradition of registration in China dates back to antiquity, the earliest registration data still to survive are the PARISH REGISTERS of pre-industrial Europe. As early as 1538 every priest in England was required to make weekly records of baptisms, marriages and burials, though it was some decades before the system operated throughout the country, and the data were not collated to produce statistics. Compulsory civil registration was first enacted in Scandinavia in the seventeenth century and did not become widespread in Europe and North America until the nineteenth century.

Today, the registration systems of developed nations provide elaborate statistical data on many aspects of social change, though the relatively expensive and complex infrastructure militates against its effective use in some poor countries. In these circumstances a SAMPLE REGISTRATION SYSTEM, or sample surveys, may be used to gain information of the prevailing demographic conditions.

RP, CW

Reading

Shryock, H.S. Siegel, J.S. et al. 1976: *The methods and materials of demography*. Condensed edition by E.G. Stockwell. London and New York: Academic Press. Chapters 2 and 3.

vital statistics   See VITAL EVENT and VITAL REGISTRATION.

wait time The length of time between an individual becoming at risk of experiencing a particular event and its occurrence. The concept is commonly used in reproductive models to express the time taken to conceive (the conception wait) and other COMPONENTS OF THE BIRTH INTERVAL.   CW

Wargentin, Pehr (1717–1783) A Swedish astronomer and the author of studies on mortality including the first ever carried out combining information provided by civil registration and data on the population at risk; Wargentin's work referred to the whole of Sweden and he profited from the advanced Swedish methods of vital registration and census taking (the first having been held in 1749). In 1766 he published what is misleadingly called 'Wargentin's life table' covering the period 1755–63. It was in fact a series of ratios of the population to the corresponding deaths (the inverse of death rates). Nevertheless, Wargentin produced all the material necessary to construct a LIFE TABLE, though his methods of analysis were superseded by later work.   RP

weaning The process by which a child makes the transition from a diet based exclusively on breast-milk to one in which breast-milk is no longer included. An alternative definition covers the transition from a breast-milk diet to the same foods as are consumed by other family members. A child receiving infant formula or special gruel, for example, would be considered as already fully weaned according to the first definition but not according to the second.

The transition may be made abruptly, but is more often a gradual process spread over a period of days, weeks, months or even years. Expressions such as 'age at weaning', without further specification of the stage in the process that is being referred to, are ambiguous.

Weaning practices vary enormously. The age at which particular foods are introduced, together with their purity and the quantities given may be significant factors in child health (for a recent summary see Winikoff 1982). The age at which children cease to suckle frequently and intensively can also affect the mother's fertility since prolonged intensive breastfeeding tends to suppress ovulation and thus, in the absence of contraception, to delay the next pregnancy (for a recent summary, see McCann et al. 1981).   HP

References and Reading
McCann, M.F., Liskin, L.S., Piotrow, P.T., Rinehard, W. and Fox, G. 1981: *Breast-feeding, fertility and family planning*. Population reports J, 24. Baltimore: Johns Hopkins University, Population Information Programme.
Winikoff, B. 1982: Weaning: nutrition, morbidity and mortality consequences. In S.H. Preston, ed. *Biological and social aspects of mortality and the length of life* Liège: Ordina Editions.

widowhood techniques A set of INDIRECT ESTIMATION TECHNIQUES developed for the estimation of adult mortality using information collected by questions on the survival of the first spouse of a respondent. Such questions are often included in single-round surveys, particularly in areas with deficient conventional sources of information on mortality.

Information on the survival of first husband provided by ever-married female respondents provides estimates of male mortality, while that on survival of first wife, from ever-married male respondents, provides estimates of female mortality. First spouses are specified in order to avoid problems introduced by remarriage after widowhood. For the theoretical development, see Hill (1977) and Hill and Trussell (1977); for details of the most recent procedures see United Nations (1983). The original methodology assumed constant mortality and nuptiality in the past, though Brass and Bamgboye (1981) have recently developed procedures for locating the time reference of the estimates obtained under conditions of steady mortality change.

In theory, widowhood techniques offer several advantages over ORPHANHOOD TECHNIQUES; there is in general only one respondent per person exposed to risk, the whole ever-married population is represented, and there is no equivalent of the adoption effect, permitting the calculation of more recent mortality levels. Applications, however, have generally been disappointing, apparently as a result of response errors at the time of data collection. Proportions reported as not widowed have shown inconsistenty from one age group or duration of marriage group to another, or between surveys, and do not inspire confidence in the mortality estimates obtained.

KH

References

Blacker, J.G.C. 1977: The estimation of adult mortality in Africa from data on orphanhood. *Population studies* 31, pp. 107–28.

Brass, W. and Bamgboye, E.A. 1981: The time location of reports of survivorship: estimates for maternal and paternal orphanhood and the ever-widowed. Working paper 81.1. London: Centre for Population Studies, London School of Hygiene and Tropical Medicine.

Brass, W. and Hill, K. 1973: Estimating adult mortality from orphanhood. *Proceedings of the International Population Conference*. Volume 3. Liège: International Union for the Scientific Study of Population.

Hill, K. 1977: Estimating adult mortality levels from information on widowhood. *Population studies* 31, pp. 75–84.

— and Trussell, T.J. 1977: Further developments in indirect mortality estimation. *Population studies* 31, pp. 313–33.

United Nations 1983: *Manual X: indirect techniques for demographic estimation.* New York: Department of International Economic and Social Affairs.

Reading

Blacker 1977.

Brass, W. 1975: *Methods for estimating fertility and mortality from limited and defective data.* Chapel Hill, North Carolina: University of North Carolina, Laboratories for Population Statistics.

Hill, K. and Zlotnik, H. 1982. Indirect estimation of fertility and mortality. In J.A. Ross, ed. *International encyclopaedia of population.* New York: Free Press. Pp. 324–34.

United Nations 1983.

woman-year   See PERSON-YEAR.

working age population   The population in the age groups from which the LABOUR FORCE is drawn. Definitions of these ages vary, but 15 to 64 is common for international comparisons. The size of the labour force is given by multiplying the working age population by the appropriate labour force PARTICIPATION RATE.

CW

working life table   The application of life table methods to describe the working life of individuals.

Working life tables have hitherto been produced by combining a normal life table with a set of labour force PARTICIPATION RATES (Shyrock et al. 1976). This approach had major problems, however, and is now being replaced by methods using MULTI-STATE DEMOGRAPHY (Willekens 1980).

Traditional approaches using life tables and participation rates cannot handle the complexities of labour force participation. For example they usually assume a single entry into the labour force and a single departure from it, so that persons who enter and leave the economically active population more than once are either excluded from analysis or assumed to be few in number. Multistate approaches using INCREMENT-DECREMENT LIFE TABLES are able to deal with this factor without difficulty, and also offer the possiblity of more realistic treatment of differential mortality between the working and inactive populations.

Complete tables of working life provide all the life table functions relevant to economic activity, of which the most useful is perhaps the number of further years an individual can expect to remain in the workforce, i.e. the working life expectancy.   CW

References

Shryock, H.S., Siegel, J.S. et al. 1976: *The methods and materials of demography*. Condensed edition by E.G. Stockwell. New York and London: Academic Press. Pp. 365–8.

Willekens, F.J. 1980: Multistate analysis: tables of working life. *Environment and planning A* 12, pp. 563–88.

working population   See LABOUR FORCE.

Z

zero population growth (ZPG) A situation in which the number of births in and immigrants to a population equal the number of deaths and emigrants from it.

Unlike the STATIONARY POPULATIONS which is a theoretical construct with specified mathematical characteristics, ZPG is the outcome of genuine circumstance and may arise in various ways. Many developed countries have growth rates close to zero and the global attainment of such a pattern is sometimes advocated as a solution to many social and economic problems. Proponents of ZPG are criticised by those who favour continued population growth, seeing people as, in Julian Simon's words, 'the ultimate resource'.   CW

Reading

Clark, R.L. and Spengler, J.J. 1980: *The economics of individual and population aging*. Cambridge and New York: Cambridge University Press.

Overbeek, J. 1974: *History of population theories*. Rotterdam: Rotterdam University Press.

Simon, J. 1981: *The ultimate resource*. Princeton, NJ: Princeton University Press.

Index

Page numbers in bold type indicate headwords in the Dictionary. Headwords are only included in the Index where there are other page references to them.